BIDDLE, JACKSON,
AND A NATION IN TURMOIL

THE INFAMOUS BANK WAR

CORDELIA FRANCES BIDDLE

OXFORD SOUTHERN

an imprint of Sunbury Press, Inc.
Mechanicsburg, PA USA

OXFORD SOUTHERN

an imprint of Sunbury Press, Inc.
Mechanicsburg, PA USA

For information about special discounts for bulk purchases, please contact Sunbury Press Orders Dept. at (855) 338-8359 or orders@sunburypress.com.

To request one of our authors for speaking engagements or book signings, please contact Sunbury Press Publicity Dept. at publicity@sunburypress.com.

FIRST OXFORD SOUTHERN EDITION: February 2021

Set in Adobe Garamond | Interior design by Crystal Devine | Cover by Darleen Sedjro | Edited by Abigail Hensen.

Publisher's Cataloging-in-Publication Data
Names: Biddle, Cordelia Frances, author.
Title: Biddle, Jackson, and a nation in turmoil : the infamous bank war / Cordelia Frances Biddle.
Description: First trade paperback edition. | Mechanicsburg, PA : Oxford Southern, 2021.
Summary: The epic fight between Nicholas Biddle and Andrew Jackson over the fate of the Second Bank of the United States comes to vivid life in this compelling biography of political intrigue.
Identifiers: ISBN 978-1-620064-87-0 (softcover).
Subjects: HISTORY / United States / 19th Century | HISTORY / United States / State & Local / Middle Atlantic | BIOGRAPHY & AUTOBIOGRAPHY / Historical | BIOGRAPHY & AUTOBIOGRAPHY / Political | BIOGRAPHY & AUTOBIOGRAPHY / Business | BIOGRAPHY & AUTOBIOGRAPHY / Literary Figures.

Product of the United States of America
0 1 1 2 3 5 8 13 21 34 55

Continue the Enlightenment!

For my niece and nephew:

Hannah Livingston Biddle and Samuel Seelye Biddle

CONTENTS

AUTHOR'S NOTE

Born in 1786 and descended from the nation's earliest colonists, Nicholas Biddle's story reflects its birth and maturation. He lived through tumultuous eras, including the War of 1812, violent clashes over States Rights' and the abolition of slavery, the rise of the Loco Foco Party, and an escalating conflict between the establishment and the self-made men who felt disavowed and belittled. Andrew Jackson became their hero. It was inevitable that he and Biddle should wage a personal and public feud. The central bank may have been the impetus. However, at heart, the two men's bitter battle reflected a changing nation: Jackson, the plain-spoken warrior, Biddle, descended from America's earliest aristocracy. Their conflict altered the political arena.

Nicholas Biddle was a child prodigy who graduated from the College of New Jersey (Princeton University) at fifteen. Later, with Jefferson's blessing, he edited the Lewis and Clark Expedition journals; and served in the Pennsylvania State Legislature before entering the Second Bank of the United States, where he famously battled President Andrew Jackson. A Renaissance man, Biddle was a gifted, impassioned orator; he could also be arrogant. His legacy was a national bank. Until Jackson destroyed it, the Second Bank of the United States was the most stable financial institution in the world.

Under Biddle's leadership, the Bank became the largest corporation in America and one of the world's largest. His policies increased its circulation and capital, developed domestic and foreign exchange, and generated a paper currency that had uniform value throughout the nation. Biddle's foresight in regulating supplies of money and bank credit brought necessary security to the investment market. He allowed an ever-expanding nation to prosper and continue to thrive. In 1829, Condy Raguet, legislator, diplomat, and subsequent author of *A Treatise on Currency and Banking* said of the financier, "There is no man of intelligence in the least connected with our pecuniary concerns who does not perceive that the purity of that currency depends mainly on the

Bank of the United States, without whose agency the whole circulating medium would be endangered."

I became intrigued by Biddle when reading his draft correspondence with James Monroe. The letters span the years when Monroe was Secretary of State and subsequently President of the United States. I am the first author to examine these intriguing documents in draft form. Significantly different from the finished copies in the Library of Congress, the letters are part of a descendant's recent gift to Andalusia, the Biddle family home, near Philadelphia. Much of the correspondence shared between the two men is marked "confidential." Biddle excised words and phrases, even entire passages, making the final versions deceptively ambivalent. Read comparatively; the letters provoked questions. Why did names appear in full in the drafts but then became mere initials in the final copies? Why were the vital passages and references deleted? What potentially risky information was Biddle communicating to Monroe, and what use did Monroe make of it? Who *was* Biddle? Was he the lordly financier the world imagined him to be, or was his story more complex, even darker?

I also found Biddle's European journals that had been believed lost; again, they inspired questions about his true purpose for traversing Europe in 1804-1807 at the height of the Napoleonic Wars. Although ostensibly employed by the American ministers to France and England, he conferred with President Thomas Jefferson immediately upon returning to America. Monroe was then Minister Plenipotentiary to Great Britain.

I believe that Biddle served as a confidential agent for the United States while in Europe. He filled the role of covert liaison for Monroe in 1818 and 1819, culminating in the Adams-Onís Treaty that redrew the nation's southern and western boundaries. Acting as Monroe's agent in 1820 and 1821, Biddle advised the President on the Second Bank of the United States' precarious state when greed and graft ran rampant. At Monroe's behest, Biddle became a director of the Bank, which culminated in his leadership of the institution as its third and final President. Was he initially placed there as Monroe's informant?

Nicholas Biddle's father and uncles fought with valor and distinction during the Revolutionary War; they guided America's birth as a country. He and his brothers inherited and acted upon a sense of patriotic duty ingrained in their being. By rights, Biddle's story begins with the heroic uncle for whom he was named. That first Nicholas, intrepid and an adventurer at heart, set the bar high, but I recognize his nephew as a natural heir to that lineage.

CORDELIA FRANCES BIDDLE

ACKNOWLEDGMENTS

Much gratitude to the Andalusia Foundation's dedicated Executive Director, Connie Griffith Houchins, with whom I spent many happy hours and who helped me interpret Nicholas Biddle's sometimes erratic handwriting. Abundant thanks also to Cornelia King of the Library Company of Philadelphia who aided and deepened my research in primary research material. Dr. Gary Nash provided substantive and welcome advice on understanding Biddle's place within our nation's history. I shall always be grateful. Jay Robert Stiefel's optimism and interest encouraged me throughout the process. And, of course, my husband, Steve Zettler, author, actor, lover, friend. Bravi to you all.

- PROLOGUE -

MARCH 7, 1778

The moon was lustrous on that spring night, the waves pearl-colored and soft, mere ripples lapping against the ship's hull. Drawn to the sight, the crew of the American frigate *Randolph* felt a momentary lull, a draining away of blood-lust and fear. The warm waters east of Barbados have a dulcet effect when the weather is calm. Early March can be as clement as June in Philadelphia.

Tranquility was short lived. The *Randolph's* position in the thirteenth parallel of latitude put the vessel directly within the trade route between Great Britain and the West Indies, a dangerous place for a vessel in the Continental Navy. Its intrepid young captain, Nicholas Biddle, knew the risks. At stake was his country's freedom. With the British blockading New York and Philadelphia, supplies of much needed munitions had grown scarce. If he and his fellow captains and shipmates could capture a sufficient number of British ships and seize their guns and powder, the colonists could continue their fight.

Intent on this mission, Biddle and his crew watched as His Britannic Majesty's Ship *Yarmouth* began bearing down hard upon the upstart *Randolph* and the lesser vessels in its company. Equipped with sixty-four guns, most of which were thirty-two pounders, the *Yarmouth* possessed over twice the *Randolph* armament. The first frigate launched for the Continental Navy braced for this unequal battle. Its attributes were a much-lauded agility and a captain famed for his bravery and his self-possession under fire. Nicholas Biddle loved the sea better than he loved the land.

Cabin boy at thirteen, he'd had ample experience with peril: a ship sunk in hurricane seas off the coast of Yucatan and a near-miraculous survival on an arid, deserted island. In 1770, at the age of twenty, he'd quit his home in Philadelphia to join the Royal Navy. War was expected between Britain and

Spain, and he yearned to join the fight. Peace dashed those hopes, and Nicholas, bored by the routine of shipboard life during peacetime, complained that he was "murdering" his time.[1] Serendipitously, in January 1773, the Royal Society proposed a Polar Eb xpedition to discover whether a route to the East Indies could be found by sailing north through the Polar Regions. When Biddle learned of the plan, he applied to join the party and was assigned a place on the ill-named *Carcass*. Her partner vessel was His Majesty's ship *Racehorse*. Another member of the party was Horatio Nelson, then a fifteen-year-old midshipman.

The expedition started too late in the year for success. Frigid air descended on the Greenland Sea. The two ships sailed as far north as Hakluyt's Headland and Moffen Island before fierce winds and strong currents forced them into a bay where growing sheets of ice soon surrounded the vessels. Five leagues of ice soon lay between the men and freedom. Doom seemed certain. When a chance easterly wind blew, the *Carcass*, having the most substantial construction, forced herself through the floes with the *Racehorse* following. The noise of the ice sheet breaking or giving way was as loud as cannon fire. "What astonishes, confounds, and frightens me most of all is that during the whole voyage, I did not apprehend danger," Biddle said of the experience.[2]

Safely returned to England and hoping to find another exhilarating expedition upon which to embark, news of the Boston Tea Party of December 16, 1773, galvanized him into action. His country needed him—just as it needed all of the Biddle family. He resigned from the Royal Navy and sailed home, arriving in Philadelphia in the late spring of 1774. Mr. Midshipman Biddle R.N. became Captain Biddle of the nascent Continental Navy, his commission signed by a family friend, Benjamin Franklin. Biddle's first command was the "little brig" *Andrea Doria*,[3] which was underequipped with only fourteen four-pound cannons. True to its legendary name (Andrea Doria had been a sixteenth-century Genoese admiral who successfully battled the Barbary pirates and drove the French from Genoa), the brig was instrumental during the Battles of Nassau and Block Island in February and April 1776. Biddle's success at stymying the enemy was so great that when the *Andrea Doria* sailed back up the Delaware following successful cruises, only five of its original crew members remained aboard; Biddle had stationed the others on the flotilla of prizes.

The thirty-two gun *Randolph* was the reward for his valor. Launched in Philadelphia on July 10, 1776, it was engineered for speed and maneuverability. "The very best vessel for sailing that I ever knew," Biddle boasted.[4] Never mind that its original masts splintered in March 1777, the ship had been refitted in

Charleston and was ready to fight again. Tonight he intended to capture the great prize that was the *Yarmouth*.

Recognizing the British warship's superior firepower and size, he chose a daring strategy. He gave the order to clear for battle and close, then sent a broadside shearing into the larger ship. He intended to cripple the enemy vessel by destroying its topmasts and rigging while maneuvering the *Randolph* out of reach of the *Yarmouth's* fire. Having dismasted the warship, Biddle and his men could then board and fight hand to hand. He had full confidence that he and his men would prevail. "I fear nothing but what I ought to fear," he'd once stated. "I am much more afraid of doing a foolish thing than losing my life."[5]

The attack took the *Yarmouth* by surprise. Its officers considered the thin-hulled *Randolph* too flimsy for warfare, a frigate built for speed rather than heavy combat. Nonetheless, they opened fire.

Biddle ordered another broadside, then another. The *Yarmouth* lost two topmasts during the initial assault. For every broadside the British ship issued, the easily maneuvered *Randolph* sent three rattling into the *Yarmouth's* masts. Fire lit the sky; the echoing blare of the cannons drowning the shattering of wood and the screams of the wounded or dying. In the sea, sizzling embers sparked and burned, making the water appear ablaze.

For twenty ferocious minutes, the battle raged, the *Yarmouth* beginning to move sluggishly with its rigging partially in threads, and the *Randolph* springing forward to deliver more blows. Severely wounded in the thigh, Biddle ignored the ship's surgeon's warnings, insisting instead on being tied to a chair where he continued to direct the attack. Heedless of pain and loss of blood, he ordered his ship to sail beneath the *Yarmouth's* stern, where he intended to deliver a final debilitating broadside. The *Randolph* had also sustained damage; it was slower than it had been and less easy to maneuver, but its officers and crew believed that victory would be theirs.

No one knows how the disaster occurred, not the four *Randolph* crewmembers who miraculously managed to survive, nor the men aboard the *Yarmouth*. One moment, all was the thud and boom and crack of cannons igniting, the next an explosion rent the skies as the *Randolph's* powder magazine detonated, ripping it apart. The sound was unearthly; the living later stated they hoped they'd never hear its like again. The conflagration looked unquenchable as the *Randolph's* splintered wood and rigging shot upward in searing arcs, then hissed, still flaming, onto the *Yarmouth's* decks or dropped red-hot timbers into the sea. Dying American crewmen also catapulted heavenward. The *Yarmouth* and lesser vessels could only attempt to maneuver as far from the disaster as possible, lest the inferno engulfed them.

Three hundred and one Americans perished. The *Yarmouth's* losses were five men killed and twelve wounded, but the *Randolph* lost all aboard save the four who'd been hurled into the sea and rescued four days later by the stunned crew of the *Yarmouth*. Captain Nicholas Biddle was among the dead. Not yet twenty-eight, he was newly engaged to be married. A young lady from Charleston was to have become his bride.

* * *

In 1840, in his encyclopedic history of the United States navy, James Fenimore Cooper wrote of Captain Nicholas Bidde:

> There is little question that Nicholas Biddle would have risen to high rank and great consideration had his life been spared. Ardent, ambitious, fearless, intelligent, and persevering, he had all the qualities of a great naval captain. For so short a career, scarcely any other has been so brilliant. His loss was greatly regretted in the midst of the excitement and vicissitudes of a revolution, and can scarcely be appreciated by those who do not understand the influence that such a character can produce on a small and infant service.[6]

"Ardent, ambitious, fearless" could have been applied to Biddle's siblings, too. Tightly knit as a family and intensely proud of one another's valor, they recognized how vital was the fight for independence. The first Biddle to leave England for the colonies in 1681 had escaped religious persecution; four generations later, his descendants refused to let anyone or anything intimidate them. Philadelphia, their home, had been central to the fight against oppression since its founding by William Penn in 1682. The Continental Congress had convened there to write the Declaration of Independence. Nicholas's eldest brother, Edward, had been a delegate to the first Congress. Another brother, Charles, had clandestinely sailed for France to purchase arms and powder, twice been taken prisoner by the British, and aided the citizens escaping the army of occupation that descended upon the city in 1777. A cousin served as Washington's aide de camp. To the British, the Biddles were traitors to the crown. They took pleasure in their reputation. Weakness and vacillation had no place in their lexicon. Courage was their byword, an article of faith they passed along to the next generation.

The financier, Nicholas Biddle, who was named for his patriotic uncle, shared those hereditary traits. Famously battling President Andrew Jackson over the issue of a central bank, the Bank of the United States, he distinguished himself not as a warrior but through his perspicacity, skills at oratory, discernment, foresight, and erudition. Like his namesake, he was also fearless.

- CHAPTER ONE -

AN AMERICAN FAMILY

The story of the financier Nicholas Biddle cannot be told without putting him within the context of his family and its place in the nation's birth. The lives of Biddle's parents, great grandparents, siblings, and cousins were intimately intertwined with the making of America from its earliest colonial days. Theirs was an immigrant narrative: the flight from injustice and oppression to forge a new identity—self-autonomy and ultimately power. The first émigré Biddles (originally Byddll[1]) William (b. 1633) and his wife, Sarah (b. 1637/8), landed in the "colonie" of New Jersey in October 1681, a year before William Penn's arrival to establish Pennsylvania.

Political upheaval and Civil War had threatened every aspect of British life during William's youth: Oliver Cromwell's "Roundheads" having deposed and then executed King Charles I in 1649. Religion played a central part in Cromwell's brutal campaign against Ireland, during which Catholics (and Loyalists who had fled England) were massacred. For a populace grown weary of war and the love of wealth and lust for power evinced by Catholics and Anglicans alike, Religious Dissenters attracted adherents eager for change. George Fox, who founded the Religious Society of Friends (commonly called Quakers or Friends), preached that all men and women should feel God's presence directly rather than through priestly intermediaries, just as the earliest Christians had. Staunch English Quakers, the Biddle family counted among its numbers Esther (also spelled Hester or Ester), a firebrand itinerant minister who traveled to Ireland, Scotland, the Continent, and the Caribbean to spread the word. Gender parity, a principle of the Faith, was essential to her. Reared in intellectual surroundings in Oxford, Esther was an educated woman. One of her surviving published tracts (*Wo to Thee City of Oxford*, 1655) can be found in the Bodleian Library.

After Cromwell died in 1658, a series of Acts of Parliaments sought to disband and destroy the Quakers. The Corporation Act of 1661 made it mandatory that all officials swear an oath based on the Church of England's sacraments. The Quaker Act (May 2, 1662) required Friends to proclaim allegiance to the king against their faith. The Act of Uniformity (May 19, 1662) held the Book of Common Prayer to be supreme. The Conventicle Act of 1664 forbade more than five Quakers from gathering outside their homes for purposes of worship or religion. The Five Mile Act of 1665 proscribed dissenting clergy and schoolmasters from practicing their professions within five miles of their former schools or parishes. Spies denounced those who disobeyed. William was imprisoned in Newgate in London for his beliefs, as were numerous Quakers. When the Great Fire of London engulfed the city in September 1666, the survivors rebuilt their homes and businesses, but dissenters' persecution escalated. William and Sarah looked to North America as a new promised land where they could experience oneness with God and follow their faith's pacifist, egalitarian tenets. With the couple were their two living children (Sarah had given birth to six babies), William Jr, eleven, and Sarah, two.

When the family arrived in West New Jersey aboard the *Thomas and Anne*, they must have believed they had discovered an earthly peaceable kingdom. Swedes, Finns, and other Englishmen had already tamed some of the lands, but most remained virgin territory. In contrast, Burlington on the Northampton River (present-day Rancocas Creek), where the *Thomas and Anne* anchored, contained twenty-eight building lots upon which had been constructed two inns, houses, barns, a tannery, cooperage, and blacksmith's shop. The monthly meeting of Friends took place in the village. Beyond Burlington stood woodlands dense with chestnut, hickory, maple, gum, and white and black oak. The Lenape village of Oneanickon lay to the south. Lenape trails or natural waterways were the sole means of travel from one homestead site to another.

Having purchased proprietary interests in seven tracts of land while he was still in England, William was entitled to 1,600 acres in the vicinity of Burlington. He decided those properties were less than ideal and exchanged them for two parcels of land that eventually included Seppasink Island in the Delaware River, six miles upstream from Burlington. Situated opposite the island, the mainland property was above the flood plain and was rich, arable, and ideally suited for farming. The island provided safe grazing from predators and an abundance of salt hay for fodder. Its purchase angered Penn, who believed that all the Delaware River islands should belong to Pennsylvania. He blamed Sarah for negotiating privately with the Lenape for ownership of the island, even though he'd been secretly attempting the same maneuver. Seppasink eventually became known as Biddle Island.

The dual tracts were worth the quarrel with Penn. On the mainland, the Delaware River's intermittent vistas opened from tall, sandy bluffs or oyster-strewn beaches, the waters in the coves crystalline instead of the turgid brown of the Thames. Sturgeon and shad spawned close to shore, flocks of migratory birds blackened the skies, and game could be found in abundance. For city dwellers who had lived in cramped quarters amidst a miasma of smoke from wood-burning fires and the constant reek of human and animal refuse, this was like the Garden of Eden. In 1684, William and Sarah built their homestead, Mount Hope. Tribal peoples continued to dwell on the land, and they and the Biddles maintained mutually supportive intercourse. William increased his landholdings, became a member of the West Jersey General Assembly, served as a justice on the Burlington Court, and was elected a Proprietor. Rather than his son, William, Jr., he named his grandson, also William (b. 1698), to inherit Mount Hope.

At first, William III's future seemed assured. His father sent him to Phila-delphia to work as a merchant. In 1730, he wed twenty-one-year-old Mary Scull, the daughter of the Surveyor General of Pennsylvania, Nicholas Scull (b. 1687). Mary was an Anglican, which meant that the groom married out of the Society of Friends. Other Quakers also left their faith, believing that Anglican-ism was more politically and commercially advantageous. Scull was a friend of Benjamin Franklin and a fellow member of the scholarly, mutual improvement society, the Junto, as well as of the Library Company that Franklin founded. He and his daughter were of a literary bent; Mary was a gifted writer, a skill she passed along to her children and grandchildren. In those early days of Pennsyl-vania, the Sculls were counted among the elite. With London tastes in the arts and a cosmopolitan sensibility, they would have been comfortably at home in the motherland.

It soon became apparent that William had inherited none of his forebears' business acumen. A proud man with a quick temper, he made dubious invest-ments with questionable partners. Wounded by a cutlass in an altercation over a debt, he lost most of the use of his right arm. Less than nine years after his father's death, he'd sold Mount Hope and all its acreage, but the proceeds barely covered his debts. He died at the age of fifty-eight in 1765 from a "lingering disorder"[2] that engendered violent dreams. His wife slept fully clothed at his side to escape his anger quickly when nightmares afflicted him. "I was married nineteen years," Mary later told her son, Charles, "and at times thought everything that gave me pain a dreadful affliction. I had nine children, one at my breast, when Mr. Biddle informed me one morning that he had ruined me and his children."[3]

Mary Scull Biddle became the heroine of her sons' and daughters' lives. She was determined to put her failed marriage behind her. If her sons needed to begin work at an early age rather than complete their schooling, so be it. They would develop strength of character by doing so. Naval hero Nicholas, who perished aboard the *Randolph*, was a perfect amalgam of his parents: steely and brave like Mary and fiery like his father. Those twin traits were found in varying proportions in all the Biddle boys.

If Mary was the glue that held the family together, her son, Charles, became its chronicler. A sailor like his younger brother and hot-tempered as a youth, he was an unlikely choice for the family historian. Given to salty language, and never one to mince words, he peppered his speech with colorful phrases like "As pickled a rascal as ever was hanged"[4] or "as great a ruffian as ever was hanged."[5] No one who knew him during his early years would have predicted that his son, Nicholas, would become the youngest person to graduate from the College of New Jersey (Princeton University), an expert in finance, and an advisor to presidents. Charles couldn't have imagined it either. Although he became an esteemed member of Philadelphia's governing class—he entitled his autobiography *Charles Biddle, Vice-President of the Supreme Executive Council of Pennsylvania*—his earliest days were spent amidst the polyglot community that comprised the port city during the middle of the eighteenth century: indentured servants, slaves, freed men and women, skilled artisans, common laborers, and mariners hailing from all parts of the globe.

As a boy, Charles ran wild. Despite his mother's efforts and those of his two eldest brothers, he started spending his hours hobnobbing with every rowdy and ruffian he encountered. "There was no kind of mischief could be proposed but what I was ready to be concerned in,"[6] he recalled of his behavior at the age of eleven. The rapidly growing city had spawned a widening class imbalance, the lowest paid being cordwainers, coopers, chimney sweeps, and the like whose precarious livelihoods put them on the fringes of respectability. Charles, the family's rebel, counted them as friends. During his brief visits home, he became surly and pugnacious—the antithesis of the upright citizen Mary hoped to rear. Reprimanded, he returned to the places where he felt most at home, the cramped alleyways that led to the docks. Because Philadelphia was the largest metropolis in the colonies and its busiest port, its wharves teemed with merchant's vessels. The seamen who operated them reveled in raucous tales of derring-do. For Charles, these were living, breathing swashbucklers, not men like his father, who ill-used their wives.

Staring downriver, he could imagine the Delaware emptying into the bay and thence the ocean. Freedom and autonomy lay there. He began taking pride in his ability to swear and made it clear he would never obey any landlubber's rules. His "pranks,"[7] as he dismissed them, became dangerous and deliberate: tying ropes across night-darkened alleyways to trip unwary pedestrians or shooting purloined pistols close to the ears of passersby. He was on his way to becoming a criminal and might have, were it not for James and Edward's intervention, fifteen and six years his seniors.

Hauling their younger brother into a room in the small, crowded home the family shared with paying lodgers; they informed him that he was breaking his mother's heart and would have no future outside of a prison cell. The boy protested; he was nothing if not independent, but his brothers persevered. By that time, James and Edward were able to aid their mother financially, and it was on her account that Charles agreed to mend his ways. Mary, though, remained apprehensive, and James and Edward vigilant.

When he reached fourteen, Mary decided the best means of calming his rebellious spirit was to apprentice him to a merchant in the city. The humdrum existence soon palled. He hated being imprisoned in a shop, being forced to run what he considered to be mindless errands, or feigning a contrite demeanor when his master criticized his fecklessness. He returned to the docks, dreaming of shipping out on a merchant ship as a cabin boy. At length, Mary acquiesced to his entreaties, although she still worried that his reckless nature would resurface. The opposite was true. "My going to sea was the best thing I could have done," Charles said.[8]

Working aboard vessels transporting cargo to the West Indies or Europe, he found the excitement his life required. Like his father, though, he possessed a volatile temper. He fought with seamen on other ships, engaged in duels, and prided himself on standing his ground with those bigger and stronger. "I got severely beaten,"[9] he would remind his children when recounting those years, but the words echoed with a sense of achievement rather than humiliation.

His sons understood that manliness required bravado, daring, and physical exertion—not bookish pursuits. Charles described near-fatal shipwrecks, lethal contagions spread among crewmembers, and narrow escapes from drowning. He rose from the rank of cabin boy to second mate to captain: the "Boy Captain" as he was nicknamed. His experiences in the southern colonies and the West Indies taught him to despise the slave trade. When new owners of a ship he commanded ordered him to sail to Africa to gather a cargo of slaves, he resigned his position and monetary share in the vessel. "I left her for nothing would have tempted me to go such a voyage. I expressed my abhorrence of this trade in such a manner as to give great offence."[10] Incapable of bridling his tongue, he also made it plain that he intended his career to be "lucrative." The penury of childhood had made him an ambitious man.

* * *

By 1775, Charles and Nicholas's thirty-seven-year-old brother Edward was a veteran of the army. After joining as an ensign at sixteen, he rose to captain of the 8th Battalion of the Pennsylvania Regiment on Foot. During one expedition in the French and Indian Wars, Edward, who had a high opinion of the chiefs and warriors, "was dressed and painted as an Indian." When he and his guide, a chief, found themselves in danger of falling into enemy hands, the chief told him, "with every token of respect, not to be in the least uneasy about being tortured, for the moment you are taken, I will tomahawk you."[11] Heedless of his safety, Edward was succinct when asked about his military record. "When my country demanded my service I did not keep back but courted Danger for her sake."[12]

Admitted to the Bar in 1767, he became a representative to the Pennsylvania Provincial Assembly and a Pennsylvania delegate to the Continental Congresses of 1774 and 1775. During the first Congress in 1774, he'd been a member of the committee that drafted the Declaration of Rights and subsequently oversaw printing the resolutions Congress passed. Elected speaker for the 1775 Continental Congress on October 16, 1774, his popularity and fitness for the position was universally acknowledged. "The house was in an uproar" the moment the announcement was made. "As many as could lay hold of him and forced him into the Chair on a unanimous vote."[13] A leader of the Whig party and radically opposed to any proposed concessions to England, Edward took thirty-year-old Charles under his wing. The seafarer newly returned home, Charles found himself awed by his brother's political sagacity and urbanity.

War with Britain was the talk on every street. From alleyways whose homes consisted of a single room stacked atop another to marble-fronted residences graced with gardens and shade trees, residents discussed the pros and cons of conflict. In the more impoverished neighborhoods, women carted spinning wheels out to their front stoops to not miss heated conversations; cobblers and saddlers also moved their wares and tools outside. Children, dogs, cats, and pigs darted through the milling throngs. Moving through the city, Charles heard voices raised either in favor of war or in trepidation. How would conflict with England affect wages? Would they plummet like they had in the early 1770s? Would more people be forced to endure the ignominy of the Bettering House (the almshouse on Spruce Street)? Would war aid only the wealthy ("worldly men"[14] as Charles deemed them) and established artisans? A Tory from New Jersey was tarred, feathered, and dragged through the city; Charles intervened and prevented the man from being beaten to death. "Huzzas" for the king met with mob retaliation. The momentousness of the debate and its consequences made his brother, Edward's, participation even more significant.

"The first day Congress sat I rode out with my brother Edward, who was a member. He told me that from the disposition of the members, particularly those from New England, he was sure much blood would be spilled before the dispute was settled."[15] Charles, like his siblings and mother, believed Edward might become "next in command to General Washington."[16] He was "brave, strong and active" as well as "esteemed and respected for his talents." Charles eagerly listened to his brother's description of the renewal of the non-importation agreement that had led to the protests over the Stamp Act. He just as eagerly greeted the men who called Edward colleague and friend. His future as a statesman seemed assured.

Calamity dictated otherwise. In January 1775, as Edward and Charles were returning by boat to Philadelphia from the town of Reading, the partially frozen waters of the Schuylkill River sent ice floes crashing against the ship's hull. Edward fell overboard. Although blinded in one eye, surviving the frigid water, he suffered painful, ill health for the remaining five years of his life. "Before this he was never sick"[17] was Charles's sorrowing assessment. It was unthinkable that the revered older brother who had been like a father to him could be so diminished. Edward and James were supposed to be invincible. But then, so was Philadelphia.

* * *

On behalf of freedom's cause, Charles's first activity was to sail to France on September 10, 1775, to purchase powder and arms. He was ordered to fly no colors and to claim the ship carried a cargo of salt if approached by a man-of-war. If he was unable to procure armaments in Nantes, he would sail for Holland and buy them there. His mission accomplished, he returned home in time to hear the Declaration of Independence formally read in the Statehouse yard on July 8, 1776. It was a stirring day, the city and its residents alive with the momentousness of the occasion. There was fear, too, for the Declaration espoused sedition, and everyone understood how harshly the mother country dealt with traitors to the Crown. Charles's brother, James, and his fellow vestry members of St. Peter's Church crossed off the king's name in the Anglican Book of Common Prayer, a traitorous act. Prominent Whigs denounced the Declaration as placing the populace in unnecessary danger.

The antagonism between the two sides escalated, both factions convinced their view was the only moral one. The rhetoric of Thomas Paine temporarily calmed the storm. Paine, Charles believed, "contributed much to reconciling the people to the Declaration of Independence." He credited Paine's work, *The Crisis,* with "rousing the people to arms. 'These are the times that try men's souls; the summer soldier and the sunshine patriot' were in the mouths of every one going to join the army."[18]

In August 1776, he joined Captain Cowperthwaite's Company of Quaker Light Infantry, composed of either Quakers or descendants of that faith. "Being desirous of having a shot at the Hessians, whom I considered as a set of horrid wretches that would hire themselves to commit any crime whatever," Charles said, "I gave up the command of a vessel to go out with the Quaker Light Infantry."[19] The decision violated the Quakers' principle of pacifism. The Philadelphia Meeting dismissed the enlistees.

After that, Charles returned to sea, joining the Continental Navy, and was twice taken prisoner in the West Indies. He never forgot the inhumane treatment of his crew aboard the infamous British prison ship, *Jersey.* All but one of his men died. There were rumors among the prisoners that the men had been poisoned.

Freed, he began receiving sporadic news of the engagements at home. The battle of Trenton became a cause for celebration. However, sailing north to Baltimore and thence to Philadelphia, he learned that his mother and other family members had fled west to Reading because the British were advancing north from Brandywine.

We could distinctly hear the firing at this battle in Philadelphia. There was an awful silence most of the day. People were coming in every minute from the scene of action, scarce any two of whom agreed in their account of the battle. We soon, however, found that our troops were worsted and retreating towards the city. I landed there, and found the place full of people flying from Philadelphia, many of whom were my acquaintances. I furnished my passengers provisions while they remained on board the brig. We lay off Bordentown. A number of vessels followed us up . . . as my brig was armed, I lay in the stream to prevent any shallop going down without a pass.[20]

The British victory at the Battle of Brandywine on September 11, 1777, meant that the enemy was now free to move northward and take Philadelphia. Panicked patriots packed up what belongings they could readily move and left the city. On September 26, 1777, Cornwallis, with 3,000 British soldiers and two Hessians battalions, entered Philadelphia. Another 18,000 men and officers in General Sir William Howe's army followed. The contrast between their well-fed figures and fine uniforms and the retreating continental troops' bedraggled appearance engendered sensations of despair.

The sudden influx of soldiers and their officers overwhelmed the metropolis. The enemy commandeered the "rebels'" abandoned homes and then dug privies in the cellars, chopped down fences, and burned furniture and church pews for firewood. The poor were evicted from the Alms House on Spruce Street to garrison some of Howe's soldiers, and the Presbyterian Church on Pine and 4th Streets was turned into a military hospital, then a stable for the cavalry. Food ran short. Looting became prevalent until British marines quelled the rioters. The newly constructed and as yet unfinished Walnut Street prison held nine hundred prisoners of war captured during the battles of Brandywine and Germantown. In charge was a villainous Irishman by the name of Cunningham who made a habit of starving and beating the prisoners, many of whom died for want of sustenance and who were then dragged by the legs to death carts. The inmates ate rats if they were fortunate enough to catch them. When a cow or other beast was butchered within the prison confines, many consumed the meat raw.

With the enemy ensconced in the city, Philadelphians endured daily indignities and terrors. Tories were lauded while patriots lived in fear. The conquerors were quick to take the city's emotional pulse. Their artillery was quartered in full view on Chestnut Street between Third and Sixth streets; the 42nd Highlanders occupied Chestnut below third; the 15th Regiment took possession of Market and Fifth Streets. Parades were performed morning and evening. The colonists were supposed to take note of all this military might and mend their wicked ways. Despite the cold winter months, the city's stench became almost unbearable. A pit dug behind the State House where the bold ideals of independence had been argued contained a vile stew of dead horses, human bodies, and human excrement. There was too little room to bury the refuse properly. Many Philadelphians believed the fight for freedom was lost.

For Tory families, however, the city's occupation was as glittering as London's "season." They organized dances and levees and introduced their marriageable daughters to eligible British officers. The festivities culminated in a "Meschianza." Held in honor of Sir William Howe on Monday, May 18, 1778, at the Thomas Wharton country estate "Walnut Grove," tickets for the event depicted the Howe family crest. The "Meschianza" included faux jousting tournaments, a regatta, a ball lasting into the early morning, a midnight banquet, and a fireworks display. Twenty-four slaves dressed in Oriental style and outfitted with silver bracelets and collars served the assembly. The ladies of the party—including the acclaimed beauty Margaret Shippen, who subsequently married Benedict Arnold—were escorted to the place while dressed "a la Turque" as if they were members of a harem. Voices singing *God Save the King* boomed out across the Wharton lands and gardens.

By then, Charles Biddle was based in Charleston, South Carolina, plying southern waters, intent on avenging his brother's death. He considered capturing the island of Tortola because he had learned that its fort was inadequately manned. With Tortola in American hands, the British would no longer control the shipping lanes. The scheme didn't come to fruition, but the possibility of the stratagem and its glorious conclusion remained with him all his days.

Between cruises, he met and married Hannah Shepard in Beaufort, North Carolina, on November 25, 1778. The courtship was brief owing to the exigencies of war, but Hannah, who prided herself on being a true southern lady, took this social indiscretion in stride. Charles said of their marriage that it was the "most happy circumstance of his life."[21] One of his proudest possessions was a certificate of bravery that he received in May 1780 from North Carolina. The signed and sealed document was kept in a prominent place in his home in Philadelphia: "Charles, Biddle, Esquire, hath upon all occasions during the present war distinguished himself for his bravery and attachment to the cause of America."[22]

* * *

A tide of pride galvanized the citizenry after the 1783 Treaty of Paris, concluding the Revolutionary War and granting independence and sovereignty to the thirteen former British colonies. For Philadelphians, the sense of elation was high because the memories of being occupied by the enemy remained entrenched in their collective memory. Charles returned to merchant seafaring after the war, but Hannah, left alone with their growing family, persuaded him to quit the trade and become a shopkeeper. The family was still living in Reading. At Hannah's urging, Charles purchased a small store, intending to eventually acquire a larger one in Philadelphia, although he mourned the thrilling days of his youth. Then politics called.

In October 1784, Philadelphia was both the nation's and state's capital. Biddle rented a house in the city to represent Berks County on the Supreme Executive Council of the Commonwealth of Pennsylvania. John Dickinson, a close friend of Charles's brother James, was then president, General James Irvine vice president. A year later, in October 1785, Charles became vice president under Dickinson. Subsequently, he served as vice president under Benjamin Franklin, whose fame when he returned to Philadelphia from France was so great that cheering throngs lined the streets. Of the group gathered to form a Federal Constitution in 1787, Charles said, "We had in the Conventions many of the best and wisest men in this or any other country."[23] His national pride blended with his populist history. When it was proposed to move the state capitol to Lancaster rather than Philadelphia, he recognized the underlying motives as friction between residents of the metropolis and the rural representatives whom he believed "could not speak their sentiments, or give their votes freely without risking their being insulted. Unfortunately, many of the principal people in the city looked upon and treated the Western members with great contempt."[24] His son, Nicholas, would later experience the same geographical discord that, in turn, impacted the popularity of a central bank.

1791 saw Charles commissioned as prothonotary of the Court of Common Pleas, a position James Biddle had also held. Ever hard-headed and independent, he insisted upon making his own decisions rather than following party lines. "I went into Council with a firm resolution not to suffer any party views to influence my conduct, and this I adhered to."[25]

All the while, Charles and Hannah's family increased in size. Mary was the first-born girl. Then came William in February 1781, James, who achieved fame as a commodore, was born in February 1783. Nicholas Biddle, the financier, was born on January 8, 1786. Charles, named for his father, came in August 1787, Thomas, in November 1790, John in March of 1792, Richard four years later in March of 1796, and Ann in March 1800. Another daughter died in 1789 at fifteen months of age. Mary Scull Biddle died the same year. Charles was devastated by the loss of his mother. One of the proudest moments of his life had been when he had finally earned enough wages to send home to his parent, and he supported her as soon as he married and established a home. Her obituary in the *Pennsylvania Gazette* on May 20, 1789, correctly referred to her as "affectionate—ardently affectionate."[26]

* * *

The yellow fever epidemic of 1793 threw Philadelphia into a paroxysm of fear. A cure seemed impossible. No physician agreed on prevention or treatment. Patients were dosed with mercury that compromised their health *if* they survived, or cannons were fired at night under the belief that the smoke might prove a deterrent. Families fled the city if they could afford to. As extensive as the exodus prior to the British invasion had been, this was worse. President George Washington quit the metropolis for Mt. Vernon.

Those who remained in the plague-infested city and ventured into the streets tied small bottles of vinegar or bags of camphor around their necks or held sponges full of vinegar to their nostrils. No one dared greet a friend or neighbor with a customary handshake. When a hearse passed, people shrank against the walls. The precautions proved worthless. Corpses lay in the streets, the living too frightened to inter the bodies. If patients could be moved, they were taken to Bush Hill, the country estate of James Hamilton (currently 17th and Spring Garden Streets), where merchant, financier, and philanthropist Stephen Girard established a hospital. However, the name Bush Hill quickly became synonymous with death. Between August and November, over 4,000 people died.

Subsequent epidemics followed in 1794, 1796, 1797, and 1798, the latter as destructive as the one five years before. It inspired Charles to purchase a country house "three miles from town"[27] on remote and pastoral Islington Lane, which is now in the city's heavily populated area of Ridge Avenue and 26th Street. Before that, in 1797, his brother James died. This loss was a bitter blow.

"No father could have taken better care of me than he did," he recalled, adding a telling, "I hardly ever remember him out of temper."[28]

On December 14, 1799, a more considerable woe shook the nation with the death of Washington. "Grief was pictured in every countenance when we had a certain account of his death," Charles wrote of the "great and good man. I have heard Mr. Robert Morris, who was an intimate with him as any man in America, say that he was the only man in whose presence he felt any awe."[29] Biddle had been well acquainted with Washington, having dined with him at his brother Edward's home. Their houses were neighboring, Biddle's at 243 High Street—now Market; Washington's at 190. Charles's first cousin, Colonel Clement Biddle (b. May 10, 1740), had fought under Washington at Princeton, Brandywine, Germantown, and Monmouth, and the two men maintained an ongoing friendship. The Biddle family had reason to view the President's death as a personal and a national loss.

* * *

When Washington died, Nicholas was a precocious and academically brilliant young teenager. At age ten, he had been enrolled at the University of Pennsylvania's college department, which his elder brother William also attended. Because he was too young to officially complete his studies, Charles and Hannah decided to send him to study at the College of New Jersey, as Princeton University was then called. He was twelve years and seven months old when he entered in 1799 and would become the youngest person to graduate, a distinction unchallenged today. His scholarly proclivities proved a conundrum to his father and brothers, who had been taught to equate success with courage under fire. Being named for his heroic uncle didn't help matters.

Up until his years at Princeton, young Nicholas's childhood had not been particularly happy. Despite Hannah's efforts at inclusion for all her children, he often experienced a sense of dislocation. His father and uncles and elder cousins' tales of valor seemed impossible to emulate. They were like a race of giants, who had bled and died for their country's freedom, and the next generation of Biddles was expected to follow their example. Where those men chose action, Nicholas preferred introspection. Where they grew impatient with debate, he reveled in the lengthy discourse, choosing intellectual pastimes over the rowdy games his brothers enjoyed.

Arriving at the college, he experienced not a moment's hesitation, although his youth inspired quizzical and sometimes censorious glances from the other students. Dressed as befitted a gentleman with knee-length breeches, stockings, tailcoat, waistcoat, and cravat, his body still had the chubbiness of boyhood, and his face was pink and smooth and his eyes wide with wonder. Nor was he yet as tall as he would become. To most, he looked like a child masquerading as a man, and cocky and even impertinent, at that. Ardor carried him along, however, as well as a hereditary resoluteness of spirit. He might have appeared awkward trundling along the pathways and lanes in Princeton while trying to mimic his elder peers' posture and gait, but his bookish soul was as bold as his forebears'. Nicholas was convinced he had entered his native land.

- CHAPTER TWO -

THE CHILD PRODIGY

When Nicholas enrolled, the College of New Jersey consisted of a single building, Nassau Hall, or "Aula Nassovica," as it was properly called. A massive sandstone edifice four stories tall and composed of two long wings flanking a central pavilion, it dwarfed the trees and lawn fronting the original King's Highway—present-day Nassau Street. Arriving in Princeton by stagecoach, young Biddle's first impression was of grandeur and gravitas, the likes of which he'd never seen, although its architect, Robert Smith, and his other works were well known in Philadelphia. No nearby structure could compare with its heft or solemn bulk. Housing recitation rooms, a library, dining hall, chapel, and dormitory, it required twelve chimneys to keep it even moderately warm. The Literary and Debating Society, the Cliosophic, occupied two chambers.

The new boy immediately gravitated to the Cliosophic, but membership in its august ranks was granted only to the most worthy scholars. Determined to join, Nicholas persevered, his voice squeaking with enthusiasm. His dedication and obvious intellectual gifts eventually impressed even the haughtiest "Clios" who invited him to become a member. They dubbed the child prodigy "Grammaticus," which may have been intended as irony. If so, Nicholas paid no heed to the gibe or its allusion to over-scrupulous bookishness. Instead, the name delighted him as further proof of prestige among his peers. Delving into the wondrous array of subjects offered, the boy who was both young teenager and college student, began his studies of Xenophon, Homer, Cicero, Horace, natural theology, the philosophy of civil government, history, logic, criticism, Latin, Greek, French, Italian, English composition, and Roman antiquities.[1] The curriculum reflected the Age of Enlightenment. It was assumed that the college's central function was to educate the nation's new leaders, which was a heady notion, especially for the impressionable Nicholas.

Eminent scholar, Samuel Stanhope Smith, was then president of the college. An alumnus, he had served as salutatorian of the class of 1769 and been a professor of moral philosophy before acceding to the presidency in 1795 after the death of John Witherspoon, his father-in-law. The latter had been a member of the Continental Congress and a signer of the Declaration of Independence. Smith was most famous (notorious to some) for his published work *Essay on the Causes and Variety of Complexion and Figure in the Human Species*, a study of the climactic differences that permitted humans to evolve into differing races— each suited to its specific topography and environment. Many viewed the *Essay* as dangerous because it questioned white racial superiority—that black Africans were innately inferior—and, by extension, the practice of slavery, which Smith despised. Nicholas copied Smith's theories with an elegant hand, hoping the refinement of his penmanship would make him appear older than his years.

> A System and Moral Philosophy by Samuel Smith DD; MAPS
> President of New Jersey College - Transcribed by Nicholas Biddle one thousand eight hundred.
> Philosophy is an investigation of the construction and laws of nature as far as the human mind alone is competent to discover them. We cannot penetrate in to the essence of things & from these determine what will be their effects, either singly or in any possible combination. An accurate attention to effects is the only means by which we can gradually approach to the knowledge of their causes, and attain something like an acquaintance with the constitution either of body or of mind.[2]

In September 1800, at the grand age of fourteen, and a year before his graduation, he was elected President of the Cliosophic. He delivered the valedictory oration to his fellow "Clios" who had completed their studies and were about to launch themselves into their professional careers, or as Nicholas said, "to enter the bounteous oceans of the world." His voice wavering between a high boyhood pitch and the assurance of adulthood, he told his audience:

> In the present state of our country, there is an extensive field for the talents and the virtues of every disinterested Patriot. With your superior advantages of improvement, doubt not that you will one day be the

statesmen and legislators of the country. . . . Your country will demand your exertions, and your minds are too noble to disobey her call.[3]

* * *

While Biddle pursued his scholarly path, Philadelphia began undergoing a physical transformation. The largest city in the United States, its population numbered over sixty-seven thousand in 1800. Built on a grid pattern according to William Penn's original design, the areas furthest east along the Delaware River had been the first sections of the city to be inhabited. At the same time, the western stretches maintained a countrified air. Leaving Nicholas's home on High Street (now teeming, commercial Market) between Sixth and Seventh Streets, and walking west toward the Schuylkill, pastures replaced homes, and streams and ponds full of fish and ducks became a common sight. To the north along the Delaware, business reigned. Steam power and mechanized industry were poised to obliterate the semi-pastoral landscape, changing the "greene countrie towne" into a bustling metropolis of textile mills, iron foundries, coopers, whitesmiths, wheelwrights, shipwrights, gunsmiths, and tanneries.

For a young man with a passion for knowledge, artist Charles Willson Peale's Museum provided a cabinet of wonders. Originally housed in Philosophical Hall, it relocated to larger quarters in the State House in 1802. The Quadruped Room welcomed visitors: each mounted specimen, whether llama, grizzly bear, or bison, placed in painted landscapes appropriate to its native climate. The Long Room, one-hundred feet in length, was filled with birds, minerals, rare shells, exotic insects, and the portraits of scientists, explorers, and Revolutionary War heroes. The greatest wonder of all, though, was a reticulated skeleton of the fossilized mastodon. The "mammoth," as the creature was known, had been discovered in a marl-pit in New York State, making spectators ponder whether such a vast animal could have once roamed the familiar streets of Philadelphia.

Everywhere Nicholas looked during his formative years, he experienced a sense of pride of place and history. His schoolwork reflected this intellectual bravado. Encouraged by teachers and tutors who voiced their collective opinion that he was a prodigy, Biddle believed them and carefully preserved the essays he considered his finest work, many of which were composed in Latin or Greek. "Whether the Arts and Sciences are Favorable to Virtue,"[4] "On the Study of Dead Languages,"[5] "The Civilized and Savage State,"[6] and "On the Advantages Arising from the Necessity of a Strong Government"[7] were among the titles. In

"To the King of the Russian Empire,"[8] he envisioned himself as a general in the Czar's army, warning of the consequences of the feudal system: "Although my personal acquaintance with you is yet small, I hope I may escape the reputation of boldness and presumption in thus addressing you. You are my sovereign. I am your subject. . . . But the truth must and shall be spoken however grating to the ears of despotism."

He also tackled slavery in a five-page essay in which he argued the moral imperative of abolition versus pragmatism. His closest friend, Edward Watts of Virginia, and his first-year roommate, Arthur Rose Fitzhugh, also a Virginian, came from slave-owning families. To the college, slavery was an accepted fact of life. New Jersey was the last northern state to abolish the practice, which it did by gradual measures beginning in 1804. Nicholas' rather laborious essay blended bravado with timidity. The youngest student did not want to alienate his companions. As abhorrent as he had been taught to believe slavery was (although he blamed Europe rather than the United States for the trade), he could not conceive a solution.

Airily declaring that the dilemma had existed since "the establishment of the constitution," he concluded that,

> Government cannot without a violation of the constitution enact any
> laws for the purpose [of manumission]. . . . It is indeed beautiful to
> contemplate man living as freely as if in a state of nature & enjoying
> all the blessings of creation. These are but the visionary dreams of the
> philanthropist or the wishes of the philosopher, but they will be far
> distant from the ideas of the politician; for however beautiful in theory,
> they will be impossible in practice.

And there he left the thorny issue. If he was unable to find an answer, he could at least wrap the debate in elegant prose.

A propensity for recklessness leavened the serious side to his nature, so did a childlike obliviousness of his physical welfare. Hannah's affectionate letters were peppered with reminders to eat and often accompanied by hampers of food that went untouched except by his friends. Charles's much shorter notes reminded "Nick" of the benefits of daily perambulations but to no avail. Nicholas considered walking and reading mutually exclusive activities. He loved his father but would have preferred a different role model.

Nicholas also had a chronic inability to account for the money his father sent him, which frustrated Charles no end. Having schooled his children in the importance of fiscal responsibility, he demanded that his son keep records of his spending. Nicholas dutifully carted home the ledger book and tried to explain each entry, but he could never make the numbers tally, nor could he explain just where his stipend went. It became an ongoing struggle. Charles might not have been surprised at his son's profligacy if he had witnessed the boisterous dinners in a Princeton tavern that Nicholas and his friends enjoyed.

There was plenty of female companionships, too, although he lacked his companions' poise and witty repartee. Often he felt like a pesky, younger brother. At thirteen, fourteen, and even fifteen, he found himself unable to exchange light banter no matter how hard he tried. Tongue-tied, he would search for a suitable topic. Failing to find one, he would begin discussing a tutorial that intrigued him or a paper he had written—no wonder the young ladies preferred his friends' company. Two exceptions were Betsy Smith, the President's daughter who was considered "rather wild,"[9] and Maria Gibbon, who called Nicholas a "smart beau," adding, "his mind is highly improved."[10] Even Maria's patience wore thin; as for Betsy, she had the entire graduating class at her feet.

* * *

While Nicholas delved deeper and deeper into his intellectual pursuits, his brothers, James and Edward, emulating their uncle and father, petitioned Charles and Hannah to join the Navy as midshipmen in January 1800. It was a period of growth for the United States Navy due to tensions with France, whose maritime forces were augmented by privateers that harried and captured American commercial vessels engaged in the West Indian trade. A subsequent treaty signed by First Consul Napoleon Bonaparte in September 1800 did little to ameliorate the problem. Charles's friend, Commodore Thomas Truxtun, visited Philadelphia to gain support for an enhanced United States Navy; and James and Edward became convinced they had found their life's callings.

Like their father and uncles, they would not take no for an answer, insisting instead that careers in the Navy were all but their birthright. At first ambivalent, Charles was persuaded to permit James to join. But he vehemently opposed Edward's choice, insisting that he was a "brilliant mathematician"[11] who should cleave to his studies. By the age of fifteen in 1799, when Edward left school, he had mastered Isaac Newton's *Principia* without a tutor's aid. Sixteen in 1800, he was already six feet tall. He believed he had achieved manhood and the ability to determine his fate, which he explained to his father.

Eventually, Charles acquiesced. He wrote to the Secretary of the Navy, who responded on February 14, 1800, by sending the young men warrants as midshipmen to serve under Truxtun aboard U.S. Navy frigate *President*. James, the elder, who would have a stellar naval career, became Edward's de facto guardian. Both parents depended upon the older to keep the younger from harm, but they worried.

As the time approached for his sons' departure in early July 1800, Charles experienced premonitions of doom, which were unusual given his personality. Accompanying James and Edward to New York to join the *President*, he found the weather "excessively hot,"[12] which deepened his anxiety. Privately, he declared the journey "the most disagreeable I ever made."[13] He went so far as to say that it would have given him "pleasure to hear the ship was burned or sunk:" strong words even for an outspoken man. In New York, they found their boarding house dirty and over-crowded. Another of Charles's friends, Aaron Burr, invited the threesome to be his guests. There, they dined with Alexander Hamilton as Burr and Hamilton were then on good terms. The boys took obvious pleasure in participating in adult discussions while awaiting their ship's departure. But Charles's apprehensions increased. "A thousand melancholy reflections filled my mind," he stated.[14] As their father's fears escalated, Edward and James, agog with anticipation, boarded the *President*. Smartly turned out in their new uniforms, they were eager for their longed-for adventures to begin.

Not until December did Charles and Hannah receive a letter from Edward. Communications between ships and ports were unpredictable, depending upon a ship outward bound to exchange mail with one inward bound. The parents were overjoyed to hear that he and James were hale and hearty and enjoying their duties. The ship was then berthed in St. Kitts. Truxton also wrote to say that he was pleased with the young men's service. Hannah hung on every word of the missives.

Two days later, a first cousin, Thomas Biddle, arrived at the Biddles' home and requested to see Charles. His demeanor was so formal that Charles laughed at his ceremoniousness. The Biddles were accustomed to paying calls upon one another in a casual fashion. Thomas's behavior had no precedence. The visitor inquired whether there had been any news from the "President," which Charles mistakenly assumed meant a personal message from President John Adams.

The misapprehension was brief. Not trusting himself with further speech, Thomas produced an official communication informing the family of Edward's death. He had perished of a fever while shipboard in St. Kitts. One moment he was lying ill on his cot, lucid and speaking; the next, he was gone. Charles was too stunned to ask further questions. He tried to keep the news from Hannah but could not. Waiting upstairs until her curiosity about Thomas's visit could no longer be contained, she raced into the parlor and grabbed the letter. Shock gave way to horror. She became inconsolable, screaming until she exhausted herself. Neither parent knew whether James had contracted the fever, too, and whether he lived. The entire household succumbed to fright, but there was nothing the family could do to alleviate it or assuage their grief.

During this anguished period, Charles repeatedly declared he would have happily exchanged his life for Edward's, while Hannah remained mute in her upstairs chamber. Popular physics were administered, and she was bled according to contemporary medical practices, but she failed to revive. It seemed that her psyche had been forever altered.

A pall settled on the house. It did not begin to lift until the family moved to another home at 159 Chestnut Street two years later, in May 1802. The cause for the relocation was Edward, whose memory seemed to permeate every brick, every stair tread, every ceiling beam. Even on Chestnut Street, Nicholas's parents' grief remained raw. Edward's death was the only time Nicholas saw his father's eyes filled with tears. The image remained with him: a strong man, unaccustomed to revealing emotion, silently weeping.

* * *

While the family mourned, Nicholas dedicated himself to the study of law with William Lewis, one of the leaders of the Philadelphia Bar. Again, family connections played a role. Nicholas's uncle, James, had been President Judge of the First Judicial District until his death in 1797; he and Lewis were colleagues and friends. As he had at Princeton, Nicholas threw himself headlong into the task. His brother, William, who had already begun practicing law, served as advisor and mentor. In the lively spirit of brotherhood within the close-knit family, he prodded, teased, and engaged in mock competitions with his younger sibling, all the while exhorting him to continue his studies of French, Italian, history, the natural sciences, and political economy. Nicholas, though, required scant encouragement. His need for intellectual pursuits dominated his personality. William also introduced Nicholas to Joseph Dennie, the charismatic founder of the literary compendium—the *Port Folio*. Born in 1768, Dennie graduated from Harvard College in 1790, became a member of the bar, and then turned to a writing career when his law practice faltered. Quixotic, impractical, a lover of philosophy and devoted to belles lettres, he was precisely the kind of person Nicholas would admire.

Dennie had been the inspiration behind the Tuesday Club, a weekly gathering of men devoted to books, writers, and stimulating conversation. It was at the Tuesday Club suppers that Nicholas met other young men who would become life-long friends: Horace Binney, Richard Rush, Charles Ingersoll, and Thomas Cadwalader, all of whom shared his literary penchant. They fancied themselves—and were—eligible bachelors about town, the tastemakers of their era. Ever vain about his appearance, Nicholas looked the part, too. He was Philadelphia's answer to the Regency dandy Beau Brummell.

For Nicholas, Dennie's appeal was obvious; equally powerful was William Lewis's influence. Raised as a Quaker, he was a vehement champion of social justice, having written and introduced the 1780 "Act for the Gradual Abolition of Slavery," the first legal motion to abolish slavery in the United States. Enacted in Pennsylvania, it forbade further importation of slaves into the state. Lewis was as outsized a character as Dennie; he spoke five languages and built a country home, "Summerville" (now known as "Strawberry Mansion"), in the quintessential American Federal style. Lewis exposed Nicholas to the injustices of an America that could promote slavery while simultaneously claiming that all men were equal. Although Philadelphia was known as the "Athens of America" because of its architectural elegance and cultural excellence, the city had dank and fetid neighborhoods where the impoverished struggled and starved. Injustice was endemic, and slaves and slave owners were unavoidable, the most conspicuous being Pierce Butler, originally a native of South Carolina. Later, Nicholas would call himself a "populist." Given his acute awareness, probing curiosity, and idealism, how could he not absorb William Lewis's ideologies?

* * *

Half a world away from the bonds of erudition and support that nurtured the bookish Nicholas, his brother, James, found himself in the midst of the Barbary Wars. By then, he had become a dashing man with wavy hair, a strong chin, and roguish eyes. He bore a strong physical and psychological semblance to his famed naval hero uncle. Like his uncle, James felt happier on ships than on land. In 1803, James served as a midshipman aboard the frigate *Philadelphia* under the command of William Bainbridge.

America's history with the Barbary States of Tripoli, Tunis, and Algiers had been fraught with broken treaties. In 1784, Barbary pirates (named for their ferocity and their sailors who armed themselves with knives in each hand and one clenched between their teeth) boarded an American brig, *Betsy*, and imprisoned her crew. They subsequently captured two more American ships and demanded $60,000 (today's equivalent of $12 million) in ransom. Thomas Jefferson, then U.S. Minister (Ambassador) to France, advised against paying. He believed the action would increase rather than decrease the depredations. Congress chose ransom, paying a yearly tribute until 1800, but peace remained tenuous.

In October 1800, the bashaw of Tripoli, Jussuf Caramalli (Yusuf Qaramalli), sent a letter to President Adams demanding an increase in tribute monies. Caramalli threatened additional attacks on American merchantmen otherwise. Without waiting for a response either from Adams or Jefferson, who was inaugurated March 1801, the bashaw cut down the flagstaff of the American consulate in Tripoli on May 14, 1801, and declared war on the United States. It was understood that only bombardment and a full blockade could undermine the bashaw's power. Two years passed in a dangerous game of cat and mouse. U.S. Navy ships patrolled the Barbary Coast, taking prizes as often as possible, but more frequently watching the enemy slip away into the safety of its harbors.

On August 24th, 1803, the *Philadelphia* anchored at Gibraltar, and from there, began patrolling the Barbary Coast to seize enemy vessels. Bainbridge and his officers and crew met with success, but the ports remained safe havens for enemy ships that could slip past their pursuers. On October 31, 1803, the *Philadelphia* sighted an enemy vessel approaching Tripoli harbor. Determined to capture it, Bainbridge opted for a dangerous maneuver, ordering his ship to sail at full speed despite a harbor entrance filled with reefs and shoals. Soundings were regularly taken when a shout of "half-six" (fathoms) rang out. A moment later, the *Philadelphia's* bow struck a reef with such force that she was partially grounded. Because Bainbridge had deep water astern, he ordered all cannons thrown overboard to lighten the ship's load; the water casks were also jettisoned. The efforts failed. As the bashaw's gunboats approached, Bainbridge commanded that the magazine be drowned and holes pierced in the hull to scuttle the vessel rather than have it taken as a prize. At five o'clock, his men hauled down the flag, and the captain surrendered rather than risk the lives of the crew.

The bashaw's men immediately swarmed aboard, carrying off anything of value they could find and forcing the prisoners into gunboats. One of the invaders attempted to rip a miniature portrait of Bainbridge's wife from his neck, but the captain fought this final indignity with such force that the would-be thief fell overboard. After that, Bainbridge and his officers and crewmen were delivered to the streets of Tripoli, where they were pushed and dragged through screaming throngs until they reached the royal palace. The route was lined with men hurling abuse at the "Amerikanos." Wounded, bloody, and ill-clad, the three-hundred-fifteen prisoners had no cognizance of how lengthy their captivity would become.

When the news reached America four months later, Charles began formulating a plan for rescuing the prisoners. Intending to outfit a "fast-sailing vessel,"[15] he also proposed captaining it. Wiser heads prevailed, one being Jefferson, who suggested that the idea, though noble, was ill-advised and might further endanger the captives. Charles acquiesced to the President's wishes, but he chafed under the directive and later regretted acceding to it. Adding insult to injury, the bashaw's men refloated the *Philadelphia*, pulled the cannons from the harbor depths, and moored the vessel a quarter of a mile from the royal residence. The American ship became a symbol of the bashaw's defiance. Refitted, the frigate could be used against the United States Navy.

In a conference with his superiors, Lieutenant Commander Stephen Decatur hatched a plan to destroy the *Philadelphia* before it became an enemy vessel. Decatur's strategy was fraught with danger. He asked for volunteers to sail with him aboard the ketch *Intrepid*. Disguised as a merchantman, the *Intrepid* would enter Tripoli Harbor, whereupon its captain and crew would board the *Philadelphia* and set it ablaze. Seventy-two men immediately presented themselves for duty. Naturally, the Biddle family knew nothing of this scheme, which could have placed James and the other prisoners in an even more perilous situation.

On February 16, 1804, amid light seas and favorable winds, the *Intrepid* approached Tripoli harbor. A Sicilian pilot capable of conversing with the Tripolitans had joined the crew. Below decks, there was scarcely room to move; the provision of salted meat had turned rancid, leaving bread and water the sole sustenance. A gale lasting six days had nearly sunk the ketch, but the severe buffeting aided the *Intrepid's* disguise. Decatur had also set out draglines, slowing the ketch's progress to appear afflicted in the extreme. All but twelve of his men were hidden, most lying flat on the decks. The captain's orders had been methodical: once he and his men boarded the *Philadelphia,* they planned to search it deck by deck, then set the frigate ablaze before returning to the *Intrepid* and escaping back out to sea. Speed was essential. There were other seemingly insurmountable obstacles, one being that gunboats and galleys surrounded the *Philadelphia*.

The *Intrepid* made its laborious way into the harbor. When the ketch came within hailing distance of the *Philadelphia*, the Sicilian pilot commenced a long discourse detailing his ship's travails. The Tripolitans stationed aboard the *Philadelphia* were fooled. They even sent a boat to aid the unfortunate pilot. The moment Decatur and his men were within reach of the *Philadelphia*, they swarmed up her chainplates and then raced through the ship as planned, killing as many of the enemy as possible.

Within twenty-five minutes, Decatur had taken possession of the *Philadelphia*. Then came the moment for which all had prepared. Taking torches to the tar and pitch, they set fire to the American frigate. Decatur and his men barely had time to jump down into the safety of their ketch before the *Philadelphia* erupted in flame. The *Intrepid* was so close to the burning ship the blaze almost consumed it as well. Pulling clear at the last minute, the men gave three cheers for victory, which roused the bashaw's men stationed on the gunboats. They opened fire on the retreating ketch as the entire bay turned orange-red, reflecting the burning *Philadelphia*. Hearing the noise, the prisoners who knew nothing of Decatur's actions assumed the worst.

Peace and the captives' release remained elusive. Not until autumn 1804 was an equally daring plan put in motion. William Eaton, the American Naval Agent for Barbary, had become acquainted with Caramalli's deposed brother, Hamet, in Tunis while serving as American consul. Aided by American marines and a ragtag mercenary force of Greeks and Arabs, Eaton and Hamet marched five hundred miles through the Desert of Barca. They captured the stronghold of Derna, south of Benghazi, on April 27, 1805. Fearing that Eaton's force would take Tripoli next, Jusuf Caramalli sued for peace.

A treaty finally secured, the American prisoners were released on June 4, 1805. They had been imprisoned for twenty months. When the news reached the United States, patriotic fervor knew no bounds.

* * *

By then, Nicholas had left Philadelphia for Europe. An offer to serve as secretary to the recently appointed Minister to France, General John Armstrong, Jr., outweighed familial concerns. Armstrong had seen duty in the Continental Army; subsequently, he became Secretary of the Commonwealth of Pennsylvania, a delegate to the Continental Congress, and a senator from New York. In the future, he would serve as James Madison's Secretary of War. Armstrong and Charles Biddle were colleagues. Determined to take advantage of the opportunity, Nicholas hurried to New York on July 30, 1804. Armstrong assured Charles that his son would be in good hands. "[The] ship I go in has been selected by my friends as the safest and most commodious that our harbor affords, tonnage between 300 and 400 [and] skillful seamen. I have taken the cabin for my family and have accordingly a berth for your son."[16]

Nicholas's departure was another blow to Hannah. She begged him to "write before you sail as letters from you are one of the greatest pleasures of my life."[17] Charles maintained his habitual formality, stressing that "it will be a great satisfaction to your mother & myself and give pleasure to all your friends to hear that General Armstrong approves of your conduct." Then he added the usual injunction that Nicholas "walk every day half hour or hour."[18]

Although the ship's departure was delayed until September 4, Nicholas had already entered the next phase of his life. His brother, James, and his uncles and father had set the bar high, but he had begun to discover that he might be as driven and competitive as they. If fame eluded him through acts of daring, perhaps he could make his reputation in the political arena. On July 19, 1804, William Lewis, who had also approached Armstrong on behalf of his mentee, sent words of advice, urging Nicholas to remember:

> what is due to yourself and to your country. . . . I shall by no means
> be satisfied with hearing you are in good health and conduct yourself
> with propriety—I shall expect more, I shall whenever I hear your name
> mentioned expect to hear that you are in pursuit of *noble ends by noble
> means* and that your success and your merit bid fair to render your
> character eminently prominent among the sons of America.[19]

- CHAPTER THREE -

THE ADVENTURER

Eighteen in 1804, when his European sojourn began, Nicholas did not return until 1807, by which time he counted James Monroe as mentor and friend. With his long, flowing hair, young Biddle looked more like a Romantic poet than a member of the legal profession. He dressed flamboyantly, too—some claimed affectedly, though he remained impervious to the criticism. Perhaps he even relished the attention. Picturing himself as an acolyte to Voltaire or Rousseau, he intended to look the part.

Worried that he might not seem sufficiently authoritative, though, he applied to his father and the governor of New Jersey for military appointments; with them would come uniforms to make him appear masterful and mature. Or so he hoped. The governor responded by designating Nicholas, a colonel in the state militia of New Jersey. Charles persuaded General James Wilkinson, a relative by marriage, to appoint Nicholas, a brevet captain in the United States Artillery. The former rank permitted him to design his uniform, which he did with gusto, resolving to cut as dashing a figure as possible. The buttons of his coat rivaled those of any Hussar's. In Europe, they received approbation, which he noted with a good deal of glee. Callow narcissism continued to betray his age.

One of his intentions during his sojourn was to maintain a series of journals, which he did, inserting poetry, some of which was painfully mawkish and sentimental, and pen sketches of fellow travelers. He used the thirty-eight-day passage across the Atlantic to increase his familiarity with the French language and Italian, German, Dutch, and contemporary Greek. Having studied ancient Greek during his student years, he hoped it would help him learn the modern language. He longed to become a paragon of erudition and culture and usually believed he succeeded in that goal. He even boasted of adding ninety-two volumes of Voltaire to his library before his departure.[1] Voluble and overflowing with self-confidence, he conversed at length with everyone he met.

For a young man in a hurry, the first week of travel was interminable. The ship was becalmed repeatedly, and after seven days, had traveled only four hundred miles. Nicholas was frenzied with restlessness, exacerbated by the close quarters and the necessity of maintaining a cheerful demeanor despite the seasickness that affected every passenger except General Armstrong and him. Armstrong's wife, sister-in-law, and children were all ill. Each day Nicholas marked the vessel's longitude and latitude in his journal's margins, but the time passed so slowly it seemed that a small bird could have winged its way across the waters faster. He found no solace in watching the endless waves lap at the ship's hull; instead, his impatience reached a fever pitch. Eventually, the wind picked up, and the vessel could proceed, but he resented the hours underway. He desperately wanted to be in France.

Arriving at last on October 10, each moment seemed transcendent. The official document securing his travels, *"Laissés passer Monsieur Nicolas Biddlé, natif de Philadelphie, dans les états unis, secretaire de la Légation,*[2] delighted him. His route through Nantes, Tours, Blois with its chateau and marvelous spiral staircase, and Orléans inspired awe. He went so far as to engrave his name *N BIDDLE 1804*[3] in the foundation wall at the chateau in Poitiers, a boyish act inspired by other inscriptions: one being a certain Christian Winkler ANNO 1627 whom he imagined as a fellow explorer from another era. Nicholas was convinced there was a fascinating and tragic tale within those stone-cut letters. In the Vendée, département of Loire-Intérieur, he pondered the uprisings that had occurred ten years prior, the result of the Revolution of 1789 that had left the region depleted economically, and her population butchered. His sensibilities to recent and ancient history were acute. Every day brought discovery.

Reaching Paris on November 6, 1804, he secured chambers on the rue du Régard. His father's financial contributions permitted him to live in comfort, although modestly, and the rue du Régard was a superior address. Nicholas had anticipated marveling at the *cité's* grandeur, its Gothic church spires, the splendid *hotels particuliers*, the boulevards, and equally fine equipages traversing them. He was unprepared for the continual flow of activity and discourse, however. Everyone engaged in ceaseless conversation: tradesman, merchant, bon vivant, and washerwoman. The noise drowned out the clattering roll of the ironbound wheels of the carriages and wagons. Philadelphia seemed silent and sleepy in comparison, and the American mode of dress and manner of perambulating woefully provincial. At the Ministry in Paris, he learned that his duties included translating for General Armstrong as he examined the Louisiana Purchase and American claims against France. This work proved invaluable in later life regarding complex financial issues, but the task failed to meet his immediate need for romance and drama. It seemed too lawyerly and dry, and he omitted references to it from the journals; he wished to chronicle only memorable events. He did not consider the Louisiana Purchase one of them.

A day following his arrival, on November 7, he was introduced to the Marquis de Lafayette at a dinner given at the Palais Royal. James Monroe and Robert Livingston, who had been negotiating the Louisiana Purchase, were among the guests. Finding himself in such stellar company, Nicholas was at pains to appear nonchalant but failed. During the course of the evening, the marquis asked him if he spoke French. "*Un peu*," Nicholas told him, although he had mastered the language. "*Parlez un peu*," Lafayette replied,[4] to which Biddle countered that the marquis must know English well having resided in America. Lafayette explained that it had been many years since he had spoken the language and consequently had forgotten it. The conversation continued when, to Nicholas's surprise, Lafayette asked his age. "I blushed when I told him I had not yet reached my nineteenth year."[5] Thereafter, Biddle made sure to lie about his age. The initial meeting proved auspicious. In the future, Lafayette would appoint him as his American banker.

> November 18, 1804. While the impression is yet fresh in my memory I sit down to record one of the most splendid spectacles which I have yet seen. About 10 o'clock this morning the General rose from breakfast & went to Mr. Livingston's thence to go to his private audience with the Emperor.[6]

Because Armstrong dispensed with his services that morning, Nicholas walked to the Tuilleries to watch the monthly review of the troops. The spectacle so awed him; his hand shook as he wrote.

> Before me was General Rappan, an exceedingly handsome young man, next to him was Caffarelli, dressed in green coats & scarlet pantaloons & boots excessively rich, next two officers whom I could not know, then General Berthres and then Bonaparte. What a sight!!

Not fifteen yards from me I beheld 'the man before whom the world had trembled,' the hero whose name has sounded in every quarter of the globe & who has rivaled if not excelled all that antiquity can produce of hardy valour and successful enterprise. I did not neglect this rare opportunity of seeing so wonderful a man & for upwards of an hour while 12,000 men passed before him my eyes scarcely for a moment left him. On the most majestic, the most elegant white horse I have ever seen, who as he went along the ranks seemed to fly rather than to walk, & who, as he now stood, seemed to regard with tranquil delight the scene before him on a saddle most richly furnished, sat the Emperor.

In his dress he seems to have desired to distinguish himself by simplicity. He had on a pair of white pantaloons, long boots coming over his knees, a plain blue coat, lined with red, two epaulets, and a plain blue cocked hat. He had a small riding whip in his hand. His hair is black & cut very short, he wears no whiskers. His face is somewhat long of a dark olive complexion, his eye hollow, but full of the expressive fire of genius. . . . The Emperor spoke once in a low tone of voice. His voice is soft and mild. Twice Genl. Mortier laughed to Bonaparte on some occasion, but the Emperor did not smile.[7]

Biddle decided to emulate Bonaparte's gravity and let others make ingratiating remarks while remaining aloof and watchful. His memories of Napoleon's coronation reflected the same awe-struck wonder. He kept his ticket, which remains in Andalusia's archives: *Dans Le Choeur. No. 6. Le Gauche du Trone, Pour un Homme.*[8]

December 3, 1804. I was waked about 7 o'clock by the servant, and when I learnt the hour I was in despair for I was told I must be at the church by six. I made all possible haste sent for a carriage, none was to be found, set off on foot for Notre Dame. Arrived at the door I stood among epaulets & stars myself without sword or stiff collar & after about an hours standing, got in. I went to all parts of the church & at last found the seat designated by my ticket which was Tribune 9, second row of benches. But the second row was already occupied by ladies, and I therefore took the hind most seat of the Tribune. The coup de oie of the church is magnificent. The Corps Legislatif, the Tribunals, and the different public bodies took their different stations.

(Then the) Bishops, the Cardinals, and the Pope appeared. He advanced towards his throne which was nearly opposite to me, and I now gazed at the successor of St. Peter. Being seated the Cardinals advanced & kissed his hand, the Bishops then advanced & on their knees kissed his knee or rather his robes under which both his hand & knee were concealed. The Pope is a hard featured man, if the extreme cold of the church did not contract his muscles more than ordinarily he is somewhere about 60 years of age & is said to be a good man. About an hour after the Emperor & Emperess came in. The Pope advanced to meet them. . . . By changing my position I however saw the Emperor before he was crowned in a very thoughtful position seated, bare, & surrounded with the Princes & great officers. . . . The Emperor was drest in a superb robe carried in his left hand, in his right the sceptre. His train was held by several great officers. Madame was also dressed elegantly & looked really handsome. Her long & fine train was supported by many of the great ladies. What a sight was this for a philosopher.[9]

That "philosopher" attended theatre regularly, dined out, made the acquaintance of every notable personage he could, and wrote more than half of his journal entries in French. Often he switched languages mid passage. He longed to become the quintessential Continental gentleman, famed for his panache and savoir-faire. Some days he penned a disgusted: "as usual" or "nothing new."[10] He craved new experiences just as he desired the acquisition of knowledge.

Despite the illustrious circle in which he moved, Nicholas had a secret heartache: Rebecca Biddle, a cousin who became the subject of his journal's private musings. References to her first appeared during his visit to Switzerland in August and September 1805. "I took out my pencil to write to Rebecca Biddle. I know not whether to regret or be pleased with the circumstances of my having left my country entirely unfettered by affect." Here he scratched out the word and replaced it with "love."

Altho' it would have tormented me by its follies, it would have added much to my pensive moments, In viewing the heavenly scenery in which the country abounds, the heart softens and almost melts . . .

then when I begin to be romantic, I look back on my country in quest of some female my mind recalls always my cousin as the young unmarried (perhaps she is at this moment no longer so) lady whom I most esteem.[11]

Draft letters to Rebecca filled his Swiss journal:

August 10, 1805 - My dear Rebecca
I have just wakened from my meditations. If you have not yet subsided into the calm of matrimony, you will not perhaps be displeased at a romantic note.[12]

Aug 23, 1805 My dear Rebecca I am now about 7 miles from Lausanne. . . . On the right the distant chain of the Jura whose tops are gilded by the sun.

Vevey Aug 24, 1805 10 o'clock am. Dear Rebecca, I am now admiring one of the scenes of nature which strike with mingled emotions of pleasure and melancholy.

Dear Rebecca, I have just come into my bedroom. . . .[13]

Loneliness heightened his aesthetic sense. The diligent young man who had compiled a shipboard list of his personal effects: "7 shirts, 6 neck handkerchiefs, 5 socks, 2 pantaloons,1 jacket, 1 towel, 1 pillowcase, 1 fork"[14] or who sat for a portrait while in Paris was not the young man venturing in solitude through Switzerland, Holland, and Austria, or gazing upon the streaming waters in the Cascade of Giessbach—"at once sublime, terrible and enchanting,"[15] or the Schöllenen gorge and the River Reuss "foaming, roaring river rushes over the rocks with headlong fury,"[16] or climbing through the Jura Mountains on muleback with only the occasional guide to keep him company.

* * *

Eventually, public affairs began to appear on his journals' pages, a curious lapse of information given the years he crisscrossed Europe and the places: Vienna, Basle, Lucerne, Zurich, Berne, Trieste, and Venice that he visited. 1804-1807 was the height of the Napoleonic Wars, and Nicholas was in the midst of the areas where battles had been or would soon be waged; the detritus of and preparations for war surrounded him. The narrow defiles of Switzerland, which he traversed, witnessed the passage of tens of thousands of men and horses and heavy arms, but Nicholas wrote as though he were traveling through a Europe that had no experience of carnage.

In Austria, he briefly chronicled the changes Archduke Charles had made in the army, what the officers were paid, and the numbers of cavalry and infantry. While journeying along the Rhine, he learned that the king of Wurtemberg had abolished his parliament, although any outsider reading the entry might scoff at its naiveté.

> This Wurtemberg country is badly governed. It is with nations as it is with men. They are not happy in proportion as they become great. The king is a fat unwieldy sinner who does nothing but hunt & is constantly quarreling with his son and his wife.[17]

In the Rhineland, he finally commented on Continental opinions of America, but his opinion was terse:

> America has no friends in Europe. There is in fact no friendship in politics, but there are peculiar causes against America. Her gov't is the despair of tyrants. It has long been a favorite doctrine that the factitious distinction of society is unnatural—since man if left to himself could not exist under a gov't where all were equal. America is trying that experiment. She has reversed every principle which secured despotism. Every monarch in Europe is interested in the fall of America.[18]

Given Nicholas's powers of observation and love of words, the entries are inconsistent with his personality and his position as secretary to the American minister to France. Two questions arise: Was Biddle obfuscating? And if so, why?

Instead of describing the battles of Ulm (September 25-October 20, 1805), or Austerlitz (December 2, 1805), or Vienna's French occupation, his journals introduce seemingly inconsequential subjects.

A large section of his narrative details how he fell under the sway of Dr. Franz Joseph Gall, who was traversing northern Europe and Denmark in 1805 to deliver a series of lectures on craniscopy, a science Gall created and that came to be known as phrenology. *On the Functions of the Cerebellum* was not published until 1838, ten years after Gall's death, but he was regarded as an expert in craniscopy long before that. Crowds thronged to hear him speak as he cataloged the organs situated in the head that he insisted controlled human impulse: the organ of cunning, of mimicry, circumspection, goodness, perfectibility, of sexual love, and the mechanic arts. Nicholas, who was now as conversant with German as he was with English and French, believed he was in the presence of a genius. Like any convert, he attempted to recognize how these organs guided human action, noting that "circumspect people hold the head higher."[19] Each person he met became a potential subject for this new science. "When my brain is occupied with any single object, I am wholly absorbed by it. I attend to nothing else."[20]

After returning to Paris, he almost immediately departed for Rome. If Armstrong protested, Nicholas made no mention of the rebuke. Nor did he explain. He simply left Paris behind, penning new entries in his journals as though casual sightseeing were his *raison d'etre*. Traveling to Nogent-sur-Seine, he wandered through the ruined Oratory of Paraclete, where Peter Abelard had originally erected a mud and wattle hut intending to become a hermit after his catastrophic love affair with Héloise.

In 1792 during the Revolution, when the razing of religious structures was commonplace, vandals destroyed the monastery buildings. A humble *pigeonnier* escaped the desecration. Nicholas took up his pencil to record his musings. "Monday September 2, 1805 I am now sitting among the ruins of Paraclete, that Paraclete so dear to the lovers of learning and beauty. The sun is just going down and presents a noble streak on the western horizon. All is melancholy, wild & dreary."[21] He concluded by observing that the remains presented "a sad monument to human frailty."[22]

Nicholas filled eight diaries with similar musings but remained mum on international politics. For a person whose purported business was diplomacy and whose aspirations were for public service, his failure to examine Napoleon's intentions toward Europe and England cannot be overlooked. Everyone he encountered must have been brim-full of theories and first-hand accounts. But, save for the abbreviated reference to the king of Wurtemberg and the observation that Europe's monarchs must despise America, Nicholas said nothing. Several motives arise: one might be that he felt that Bonaparte was too heroic a figure to criticize and that he idolized him because he had attended his coronation and been awed by its majesty. A second might be that, like his father's generation, he believed France was an American ally and Britain an enemy. A third would be closer to the truth.

All governments employ persons of high or low rank to gather information. Bonaparte used spies; so did the countries allied against him. America also needed people who noticed everything while feigning interest elsewhere and who could subsequently transfer personal knowledge to the nation's leaders. Napoleon was poised to conquer Europe, Russia, and North Africa. America's treaties and commerce would alter dramatically if a French empire extended throughout the Mediterranean Sea into the Black Sea and the Atlantic Ocean. Recognizing how great a threat Bonaparte posed, newspapers in America followed the outcome of every battle. Jefferson and members of the State Department and Congress required knowledge of Europe's theatres of war, but correspondence home was liable to interception and scrutiny. A person with a prodigious memory, capable of recalling the minutest detail without depending on notes, was critical to American interests.

Consider the figure Nicholas cut: a cultivated young man of independent means who desired enlightenment and was eager to assimilate new cultures and ideas as any student in any university. How innocent he appeared as he smiled and chatted and waited to have his *Laisses Passé* examined at each border, pleasantly joking as he permitted every guard to riffle through his effects. Crossing from France into Switzerland, he meandered along the Rhine and Danube and roved through Bavaria and Austria. Conversant in numerous languages, his manner lively, he greeted everyone as a boon companion. The thrill of the unfamiliar was all he appeared to ask and invite as he ventured along his way, journeying from town to town, city to city.

He never described the French infantry and cavalry, although he traveled within easy proximity or pondered how the Austrians and Russians could sustain their thousands of men and horses. Nor, did he write that the earth in Switzerland and Austria had been trampled into mud, or that food and fodder was nonexistent in some places, or bridges destroyed and villages pocked by cannon fire. He eliminated any mention of the Austrian general Mack whose loss to the French at Ulm set in motion the near destruction of the Austrian and Russian armies, or that Vienna was no longer home to the Hapsburgs but the domicile of Napoleon. The latter installed himself in splendor at Schonbrunn Palace, once the beloved summer retreat of Austrian emperors.

Instead, he wrote flowery ruminations, made pencil sketches, described art and architecture or dinners with persons of means, and reflected on the natural and scientific world. Only in Florence did a glimpse of another role appear:

"When we consider the quantity of the beautiful and valuable art which Florence contains I am surprised that more was not taken by the French who were so anxious to collect the monuments of the arts."[23] Criticizing the conquering nation—even in a minor fashion—could bring unwelcome scrutiny. Nicholas buried the observations with a long stream of commentary on the art of Cimabue, da Vinci, Michelangelo, Perugino, Titian, and Veronese, concluding in a gush of rapture that "no man can look with indifference on the Palais Riccardi"[24] He concluded his Florentine sojourn with a lengthy description of a ball given by the Queen of Tuscany in which he castigated himself because "I danced very badly."[25]

A recent addition to the archives at Andalusia, the country home Biddle inherited from his wife's family, is a single sheet of paper hand printed with the words "Memorial Lines" and what is surely a code. Nothing else is written on the page, nor the reverse. At the time of Nicholas's European journey, cipher letters were common even among long-standing friends, the means of translating them kept concealed by both parties until the need for private communication arose. Without the aid of a code, a missive sent from one person to the other couldn't be deciphered. Nicholas's "Memorial Lines"[26] provide a tantalizing glimpse into his possible mission.

a	e	i	o	u	au	oi	ei	ou	4
1	2	3	4	5	6	7	8	9	0
b	d	+	f	l	s	p	k	n	z

Perhaps the newly discovered "Memorial Lines" answer why he traveled to Washington City in 1807 to meet with Jefferson, rather than first return to his family in Philadelphia. The choice baffled his parents, who expected him to come home after his long absence, and who went to the Lazaretto where ships docked before passengers being cleared to sail up the Delaware. They anticipated a happy, surprise reunion there and were dismayed at being informed he had already disembarked at Cape Henry at the mouth of the Chesapeake to journey overland to Washington.

The scholar with the dandyish air and theatrical garb was a perfect cover—if cover it was—but it was also exceedingly dangerous. Spies for all nations risked incarceration and death. Maybe Nicholas was not so different from his namesake, after all.

* * *

I had long felt an ardent desire to visit Greece. The fate of a nation
whose history was the first brilliant object that met my infancy, &
the first foundation of my early studies was so interesting that I had
resolved to avail myself of any opportunity of witnessing it. The soil
of Greece is sacred to Genius & to letters. The race of beings whose
achievements warm our youthful fancy has long disappeared. But the
sod under which they repose: the air which listened to their poetry and
their eloquence: the hills which saw their valor are still the same.[27]

Biddle continued keeping journals when he traveled to Greece in 1806. Although the passage is similar in tone to his European diaries, he was finally free
to expound on international politics. American vessels anchored at Messina and
other ports where he called, so his missives were safe from prying eyes, which
allowed him to send candid letters home or write openly about Napoleon's intentions. His goal of "collecting information in order to extend our commercial
relations in the Levant & in this way being useful to my country"[28] enabled him
to gauge France's military prowess relative to the nations allied against her and
to describe his findings succinctly and clearly. He dispensed with platitudes and
a feigned indifference to Bonaparte's intentions. "The extension of the French
power along the western shore of the Adriatic lays open all Greece to their arms,
& the possession of it will be of infinite importance, as the direct road to Egypt
and thence to India. The conquest would be easy."[29]

In January 1806, two months before Biddle's departure from Naples for
Greece (March 28), France invaded the Kingdom of Naples. André Masséna
led the French forces, handily vanquishing the Neapolitans on February 14.
Napoleon then installed his brother, Joseph Bonaparte, as king. Simultaneously,
the defeated Ferdinand IV and his court fled to Sicily, where he came under the
Royal Navy protection and a British garrison.

Nicholas soon discovered that the Mediterranean, Adriatic, and Ionian Seas
and their contiguous lands were up for grabs. The British maintained troops in
Malta. Russia controlled the Ionian islands of Zante, Cefalonia, Corfu, Cythera,
Ithaca, Leucadia, and Paxos: the Septinsular Republic as it was known. French
privateers and Russian warships jostled for supremacy, although the Royal Navy
maintained the largest and most conspicuous presence. This uneasy peace could

not last forever. The immediate history of the region had been equally volatile. Nine years prior, in 1797, the French had defeated the Venetian Republic. For a year, Zante came under the French department Mer-Égée until a fleet comprised of Russians and Turks captured it in October 1798. Although the Ottoman Empire ostensibly governed the Septinsular Republic, Russia provided the fading empire's military might. The Russians harbored a deep mistrust of the French, which presented Biddle with his first serious predicament. Carrying a French passport, he came under intense scrutiny when a Russian soldier examined it. The document "set him on fire,"[30] according to Nicholas. Despite employing all his charm, he had difficulty persuading the soldier and his commanding officer that he was merely a "neutral officer" traveling to a "neutral country."[31]

After a good deal of diplomatic posturing from Biddle, including repeated assurances of his supposed neutrality, he was permitted to proceed. He departed Naples on Friday, March 28, 1806, aboard the polacre brig, *Themistocles*. Major Joseph Barnes of Virginia, the American consul for Sicily, was his companion. Nicholas was then reading Cicero's *Orationum Selectarum Liber Unicus*. His copy, published in 1715, remains in the library at Andalusia. He affixed his signature to it while at Messina, and with characteristic hyperbole, wrote about the destiny he envisioned for himself:

> Who would have thought this year since this day should find me where
> I am; that eighteen months since when my only prospects were those
> of completing the routine of my profession, pleading the defenseless
> cases of vice & misfortune, & then dying like a mushroom on the soil
> which had seen me grow, that I should now be bending my devious
> course among foreign nations. . . . Every good citizen owes himself
> to his country & his family, & and I feel at every step of my path, I
> become a better citizen. The more I have seen of nations the stronger
> has become my attachment to the institutions of that country which
> bears in its bosom the sacred principles of freedom, where all my hopes
> & my ambitions tend.[32]

The city of Messina, he found dismally impoverished. A series of earthquakes and tsunamis had ravaged Calabria and Sicily in February and March 1783, killing upwards of 100,000 and destroying the port's harbor walls. The area hadn't recovered by the time Nicholas arrived. " 'Mori di fame'—I die of hunger assails a stranger at every avenue."[33] Despite the pervasive poverty, the wealth of the city's commercial interests impressed him: "The commerce of Messina is greater than that of any port in Sicily." King Ferdinand, he declared "uncultivated by education and unweeded by control;" his queen appeared "capricious arbitrary & tyrannical," although Nicholas inserted a pointed, "The govt has been particularly favorable to America."[34]

From Messina, he traveled to Malta in late April, where he hoped to find his brother James who had been stationed there after he and his fellow prisoners were freed from captivity in Tripoli. An exorbitant ransom of $60,000 had been paid for their release. The terms of the treaty of June 1805 forbade future demands for tribute monies. No American wanted to continue pandering to a treacherous regime.

Eager to send home good reports regarding James, Nicholas was disappointed to learn that his brother had already departed Malta. In port, though, he found the U.S. frigate *Constitution*; many of its officers were James's friends and shipmates. Captain John Rodgers, who had been appointed commodore of the Mediterranean Squadron in May 1805, commanded the *Constitution*. He invited the young man to dine aboard almost daily, which allowed Nicholas to hear about his brother's exploits from trustworthy witnesses, if not from the source itself. Fourteen years Biddle's senior, Rodgers's hospitality and candor with a man the age of his junior officers was unusual. He believed his guest was in Malta on official business. With Rodgers's intimate knowledge of America's interests in the Mediterranean, he was the perfect man for Nicholas to interview.

Rodgers and Biddle discussed the peace treaties between America and Tripoli and subsequent ones with Tunis, Morocco, and Algiers. The two conversed in depth aboard the *Constitution*, and once during a solo horseback excursion, ostensibly to enjoy the locale sights, but in reality to avoid being overheard. "Much as I dislike equitation, there was no declining. We rode out about a circuit of 8 miles. During this ride he spoke with frankness on all the concerns of the navy."[35] The two men traversing Malta's alternatively sere and anemone-strewn terrain conjures a tantalizing image: the battle-hardened, politically-savvy Rodgers and the young adventurer in his self-styled "uniform" grimacing in discomfort across every hard-won half-mile while Rodgers blithely pointed out fortifications, harbor works, and got down to brass tacks. Blunt in his assessments, the commodore said he mistrusted Britain's motives and maritime strength.

His opinions began to mold Biddle's who thereafter declared, "Malta cannot subsist alone and must therefore belong to the most maritime power," and "The possession of Sicily by the French far from endangering Malta will render it more important." He concluded, "The port is very secure."[36] As he examined the roles of the nations allied against Napoleon and the Ottoman Empire over which Russia and Britain hovered like carrion birds, he recognized there was room for American interests. "I believe our country might derive benefit by opening some channels of commerce."[37] However, it was impossible to imagine that Napoleon would not continue to dominate Europe. The man's rise had been spectacular, his acumen at waging warfare so lauded, and his foes so effectively crushed that to conceive of him and his military forces destroyed within six years was unthinkable.

* * *

From Malta, Biddle sailed to Zante in May 1806, taking note of a British convoy patrolling the coast of Corfu, even though Russia governed the island. In Zante, eight hundred Russian soldiers made the place resemble an armed camp. Querying the English consul about the significant military presence, he learned that the government of Zante regularly dispatched ministers to Petersburg and Constantinople, trying to placate both nations. This was not the Greece of Homeric legend. Nicholas's indignation rang out time and again.

> The race so honored, so proud whose oracle dictated to nations groans under the rod of a Turkish despot. . . . The Turks pay no taxes; the whole burden falls upon the Greeks—all the offices are in the hands of Turks. The Turks always go armed; all kinds of weapons are forbidden to the Greeks. . . . A Pasha has complete power of life and death over every man in his kingdom.[38]

On one occasion, Biddle watched a village elder remonstrate with a mounted Turkish soldier. The soldier drew his sword, pressed his horse forward, and "drove him before him like a dog."[39]

Arriving in Patras on the mainland, his outrage turned to elation. "I have at last touched the holy soil of Greece,"[40] he wrote to his brother Tom. Delphos sent him into raptures.

> May 16, 1806 Friday. Why have I not the pencil on an artist to transmit to you the scene before me? I am sitting amongst the ruins of

one of the proudest cities of Greece. Temples to which no names can
be assigned, & apertures in the rocks are all that remains. Yet I have
seen few ruins so noble.[41]

In Athens, he gushed, "My heart beats as I date my letter from the venerable
presence of the mistress of the world."[42] Amid these awestruck recitations, he
took time to denounce Thomas Bruce, 7th Earl of Elgin, whom Nicholas considered a Barbarian. He accused him of plundering the Acropolis.

A man named Elgin, a Scotsman & a lord, was sometime since the
British minister at Constantinople. He availed himself of the interest
of his situation to procure permission to take from Greece whatever he
chose that had no proprietor. Armed with that order & the resources
of a large fortune, he began his work of destruction. For him the
temples had no sanctity. Without taste without judgment without
selection all that could be bought or stolen was put into boxes & sent
to England . . . Elgin robbed for gold.[43]

Dispensing with Elgin, he waxed reverential again.

Greece has given me more satisfaction than any thing I have seen since
of left America. Tired of the noisy quarrels which agitate the greater
part of Europe, I was glad to find a retired corner undisturbed by the
sound of foreign cannon, and forgetting for a moment the events
of the day, bury myself among the ruins & recollections of former
times.[44]

His circle in Athens then included the French consul and the Russian,
English, and Austrian consuls. The wars among their home nations were ignored during long, convivial evenings in the French consul's residence, where
the party gathered on a roof garden overlooking the Acropolis. Encouraged by
men a generation older than he, Nicholas waxed grandiose in his self-analysis.
Had he not been so endearingly high-minded, he might have been insufferable.

I believe the turn of my mind, or what may properly be called my
genius, has at length decided itself. To govern men, and particularly by
means of eloquence seems to me the object most worthy of ambition

in a free govt. It is the avenue, which leads to glory. Yet much, very much is to be done in order to acquire glory. The routine of [an] attorney, pleading, is beneath imitation. When I consider how much must be done before I can reach what I desire, when I examine how very few advances I have as yet made towards it, I feel not the debasing sentiment of despair, but a mingled sensation of the dignity of my pursuit & the labors thro' which it must lead me.[45]

* * *

Nicholas left Greece on June 29, 1806, declaring, "A young American leaves his country not to diffuse but to acquire information, & he should therefore remain near the source of them. I have now gone much beyond my original hopes or expectations. I have many duties to perform to my family, my profession & my country."[46] Traveling by stages, he experienced miserably lonely periods of quarantine in lazarettos along the way. Finally, he returned to Paris. There, his official duties were so light that he had ample occasion to dine with the Marquis de Lafayette and the author Madame de Stael, who was famed for her salon, and undisguised dislike of Napoleon.

By February 1807, he was on the move again, journeying to Belgium and Holland before sailing to the British Isles to tour England and Ireland before returning home. In London, he met James Monroe, the American Minister Plenipotentiary. Impressed with the charismatic and irrepressible youth, Monroe asked him to serve as his temporary private secretary. Despite the discrepancy in their ages (Monroe was twenty-eight years Nicholas's senior), they were soon on cordial terms. Biddle's journals refer to him as "Mr. M." In Monroe, Nicholas found his *beau idéal*: a man of ambition, passion, and daring. Yes, he could be irascible and easily offended, but his steadfast, courageous nature outweighed his flaws.

Devoted to his country, Monroe had distinguished himself during the Revolutionary War and was nearly fatally wounded during the Battle of Trenton. After studying law, he served in the Virginia Assembly and Continental Congress. In 1794, George Washington appointed him Minister to France, relying on his diplomatic skills and fluent French to negotiate a political climate that was in a state of constant, dangerous upheaval. Monroe's wife, Elizabeth, née Kortright, reared in wealth in New York City, immediately became popular. Dubbed *"La Belle Américaine,"* she was ten years younger than her husband, also fluent in French, elegantly attired, and ensconced in their newly-purchased miniature palace *La Folie de la Bouexiere*. In 1795, she helped secure the release from prison of Adrienne de LaFayette, wife of the Marquis. Monroe supplied Mme. de LaFayette with an American passport and the finances necessary for her and her children to escape France.

Aiding supposed enemies of the state drew the wrath of the French government. Monroe's popularity plummeted. His woes increased when John Jay, envoy extraordinary to Britain, negotiated a "Treaty of Amity, Commerce and Navigation Between His Britannic Majesty and the United States of America" in 1795. Outraged that America should side with her ancestral enemy, France recalled her minister to the United States on September 1, 1796. Monroe's position became untenable; he was also recalled, incurring additional debt by shipping home the expensive furniture he and Elizabeth had purchased for *La Folie*.

In 1803, Jefferson sent Monroe back to France with instructions to negotiate the Louisiana territory's purchase. Robert Livingston, whom Jefferson had dispatched to Paris in 1802 to serve as minister plenipotentiary, resented Monroe's interference. Enmity between the two men arose, but the purchase of nearly 1 million square miles of new territory proceeded. His work in Paris accomplished, Monroe departed for England in July 1803. Initially lauded because of the Louisiana Purchase, which the British regarded as a resounding defeat of the French, he soon became embroiled with the issue of impressment, the seizure of English-speaking sailors to man Britain's warships. His increasingly antagonistic opinions of British motives and politics colored those of his secretary.

Despite Monroe's condemnation of Britain's policies concerning American interests, Biddle found the city delightful and the Monroes' London home on Portland Place a haven amidst the pomp of the Court of St. James. Here was Philadelphia on the grandest of scales: Whitehall Palace, St. James' Palace, the manicured greenswards fronting the Georgian residences of Fitzroy Square, handsome thoroughfares, St. James Park with its pleasure canal, Queen's Garden, Lincoln's Inn, the Admiralty, and The Temple. Portland Place was a fashionable address with spacious terraced houses designed by the neoclassical architects and designers, Robert and James Adams. True, the streets beyond broad Portland Place could be chaotic, but there were booksellers aplenty and smart equipages with liveried footmen everywhere Biddle looked. He took lodgings in Coventry Street above George's Coffee House, an excellent spot to observe British mores and ideology.

Monroe indulged his secretary, treating him almost as a son, and even allowing him to challenge a well-regarded classicist, behavior considered grossly unorthodox then as well as now. Correspondence between Biddle and Monroe during the months in London reveals a young man continuously attempting to impress an elder he emulates. Letters and notes flowed between the two daily: Monroe dashing off a request asking Biddle to "walk up" to "confer together . . . as early as convenient,"[47] was an ongoing theme. Referring to a communication from Lord Holland, he stated a blunt "I do not know what to say on it."[48] Biddle's responses were painstakingly copied: word choices and phrases tried and changed before a final draft was completed, his handwriting careful as opposed to Monroe's firm but hurried scrawl.

Twenty-one in 1807, Biddle was a year older than the Monroes' eldest daughter, Eliza, a vivacious beauty like her mother, and like Elizabeth, a model of Continental manners and modish deportment. Maria Hester Monroe, then five, served as a saucy counterpoint. Elizabeth Monroe revered her husband; he doted upon her, making their household an exceedingly happy one. A frequent guest was the painter Benjamin West, whom Biddle, with habitual gusto, venerated. He declared the artist a "genius." Their conversations ranged from Rubens to Elgin (West also derided Elgin as "a sad barbarian who collected merely to sell and whose boxes are now lying in some corner of London") to the aesthetic tastes of Philadelphians, whom West preferred over New Yorkers whose chief interests were "mercantile."

Knowing he had an eager audience in Nicholas, the artist expounded upon his early years as an artist and his difficulties with his father.

> Some of the old Quakers spoke to him and represented that his talent
> was a gift from God whose will was not to be contradicted. Therefore
> his son should be permitted to follow his genius. When I went to
> Rome, said West to me, such was the effect which a passage from a
> little town on the Delaware to the mistress of the world & such the
> enthusiasm for her art that his mind was overwhelmed by it.

"He is really a good old man," was Nicholas's conclusion, "fond of talking of himself, & like all old distinguished men I have ever seen equally fond of flattery."[49] Biddle ignored his own love of flattery.

Urged by the Monroes, he visited Bath in May and was charmed by the sophisticated spa town with its Royal Crescent, Circus, theatres, and daily promenades in the Upper and Lower Rooms and the Grand Pump Room. Handsome, accoutered in the latest fashions, he cut an impressive figure, although he sneered at the haute monde's behavior. "The manners of English society are much talked of—The nation has many good qualities but as a social people they have very little to recommend them."[50] What was the impetus for this withering critique? Had a young woman he admired slighted him? The wording reveals pique as well as humiliation. He considered himself equal to any English socialite, and Bath teemed with dandies his age disporting themselves extravagantly, as well as a plethora of marriageable young ladies. Perhaps, the parents of available young women dismissed Nicholas because he hailed from a former colony. Their disapproval would have cut him to the quick.

In London, he attended debates in Parliament, stating, "Lord Bathurst is a clumsy, hesitating, awkward speaker" and that "the noise of the gallery is brutal."[51] He also studied Britain's political, diplomatic, and mercantile affairs, remarking on "long annuities, short annuities, Irish Annuities, South Sea Stock, New South Wales Sea Annuities, India Stock, Navy Bills, India Bonds, and Victualling Bills;" monetary matters that would prove useful in future. In June 1807, he observed:

> As far as respects America it is not too early to collect the sentiments of England. . . . We should remember that there is behind the curtain a rooted animosity against us. The rapid progress of our commerce & the unexcelled advancement of our prosperity which every port in Europe bears such melancholy testimony. That part of England therefore which knows America fears her. They perceive that their own importance depends on their maintaining the superiority of the sea & they feel that there is no nation capable of disputing that superiority more than America. Like the waves of the ocean, the vigor and industry of America is beating against the dyke of the Navigation Act with they must one day surmount or undermine.
>
> The temper of England was well seen during the debates in Parliament. . . . On that occasion the member of the present ministry expressed sentiments of very strong hostility against us. The navy is particularly anxious for war—as the officers would all make fortunes in a short time. The shipping interests and the West India merchants are also among our opponents. On the other hand we have all the

manufacturers, the landed interests generally, and most of the prudent and dependable men of the country.[52]

As to Livingston, Biddle despised him with the same fervor with which he admired Monroe.

> The friends of Livingston (Robert known as the Chancellor) try to give him the credit of the Louisiana purchase. He has in my opinion none whatsoever. The whole family of Livingston's is politically rotten and corrupt. I believe him an unprincipled politician. . . . On M's arrival in France, Livingston wrote him a letter of compliment. . . . In that letter he mentions his hope that he (M) might be able to effect something, but he fears that unless M brought news of a war (that is a war with Spain on our part) he would be unable to do anything in the way of negotiation . . . I have seen the letter myself. M found it much more difficult to manage him (L) than the French gov't.

Livingston's sole impetus, Biddle concluded, was "to get money into his own hands.[53]

A draft of a letter written to Monroe in July 1807 epitomizes the younger man's efforts to impress his idol. In tortured prose, excised words, and revised phrasing, Biddle's self-assurance vanished, replaced by desperation for guidance.

> July 6, 1807 The observations you made in our walk yesterday were of so interesting a nature, that I hope you will excuse my recurring to the subject of them. About to ~~engage~~ enter on a scene where I may not be permitted to remain a spectator only, & in which all my success will be influenced by my first steps, I feel a natural anxiety to prescribe a course of conduct which may become the rule of my political life. The violence of party which disgraces our country is indeed discouraging to one who feels no disposition to become the follower of any seat, or to mingle political animosities with the intercourse of society. . . .
>
> You, Sir more than any other character with whom it has been my ~~good fortune~~ happiness to be acquainted, have passed thro' all the stages of political advancement honorably for yourself & usefully for your country. From you therefore I am particularly desirous of

receiving advice which be useful to a person who like myself has a profession the pursuit of which is a primary object, but who for many motives adheres to our political distinction.[54]

Interestingly, with all his observations on British mores and politics and his close alliance with Monroe and his family, Biddle never commented on the March 25, 1807, Act of Parliament abolishing the English slave trade. The abolition of the slave trade must have been discussed, given Elizabeth Monroe's anxiety while at her husband's Virginia plantation, her constant fear of his slaves and their overseers, and the necessity of bolting the doors of their small living space every night. Undoubtedly, it was everywhere else in England.

Slavery, however, was an issue upon which the Monroes disagreed. The husband believed that a plantation, whether as large as his friend, Thomas Jefferson's, or as small as his own, required enslaved peoples' labor. Elizabeth Monroe understood his rationale but dreaded—with good reason—a slave uprising. It may have been that Biddle's adulation of Monroe caused him to ignore the Act and its repercussions because it's certain that his inquisitive nature would have been intrigued by the decades-long debate between economics and moral responsibility. Given his volubility on other aspects of British life and public affairs, and America's similar 1807 Act Prohibiting the Importation of Slaves, Nicholas's reticence on the topic of slavery is marked.

During his three years abroad, Biddle had learned much about international politics and the hunger for power and fortune that motivates human nature. As yet, though, self-regard remained his primary characteristic. Most prodigies who are extolled at an early age fail to discover their frailties until later in life, if at all. Nicholas's persona can be examined in light of his first academic achievements, but a better explanation lies in the family's men and his place within their midst. Recognized for his intellect, he had been rigorously schooled, then afforded coveted positions with the ministers to France and England. His journals and letters home repeatedly referred to his service to his country, which was not an idle or boastful concept. Like his father, uncles, and brothers, serving his country was birthright and duty. The Biddle men knew that contributing to their nation's security and health was a familial obligation, essential rather than choice. During his travels through war-torn Europe amidst danger and the thrill of narrow escapes, he proved his worth to himself and his relations. If he was arrogant—and he was—he could point out his family's tradition of honorable self-sacrifice.

- CHAPTER FOUR -

THE YOUNG LAWYER

Nicholas Biddle left England in September 1807, traveling directly to the capital—then called Washington City—to deliver reports from Monroe to President Jefferson and Secretary of State Madison. He included his observations regarding Europe's political climate. His single-minded focus on his mission made him heedless of his parents' disappointment at not being the first ones to welcome him home. His brother, William, wrote to him in Washington on September 27 to express his parents' sense of hurt and pride. "Papa and I went to the Lazaretto yesterday," adding, "You are performing a public duty."[1] William concluded that the family considered it "proper" that Nicholas should be in the nation's capital rather than enjoying a reunion with his family, then ended the letter with a postscript dictated by Charles. For Charles, the wording was the height of discretion, although he could not resist revealing that he was in on the secret.

> Papa desires me to say to you, that you must not suffer your impatience to be at home to prevent you from accomplishing fully any business with which you are charged by Mr. Monroe. A stay of some days at Washington or even a journey to Monticello may be deemed necessary.[2]

Washington, in 1807 could scarcely have been called a metropolis. Its residents dubbed it "Wilderness City," or "Capital of Miserable Huts," or "City of Streets Without Houses." There was such a dearth of decent dwellings that members of Congress were forced to live across the Rock Creek in Georgetown, at that time a separate port on the Potomac whose ships transported Virginia and Maryland tobacco to England and the Continent. Despite the abolishment of the Atlantic slave trade in Great Britain and the United States, an internal trade continued to prosper, sending slaves from Virginia and Maryland to the deep south to labor on cotton plantations. Georgetown's merchants kept handsome residence in proportion to their growing means, but in many of the dank cellars in which slaves prepared meals for their masters, it was impossible to stand upright.

Major Pierre Charles L'Enfant had drawn the original plans for Washington City. A Frenchman and son of a successful painter affiliated with the Royal Academy of Painting and Sculpture in Paris, he had joined the Continental Army's Corps of Engineers at the rank of captain. Tall, with a beaky nose, he emanated Gallic disdain. L'Enfant's sumptuousness of design was as well known as his disregard for budgetary constraints. His vision for Washington City reflected his love of grandiosity: a place of broad and radiating avenues and monumental buildings arranged to provide noble vistas. The site lay in the fork between the Potomac River and Eastern Branch. Andrew Ellicott, a civil engineer, succeeded L'Enfant in the city's creation, preserving the nation's coffers though not L'Enfant's reputation. Despite Ellicott's pragmatism, Washington City had been hastily constructed and appeared so. It was a sorry sight.

Paying his respects at President Jefferson's house, Biddle was informed that both he and Secretary of State Madison were away at their plantations in Virginia. In possession of critical reports, he was forced to wait for their return. At the time, a good deal of conversation in the nation and capital centered on the British attack on the United States frigate, *Chesapeake*, an uneven sea engagement that had occurred three months prior in June 1807, and became known as the *Chesapeake-Leopard* Affair. Just back from England, a witness to Napoleon's subjugation of Europe, and intimately acquainted with Monroe's efforts to end impressment, Biddle found his opinions on the matter sought after despite his youth and lack of experience in government.

The crisis began as an uneventful cruise when the thirty-eight gun frigate *Chesapeake* departed Hampton Roads for the Mediterranean on June 22, 1807. Aboard were four seamen whom the British government claimed were deserters from the Royal Navy, but who insisted they were impressed Americans who had managed to escape to an American ship. The larger and more heavily armed *Leopard* (equipped with fifty guns) was then lying off Annapolis. The *Leopard* took the lead of the smaller vessel, then turned and hailed her. The American ship, believing the gesture was friendly and that there was news to impart, hove to at which point the *Leopard's* master declared it his right to search for deserters. By then, the two vessels were within pistol range of each other, making the *Chesapeake's* refusal all but impossible. Its commander stated he had no deserters on board and didn't intend to allow his seamen mustered and searched. The *Leopard's* master ignored the reply, ordered a warning shot fired ahead of the American vessel's bow, then followed it seconds later with an entire broadside. The battle was swift, lasting less than twenty minutes. At the conclusion, the *Chesapeake* counted eighteen wounded, one being the commander, and three dead. With the American ship all but disabled and its foremast and main mast destroyed and mizzen mast severely compromised, the British boarded it and removed the four seamen to try them for desertion.

The attack infuriated the public. "UNMERITED OUTRAGE"[3] exploded the June 29 edition of *Poulson's American Daily Advertiser* in Philadelphia. On June 30, *Poulson's* reprinted a call to arms from the *Norfolk Herald*, urging citizens "to discipline ourselves and be in readiness to take up arms in defense of those sacred rights which our forefathers purchased with their blood."[4] *Poulson's* included a list of those killed and wounded. The irate rhetoric continued on July 4, "MORE BRITISH OUTRAGE; Schooner *Wasa* chased up Chesapeake [Bay] by an English cutter and had several shots fired at her."[5] The same newspaper issue ran a letter "TO THE CITIZENS OF THE FIRST CONGRESSIONAL DISTRICT [of Philadelphia]" insisting that "National wrongs require national redress."[6]

Charles Biddle was among the signers. On Monday, July 6, when it was reported that four thousand people had attended the slain seaman's funeral, Robert McDonald, Thomas Jefferson's proclamation of July 2, was reprinted. It had been signed and sealed by the president and secretary of state and stated that "vessels bearing commissions under the government of Great Britain, now within the harbors or waters of the United States, immediately and without any delay to depart from the scene."[7] War upon England became a rallying cry and began to adversely affect the presidency of Thomas Jefferson and challenge the viability of his supposed successor Madison.

While the populace seethed, blaming the legislature for not financing a strong navy, Jefferson issued a proclamation on October 26, banning British warships from entering American waters. To accomplish the blockade, Congress began debating (and authorized on December 18) the construction of one hundred eighty-eight new gunboats. Nevertheless, the challenge to America's sovereignty continued to rankle, drawing anger toward Jefferson and Madison.

Biddle's recent experiences in England lent credence to his opinion that the British "navy is particularly anxious for war."[8]

Aware of the storm brewing over Jefferson's successor, Biddle wrote to his mentor on October 31, 1807. It was the first time he had corresponded with Monroe since leaving England. He explained that he had finally met with Madison, discussing the "subject of our affairs & communicated as you desired what I know with regard to their progress," then added a tersely worded and cryptic "Nothing material has occurred since my return with regard to that business."[9]

In Biddle's opinion, most Americans, initially having been roused to fury with England, had now tempered their assessment. "Such a war would be in the highest degree unpopular," he told Monroe while urging him to come back to the United States with all due speed. "I hope you persist in your intention of returning home shortly. It is everywhere said that your interests suffer by your absence. Your friends are very anxious that you should be here during the present session of Congress."[10]

When Biddle wrote, one of the major issues facing Congress was the Embargo Act of 1807. Jefferson viewed the embargo as an alternative to war with Great Britain over the impressment problem. Enacted on December 22, 1807, the embargo produced a severe economic depression at home while the commerce of England and France, its intended targets, escaped unscathed.

* * *

Amid America's mounting fiscal woes, Monroe returned in the spring of 1808. Ignoring the depression and its causes, Biddle sent Monroe a letter of welcome while steering clear of politics or what future position in government Monroe might hold. Instead, Biddle said he wished that the family had disembarked in New York, which would have enabled the Monroes to visit Philadelphia on their way south. The tenor of the missive was cheery in the extreme. Nicholas was anxious to build upon the bond the two men had established in London. Although his European sojourn had led him to hope he was meant for loftier work than being a member of the Bar, he had embarked on a legal career. However, he admitted to Monroe that he had begun "somewhat inauspiciously."[11] His first client was Aaron Burr, a long-time friend of his father's, who had plummeted from grace following the infamous duel with his nemesis, Alexander Hamilton, in July 1804.

Born in 1756 and called "Little Burr" while at Princeton because of his slight stature, the tempestuous Burr's letters to Charles habitually concluded with "God bless you ever. A Burr."[12] or "Your very affectionate friend Aaron Burr."[13] Apologizing for some minor slight, he told Charles, "If the Heart was made accountable for the errors & omissions of the Head, I should have a heavy reckoning on my hands," then concluded the communication with a telling, "I took a large dose of opium."[14] When Burr became Jefferson's vice president, Charles advised against it, arguing "that it would be better for him to remain at the Bar, where he was making a fortune, than to be Vice-President of the United States."[15]

Then came the duel during which Burr killed Hamilton in Weehawken Heights, New Jersey. Regarded as a murderer, he turned to Charles, writing two hurried letters begging for aid and sending them by a private messenger. The necessity for secrecy was great. Burr was on the run and could not afford to be recognized. The second missive was shorter than the first. As usual, he needed money. "My movements are interrupted until I can dispose of a bill for 350 dollars. I am ashamed to trouble you with these trifles."[16]

Although Charles understood how reviled Burr had become, he felt honor-bound to invite his friend to Philadelphia. Because it was summer when yellow fever and other ailments were rampant, Hannah and the children resided in their country home on Islington Lane, making it easier to accommodate the surprise guest. Charles became a lightning rod of anti-Burr sentiment, even among his closest acquaintances. "I never knew Colonel Burr speak ill of any man,"[17] he countered with his habitual heat while admitting that, "If in this he [Burr] acted as a sinner, Hamilton did not act as a saint in accepting it."[18]

Efforts to extradite Burr were unsuccessful. There were even assassination rumors afoot. About to embark on what he hoped would become an illustrious career, Nicholas yearned to distance himself from the tumultuous situation. At the same time, Burr attempted to appease his savior's son by writing a letter of recommendation to a friend in Paris. "He is the son of my old & faithful friend, Charles Biddle, a man of fortune & respectability in this city . . . an amicable young man of uncommon distinction and implicit honor. He will inform you of the state of things in the U.S."[19]

Nicholas resented the interference with its implied obligation as well as a hint of involvement in the sordid affair. He had no intention of becoming Burr's spokesman. Although the two had Princeton in common (Burr had also been a president of the Cliosophic, his father had been the institution's second president, his maternal grandfather its third), Nicholas refused to chat con-genially about campus days and scholarly pursuits. He fled his father's house, hurrying to New York in preparation for his departure for France. The relationship between father and son was severely strained by then. In his autobiography, Charles spared little space to Nicholas's leave-taking while devoting pages to Burr's misfortunes. "If General Hamilton had not opposed Colonel Burr I have very little doubt but he would have been elected Governor of New York," was the loyal assessment.[20] He felt that his son had betrayed his friend.

In France, Nicholas had been immune to Burr's travails, but Charles remained defiantly faithful, corresponding with "the unfortunate Burr," as he now referred to him, after he left Philadelphia. Burr developed a grandiose scheme that involved procuring a tract of land in the Mississippi Territory to settle it with military men. Believing that the residents of Mexico were "ripe for revolt," he told Charles his plan "would make the fortunes of all those concerned in revolutionizing the country."[21] Charles disagreed and eventually withdrew all support. Burr countered that Andrew Jackson had promised his aid and that arming the Mississippi Territory would be a deterrent to a possible invasion by Napoleon. "Burr was always of the opinion that Bonaparte would give us some trouble in New Orleans," Charles observed, "and wanted, long before this time, to take measures that would put it out of his power to do us any injury; but Mr. Jefferson either was afraid of Bonaparte, or had a better opinion of him than he deserved."[22]

Burr made the mistake of confiding his plans to General James Wilkinson, commander of the American army in the west, who was then illicitly receiving payments from Spain. (At Charles's request, Wilkinson had made Nicholas an artillery officer prior to his European journey.) To keep his own felonious practices secret, the general informed Jefferson that Burr intended to found a dynasty in Mexico. Jefferson, who had conceived an abiding mistrust of his one-time political ally, had him arrested on charges of treason.

In February 1807, Burr sent a plaintive appeal asking Charles to attend his trial, but Charles, finally considering his family's reputation, refused. The trial, which began May 27, 1807, in Richmond, Virginia, gripped the nation. Here was a hero of the revolutionary war and a former vice president charged with the greatest crime against his country. The *Richmond Enquirer* described an "immense concourse of citizens from various parts of the Union converging to witness the proceedings."[23] A "cyphered letter" outlining the colonel's nefarious plans and presumably written by Burr was admitted as evidence.

However, it was discovered that Wilkinson had penned the letter himself, so the question arose whether the missive was a copy of an original, as the general claimed, or a fraud. It was then understood that "Wilkinson would go almost all lengths to hang Col. Burr,"[24] and his double-dealing became public knowledge. "For a great number of years no three men were more intimate friends than Wilkinson, Burr, and Truxtun. I was intimate with them all," was Charles's weary assessment.[25] Complicating matters, Wilkinson was married to Charles's first cousin, Ann, which meant that Charles received complaints from both parties. Burr penned a tragic, "it has pleased Heaven to take from me all the richest treasures ever conferred on me."[26] While Wilkinson fumed about "knaves, swindlers, gamblers, drunkards, villains"[27] besetting him on every side.

After a long, exhaustive trial, Chief Justice John Marshall acquitted Burr in October, ruling that there was insufficient evidence to try him for treason. Devastated in spirit and hounded by creditors, some former friends and supporters who had loaned him money, Burr quit Richmond for Philadelphia. Again, he turned to the Biddles, this time regarding civil suits over his mounting debts. Nicholas had joined his brother, William's, law firm after returning from England. The younger brother took charge of the offices at 100 South Front Street when William was elected to the Pennsylvania state legislature.

By default, Nicholas became Burr's legal counsel. As he explained to Monroe:

> After his acquittal at Richmond, Burr came here broken in fortune
> and character, & has been pursued by creditors. I have no partiality for
> Burr himself, and I have an abhorrence for certain parts of his conduct.
> But an acquaintance of long standing with the family was the occasion
> of his asking my assistance.[28]

Charles was more blunt. He feared for his old friend's sanity. "It would not have surprised me on going there to have found he [Burr] had ended his sufferings with a pistol."[29]

* * *

Despite his dislike of Burr, Biddle found the practice of law appealed to him more than he had imagined. His European connections served him well. Authorized to represent the American consuls in Paris and London and through them a widening sphere of men of affairs, he began concentrating on civil law for which he had a natural propensity. He liked strategic thinking, had a strong competitive streak, and was articulate and eloquent in his arguments. About his "commencement of the practice of the law," Monroe told him, "I sincerely wish you success because I think you merit it," then extended an invitation for the young attorney to visit the Monroe family at their estate in Virginia, which he indicated "merits rather the name of a cabbin [*sic*] than a cottage."[30]

Nicholas declined and applied himself to his career. As he began carving a place for himself as an intellectual rather than a warrior Biddle, he felt he was achieving distinction within his family and city.

By then, he had discovered that he could maintain both a career and a nearly all-consuming avocation with the literary, political, and critical compendia *Port Folio*. The publication, founded in 1801, was without peer in the nation, attracting a cultured, erudite audience eager for discourses on a wide variety of subjects ranging from "Classical Learning," "Literary Intelligence," dramatic and humorous poetry to political treatises and theatre reviews. "Memoirs of Anacreon," which ran serially, included footnotes and references in ancient Greek. Editor, Joseph Dennie, contributed under the pseudonym Oliver Oldschool, Esq. In 1808, the *Port Folio's* emblem consisted of a young man pouring over a stack of books and burning the proverbial midnight oil. "One of the most essential duties of a literary journalist," the publication asserted, "is not only to take care that the republick [*sic*] of letters should suffer no detriment, but that the dignity and honour of the wise and the learned should be constantly indicated to all who aspire to intellectual eminence."[31]

The words might have been written to describe Nicholas.

Mental illness exacerbated by alcoholism made Dennie's work erratic. His considerable charm counteracted those problems, at least in the beginning when the stable of pseudonymous authors included Charles Brockden Brown, Benjamin Rush (signing himself as Marcellus), and John Quincy Adams, who had been Dennie's Harvard classmate. When Dennie's growing addiction put the *Port Folio* at risk, restructuring became necessary. Biddle stepped in and saved it, turning the magazine into a monthly publication instead of a panic-inducing weekly. An irreverent Nicholas is easy to detect in the words, "The *Port Folio* Magazine contributes to the interests of individuals, to the power of Philadelphia, and the aggrandizement of our empire. The place of publication is unquestionably auspicious to all the projects of Genius, Science, and Art."[32]

"Levity," "Philosophical Intelligence," "Literary Intelligence," "Scientific Papers," "Rhetoric," were among the offerings, as well as "The Sententious World," consisting of epigrams like: "The common soldier's blood makes the general a great man."[33] Biddle began his new role as author and editor with a meticulously researched treatise on Nicolo Machiavelli, "Vindication of Machiavelli," in which he sought to prove that the author of *The Prince* was not a "despot in politics."[34] His efforts to turn his subject into a product of his time rather than a political mastermind met with only moderate success but proved a catalyst for debate and brought him the admiration of his "Tuesday Club" peers.

In 1809, the publication analyzed the "Military Character of Different Nations," in which the French—not without criticism—were awarded the highest marks. Given Biddle's European experiences, he was probably the author.

> The German troops are slow in their attack, indifferent in battle, and slow in their retreat. They leave behind them the most prisoners because the French make their escape and the Russians will suffer themselves to be cut to pieces rather than run from their post. When the Russians attack, they must either conquer or die. They know only to go forwards, but never backwards.[35]

The assessments were both timely and topical because Napoleon's subjugation of Europe had by then extended into the Peninsular Wars, causing renewed apprehension by American citizens who wondered whether New Orleans or Canada might be the emperor's next target. After Nelson trounced the combined French and Spanish navies at Trafalgar on October 21, 1805, Napoleon began to fear that an allied attack might come from the Iberian coast and move northward into France. In 1808, he dispatched 100,000 men to Spain. On June 7 of that year, the French sacked Cordova. Spanish forces rallied in defense of Saragossa, temporarily halting the invasion. Joseph Bonaparte, who had been named king, fled Madrid. On December 3, Napoleon and his *Grande Armée* recaptured the city, but on the 22nd, he was on the move again, traveling with 50,000 men across the snow-covered Escurial Pass. In five days, his army traversed more than one hundred miles. Defeating him seemed implausible. The safe passage of merchant ships, including American vessels, in and out of the Mediterranean became increasingly dubious.

The mood in the United States turned restive. On Friday, January 6, 1809, *Poulson's American Daily Advertiser* reported that Congress proposed creating a federal militia of 50,000 volunteers, each serving two years, thereby "placing the country in a more complete state of defense" because "the danger and probability of war appeared to thicken upon us every day."[36]

The delay in receiving news from Europe exacerbated fears. A passage of forty-nine days was considered swift, but anything could happen in that space of time. On January 17, *Poulson's* reprinted a grim communiqué from the *Liverpool Courier* of November 2, 1808. "Buonarte [*sic*] about to let slip the dogs of war against Spain."[37] Accounts of attacks on Gallicia, Aranjuez, and Castilia appeared in *Poulson's* January 27 and an announcement that Britain had advised the Spanish royal family to emigrate to Brazil. By late March, reports indicated that the allies were losing and that the French had begun capturing American seamen and forcing them to serve on French ships of war. Then came the most disturbing communication yet, a proclamation made by Napoleon:

> Spaniards—You have been blinded by perfidious men. They have seduced you to take up arms, and drawn you into foolish and senseless warfare . . . I will treat you only as prisoners conquered and place my brother on another throne. I will put the crown of Spain on my own head; and I will be respected even by the worst, for God has given me the power and disposition to surmount all obstacles. In our Imperial Camp at Madrid 7th of December. (signed) Napoleon.[38]

While the United States government and her mercantile interests kept a weather eye on Napoleon and worried if he would succeed in his plans to conquer the entire European continent, Philadelphians balanced the menacing with the mundane as they went about their daily lives. Zachariah Poulson, Jr., librarian at the Library Company and the publisher of the newspaper that bore his name, ran advertisements offering for sale the "Holy Bible Explained,"[39] as well as the services of young black indentured males: "For Sale—the time of two Mulatto Boys—one has 10 years and the other 9 years to serve. Enquire at 46 Chestnut Street or at the grocery. . . . A likely Black boy who has five years to serve."[40] Although the notices did not advocate slavery, they were comparable.

A brazen, broad-daylight kidnapping of a twelve-year old girl made front-page news when her father, a carter, begged for her return, promising "100 Dollars Reward," a vast sum.[41] That domestic tragedy competed for space with the prosaic: "Street dirt at auction 7th and Vine"[42] and advertisements for "Souchong and Hyson Teas, Madrass Goods, Havanna Sugars, and Black Italian Crape."[43] An illustrated advertisement, "Vive La Plume—Metallic Pen Manufactory,"[44] depicted two pens resembling crossed swords. Although the image presented an insouciant suggestion that the pen should be weightier than Bonaparte's cutlasses, it was clear that Napoleon dominated almost every aspect of the public's imagination.

* * *

Despite the crisis in Europe, James Madison began his presidency on a positive note in his speech delivered to Congress on May 22, 1809. Just prior to leaving office, Thomas Jefferson had signed the Non-Intercourse Act, repealing the unpopular Embargo Act 1807 that had all but crippled America's foreign trade while doing nothing to curtail Britain's policy of impressment. Madison declared that commerce between Great Britain and the United States would become "renewable" after June 10 of that year.[45] In addition, he proposed reducing the federal militia from its current total of 100,000 men. Although a Navy report regarding the expense of maintaining gunboats cautioned vigilance, the troubled history of ratified and nullified treaties with England appeared to be over. A celebratory ode entitled "Commerce Reviving" sung to the tune of "Rule Britannia" heralded the new accord. Elation was short-lived. In August, Madison withdrew trade agreements with Great Britain; and in November, his message to Congress referred to the "insecurity of our commerce."[46] Immediately thereafter, the British minister to the United States, Francis James Jackson, was recalled.

While America and Britain's relationship again deteriorated, Napoleon continued tyrannizing Europe. A revolution occurred in Sweden on March 15, 1809, during which a military coup deposed the king and took him prisoner. France was blamed for instigating it. Portugal remained a battleground. The war against Austria resumed, and Napoleon issued a manifesto to Hungary: "Hungarians—the moment to obtain your freedom has arrived. I offer you peace. Your union with Austria is the source of all your misfortunes."[47] The "Annihilation of the Pope's Temporal Power" (June 10, 1809) was reported on August 11. Occasional moments of hope tempered the calamitous news. Following the battle of Ratisbon, came a gleeful communication that Bonaparte was unable to pay his troops and that he had commanded the sick and wounded to return to battle. His *Grande Armée* appeared to be fighting on too many fronts at once; finally, the tide was turning in favor of the allied armies of The Holy Roman Empire and Russia.

The news proved unreliable.

As the year in America drew to a close, information that composer Joseph Hayden had died near Vienna (May 31, 1809) was overshadowed by Napoleon's declaration of victory over Hayden's beloved city. One hundred cannons were fired from the ramparts to herald his supremacy. The Emperor of France now proclaimed himself Emperor of Austria, King of Hungary and Bohemia, King of Italy, and Protector of the League of the Rhine.

* * *

A by-product of the rampant warfare consuming Europe, Russia, and England was a focus on America's western frontiers as spaces for development and commercial expansion. A treatise on the habits, language, and behaviors of the Creek Indians, written by Col. Benjamin Hawkins, Agent for Indian Affairs south of the Ohio River, and published in 1809, gave traders and settlers a workable understanding of the tracts of land they should consider inhabiting, and the peoples among whom they would dwell.[48] In June 1809, Madison referred to "lands ceded to the United States by the Cherokee and Chickasaw Indians,"[49] a sizeable area ripe for settlement. The December 8 issue of *Poulson's* provided a comprehensive list of the western territories and the various Acts of Congress by which Louisiana, Indiana, and Mississippi had been ceded, or given governance, or divided into separate territories or governments.

The expedition led by Lewis and Clark was about to alter Nicholas Biddle's career. Published in 1814 as *The Journals of the Expedition Under the Command of Capt.ⁱ Lewis and Clark to the sources of the Missouri, thence across the Rocky Mountains and down the river Columbia to the Pacific Ocean performed during the years 1804-5-6 by order of the Government of the United States.* Biddle edited over one million words detailing the flora, fauna, topography, geography, and, most significantly for white expansion, the activities and relationships of the tribal peoples of the west.

As an introduction to the finished work, Thomas Jefferson described the expedition's inception and the character of Meriwether Lewis, who had served as the President's private secretary for two years. He had chosen Lewis to lead the exploration, and his death affected Jefferson deeply. Penned at Monticello, he dated the missive that served as introduction August 18, 1813, the anniversary of Lewis' birth: "Meriwether Lewis, late governor of Louisiana, was born on the 18th of August, 1774."[50] Jefferson further noted that the Lewises were among the "distinguished families of that state" (Virginia). A great-uncle, John Lewis, had been a member of the king's council before the Revolution. Fielding Lewis, another great-uncle, had married one of George Washington's sisters. In addition to detailing Lewis's lineage, Jefferson marveled at Lewis's fortitude:

Of courage undaunted, possessing a firmness and perseverance of
purpose which nothing but impossibilities could divert from its direction; careful as a father of those committed to his charge, yet steady
in the maintenance of order and discipline; intimate with the Indian
character, customs, and principles; habituated to the hunting life . . .
honest, disinterested, liberal, of sound understanding, and a fidelity to
truth so scrupulous, that whatever he should report would be as certain
as if seen by ourselves . . . I could have no hesitation in confiding the
enterprise to him.[51]

The expedition had been Jefferson's long-held hope. Scientific and political, its purpose was to examine the geography, flora, and fauna of hitherto un-
explored regions and examine the customs and alliances of indigenous peoples.
Although the phrase "manifest destiny" was not yet in usage, territorial expansion was a given. As early as 1783, when the American Revolution was over
in all but name only, rumors circulated that the British planned to send an
expeditionary force from the Mississippi River to the Rockies and thence to
Pacific Coast. If so, might they colonize the area, challenging American settlers
who had pushed west beyond the Blue Ridge Mountains and thereby curtailing
the new nation's maturation? The fear of Britain's colonial designs was real.

It was not until 1786, when Jefferson was serving as minister to France that
an opportunity for a western expedition arose. The explorer John Ledyard was
then in Paris; he had accompanied Captain James Cook to find the Northwest
Passage to the Orient (1776-1779). According to Jefferson, the Connecticut
native, being "of a roaming disposition, he was now panting for some new
enterprise."[52] That enterprise would carry Ledyard through Europe and Russia, across the Pacific to the "Nootka Sound, fall down into the latitude of the
Missouri, and penetrate to and through, that to the United States."[53] Ledyard,
Jefferson added, "eagerly seized the idea." Although Empress Catherine considered the plan outlandish, she gave her approval for Ledyard to enter Russia. The attempt failed when she changed her mind, had the explorer arrested,
thrown into a coach and driven without pausing except to change horses until
he reached Poland where, dangerously ill, he was all but tossed out of the carriage and "left to himself."[54]

The notion of an exploratory expedition lay dormant until 1792 when Jefferson suggested the idea to the American Philosophical Society in Philadelphia.
Founded by Benjamin Franklin in 1743 to promote "useful knowledge," it was

the first scientific society in America. Jefferson had been elected as a member in 1780 and became its third president in 1797. He proposed "a subscription to engage some competent person to explore that region in the opposite direction . . . by ascending the Missouri, crossing the Stony [Rocky] Mountains, and descending the nearest river to the Pacific."[55] Meriwether Lewis immediately applied to Jefferson, but the French botanist André Michaux was chosen instead. His work was cut short due to diplomatic entanglements between France and Spain over the Louisiana territory. Some believed Michaux was a spy.

By 1803, it had become necessary to review previously established trading practices with the tribal peoples. In a confidential message sent to Congress on January 18, Jefferson recommended adding and including the tribes along the Missouri River. To do so would require an expedition into their territory and beyond. Certain that his secretary possessed the skills and military discipline necessary for the task, the President suggested Lewis, who journeyed to Philadelphia and Lancaster, Pennsylvania, to improve his knowledge of the natural sciences as well as "the astronomical observations necessary for the geography of his route."[56] Lewis studied practical astronomy and surveying with Andrew Ellicott in Lancaster, and botany in Philadelphia with Benjamin Smith Barton and Benjamin Rush, and paleontology and comparative anatomy with Caspar Wistar—all members of the Philosophical Society.

"Deeming it necessary he should have some person with him of known competence to the direction of the enterprise,"[57] Lewis proposed his friend William Clark, the much-younger brother of General George Rogers Clark, who responded, "I will happily join you."[58]

Clark also communicated with Jefferson, who had approved the addition to the party. "I will cheerfully and with great pleasure join my friend Capt Lewis on this vast enterprise."[59] Bold flourishes underscored his signature.

The expedition began May 14, 1804, near St. Louis on the river Dubois. The Corps of Discovery, as it was called, did not return to St. Louis until September 23, 1806. In the intervening twenty-eight months, they suffered intense cold, at one point forcing them to change sentinels every hour lest the sentry freeze to death, drank poisonous water, withstood attacks by men and animals—especially the "white bear" (grizzly). They suffered hunger and near starvation, torrential rains, were forced to eat their horses, and made "providential" escapes from death. Reaching the Pacific, they were dismayed to find signs of venereal disease among the coastal Chinooks, which they accounted for by evidence of Western traders and whalers. Some of the men wore cast-off sailors' jackets, trousers, or coats. A woman bore the name J. BOWMAN tattooed on her arm. Toward the conclusion of their journey, they learned they had been given up for lost. Only Jefferson believed they were still living, but his hopes were a matter of intuition rather than fact. When the explorers reached St. Louis (then a mere village), the entire population turned out to welcome them.

In addition to journals and notes "in their original state" that Clark sent Jefferson "for your own perusal,"[60] there were boxes containing examples of flora and fauna "part of the upper head of the Mammoth [discovered at Big Bone Lick, Kentucky] . . . part of a Small Elephant jaw . . . 5 Elephant Teeth."[61] Transported by sea via New Orleans, Jefferson dispatched part of the collection to Philadelphia and the Philosophical Society, while shipping the remainder to the National Institute of France. Jefferson told Clark that the mammoth was a distinct species called "Mastodont" owing to the formation of its teeth.[62]

Made governor of the Louisiana Territory, Meriwether Lewis's temperament was ill-suited to a sedentary existence. Spending his remaining years in a richly appointed home while being forced to endure polite conversation dismayed him. Except for his time serving as Jefferson's secretary, he had always been a man of action who thrived on physical challenges. The odyssey to and from the Pacific Ocean had been long, grueling, perilous, and exhilarating. Every day had produced new trials that demanded shrewdness, perseverance, and audacity. Within his newly circumscribed life, the bouts of depression that Jefferson had recognized as a family trait manifested themselves again. Then, too, he probably intuited what devastation white expansion would wreak on the native populations he had come to admire. He had been commissioned to study tribal languages and behavior; that information could and would be used to deleterious effect.

Exacerbated by alcohol, his behavior grew increasingly erratic. On a journey east to Washington, he was described as having "symptoms of derangement."[63] His death on October 12, 1809, was shrouded in mystery. No one wanted to suggest that the hero who had traversed the nation had taken his own life; murder seemed a preferable option, but both motive and perpetrator were elusive. Jefferson believed Lewis had committed suicide.

William Clark was left to create a narrative of the remarkable journey. He went to Monticello to confer with Jefferson. From there, he traveled to Philadelphia, hoping the men who had aided Lewis in his scientific preparations would help find an editor and publisher (an original publisher had withdrawn after Lewis's death). In Philadelphia, Clark learned about a young magazine editor named Nicholas Biddle, who was making a name for himself in the nation's literary circles. After returning to Virginia, Clark wrote Biddle in February 1810, asking him to edit the journals. The request took Nicholas wholly by surprise. He declined, citing health and time constraints.

A mere two weeks later, he changed his mind and fell into a panic over his prior communication. He begged to be reconsidered and fretted lest a "better choice" had been made in the interim. "I will therefore very readily agree to do all that is in my power for the advancement of the work; and I think I can promise with some confidence that it shall be ready as soon as the publisher is prepared to print it."[64]

Creating a cohesive narrative from years' worth of notes was an enormous undertaking, but impetuosity remained Biddle's hallmark. "Having made up my mind today I am desirous that no delay should occur on my part." He informed Clark that he planned to travel south by stagecoach via Hagerstown, Maryland, and would be at the explorer's home in Fincastle, Virginia as soon as possible—maybe even before his missive arrived. If he could have recalled his previous letter, he would have.

On March 22, five days after sending Clark his appeal, Nicholas commenced his journey. The route west and south through Frederick, Winchester, and Staunton took him into the Blue Ridge Mountains. The weather was execrable. Persistent rain delayed his progress. The coach would climb one steep hill and then slowly descend a rutted mud road only to face another higher elevation. The crowded vehicle grew more and more cramped as its passengers tried to stretch out and ease their jouncing limbs. No lofty vistas raised the grumbling travelers' spirits; instead, they peered through the pervasive murk or furtively examined each other. Nicholas doodled in his journal, drawing two mountain peaks, a tree, and a fellow passenger's profile. He may have been facile with words, but he was no artist. A rhyming verse fared no better. He wrote that he'd "exchanged the gayer scenes of city strife/ For rural peace & meek sequestered life."[65]

The remainder of the diary he kept in French, which poses questions. Was he utilizing the long hours by practicing a language he already knew, or didn't he trust the other travelers to read his notes? Or, did he fear a rival might lurk on the opposite seat? The slow slog made him wretchedly uneasy. Impatience robbed him of his famous charm, making him a singularly uncongenial companion.

When he reached Santillane, William Clark's wife's family home, his host was as astonished by his guest's unexpected arrival as Nicholas was to find himself face to face with the famed explorer. His ardor deprived him of any gravitas he intended to impart, but he impressed his host with his exuberance. Nicholas spent nearly three weeks at Santillane discussing the project, examining Clark's library, and letting the enormity of the exploration begin to take shape in his imagination.

* * *

Returning to Philadelphia, Biddle immediately set to work. The partnership between editor and author(s) became a matter of specific questions posed and equally precise answers received. Biddle wanted to make certain the book accurately conveyed the technical elements of the journey, as well as its spirit. Jefferson's 1803 injunctions had been explicit. He told the party to report back on every aspect of the tribal people's lives:

> The extent and limits of their possessions;
> Their relations with other tribes or nations;
> Their language, traditions, monuments;
> The ordinary occupations in agriculture, fishing, hunting, war, arts, and the implement of these;
> Their food, clothing, and domestic accommodations;
> The diseases prevalent among them, and the remedies they use;
> Moral and physical circumstances which distinguish them from the tribes we know;
> Peculiarities in their laws, customs, and dispositions;[66]

Having traversed Europe during the Napoleonic Wars and delivered his own and Monroe's reports to the federal government, Biddle understood the necessity of documentation. Where precisely did the party portage across the Columbia River or cross the Rock (Rocky) Mountains? What about tribal languages, practices, and customs, as per Jefferson's instructions? Biddle suggested enlarging the scale of the maps Clark submitted.

To aid the project and help translate sign and spoken languages, Clark sent George Shannon to Philadelphia. Eighteen when he enlisted in the expedition, Shannon had been the youngest member of the permanent party. Shot in the leg in 1807 while accompanying the Mandan chief Sheheke back to his people after visiting the President in Washington, he had undergone an amputation and wasn't expected to live. After recuperating, he returned to his native

Kentucky and attended Lexington University, where he was "highly spoken of by his acquaintances."[67] Clark had full faith in his emissary and assured Biddle that he "possesses a sincere and undisguised heart," and that "he has been studiously employed in pursuit of an education to enable him to acquire a profession by which he can make an honorable respectable living."[68] Shannon wanted to study law in Philadelphia. Clark hoped Biddle would help him.

Biddle's first letter to Clark was dated July 7, 1810, and contained twenty queries that required clarification or explication—what he called a "catechism of inquiries."[69] He further told Clark that "I have been very industrious with it, and although I find it occupies much more of my time and is more laborious than I expected, I am by no means discouraged." (In the letter's final version, he reordered the words, making "laborious" less prominent.)

Rising "habitually at 5 o'clock every morning & by constant exertion," he said he was "advancing," but also admitted that he required additional reading material to help him understand the region and tribes. He asked a friend in Paris, David Warden, to supply a copy of Jean-Francois-Benjamin Dumont de Montigny's, *Mémoires historiques sur la Louisiane* (published 1753), which up until then had been the definitive work on the Louisiana Territory and lower Mississippi valley. Biddle made use of two other diaries kept during the expedition: that of Patrick Gass, already published and unfortunately expurgated, and John Ordway, which Clark purchased and gave to the editor.

Biddle's inquiries dealt with place names and spellings, which the journals listed imperfectly, as well as the interactions, sociology, family life, and superstitions of individual tribes. Of great importance was the ability to communicate.

> Were there particular gestures you would make? Was the Cheyenne
> nation the same as the tribe the French called Le Chien or Dog Indian?
> What is, in fact, the Indian name for medicine or Great medicine?
> Have the Mandan or any other Indian you met any particular mode of
> reckoning the week, month, year?

Biddle also asked for additional descriptions of trade practices, fortifications, and the physical aspect of villages. He understood that Clark's memory needed to stretch back six years in time and was gentle with his prodding, mitigating his demands with "If you recollect. . . ." As professional as he appeared in his editorial role, his imagination had taken flight, and his mind's eye envisioned each moment of the expedition as though he were traversing the terrain in company with the party. "Today," he told Clark, "I have sent you into a hollow to look for wood to make canoes after the unhappy failure of your iron boat."

That failure occurred Tuesday, July 9, 1805, near the confluence of the Missouri and Medicine Rivers. The party had employed a combination of buffalo and elk skin to cover the boat's iron frame but discovered that the elk hides were inferior, causing the boat to leak. By then, the plentiful herds of buffalo had deserted them, forcing Clark and ten members of the expedition to improvise by making dugout canoes. Material for ax handles was scarce and inferior; thirteen handles broke in a single day. Mosquitoes and swarms of large black gnats attacked them, especially their eyes; painful hand abscesses, called whitlows, afflicted some of the men; and Nathaniel Hale Pryor, a sergeant, dislocated his shoulder. Remedied, it remained exceedingly painful. It was not until Saturday, July 13, that the party could proceed. Amid these trials, the men kept notes on the natural world: enormous gray eagles they believed were a distinct species, a kind of white chub fished out of the river, kingfishers, turtledoves, brown curlews, otters, antelope, bow-alder, and sweet-willow. Reading the report in Philadelphia five summers later, Biddle was transported.

Clark answered each of Nicholas's queries, providing a pronunciation guide to the tribal words and enclosures listing the various names of the nations and places. For instance: Medicine River was called "Måh-ho-påh-åja"—with the accent on the final a; medicine was "mahopah."[70] The Ottoes, he said, "believe that they come from the Earth and will return to the earth, and again return on earth." He added that he was busy preparing a larger map "on a scale which I think will please you." He expressed his gratitude for Biddle's diligence, concluding his letter with "Prey [sic] write to me as often as you can conveniently— The post is waiting, and I have not time to read what I have wrote."

By July 1811, Biddle felt he had finally gotten the narrative ready for publication. Now came the tricky matter of Clark's rank. Promised that he would be appointed a captain and therefore equal in command to Lewis, Clark had been shabbily treated. He remained a second lieutenant. He understood that he had been ill-used, as did Lewis, and the two men had agreed to create a semblance of parity for the good of the expedition. Clark explained this personal history, then added,

> I do not wish that any thing relative to this commission or appointment should be inserted in my book . . . and I do assure you that I have never related as much on the subject to any person before. Be so

good as to place me on equal footing with Capt. Lewis in every point of view without explaining any thing which might have taken place or even mentioning the Commission at all.[71]

Finished with the original journals, Nicholas placed them reverentially in the American Philosophical Society, where they remain to this day. By then, his professional vistas had altered. Nominated by the American Republicans for the Pennsylvania State legislature's lower house, he was elected in October 1810. His father was on the same ticket as a candidate for the state senate. The possibility of serving with Charles brought Nicholas deep satisfaction. He had always desired his father's approval.

Before embarking on his political career, Nicholas asked Paul Allen, a colleague from the *Port Folio,* to do a final revision on the Lewis and Clark journals. It was Allen's name that appeared in the published work, although everyone recognized Biddle's role. In 1811, Monroe wrote to thank him for handing "to the world & to posterity the voyage of Mssrs. Lewis & Clark to the Pacifick [*sic*] Ocean . . . an event so remarkable and important in the annals of our country."[72]

Thomas Jefferson expressed his gratitude, too, writing from Monticello on August 20, 1813. "In a letter from Mr. Paul Allen of Philadelphia, I was informed that other business had obliged you to turn over to him the publication of Gov^n Lewis's journals of his western expedition . . . I am happy on this occasion of expressing my portion of thanks all will owe you for the trouble you have taken with this interesting narrative, and the assurance of my sentiments of high esteem and respect."[73]

Bradford and Inskeep, the *Port Folio* publishers during Biddle's tenure, brought the journals to press in 1814. Sadly, William Clark never received payment because the publishers went bankrupt the same year. Despite the bankruptcy, the journals' importance endured. Biddle's authoritative editing fashioned from rough notes an epic tale of adventure. Empathizing with Lewis's self-doubts, he pictured him as an even greater hero because he battled tragic character flaws. Clark and the remainder of the party, Biddle saw as the quintessence of patriotism. Readers agreed, turning the explorers into latter-day gods. Twenty-two additional printings of Biddle's *History* were published throughout the nineteenth century, transporting the public over treacherous mountain passes and down cascading rivers. Rightly, the expedition became the stuff of legend.

- CHAPTER FIVE -

"PRAY GOD FOR A LUCID INTERVAL"

Biddle began his political career by chairing the Committee on the Education of the Poor. Although the Pennsylvania Constitution had authorized the establishment of schools "in such a manner that the poor may be taught gratis,"[1] only Philadelphia's Aimwell School for the Free Instruction of Females served that purpose. Biddle, for whom education was paramount, found the situation egregious. He might have wondered why he had been assigned the chairmanship of an essentially toothless body; instead, he studied Noah Webster, Richard Rush, and other activists for free education. He understood that equality could never be achieved without the opportunity for educational parity. He drew up a plan for creating neighborhood schools within the state's counties, each easily accessible to the residents and led by a well-paid schoolmaster. The poor would learn free of charge; the wealthier would pay tuition. Biddle envisioned a system that provided not only educational equality but also encouraged social non-discrimination. This egalitarian dream came to naught. At least not until Biddle reached the final decade of his life.

The same held true for another project dear to his heart—the construction of a canal connecting the Delaware and Susquehanna Rivers that would not only improve commerce but bring far-flung communities into bonds of mutual support. His idealism met the hard reality of partisan politics. The Republican Party, of which he was a member (albeit in name only), cared more about fiscal conservatism than spending funds on infrastructure or universal education. He also encountered resistance as a member of the Reorganization of the Militia. His sojourn in England and the Continent had convinced him that a new war with Great Britain or France, or both was certain. An enhanced defensive force was vital. He wrote to other legislators in other states, but again in vain. Cocky, driven, and with a gift for oratory that impressed his peers—even if grudgingly, Nicholas ignored the deep-seated division between Philadelphia and the rural and western communities that his father had previously recognized. He wanted to make sweeping changes, and he wanted to do so quickly.

He found his severest test in the national bank debate, an institution he and his father championed. Chartered in 1791, on the recommendation of Alexander Hamilton, Secretary of the Treasury, by 1810, the Bank of the United States had become a political football. At the time of its establishment, Jefferson, Washington's Secretary of State, and Madison, a member of the House of Representatives, had opposed the idea of a central bank, believing that specie was the only safe form of currency and that paper—even utilized with oversight—could become subject to exploitation or misuse. With the bank's original charter set to expire in 1811, the question of a national bank became hotly contested by Republicans on both sides of the ideological argument while the Federalists, no longer a strong party, demurred. At the heart of the intra-party fight was not the bank but Madison. Republicans, who were loudest in their denunciation of the Bank of the United States, exploited the issue to prevent Madison's re-election and gain control of their party. Charles Biddle declared the issue "the most important business that was before the Legislature this session."[2] He had been a director of the bank since its original institution.

On December 13, 1810, Jacob Holgate, a member of the Pennsylvania State Legislator representing Philadelphia County and a particularly rabid opponent to a national bank, declared that the institution was unconstitutional and controlled by foreign interests, which, naturally, stoked fears. Napoleon's grip on Europe continued to plague American commercial interests, and the specter of foreign domination loomed large. In his introduction to a resolution to "to prevent the charter of the bank of the United States from being renewed,"[3] Holgate appealed to the state's rural populace and lawmakers, many of whom mistrusted those residing in urban areas. Extolling "the yeomanry of America," whom he said:

> Are its pride, its bulwark and its hopes. Their interests, the dearest affection of the human mind, their simplicity of manners and their habits, bind them to our republican institutions, and to the defense of the independence of our country. Neither the allurements of wealth, the whisperings of hope, nor the dazzling visions of fancy could persuade such men to betray their country.[4]

Lest the allusion to the city folk's greed, guile, and venality be lost, he conjured up the memory of traitor, Benedict Arnold, who "sold his country and blasted his laurels, to pamper his artificial appetites and gratify his love of pomp and splendor."[5] The War for Independence also had echoes in the denunciation of a national bank. "The bank of England has placed the government of England in the hands of a monied aristocracy, who rule the nation with a rod of iron."[6]

Holgate concluded by demanding:

> That the senators of this state in the senate of the United States be, and
> they are hereby instructed, and the representatives of the state in the
> house of representatives of the United States, be and they hereby are
> requested to use every exertion of their power, to prevent the charter of
> the bank of the United States from being renewed, or any other bank
> from being chartered by congress . . . the copies of the resolution to be
> provided to governors of our sister states and each of the senators and
> representatives in the congress of the United States.[7]

The resolution was left on the table. The members went home to their families to celebrate Christmas and the advent of the New Year. Holgate, a clever speaker and wily politician, must have believed he'd won the day and that his proposal would find no opponent.

* * *

Certain he had prevailed, Holgate demanded a vote as soon as the recess concluded. He intended to kill the Bank before any of his colleagues had second thoughts. While the legislators straggled in to take their seats on Thursday, January 3, 1811, Nicholas Biddle rose to his feet to debate the resolution. His twenty-fifth birthday was five days hence, and to Holgate and other like-minded legislators, the young man looked anything but impressive. Dressed in the city's latest fashions and adhering to the rules of cosmopolitan etiquette, he seemed like a lightweight. His brief history as a legislator failed to improve the image because he had focused on what his more seasoned colleagues viewed as useless causes. Holgate decided to let young Biddle say his peace—and then leave the chambers in ignominy.

The courthouse in Lancaster, which served as the state's capital prior to the move to Harrisburg, was chilly. Men clustered by the fireplaces, chatting idly about their excursions home. No one seemed inclined to work or pay attention as Biddle requested the Speaker's permission to address the assembly. The members assumed the remarks would be pro forma, an effort by a new member to impress the august body. If they bothered to listen, they did so with the condescension of legislators who knew the father and expected the son to follow his parent's example. Charles, although given to strong views, preferred plain speech to oratory. Brevity was his trademark.

Nicholas began in a measured, civil tone that initially disguised the strength of his convictions.

> I had hoped, Mr. Speaker, to have been spared the unpleasant necessity of discussing these resolutions, which have excited throughout the country so much irritation and alarm. But a decision is suddenly demanded; and I have therefore no other alternative, except either to surrender my own opinions, or to follow the straightforward path of duty, however it may lead me across the feelings of this house and the prejudices of the people.
>
> In public, as well as private life, Mr. Speaker, the first virtues are frankness and candour—instead therefore of a silent, sullen opposition, I mean to tell you plainly and simply that you are wrong.[8]

If there were gasps of dismay at his effrontery, Biddle ignored them. Point by point, he began to address each of Holgate's charges. He had done his homework, as the thirteen pages of surviving notes attest.

> What said congress in establishing a national bank? Whereas, 'a bank for the United States will be very conducive to the successful conducting of national finances' will give facility to loans, and 'will be productive of considerable advantages to trades and industry in general.'
>
> If then, for state finances and state trade, Pennsylvania could incorporate a bank, why could not congress for the finances and the trade of the United States? Are their finances less worth preserving—are the powers of congress over them more limited—is not 'trade in general' almost the exclusive care of congress—and why should we pretend that they cannot use the same means of advancing the commerce and the finances of the union, that we employ for our own?[9]

He paused. The other legislators were unsure whether he intended to continue. The anti-bank faction must have been hoping their young colleague had lost his way within the thicket of historical fact, and that speaking extemporaneously was a skill he lacked.

Resuming, his approach changed, he began using methodical arguments as if he were explaining basic facts to a child:

> When taxes and duties are collected, what is to be done with the
> money? Is it to be put in boxes and sent to Washington?
>
> You are to raise an army, you must therefore pay money over the
> whole frontier of the United States. You are to raise a navy, and you
> must pay at the remotest ports on the Atlantic or the lakes. You have
> to pay much where you receive nothing. Then you are reduced to the
> necessity of sending the coin itself, at great expense, and incumber-
> ing the rear of your armies with specie wagons. . . . For this purpose,
> there is no other resource but a paper circulation, known and trusted
> throughout the United State. But if you mean to pay national debts
> with paper, it must be with a national paper . . . the institution from
> which it issues must be stamped with something like a national
> character. . . .[10]
>
> Can the United States government place its millions in a bank
> whose capital may not exceed the amount of a single day's deposit,
> whose affairs they have no right to inspect: nay, all whose operations
> are exclusively controlled by another government? How, I pray you,
> is any state bank to do this; or what are to become of the finances of
> the union, in the confusion of at least seventeen independent distinct
> banks, with no power to compel punctuality, and with no security for
> their stability?[11]

By this time, the assured and fiery speech had attracted attention. Absent legislators had begun appearing, crowding together. The room remained hushed while Biddle cited year after year and fact by fact the national bank's inception and implementation, its necessity in former times of war, and its future relevance. Mocking Holgate's words, his voice rose.

> But the bank is denounced as being totally subversive of the interests
> of agriculture, as tending to deliver the 'bold yeomanry' to the country

into the hands of a monied aristocracy. And yet, sir, to my mind no principle of national economy is clearer, than that the most natural way of protecting the poorer classes of society is by a bank: an institution, sir, which enables the farmers to reserve his crops for a better market, instead of sacrificing them for his immediate wants.[12]

As a Philadelphian, Biddle recognized the interdependence of commerce and the laboring classes, a fact he believed his colleagues from rural Pennsylvania and the countryside surrounding the city disregarded. By 1810, industries utilizing large-scale machinery and employing hundreds of skilled and non-skilled workers dotted Philadelphia. The numbers of those businesses were on the rise, exacerbating the tensions between the city and its agricultural environs.

Suffer me now, Mr. Speaker, to attract the attention of the house to the disastrous consequences of the dissolution of the bank.

The immediate effects of it upon the revenue of the United States are too apparent to escape observation. The resources of the union are almost wholly drawn from commerce. As the treasury must be supplied from the collection of duties, it must depend on the ability of the merchant to pay their duties by means of the bank—by the loans from the bank, and in the notes of the bank. Their loans amounted to fifteen millions of dollars. On the sudden you declare that there shall be no longer any loans; the fifteen millions cease; ten millions of hard dollars are withdrawn from circulation; and with the charter of the bank expires the provision with renders the duties payable in notes. . . . And what period have you chosen for this? Why, the very moment when the merchants throughout the whole union ought to receive an unusual extent of credit and accommodation . . . at the moment when the cessation of the Vera Cruz trade, and the large exportations to China have occasion a most extraordinary deficiency of the precious metals.[13]

Following additional references to foreign trade, Biddle turned his focus to Pennsylvania. He was determined to win over Holgate's band of naysayers even though he correctly suspected them of having ulterior motives regarding a national bank, preferring to create rural institutions that would keep money and power in the hands of community leaders.

The effect of this dissolution however may be more distinctly seen by confining our view to Pennsylvania. About one million of dollars, a third of the whole stock of the bank owned in the United States, is held by citizens of this state.[14]

In this situation, without credit or money, while your commerce is stopped, and your manufacturers languish, do you think its effect will be confined to the city? It will be known beyond the mountains; there is not a fibre [*sic*] of the whole body that will not feel its deleterious influence. In the total want of money, who is to purchase land, who is to buy produce? Amidst this general distress, while the demand for specie will place the poorer classes at the mercy of the rich, and the great money lenders will issue aboard to prey upon their fellow creatures. . . . In the sweeping ruin which will overwhelm humble and useful industry in the general submersion of small traders, the only beings who will be seen floating on the wreck, are those very 'monied aristocrats' whom the resolutions denounce with such indignation.[15]

Look round, sir, at our situation. . . . We are now preparing our non-intercourse for England which may drive us into a war with that country. With the dreary prospect of such a misfortune, with a sort of war already on our southern frontier—when the government needs all its strength to meet such dangers—is this a time to disorder its finances? When the nerves of the whole nations should be braced and strong, are we to prepare for combat by cutting the main artery of all its resources . . . ? When even in spite of these calamities we are still the happiest people on the earth, is this a time, Mr. Speaker, to hazard the remaining prosperity of our native country by such wild, and rash, and desperate experiments?[16]

Biddle spoke until two-thirty, at which time the house adjourned. The final words in his handwritten notes were "Pray God for a lucid interval."[17] The speech, which ran to twenty-six published pages in William Hamilton's *Debate in the House of Representatives of Pennsylvania, on Mr. Holgate's resolutions relative to the Bank of the United States. Session 1810-11* did not end the discussion. As Biddle had surmised, the resolution ran deeper than dislike and mistrust of a national bank headquartered in Philadelphia.

On January 28, the anti-U.S. Bank members introduced a bill for incorporating a local bank in Chambersburg, Pennsylvania, and the argument caught fire again with one legislator shouting, "We want, sir, banks in the interior of the country, the profits of which will be divided among ourselves. We know of no right the Philadelphians have to be the exclusive bankers of the state. We cannot perceive any witchcraft in their paper, that makes it better than the paper of a country bank."[18] The remark produced guffaws of derision. Invoking the "money concerns of the cities of Philadelphia and Baltimore" to growing scorn, it was further declared that "the erection of country banks would destroy that dependence on the city, and would prevent her from grasping and employing to her own purpose, almost all the specie of the state."[19]

Biddle shot back, "One would think that a bank was a wild beast, or some pestilence against which we are to keep our eyes open night and day, lest we should be taken by surprise."[20]

But argue as he might, he and his fellow supporters of a central bank were fighting a losing battle. Explaining that the United States Treasury could not borrow without a national institution's assistance had no effect. America was at peace; why would its treasury need to borrow money? Biddle knew that the naysayers' reasoning was shortsighted and specious, but what was he to do?

* * *

In courtship and love, however, Nicholas found greater success. Jane Craig, a demure seventeen-year-old, whose family's country estate, Andalusia, lay north of the city on the banks of the Delaware, caught his eye. Or, rather, her mother, the vivacious Margaret Murphy "Peggy" Craig, did so on behalf of her retiring daughter. In her estimation—and the estimation of other mothers of marriageable daughters—Nicholas was a catch: handsome, debonair, and with a potentially brilliant future. Jane and Nicholas's courtship, although not precisely "arranged," was certainly managed. Of course, Jane was not permitted to write to her would-be lover in the early stages of their relationship, nor he to her, but Peggy could and did, sending off frequent, breezy notes, and inviting the young man to Andalusia as often as his duties in the state legislature permitted.

Born April 6, 1793, Jane's upbringing had been mostly spent in the countryside's seclusion. She rode horseback, studied French, geography, and English composition, and daily practiced the piano and harp. She knew of no happier spot, not her parents' house in Philadelphia nor her unmarried Craig aunts' home on Spruce Street, and certainly not the city of Chester where her merchant father maintained trading ships and where she and her older brother James had been dispatched during the 1793 Yellow Fever epidemic when she was an infant. At Andalusia, quiet Jane sparkled. For Peggy, the estate's solitude had an additional benefit; no other unmarried young ladies intruded as competition. As they were encouraged to stroll the grounds without a chaperone, the couple spent hours walking among the orchards and gardens or sitting in intimate tête-à-têtes while they admired the view from the veranda. Peggy orchestrated it all; she was certain Nicholas's star would rise, and that he would make an ideal husband for her Jane.

Lauded for her "commanding energy and firmness of mind,"[21] Peggy was a force of nature. Petite in stature with long flowing hair coifed in the style of Gainsborough's grand ladies, she saw what she wished to see and rarely held her tongue. Jane was her mother's opposite. Although their features were alike and both had the same dulcet eyes, Jane was quiescent where Peggy was effervescent, contemplative instead of gregarious. Often speechless in her mother's ebullient presence, Jane could appear shy and withdrawn, preferring solitary country rambles and sedate clothes in subdued colors. Her sartorial choices and reclusive manner caused friction between parent and child. Peggy wanted her only daughter to shine as brightly as she. She envisioned Nicholas as a flame setting fire to Jane's gentle soul, hopefully turning her into another Peggy. "Jane," she once remarked, "has a heart already alive to every noble and virtuous sentiment, and a brilliant capacity for everything she undertakes," but the description better suited the mother than the daughter.

A native of Ireland, Peggy had accompanied her uncle, Caldwell Craig (no relation to her husband), to his sugar plantation on the island of Tobago in 1779 when she was eighteen. The next year she married John, and the couple moved from Tobago, where John maintained commercial interests to his home in Philadelphia. No sooner did she arrive than she took the city by storm with her "captivating manners," her fluency in French and Italian, her "masculine judgment" (a compliment indicating that she was decisive and self-confident), and lively wit. She was well educated, which was an anomaly at the time, "slow to believe in the misconduct of others," and her kindness "came from the heart."[22]

Before her marriage, Peggy had been an unrepentant flirt; she saved correspondence from former suitors who'd courted her while she resided in England. What her husband thought of this collection is impossible to surmise. Perhaps she kept it hidden, but equally probable that she liked to recollect her glory days when she had modeled herself after a French coquette, and that John took a kind of possessive pride in his wife's early conquests and the fact that he had won her against such formidable competition. Peggy's young men had sent gushing notes in French or selections of Italian verse. One paramour disguised his name, Dalrymple, by spelling it backward Elpmyrlad, or the abbreviated "Dal."[23] All presented her with songs and poems inspired by her beauty; "Dal" brought "four birds and a fish the produce of his mornings labours" and signed himself "a penitent offender."[24]

Although that seductive history was bound up in ribbons and consigned to a drawer, Peggy still loved to charm men: John being her chief target. Whenever his business caused him to be absent from her, letters (often more than once a day) flew back and forth between them. He was her "beloved husband,"[25] while he called her "My Dear, Dear Peggy" and "my little woman," and signed his letters "toujours votre fidele J. Craig."[26] Her notes were equally conversational but no less affectionate. "I wanted to know if you could afford to treat me to a gown which is a very uncommon and rare bargain." There was some haste in this request. In typical Peggy fashion, she needed an answer "immediately. Yes or no will do."[27] Of course, he said yes.

Despite her progressive behavior, she believed in the portents of dreams and premonitions. Once her children were born, she fretted continually about their welfare. Her father-in-law had died of Yellow Fever during the epidemic of 1793, and he was a hardy soul who had hailed from Scotland. How much more fragile her babies: James born May 10, 1787; Jane, April 6, 1793; John Charles, February 19, 1802; and another John who'd been born January 20, 1795, and was "taken from the world" November 24, 1796.[28] "My children," she explained to her father in far-off Dublin after apologizing copiously for failing to put her letters home on the latest outgoing vessel, "are now an inexhaustible source of pleasure to me and their father."[29]

Peggy's indefatigability failed her when John died on May 29, 1807, after a one-week illness. Misdiagnosed with gout, he had been expected to make a full recovery. Instead, it soon became clear that the problem was inflammation of the bowel. His death, though relatively quick, was anguished, and Peggy was unable to ease his pain. Shock and grief robbed her of words. John's death "left me a wretched widow on Friday evening the 29th of May, 1807"[30] was all she wrote.

In that terse statement lies a wealth of imagery: the pretty woman accustomed to a life of emotional ease and mutual adulation. Cosseted, rich, secure in her many loves, she found herself suddenly bereft and utterly alone in her adopted land. It must have felt as though an abyss had opened beneath her feet. If John, the pillar of her existence, could vanish with so little warning, nothing and no one was safe. From that time forward, her children became her single-minded focus. Though she still loved to charm, an underlying sense of vulnerability stalked her, which she attempted to escape by channeling her energies first into Jane and then her sons.

* * *

Under Peggy's guidance, Nicholas and Jane's love burgeoned. Peggy flattered him by calling him "the best, the most virtuous of men."[31] Jane flattered him by hanging on his every word. Nicholas was captivated by Jane's guilelessness and her open, affectionate nature. Jane reveled in being adored. In small ways, she began to outshine her mother, which met with Peggy's approval. Music had always been Jane's passion, and her parents had been at pains to keep her in sheet music imported from Europe: "Les Charmants Oiseaux," "Romance de Gulnare," and "Ses Yeux Bleus" being among her favorites. Her proficiency on the guitar and singing of "La Cachuca" and "Bolero del Olé" enthralled Nicholas. Again, Peggy encouraged her daughter to reveal rather than hide her gifts. Every mother understood that performing transformed the shyest of girls.

The couple married on Thursday, October 3, 1811, at Andalusia. The year before his death, Jane's father had hired architect Benjamin Henry Latrobe to increase Andalusia's size and regency charm. Originally called Craig Hall, the name Andalusia had been inspired by John Craig's trade in South America and Spain, and his partnership with Don Francisco Caballero Sarmiento, who married his sister, Catherine. The house and its surroundings looked like the picture of romance, making it an ideal backdrop for a wedding. The temperature was unseasonably warm as the small family party gathered in the parlor to observe the nuptials. Outside, a few migratory birds sailed overhead, but the chirping of crickets and the buzz of bees drowned their calls; and the sun shone with a hazy gold as on an August afternoon. The Great Comet of 1811 that passed closest to the earth on October 20th spectacularly lit the night skies before and after the wedding. Shadows of trees and shrubbery, people and buildings stretched across the lawns as they would at midday; the windows of the house and outbuildings glinted. The phenomenon inspired scientists and amateurs worldwide, and artists and poets took inspiration in the comet's starry trail. Napoleon felt it was a sign granting him success in his invasion of Russia. For Jane and Nicholas, it was nature's gift to their union.

For Nicholas, marriage brought the dignity of manhood. The person who had balked at every fetter not to his liking, toured the globe with little heed of his parents' fears and concerns, sought danger rather than comfort, now experienced the joy of loving another person more than himself. During the recitation of their vows, Jane's hands in their crocheted and beribboned gloves looked tiny in his grasp, and her child-sized silk shoes—*droit* and *gauche* penned on the insteps—seemed like nursery reminders of which foot should be placed in which slipper. He felt proud and humbled.

Peggy bolstered his self-esteem, relying on him to take up the task of protecting her daughter. "Mon cher Nicolini," she called him, or "mon chere Nichole," adding a gushing, "My Darling my Adored Children I live but for you."[32] Or, "God bless you, my Darling, my best earthly treasure. I embrace you & your chosen with the tenderest affection."[33] If Peggy had been insincere in her endearments, her love might have seemed stifling and even controlling, but neither Jane nor Nicholas considered her intrusive or domineering. She was simply Peggy, ever effusive, or, in her own words, a "warm hearted Irish woman."[34]

Jane's altered status as a married woman and Peggy's faith in Nicholas failed to alleviate her fears. Physical distance and the new lack of intimacy exacerbated her foreboding. In one nightmare, she envisioned her daughter lying prone in a barn's hayloft with her head and jaw tied in a kerchief. The dreaming Peggy tried to reach her ailing child, but no matter how high she climbed up the ladder, the more inaccessible became the loft. Her exertions came to naught; she never reached the patient. "Down I went in despair," she told Jane, only to "awake about break of day so exhausted by tears and perspiration."[35] Or she might scold, "You have a very bad practice of dressing without a dressing gown. Listen to your mother, my beloved girl, in her old days."[36]

While in Baltimore on their wedding trip, the couple stayed with Robert Oliver, Jane's uncle, in his home on Gay Street. Even absent, Peggy remained a central figure. "Here are Jane & myself, darling mother," Nicholas wrote, "returned to our room to employ the few moments of leisure permitted to us. . . . We have had a multitude of visitors, many enquiring after you."[37]

When Jane sent notes to her mother, as she did daily, Nicholas often added a postscript. He remained fond of rhyming couplets all his life.

> Alas my dear mother what will beset me?
> I wish'd to write first but Jane would not let me.
> So now if I thump my poor noddle all day,
> I fear I should have very little to say . . .

Yet dear mother I cannot refrain

From putting in verse that the love of my Jane for you is not greater—
  indeed is as fickle as

The warm cordial heart of your own dear Nicholas.[38]

From Baltimore, the newlyweds traveled to Washington where the Monroes entertained them. Monroe, now Secretary of State, praised Biddle on his articulate and vehement defense of a national bank, then introduced the couple to President and Mrs. Madison, who also entertained them. All the while, eighteen-year-old Jane strove to appear more mature and sophisticated than her years while she met other leaders of the nation. She had none of her mother's self-confidence, nor did she possess Nicholas's easy rapport or his familiarity with the halls of power. It was evident to her that Monroe valued her husband's opinions, but instead of emboldening her, the Secretary of State's regard made her feel inadequate. While the two men conversed about shared experiences in London or Nicholas's refutation of Jacob Holgate, she remained silent or smiled dutifully. Unwittingly, Peggy undermined her daughter's new status, writing from Philadelphia about a stellar speech that William Pinkney had delivered in the State Senate in Baltimore. Pinkney had worked with Monroe in London in 1806; he would become Madison's Attorney General in December 1811. Peggy expected Nicholas to triumph politically. Jane must have quailed at the thought.

- CHAPTER SIX -

A SECOND WAR OF INDEPENDENCE

Biddle's hoped-for "lucid interval" never arrived. Partisan politics carried Holgate's resolution regarding the Bank of the United States: sixty-eight to twenty. The preamble and its aggressive tone was eliminated, a fact the supporters of a national bank viewed as a positive sign that the battle might be won eventually. Legislators on both sides of the argument praised Biddle's eloquence and clarity. However, the mistaken belief that the bank shares were held by "foreigners"[1] remained, as did an inherent mistrust harbored by members from the western areas of the state toward those from Philadelphia. With his cosmopolitan manners and mastery of Continental languages, Biddle was the antithesis of the rough-hewn folk who were settling the state's farthest reaches. The legacy of the failed Whiskey Insurrection of 1794 still had a populist appeal among those whom Charles Biddle labeled a "hardy, warlike race."[2] The tar and feathering of federal officials attempting to collect tax on distilled spirits continued to enkindle a David versus Goliath image: the humble local farmers utilizing their surplus grain and corn to produce homegrown whiskey despite the national government's overbearing laws. For a country born out of rebellion, fighting against perceived oppression was considered both justifiable and laudatory.

The twenty-five year old neophyte legislator probably felt that he had received a psychological tar and feathering because he chose not to run for reelection in 1811 but retreated to Philadelphia to nurse his wounds. Despite his rhetoric, he had discovered that high-flown speech (correct though he believed the message) was insufficient. For someone who had revered words and their power since childhood, this was a stunning and terrible lesson. Then too, it was his first defeat, and he was descended from men and women who had never accepted failure. Having been acknowledged as a prodigy from his earliest years and then gaining entrée to the highest circles of diplomacy and politics at the age of nineteen, he had never met with adversity. Instead, indulgence and praise had been the norm. Given his history, he could scarcely imagine becoming a humble novice scrabbling for votes from men he disparaged.

His father remained in the upper house of the legislature, but Nicholas crept home. Yes, he had Jane and their forthcoming marriage, but as for his dreams of ascendancy in the political arena, they seemed to have been quashed. Even Peggy's exhortations failed to rouse him from his despondent state. On July 4, 1811, he delivered an oration to the Pennsylvania State Society of Cincinnati that he hoped might eradicate the memory of his blighted efforts on behalf of a national bank. The Society had an august membership; being asked to address their gathering to celebrate the nation's birth was a considerable honor. The meeting began at ten in the morning in the State House and ended with lunch at the Mantua Hotel near the Upper Ferry crossing the Schuylkill. The area was newly settled on land formerly owned by Judge Richard Peters, who had taken the name from Mantua, Italy, the birthplace of Virgil. Biddle appreciated the association. He was in his element once again. Being admired and encouraged by men of rank and distinction soothed his psychic pain. Waxing both patriotic and poetic, he referred to "the men of the revolution" who "did not stop to calculate the dangers of defending their freedom."[3] His speech continued:

> What a hopeless contest! A powerful nation, old in war, strengthened by alliances, was directing its vengeance against a feeble and dispersed population. . . . The want of arms, the want of discipline, the want of every thing that renders a common army formidable, were supplied by the gallant patriotism of our country.[4]

Having praised Washington and the multitudes of lauded as well as unsung heroes in the fight for liberty, and vowing that they should never be forgotten, Biddle turned his attention to Europe and "despotism." Every experience, every observation he had made there four years prior came rolling out.

> A foreign soldier usurps the throne of Charles XII, and Austria, that Austria, who balanced with the Bourbons the fate of Europe, sitting among the ruins of her own Germany, turns westward her humbled pride, and bows before her hereditary rival. Spain, whose alliance we once courted, is now suffering the bitterness of affliction . . . while

on the shores of America, the last of the kings of Portugal wanders, a lonely exile from his ruined country. Not a state, scarcely a fragment, a solitary monument, of all the Italian governments, is now standing. . . .

Approach near this gloomy picture; and see over the prostrate fragments of so many nations a fierce and criminal ambition brooding with a savage delight on the misery it has caused, and coldly listening to the groans its cruelty has excited. Scarcely a valley in Europe which has not startled at the sound of arms: not a stream which had not swelled with tears of been tinged with blood. Her fields are desolated; her uncertain harvests trodden under foot . . . her villages abandoned to pillage and conflagration . . . her youth torn from their homes to be sacrificed in foreign wars.[5]

Then he contrasted Europe's misfortunes to America's "blest"[6] repose and happiness. "Around us all is prosperity and peace,"[7] he said before conjuring up impressions of Britain in 1807, during which he had discerned that their navy wanted war. The oration's conclusion had the ring of a threat. "Let those who would disturb its peace but touch the soil of this country. . . . The republic was cradled in tempests; what storms shall it now dread? In our infancy we strangled the serpent; our manhood may defy the world."[8]

Biddle chose his belligerent verbiage advisedly, because by November 5, 1811, when James Madison delivered his annual address to Congress, the possibility of a new war with Great Britain seemed inevitable. Since 1793, England and France had been battling each other almost continuously. As a neutral power, the United States was caught in their hostilities, disrupting the nation's commerce and curtailing its maritime rights. The Federalists (many of them Northerners) bitterly opposed the notion of another war with Britain.

The Republicans, led by the Southerners and the Virginia "dynasty," believed they had no choice but to fight England in a Second War of Independence, as it became popularly known. The dynasty included Madison, Monroe, and Jefferson, who, although retired, remained active behind the scenes, conferring via correspondence from Monticello. Ever since the Lewis and Clark expedition's success, he had advocated claiming lands along America's frontiers. Others shared his opinion of expansionism; they also believed that Upper and Lower Canada were ripe for the taking. Conquering the British there and in the southern and western U.S. territories would finally remove England's hovering presence in North America and put an end to that nation's alliances with hostile tribal peoples who attacked American settlers. Defeated or dispersed, the tribes would then leave the lands free for increased population by U.S. citizens. Or so it was hoped.

The rift between Federalists and Republicans grew over the war issue, as did the mistrust by northern commercial interests toward the South's slave-based, agrarian economy. Both sides agreed, though, that Great Britain's impressment of American seaman (an estimated 6,000 between 1803 and1812) must end. With Britain controlling the seas, and with superior and better-equipped ships and islands in the West Indies, as well as Bermuda and Halifax from which to refit her vessels, America's ports were in constant danger of being blockaded. British ships of war cruised at easy distances from the coast. America rightly claimed she was being forced into action because of Britain's bellicose tendencies against her former colonies, while the British argued that theirs was the beleaguered nation.

Neither Federalist nor Republican mentioned Napoleon during the war debate, although his policies had resulted in Britain's continuous need for seamen to man her warships; England also felt threatened by America's ongoing trade with France. The Louisiana Purchase of 1803 had added $15 million to Bonaparte's coffers. Britain's close proximity to France naturally made her jittery, and there were those in America who felt Napoleon might have designs on the United States, too. Every day, newspapers carried detailed descriptions of the *Grande Armée's* battles as it moved inexorably north and east through Europe toward Russia, adding soldiers conscripted from the conquered nations until the force was said to number 400,000 men. If Tsar Alexander's forces proved as easy to defeat as Austria's and Prussia's, invading America might well be next. Such was public sentiment when Madison signed a proclamation of war, June 18, 1812.

* * *

A firestorm erupted over the President's decision. The populace soon learned that Madison and Congress had met behind closed doors for two days; it was further reported that the tally of votes supporting hostilities was incorrect. John Randolph of Roanoke led the attack on the President. His speech was recorded in its entirety in *Poulson's* on June 19. Acerbic as always, he accused the minister plenipotentiary to France, Joel Barlow, a poet and Jeffersonian, of "dancing attendance on her court" while doing nothing to further America's causes. He saved his biggest guns for Madison, whom he insisted had conspired to fight on

Napoleon's "behalf."[9] On June 20, it was revealed that a Russian plot to murder Alexander and his brother Constantine and replace them with the Dowager Empress had been led by two hundred members of Russia's nobility and that most of them had resided in Paris.

The vitriol between those supporting the war and those opposed to it devolved into physical violence during a June 22 riot in Baltimore when the printing presses of the *Federal Republican* (anti-war) were destroyed and the building razed. A seaman named John Irvin aboard the *Essex* in New York refused to sign an oath of allegiance, claiming he was British. In retaliation, a mob caught him and tarred and feathered him. While both sides of the issue fought each other, American land forces began campaigns in the north and west, a British vessel captured an American one on Lake Erie. August brought news of widespread riots in the north of England, where members of the Luddite Association were smashing looms and burning textile mills. The Napoleonic wars' harsh economic climate had given rise to the Luddite movement—livelihoods and lives sacrificed to a growing dependence on technology. The army was called in to quell the Luddites' bloody riots.

On September 1, 1812, newspapers reported that Bonaparte had declared war on Russia. The entire earth seemed to be one gigantic battleground. It was of little consolation that William White, Bishop of the Protestant Episcopal Church, called for a "Day of Fasting and Prayer to implore the Righteous Governour of the world to guide, by His holy influence the rulers and the people of the United States."[10] Prayer had not stopped Napoleon or protected free African-American boys in Philadelphia from a recent and alarming spate of kidnappings that carried them into enslavement in the southern states.

"FRIENDS OF PEACE" vs. "ADVOCATES OF WAR"[11] *Poulson's* trumpeted in support of forty-three year old DeWitt Clinton, Mayor of New York, when he became the Federalist's nominee to oppose James Madison. Jared Ingersoll of Philadelphia was nominated to run for vice president. August 20, 1812, witnessed the USS *Constitution's* victory over HMS *Guerriere* four hundred miles southeast of Halifax off of the Boston Light. For a young American navy that consisted of a mere twenty-two commissioned vessels as opposed to Britain's force of eighty-five ships, this proved a boon to morale as well as to the nation's. A seven-verse song dedicated to the men of the *Constitution* concluding with the line "Her Yankee thunders roar,"[12] and a commemorative book including an engraving of the action and a portrait of Captain Isaac Hull in full uniform appeared within days of the *Guerriere's* stunning defeat.

Seesawing emotions became a matter of course. When a hurricane flattened New Orleans in September, destroying lives and levees, hospitals and houses, crops (especially the vital sugar crop), and sinking or crippling sixty ships and leaving all river craft "smashed to atoms,"[13] the beleaguered nation could only wonder what fresh catastrophe awaited. The grim memories of the American Revolution were still fresh. Not even the war advocates wanted a reprise of those blighted days when it seemed that the colonists' fight for freedom might be lost.

* * *

As the rancorous rhetoric intensified, Biddle remained in retreat from the public eye. After quitting the state legislature, he had slipped inside the sanctuary of literary pursuits, becoming the *Port Folio's* full-time actual editor when Joseph Dennie died on January 7, 1812. Even among style-conscious Philadelphians, Dennie had cut a remarkable figure, his breeches tied with "long bows of colored ribbons," his "pumps ornamented with great silver buckles" and his hair "powdered, frizzed and made heavy with pomatum, while adown his back hung a false tail or queue wrapped in yards of black silk."[14] Biddle nursed the ailing man during the last months of his life. Believing that financial worries exacerbated his alcoholism, he paid Dennie's bills and then introduced him into his family circle, hoping that a dose of home and hearth would help. Peggy, whom Dennie had long wished to meet, shared her enthusiasm with him about "1,000 literary schemes and projects."[15]

Biddle was determined to rescue the man, but Dennie's addiction proved too great to overcome. A stroke partially paralyzed him; his condition worsened, affecting his internal organs and making communication difficult. When he died, his "face could scarcely be recognized."[16] Biddle arranged for interment at St. Peter's Church. John Quincy Adams provided the tombstone's inscription. "Formed for converse with the muses, He devoted his life to the literature of his country."

Dennie's death gave Biddle another excuse for staying within the closed sphere of belle-lettres Philadelphia, out of reach of the vitriol of Holgate and his adherents. At the end of January, he tried to explain his new status to Monroe, "We all remain very quiet or very supine in Philad'a. After so long a repose the people will scarcely believe that there may be a change in our situation."[17]

Although referring to the "alarm of war," he excused himself from active participation. The words still ring false, as though Biddle were persuading himself rather than Monroe of his worthiness.

> Being myself detached for the immediate pursuit of the law, I have given myself to much more agreeable studies, the higher branches of national jurisprudence & politics . . . one should I think prepare himself to render according to the measure of his talents all the service which his country may ever demand in return for its protection.

The letter ended with a forlorn hope that Monroe might visit, but the secretary of state had urgent issues to tackle and neither the time nor inclination for a social call.

If Biddle gave any thought to future political ambitions, they remained amorphous while he sequestered himself with Jane. Had he been a small boy, he might have been accused of sulking. Exacerbating his malaise was the return of his brother-in-law in late July following a three-year sojourn in England. The charismatic James had always been Peggy's favorite. His reappearance pulled her attention away from Jane and Nicholas, making the latter feel inconsequential and dull in comparison. Debonair and notoriously careless with money, Craig had left a string of disappointed ladies in his wake before leaving Philadelphia; he also deserted a slew of women in Europe. Peggy despaired of seeing him settle down. As she explained to her Irish relatives: "I fear he is not much inclined for matrimony, but it's best to let everything take its natural course."[18]

Despite her good intentions, this was hard advice for Peggy to follow. She had played matchmaker for him numerous times, been petitioned by her son's former flames, and remonstrated with him on his fickleness. A war between America and Great Britain gave her greater reasons to worry about his welfare. British cruisers now patrolled the Atlantic with orders to detain any enemy ship. Should James sail for home during this dangerous time, she was certain that she would never see him again. For this reason—or because he was undecided about how or when he would return to the bosom of his family—James informed Nicholas of his proposed arrival instead of his mother, cautioning him to keep the information secret. Although only a year separated the two men, Nicholas was thrust into the role of elder statesman of the family, a position he continued to play regarding his profligate brother-in-law.

Nicholas felt eclipsed, but his emotional stamina faced a greater challenge when he suffered a fall while descending from a carriage at the end of the summer and fractured his leg. Impetuosity had combined with his habitual disinterest in physical exercise. Total bed rest was prescribed if he were to regain full use of his limb. This final indignity was too much. He rebelled. Jane argued and cajoled, trying to keep him idle, but he found ways around the doctor's orders, hobbling about and impeding his recovery. Although he was in almost constant pain, no one could reason with him.

Determined to keep James under her watchful eye and convinced that Nicholas would be a stabilizing influence, Peggy concocted a plan to have all her children quit the city and its dangerous seductions. Wholesome country living would cleanse the spirit and strengthen family bonds. In her mind's eye, she envisioned her loved ones stepping backward in time. James could ride; Jane could sing or play the piano or harp, and Nicholas could slowly learn to walk again. Jane agreed with her mother's proposal, believing that her husband would recuperate better while under the care of two nurses instead of one. Neither she nor Peggy recognized the effect this enforced idleness might have on Nicholas. Perhaps he also discounted its impact, or maybe he welcomed his new persona as a country squire, removed from the cares of the world while pottering about with his books, or handwriting treatises on "American Politics," "Studies of European History," "Locke's Two Treatises of Government," "Historical Stories," or "French Law & History."

Try as he might to ignore the war, Nicholas's brothers' active service challenged his soporific state. James, Thomas, John, Charles Jr., and Richard were all in the thick of it, communicating with him about their military exploits whenever possible. On November 27, 1811, James, then a naval lieutenant, had received confidential orders from Paul Hamilton, the Secretary of the Navy, dispatching him to France aboard the American ship *Hornet* to offer safe passage to Pierre Samuel du Pont de Nemours of Paris.[19] Du Pont (father of Éleuthere Irenée, founder of E.I. du Pont de Nemours and Company) was a friend of Thomas Jefferson and had advised him on the Louisiana Purchase. Having escaped the reign of terror in 1797, he and his children immigrated to the United States in 1800. Two years later, the father returned to his native land, holding government posts under Napoleon but becoming increasingly critical of the regime. He wrote Madison on July 4, 1811, requesting that his children be permitted to write to him under diplomatic cover and transmit money to him via the United States Treasury. The President arranged du Pont's journey on board the *Hornet*.

James understood the risk of helping a government official escape Napoleonic France and conducting him across the British-controlled Atlantic Ocean. He kept no record of their conversations or whether he met with Lafayette, who would continue his long-distance friendship with Nicholas. The lapse in communications was unusual because the family frequently wrote to each other, nor did they keep secrets. Returning in May 1812, he penned a shipboard note to Nicholas, but the content referred almost exclusively to his brother's work on the Lewis and Clark journals. "[The] work is looked for enthusiastically in Paris, & a translation will be undertaken the moment a copy reaches Paris . . . sales will be "rapid and extensive."[20] He added a postscript stating that he was bringing home French newspapers for Nicholas's use in the *Port Folio* but made no mention of his influential guest. A single sketched image survives from that mission: that of James leaning out of a carriage window while urging the coachman to make the horses gallop faster. "Bearer of dispatches to France"[21] was the title.

Having escorted du Pont to America, James served aboard the sloop-of-war *Wasp* under the command of Jacob Jones. She sailed south toward Bermuda from the Delaware River in October and ran into a gale on October 16, 1812, during which she lost her jib boom. Damaged and fighting heavy seas, the *Wasp* encountered the HMS *Frolic*, also battered and unable to maneuver easily. The two ships closed on each other. The battle lasted forty-three minutes, killing all British officers and killing or wounding more than half the ninety-man crew. The *Wasp* suffered minimal casualties. James was the first American officer to board the disabled *Frolic*. He took over the ship's command, and while he and the *Wasp*'s crew attempted to make the captured vessel seaworthy again (her masts had fallen owing to a final broadside), HMS *Poictiers*, a seventy-four-gun ship of the line, hove into view. After a brief chase, she captured the *Wasp*, taking James and his fellow crewmates prisoner.

Nicholas, snug at Andalusia, felt roused into action. He immediately appealed to Monroe for help—if help was possible.

> This morning rec'd a letter from my brother, James Biddle, 1st Lieutenant of the *Wasp*, dated at sea on board the British 74 the *Poictiers* in which he stated that the *Wasp* had engaged a British brig the *Frolic* of 18 32 pound carronades & two long nines (the *Wasp* having only 16 carr's) & after an action of 43 min. succeeded in taking her—the *Wasp* had only 5 men killed—but the slaughter on board the enemy was dreadful. While in possession of the prize, the *Poictiers* unfortunately bore down and there was no resistance to make. Altho' I feel for a misfortune which throws one whom I love into the hands of the

enemy, yet I rejoice most cordially that it should have reflected such lustre on our arms.[22]

At the same time, Thomas, an army captain, was headquartered near Platts-burgh, New York, on Lake Champlain's western shore at the Saranac River's mouth. The area had been ceded to Britain from France due to the 1763 Treaty of Paris, and the British were determined to keep it as a buffer between America and Canada. They appealed to their allies, the indigenous peoples, for aid, promising them autonomy and land and supplying them with ammunition. It was already clear to the tribes that the Americans, the "Big Knives," had no such supposed altruism in mind. They coveted the territories in which the Pot-tawatomie, Miami, Creek, Lenape, and other nations dwelled.

In early autumn 1811, the Shawnee chief, Tecumseh, had attempted to create a coalition among the Cherokee, Chickasaw, Choctaw, Creek, and Seminole nations on behalf of their "Father," King George III, by visiting Tennessee, Georgia, and the Mississippi Territory. While Tecumseh employed diplomacy and military skills, his younger brother, Tenskwatawa, known as the Prophet, created a religious movement among the northwestern tribes. The Prophet urged his followers to return to their hereditary ways. On No-vember 6, an American army under the command of William Henry Harrison encamped near Prophetstown, which lay at the confluence of the Tippecanoe and Wabash Rivers. The next morning, the Shawnee attacked the invaders. Although initially successful, they were soon overwhelmed, resulting in the wholesale destruction of Prophetstown and the grain supply that would carry the Shawnee through the winter months. The Americans intended to starve the survivors.

Massacres on both sides became commonplace, with newspapers decry-ing the tribal people's brutality, which roused vehement calls for revenge. Em-battled on their ancestral soil, the indigenous population retaliated by besieging and attacking frontier forts in Michigan and Indiana Territories. Although the Shawnee were castigated as pitiless assassins, their American opponents were just as savage. Andrew Jackson, then a forty-five year old major general, made it clear that he believed that the annihilation of one tribe might induce the others to slink away in fear.

As the year 1812 drew to a close, America's prospects looked dire. Adver-tising cards urged the public to vote against Madison. "An Honorable Peace" vs. "A Disastrous War (and a French allegiance)." "If you wish commerce destroyed . . . sons, bothers, yourselves forced from your farms, workshops, families" and "drafted into militia . . .VOTE WAR TICKET."[23]

The numbers of votes already counted were published. The tally competed for space with evil accounts of Napoleon's Russian campaign. The emperor was likened to the all-destroying beast from Revelations as his name consisted of eighteen letters or three times six, which was interpreted as 666.[24] *Poulson's* described a Russian count who destroyed his country estate and torched his crops rather than allow the enemy to encamp there. He left a note nailed to the smoldering ruins that he'd had set the blaze himself.

Then, on December 23, word arrived that French-occupied Moscow had been burned to the ground. Or, as the conqueror himself declared, "*Moscou n'existe plus.*"[25] "Moscow no longer exists."

* * *

Madison was declared the winner on the last day of 1812, but the numbers were close, and he entered his second term under a cloud of mistrust and unpopularity. The Biddle family, though, had much to celebrate. In an exchange of prisoners, James had been released from a British jail in Georgetown, Bermuda, and sent to New York. Nicholas wrote Monroe on November 29. "I am anxiously expecting every day the arrival of my brother who remains with Captain Jones at New York. . . . We are all very proud of their gallant actions."[26] At twenty-eight, James had become a seasoned mariner but was as audacious as when he had first set sail at sixteen.

While James received commendations (and on March 5, 1813, an appointment as Master Commandant in the Navy), Nicholas's injured leg continued to afflict him. After their sojourn at Andalusia, he and Jane had returned to Philadelphia; Jane was pregnant, further curtailing their movements. Not that Nicholas chafed against his enforced quietude. He enjoyed the cocooning nature of home life: first-time parents expecting a baby and reveling in the nurturing attendant to Jane's care. It was as if the tumult of war had been stilled while husband and wife awaited the infant's arrival. Comparisons to his warrior siblings, uncles, and father caused him distress, however. While his brothers leaped at their country's call for service and self-sacrifice, Nicholas sat at a desk, putting words on paper. Yes, he might claim that those words fired imaginations and helped accomplish mighty acts, but he had too much of the Biddle fervor within him to believe his own argument. Despite his love of erudition, he yearned to be as physically bold as James and Thomas.

* * *

Born April 23, 1813, the infant Nicholas Craig Biddle drew immediate praise from Peggy. "I am grandmother to one of the most beautiful boys I ever beheld," adding a less glowing portrait of the mother who now competed for the doting grandmother's attention. "Jane is fat and hearty and much improved in her looks."[27] Naturally, Peggy swooped in and carted the young family off to Andalusia. Nicholas was reduced to becoming "a sort of farmer at least for the summer" wholly consumed by "my books, my family, my son."[28]

Despite his inactivity, by early November, he was still experiencing debilitating pain and physical weakness. Walking had become a chore. As he told his bother, James: "[In] hopes of curing that old strain which has annoyed me so long . . . I have accordingly established myself in my office on a sopha [*sic*] & while I write this the bleeder is sticking about a hundred leeches on my knee having yesterday performed the same office to my hip, so that I am fairly nailed down."[29] He concluded with the sheepish disclosure that he was adding patriotic songs to the new issue of the *Port Folio*, which must have seemed a small accomplishment compared to James's efforts on behalf of the country.

Although "nailed down" amid a household consumed with the care of a growing baby, Biddle could not escape the war's depredations. "Peace has left us not to return"[30] was the prevailing sentiment in early January 1813 when Congress considered a bill to add 20,000 men to the military. The conflict's price also made news when an Act of Congress permitted the United States government to borrow $16 million. John Armstrong had become Secretary of War; it was even bruited that he would be a likely presidential candidate. Armstrong's appointment gave Nicholas further cause for chagrin because it reminded him of the glorious future he'd envisioned while laboring for the minister in Paris. How long ago those idealistic years seemed.

The weather exacerbated his despondent mood. The winter of 1813 in Philadelphia was the coldest in twenty years; zero minus fourteen degrees became a new normal; chill blains and frostbite were common. Parents were instructed to keep children indoors, although child laborers continued to suffer terribly, as did everyone living on the poorer streets and alleys where houses were shoddily constructed of wood rather than brick. Fires became a frequent by-product, but often the brigades failed to reach burning homes because of the depth of the snow and ice. One positive outcome of the bitter cold was the ease with which sleighs brought goods to the market. The outlying dirt roads that could become deeply rutted and almost impassable under ordinary winter conditions were covered in rock-hard snow.

A naval victory (the United States frigate *Constitution* versus Britain's *Java* off the coast of Brazil) lifted spirits when news reached home during the last week of February. The *Constitution's* victory near-distant Brazil illuminated the war's global reach; if the United States Navy could prevail, could it break Britain's dominance over the world's oceans? The celebration was short lived because on March 1 came reports of a total rout of General James Winchester's forces south of Detroit and the wholesale massacre of the fleeing American soldiers. Nine days later, Philadelphians learned that the British had captured Ogdensburgh, New York, on the south bank of the St. Lawrence River. "Silent streets, deserted warehouses, dismantled ships, public calamity and private grief"[31] became a matter of course. Those who had battled the British during the Revolutionary War had a terrible sense of déjà vu.

The next day, the debacle of Madison's minister to France, Joel Barlow, came to light. Having failed to gain an audience with Napoleon in Paris, Barlow had raced to Vilna at the emperor's behest, where another meeting was denied. Some maliciously spread rumors that Barlow intended to congratulate Bonaparte rather than pressure him on American affairs. The *Grande Armée* was then engaged in a headlong retreat from Russia through Poland, traversing unthinkable distances and casting aside valuable weapons, as well as the wounded and dying who were left to succumb where they had collapsed. Hospitals along the route soon filled to overflowing, spreading disease to nearby villages. When frozen terrain made burying the dead impossible, the bodies were stacked outside the towns and burned. Unable to procure horses or a carriage to bring him safely back to Paris, Barlow was caught up in the vast, disordered flight. He died of pneumonia.

Residents of Philadelphia lived in a state of constant apprehension during March and April 1813, when a British squadron sailed into the Delaware Bay, bombarding the village of Lewes, Delaware at the mouth of the bay before sailing so far up the river it reached Reedy Island opposite Port Penn, from whence it could easily access Wilmington and Philadelphia. Volunteer companies were organized and marched south along the river to protect the du Pont powder mills and Wilmington. In May 1813, James Biddle was ordered north to destroy the enemy's whale fishing fleet off Greenland, Newfoundland, and Labrador. That mission accomplished (with only moderate success), he sailed south to New York, so the *Hornet* could be refitted before setting out again for the waters off New London, Connecticut, an advantageously situated port protecting Connecticut, Rhode Island, and the entrance to Long Island Sound.

Safeguarding America's shoreline had taken on new urgency. With its superior number of ships, Britain had begun attacking coastal cities and towns at will and promising freedom for all American slaves who escaped from their masters. The slaves' flight left their former plantations even more vulnerable. Villages along the Chesapeake River became easy targets. Fredericktown and Georgetown in Cecil County, Maryland, were sacked and burned in early May. In June, Hampton, Virginia, was destroyed. Mid-July saw an enemy fleet a few hours' sail from the nation's capital, causing widespread flight. In August, the enemy burned Chestertown, Maryland. Baltimore and its contiguous communities lived in terror daily.

With each loss, the British gained necessary stores and equipment—and manpower. Goods too unwieldy to move were set on fire. There were widespread reports of rapes. Churches were pillaged, intensifying notions of the enemy as the devil. At the same time, Thomas, stationed at Fort George on Lake Ontario, wrote Nicholas that after winning the fortified post from the British at the end of May, the Americans had been under constant enemy fire and that he had slept in his clothes for three months.

James sent equally galling news. After the British frigate, *Shannon* captured the *Chesapeake* at the Battle of Boston Harbor on June 1, 1813. James's squadron (led by Tripolitan hero Stephen Decatur) found itself chased into the Thames River in New London on June 18. The treacherous waters of "The Race" off the southern end of Fishers Island opposite the Thames' mouth could be navigated only under specific tides and winds, which meant the small fleet was effectively trapped. Unable to protect American shipping, they watched helplessly as the enemy harried or destroyed fishing and commercial vessels along the Connecticut coast. New Haven and Saybrook were left defenseless, as were inland towns along the Connecticut River. Although the residents of New London provisioned the blockaded ships, the war continued without their aid.

Months passed in this dismal manner, but the vessels were unable to break free despite subterfuges and providential fog banks. Two forts guarding the river prevented the British from entering New London's harbor, but that was scant cause for celebration for James, who hated being removed from the action. Nicholas promised to journey north and visit his brother, but his son's sudden illness kept him home. Jane and her mother grew frantic with worry. The new father failed to comfort them.

The year wore on. Wilkinson's army was driven out of Canada; before evacuating Fort George, American forces razed it and spiked the canons to prevent the enemy from using them. The latter action drew outrage from the cash-strapped populace, but the beleaguered troops were too burdened to haul them to safety. On December 15, 1813, *Poulson's* printed "Reflections of a Volunteer, posted as a Centinel [*sic*] near Fort George." The anonymous writer described pervasive and lethal illnesses within the camp, comrades incapacitated, and constant war whoops emanating from the surrounding forests that shattered any nightly hope for rest.

> This is a dismal night—the storm rages with increased violence. It begins to sleet—the cold increases. . . . Day after day I feel my spirits flag. Where now is that fierce desire for military fame, which forc'd me to the field. Why am I here? Must fire and famine waste our sea-girt villages and border towns, and must a nation's blood in rivers flow?[32]

* * *

For Nicholas and Jane, the year 1814 began in tragedy. Peggy died on January 28 at the age of fifty-three. Never physically robust, her vibrant personality had fooled everyone not intimately connected to her into believing that she was as incapable of weakness in body as in spirit. A heart attack struck her down January 25; incapacitated, death came three brief but tortured days later. Jane stayed at her mother's side, nursing her throughout the ordeal while her initial fears turned to dread. Nicholas hurried in and out of the sickroom, trying in vain to get Jane to rest or eat. When they spoke, their words echoed with the futile hope that Peggy would recuperate and prove the doctors wrong.

Jane's prayers and ministrations failed to revive her mother, and she entered into a state of shock. She found her mother's death not only crushing but incomprehensible. How could this loving and effervescent woman be gone? How was it possible that Jane would never hear her voice again, or chide her for fretting about James's philandering, or baby Nicholas's welfare? "Do not be uneasy again, dear mother. You see how naughty it is to let such feelings take a hold of you."[33] How long had it been since she'd penned those words? Or spoken similar sentiments urging Peggy to ignore imagined ill omens?

Bereft, Jane could only sift through her memories, or reread her mother's copious letters, or gaze at the loving notes shared by her parents. Even the amorous messages from Peggy's one-time admirers brought tears. Drifting through the eerily hushed rooms at Andalusia, she relived every moment of her shared life with her mother. Her heart felt hollow, and her eyes, which had always held a hint of melancholy in their downward slope, grew irreversibly sad.

Less than a month later, a dire illness attacked baby Nicholas. The onslaught was swift and terrible. No physician could find a cure or soothe his suffering, which worsened moment by moment. Jane watched in horror as her child screamed and gasped for breath, and finally died. After that, she wrapped herself in inconsolable silence. Nicholas did, too. No expressions of sympathy from family or friends could banish their sense of hopelessness. Before the burial on February 28, 1814, at St. Peter's Church, the associate rector, James Abercrombie, searched for words of solace in a note to Jane. "My dear, affectionate young friend. . . . Your present bereavement by the death of your beloved Infant who possessed every charm that could awaken the tenderest and most anxious affection of his parents. . . ."[34] Although Jane knew that Abercrombie's wife had died in 1805, and his daughter two years later at the age of 18, she felt little kinship with him. He was of her father's generation and had been blessed with ten children. Well-intentioned though the message was, it inflicted additional sorrow. "For human hearts are justly said to be in unison; when the hands of calamity strikes hard on one others vibrate and tremble also."[35] Still mourning for her mother, Jane wondered whether the hands of calamity were about to strike a third time.

Filled with despair, she stopped eating or speaking more than a necessary sentence or two. It was clear she suffered from melancholia, an accepted medical diagnosis at the time. Nicholas feared for her psychological and physical health. He resigned from the *Port Folio* to stay by her side.

Winter dragged into Spring. At the end of March, the Battle of Horseshoe Bend in the Mississippi Territory (now Alabama) brought the good news that the wars with the Creek Nation had finally reached an end. The terms of peace were draconian, however. Dictated by Andrew Jackson, who led the American troops, the Creeks, including those who had allied themselves with the United States versus the British, were forced to cede all the remaining Creek territory in Alabama and Georgia—23 million acres. No longer would they be permitted to hunt as their ancestors had; they must turn to farming, raising cattle, and growing cotton. Their game, Jackson told them, had been destroyed. Although Nicholas had no cognizance of his future opposition to Jackson, he viewed the decree as an affront to Lewis and Clark's legacy.

Jane's health continued precarious. Her doctor prescribed a total change of scene. Nicholas readily accepted the plan. Jane did so with reluctance. She could scarcely imagine her broken heart healing, no matter how many new places she visited. She acquiesced to her husband's cheery pleas, although both surmised that their communal loss would travel with them. The couple left Philadelphia in early June, first visiting the Olivers in Baltimore, and then continuing south to the medicinal mineral springs of western Virginia where they spent the summer. Biddle's friend—and Peggy's—John Vaughan, had written to Jefferson May 28, requesting an invitation to Monticello. "My particular friend Mr Nicholas Biddle, with his Lady, daughter of the late Mrs Craig, are travelling to some of the springs in Your State, to reestablish health & tranquility of mind, which had been much affected by their late Domestic afflictions."[36]

The former president either ignored Vaughan's wish or never received the letter because Jane and Nicholas stayed by themselves and to themselves, which was just as well. Without Peggy to prod her, Jane had reverted to her naturally contemplative state; her quiescence, though, acted as a salve providing the necessary time for her to ruminate and heal. Starting at Warm Springs, which was nestled in a verdant hollow and surrounded by high mountains, they found the sulfur smell almost overpowering. However, the hot water for the daily immersive baths was invitingly clear. In the morning, huge white puffs of steam rose against the greenery, giving the landscape an otherworldly beauty. It reminded Nicholas of his visit to Neapolitan Baia and Virgil's Cumaean Sibyl, who provided prophecies from within sulfurous clouds.

Next, they visited White Sulfur Springs, also known as the Fountain of Health. Like Warm Springs, the accommodations were rustic: log cabins amidst narrow walkways leading to the various bathing pools. Sweet Springs came last. Much as she wanted to show Nicholas that her depression was lifting, Jane found the trek increasingly dismal. "This miserable hole in which we must stay," she wrote her sister-in-law, Mary Biddle, on August 17, 1814, adding that the "country about here is very pretty, but it is so hot that we hardly ever venture out until after sundown" at which point fleas and mosquitoes descended upon them in "abundance."

She and Nicholas were so bored by the lack of stimulating company that they spent "almost the whole day in our rooms lolling on the bed and reading,"[37] Jane's irritability was the first sign that she was beginning to improve. She had inherited more of her mother's fortitude than she knew. Restless, impatient with herself, and with the stultifying atmosphere, she wanted to go home. Nicholas acquiesced to her wishes. In the first week of September, they started for Philadelphia.

Finally, reaching the town of Staunton in the Shenandoah Valley they learned that the British had attacked and burned Washington on August 24, 1814. The couple could scarcely believe the reports: that the president's house, the capitol, treasury, and offices of war and state department now lay in ashes. Exploding magazines and depots of gunpowder had created such a ferocious conflagration that the residents of distant Baltimore had witnessed the blaze. It was said that British troops, newly augmented by battle-seasoned veterans of the Peninsular Wars, had made themselves at ease around Madison's dinner table and consumed the elegant meal that had been prepared for him and his cabinet before looting the building and setting it afire. Recognizing that Baltimore and Philadelphia were in imminent peril, Nicholas and Jane tossed aside plans for a leisurely journey east and north. They hired whatever conveyances they could find to bring them home as fast as possible. They had hoped to visit the Monroe family, but that was out of the question.

* * *

By then, Charles Biddle had been elected chairman of Philadelphia's Committee of Defense. Fearing that the enemy would attempt to occupy the city as it had done in 1777, the committee had hastily raised $425,000 for arms, building additional fortifications and augmenting the militia. In case the fight grew protracted, members of the committee also made provisions for caring for the families of drafted militiamen and volunteers. Again, Philadelphians watched and waited. Blame for the capital's destruction circulated, from the army's focus on invading Canada (and thereby leaving Washington ill-protected) to an increase in British spies, one of whom was reputed to have visited the president's house only days before the invasion. On September 5, *Poulson's* cautioned its readers to "Look out for Spies." William Jones, Secretary of the United States Navy, drew scathing public rebuke for burning the capital's naval yard and its ships and munitions, even though his timely action prevented the vessels from falling into enemy hands. His decision further damaged America's already diminished fleet.

In mid-August, Britain's navy had bombarded the Connecticut village of Stonington, north of New London; by late August, her ships were in possession of Montauk Point at the end of Long Island. Nantucket's citizens, starved because their fishing industry had been crippled, declared neutrality, opting to supply the British to recommence whaling. Block Island, off the coast of Rhode Island, had already been consorting with the enemy for the same reason. Britain now had full control of America's seas, crippling the young nation's commerce and trade. Following the destruction of Washington, the enemy was free to sail north through the Chesapeake Bay. Attacking Baltimore became a matter of time rather than of conjecture. Philadelphia would be next.

On September 13, 1814, came the assault on Baltimore's Fort McHenry, the star-shaped fortification guarding the harbor entrance. A chain of sunken American vessels kept the British ships navigating close enough to destroy McHenry by their barrage of cannon and rocket fire. They persisted in their attack for twenty-five hours before a lack of ammunition forced them to abandon the plan to capture Baltimore. Francis Scott Key, a witness to the fight, published his poem "Defense of Fort M'Henry" on September 17th.

Although Baltimore escaped unscathed, Philadelphia's safety remained uncertain. Many feared the worst. The cost of the war was mounting, too. Initial war loan subscriptions equaling eleven million dollars[38] could no longer cover the growing debts of cities like Philadelphia that needed to protect themselves. The moment Nicholas and Jane returned home from Virginia, he started working with his father arranging for the city's safety. Financial resources had become scarce. Nicholas turned to Monroe, the acting Secretary of War, writing him the day after the British attack on Fort McHenry. He had gotten into the habit of seeking Monroe's assistance for family members who wished military advancement—even for Charles in November 1813 when he wanted to accede to a post left vacant by the death of Brigadier General William MacPherson. In each instance, Nicholas's handwriting displayed a sense of unease, the lines sloping increasingly upward and to the right. Loyal to one another though the Biddles were, it was apparent Nicholas disliked asking for favors.

This time, no such hesitation appeared. He was requesting aid for his hometown not personal intercessions. Explaining his role on behalf of the Committee for Defense, Biddle described the precariousness of the city's position, saying, "At the present moment we are all occupied in preparing to repel the enemy."[39] As he sent Monroe his appeal, the Philadelphia militia marched south to the Brandywine Creek, the scene of the pivotal battle of September 1777 that had allowed the conquering British to capture Philadelphia.

Having re-entered the public arena, Nicholas decided to run for office again. Jane, who was now strong in body and soul, agreed with his proposal.

Both viewed the decision as a logical career step. Running unopposed as a Federalist who believed in a strong central government, he was elected to the State Senate in October 1814. Because of the war, party affiliations were shifting and breaking down. "Old School" Democrats engaged in ideological battles with established Democrat-Republicans, who, in turn, battled Federalists. Wealth, geography, and a new class of immigrants kept the parties in turmoil with ever-shifting alliances. Biddle knew he would be rejoining the fray, but he felt confident that his ability to compromise and persuade had increased. The session was scheduled to begin in December; in the intervening time, he hurried to Washington to meet with Monroe in hopes of securing the funds necessary to save Philadelphia. He and Jane were expecting another child.

- CHAPTER SEVEN -

MONROE AND BIDDLE

The Treaty of Ghent brought an end to the war. Signed December 24, 1814, the negotiations between representatives of the United States of America and His Britannic Majesty required persistence, diplomacy, and over four and a half months of tense and often-hostile deliberations. While Americans John Quincy Adams, James Bayard, Henry Clay, Albert Gallatin, and Jonathan Russell were formulating the treaty's details in the medieval town on the River Leie, the Congress of Vienna was finally bringing peace to Europe. The conclusion of the Napoleonic Wars required multiple agreements between participating nations and the redrawing of political boundaries (including possession of Ghent). Although the British were privy to a constant flow of information from Vienna, the Americans were not, and thereby had no knowledge which of the nations allied against Napoleon might have sided with them in their contest with Britain. Under the circumstances, as Gallatin explained to Secretary of State Monroe in his Christmas Day letter, the treaty was "as favorable as could be expected."

That was the extent of the former Secretary of the Treasury's enthusiasm. Gallatin further admitted that he considered the document drawn up in Ghent more of "an unlimited armistice than a peace."[1] Despite his pessimism and his belief that Britain remained "desirous of obtaining the northern part of Maine,"[2] he added, "As to the people of Europe, public opinion was most decidedly in our favor."[3] He felt that America had proven herself worthy against a formidable foe, and would heretofore command international respect.

News from Ghent took six weeks to reach America. Henry Carrol, one of the legation secretaries, brought the United States' copy of the treaty with him aboard the British sloop-of-war *Favorite*. He sailed from London on January 2. The letter accompanying the document read in part, "The bearer of this carries with him the olive branch of peace—The treaty was signed at Ghent on the 24th inst., and has been ratified by the Prince Regent, but hostilities are not to cease until ratified by the President."[4] Landing February 11 in New York instead of Washington due to inclement weather, the glad tidings became public knowledge before the treaty made its way to the capital. Divisive and unpopular from the beginning, the war's conclusion all but negated the Federalists' work at the Hartford Convention (December 15—January 5), where New England delegates met in secret to plot the end of Republican-dominated politics with its "lust and caprice of power, the corruption of patronage" and "unjust and ruinous wars."[5] One of their mandates had been to insist that: "the same person shall not be elected President of the United States a second time—nor shall the President be elected from the same state two terms in succession."[6] Before the meeting, the New England Federalists envisioned a possible, even a probable, dissolution of the union. Although Madison had been one of the targets of their anger and frustration, they were as relieved as their Republican counterparts that the grueling and costly conflict was over.

Congress unanimously ratified the Treaty of Ghent on February 15, 1815. Biddle, returning to Philadelphia from the Pennsylvania State Legislature in the new capital of Harrisburg, immediately sent Monroe his congratulations.

> I arrived here only yesterday, but cannot defer the pleasure of congratulating you most sincerely on the glorious termination of the war. It will have rendered signal service to both nations—to England it has taught respect for our arms—and to ourselves it has been a great volume of political experience, and our reputation throughout the world has acquired a brilliancy which a century of peaceful prosperity could never have imparted.
>
> It must have been a source of great satisfaction to yourself as it is to your friends that not the least glorious part of the war has been conducted under your immediate auspices. . . . For your zeal & devotion to the public cause in that great hour of trial you must find your reward in the [knowledge] of having fully discharged your duty.[7]

Celebrations made the country one great festival. Balls, teas, and fetes took place in every city and town, the events lasting well into April (Madison proclaimed the second Thursday in April as an official day of thanksgiving). In Philadelphia, the evening of February 15 saw a grand illumination. Every window in every public building and private residence shimmered with candle or oil light, turning the entire city snowy white. In the harbor, all the ships were illuminated, making the Delaware River gleam. An estimated 100,000 people gathered throughout the city, cheering and singing amid a constant flow of carriages and sleighs filled with revelers. Of course, recruiting militia members had been suspended, which added to the public outpouring of joy.

The "glorious termination of the war" had not extended to New Orleans, however. Only two weeks after the treaty was signed in Ghent (but before the information had reached American shores), the British mounted an attack on New Orleans. Britain's navy had begun massing in the Gulf of Mexico in mid-December. To protect the city's artillery batteries, Major General Andrew Jackson declared martial law, commandeered men and materials, and ordered the construction of a series of earthworks. On January 8, 1815, Edward Pakenham, brother-in-law to the Duke of Wellington, the hero of Waterloo, threw his full force at the works. Although outnumbered and not as battle-tested as the British, the Americans had the advantage of their position, permitting them to fire down upon the enemy as they attempted to climb and breach the earthworks. The British had neglected to bring scaling ladders, making their ascent all but impossible. For such a brief fight, the carnage was "immense,"[8] as Jackson explained to Monroe. He estimated that in "upwards of an hour,"[9] 2,600 British soldiers died as opposed to seven Americans killed and six wounded. Pakenham was among the slain.

Slow communications delayed news of the peace treaty from reaching New Orleans until March 13, at which date Andrew Jackson lifted martial law. By then, though, the British had moved to Amelia Island on the Florida coast, attacking it on January 24 and plundering its stores and homes. Savannah, Georgia, would have been the next target had His Majesty's Britannic Navy not been instructed to stand down. It was an anxious time for those in the wealthy port city who knew that the war was over but also realized the enemy might not have been apprised. Although waged after the ratification of the Treaty of Ghent, the Battle of New Orleans made Jackson a folk hero.

* * *

For the first time since Napoleon proclaimed himself emperor, peace reigned on both sides of the Atlantic. In the United States, however, partisan politics continued to bedevil the populace. The patriotism that had erupted after each combat success—a display of panoramic paintings depicting the 1813 naval battle between the *Constitution* and the *Guerriere*, for instance—competed with the sobering reality of the war's psychic and pecuniary cost. In addition, the proposals raised by the Hartford Convention continued to rankle Republicans.

In the Pennsylvania State Senate, Biddle found himself caught in the middle of the argument. The actions taken in Hartford appalled him, and the doctrines of disunion and state sovereignty ran counter to his belief in a strong central government. Asked to chair the committee to write Pennsylvania's reply to the Hartford delegates' request to endorse their resolutions, he found himself battling his own party's ideologies, asserting that "the maintenance of the general government in the full exercise of its constitutional powers is vital to the freedom and greatness of the nation."[10] At that point, Biddle realized that the two parties had mutated. Federalists in the North and South had long shown opposition to the war. Northern Federalists had been active in their antipathy, withholding their militias from serving in the federal military. As of March 7, 1815, when his committee submitted its completed document, he no longer considered himself a Hamiltonian Federalist but a Republican.

Fellow Philadelphia resident Alexander James Dallas became Secretary of the Treasury in October 1814. By then, the war had nearly bankrupted the nation. In November 1814, the government defaulted on the national debt, although Congress was unwilling to raise taxes to pay for the ever-increasing costs of munitions, men, and ships. Desperate for troops, the bounty for enlistment had increased to $120 and 320 acres of land, the modern equivalent of approximately $30,000 for the combined numbers. Dallas believed that the creation of a new national bank was necessary to rescue the country from fiscal irresponsibility and the foolhardiness of another war with England.

Like the First Bank of the United States, which Alexander Hamilton had conceived, devised, and brought to life, the Second Bank, in Dallas's words:

> Ought not to be regarded simply as a commercial bank. It will not operate upon the funds of the stockholders alone, but much more upon the finds of the nation. Its conduct, good or bad, will not affect corporate credit alone, but much more the credit and resources of the government. In fine, it is not an institution created for the purposes of commerce and profit alone, but much more for the purposes of national policy, as an auxiliary in the exercise of some of the highest powers of government.[11]

Hamilton's sanguine opinion in 1781 had been that "Most commercial nations have found it necessary to institute banks; and they have proved to be the happiest engines that ever were invented for advancing trade."[12]

However, as Biddle found thirty years later in 1811, when he made his fervent but unsuccessful speech defending the First Bank of the United States, the central bank had entrenched enemies. That same year John Adams had gone so far as to declare, "Our whole banking system I have ever abhorred, I continue to abhor, and shall die abhorring."[13] When the issue of chartering a Second Bank of the United States arose, banking and bankers still elicited something like primal terrors among the naysayers. At the same time, those promoting the system viewed the antis as hopeless rubes who would probably revert to a medieval mode of bartering goods for services if allowed to have their way. *Poor Richard's Almanac* had put it succinctly, "He that goes a-borrowing, goes a-sorrowing." Never mind that its author, Benjamin Franklin, had understood the necessity of borrowing to grow business or had also advocated using paper money as early as 1729.

* * *

America had been conflicted about the role or necessity of banking since its earliest days when settlers arrived in the colonies to hew farmland from the wilderness and, in return for property and freedom, send profits back to business enterprises in the old world. By nature fiscally conservative, although bold in venturing to unknown terrain, they confused or conflated banking with their homelands' dreaded monarchies. When Thomas Paine stated in *Common Sense*, "no nation ought to be without debt," the farmers and farriers and village artisans must have quailed. In addition, they had experienced the economic depression following the Revolutionary War and could and did refer to a not-so-distant past when specie had been scarce or nonexistent. In their memories, barter, not coinage, meant survival. Even farmers living close to cities who had transported their produce to sell to local citizens recalled encountering a dearth of buyers with ready cash.

Moreover, as everyone knew, banks could be robbed. America's first bank heist occurred in August 1798 in Philadelphia during a Yellow Fever epidemic when citizens fled the city and its contagions. In an infamous, inside job, thieves made off with upwards of $162,000 from vaults belonging to the Bank of Pennsylvania that were then housed in Carpenters' Hall. The loss was more than monetary; it was an insult to national pride. Carpenters' Hall had been the site of the First Continental Congress; the fathers of the future nation had gathered there.

* * *

Sixteen years before that daring theft, The Bank of North America, which became the precursor to the Bank of the United States, opened its doors for business in Philadelphia in January 1782 at 307 Chestnut Street. Founded by Robert Morris and chartered in 1781 by both the Continental Congress and Pennsylvania legislature, the bank was intended to provide sorely needed financial aid for the patriots' war efforts. From the beginning, Morris's enterprise inspired partisan politics that would have eerie echoes among subsequent generations of legislators. For one thing, the twelve directors were elected from the ranks of stockholders, the majority of whom came from a small cadre of Philadelphia's elite. Thomas Willing, the first president, was a business partner of Morris's; Willing's son-in-law, William Bingham, one of the wealthiest men in the colonies, also served as a director. Clement Biddle, who had served with Washington's army at Valley Forge and became quartermaster general of the Pennsylvania troops in 1781, was another director. There were no term limits, therefore little rotation. For an outsider, the situation was notable for its lack of transparency.

With the Peace Treaty of Paris came a post-war financial depression, and the historical rift between men of means versus the struggling small landholders and the poor resurfaced. Without a common enemy, it became clear to those perched on the bottom rungs of the ladder that those on top had no intention of yielding their coveted positions. The depression deepened because of a surplus of land confiscated from former Tory estates, diminishing the value of the possessions the farmers held most dear: their properties. Farmers and small tradesmen found themselves in desperate straights, exacerbating the long-standing mistrust rural America felt for its metropolises. The Bank of North America drew criticism because its policies seemed to favor Philadelphians over residents in the state's western reaches. It was necessary to renew or pay notes every forty-five days to borrow money; for those living in Westmoreland, Fayette, or Cumberland Counties, this was a physical impossibility.

The directors of the Bank of North America were loath to issue sufficient amounts of paper money to meet new demand, making matters worse. They believed public confidence would falter and pointed to a long-standing distrust of paper. The problem was that the mistrust was mostly among the mercantile elite, while the farmers, with their cyclical needs for loans to tide them over until harvest time, embraced paper. The directors' decision intensified the hostility of the agrarian interests. The institution was derided as being "mischievous"[14]—the most polite of the denunciations.

The critics also blamed the Bank for what they perceived as preferential treatment for foreign shareholders, further inflaming the argument and adding a damning insinuation that the Bank of North America might soon come under European powers' dominion. Morris had dealings in France (he controlled the sale of American tobacco to France) and was part-owner of the *Empress of China*, which, in 1784, became the first American ship trading in the Far East. Discontent at this impotent position turned to rage among a group led by three Scots-Irishmen who had despised the eastern Pennsylvanians from the beginning and had welcomed the War of Independence to wrest control of the state government from the Philadelphians' hands.

That anti-bank bloc appealed to the State Legislature for a vote on the Bank's charter. April 1786 witnessed a debate during which personal attacks became a matter of course. The dreaded words "monopoly" and "aristocracy"[15] were lobbed at will. Morris declared that he wished "more delicacy were observed"[16] and mocked his attackers for their illogical and meandering refutations. The result was that the Bank of North America lost its charter. However, it continued to function until Benjamin Franklin became President of the Supreme Executive Council of Pennsylvania (Charles Biddle served as Vice President), and again promoted it. "An Act to revive the incorporation of the subscribers of the Bank of North America"[17] passed the Assembly on March 17, 1787, two months before the Constitutional Convention began in Philadelphia.

In December 1790, during the Third Session of the First Congress of the United States, Alexander Hamilton, Secretary of the Treasury, submitted his plan for a national bank to serve both the federal government and the nation's needs economically robust and growing population. Unlike a commercial bank, Hamilton's national bank would be able to make loans to the Treasury, collect taxes, and aid in administering public finances. Each committee member assigned to review the proposal believed in a strong federal government; all but one, Philip Schuyler of New York, Hamilton's father-in-law, had participated in the Constitutional Convention. The opposition was swift and forceful, centering mostly on the argument that the plan was unconstitutional. In addition, there was a pervasive suspicion that a national bank would compete with and overwhelm state banks and that it would interfere with the states' sovereignty.

The agrarian interests likened the idea to the "ecclesiastical corporations and perpetual monarchies of England and Scotland."[18]

Secretary of State Thomas Jefferson argued that a national bank would go against the Constitution, thereby igniting an internal feud in Washington's cabinet. Jefferson cleaved to an agrarian ideal, one in which every family and household would have the means to provide for themselves, to grow their food, and produce their clothing without engaging in commerce. Of course, Jefferson's Monticello ran on slave labor, which debunked his utopian argument. Hamilton considered Jefferson's idea outmoded if not downright absurd. If America was to succeed, it must promote entrepreneurism, which required ready credit and confidence in the central government.

The debates over a central bank, impassioned, eloquent, often fraught with fear, and ever-circling back to the Constitution's battleground, ended on February 25, 1791, when George Washington signed the bill incorporating the First Bank of the United States. Subscriptions were delayed until July 4 to allow time for those living at a distance from Philadelphia to participate. The $8 million available publically was immediately oversubscribed. Thomas Willing, former president of the Bank of North America, was elected president in October; his son-in-law became one of the twenty-five directors: nine from Pennsylvania; seven from New York; four from Massachusetts; and Connecticut, Maryland Virginia, and North and South Carolina represented by one director apiece.

Carpenters' Hall was the bank's original home before moving in 1797 to a grand, neo-classical building on Third Street between Chestnut and Walnut. Eschewing the warm and homely brick of the State House, Carpenters' Hall, and other public and private edifices, the Bank of the United States had a front façade constructed of Pennsylvania blue marble and a tympanum containing an eagle holding arrows and a shield in its talons. Six Corinthian columns supported the entablature; eight more Corinthian columns rose to an interior balcony; forty smaller columns supported a dome and skylight. The place was built to impress. Branches opened in Boston, New York, Baltimore, and Charleston in 1792; in Norfolk, VA in 1800; in Washington City and Savannah in 1802; and in 1805 in New Orleans.

The year the first Bank of the United States opened, Pelatiah Webster, a Philadelphia merchant, author, and a self-taught economist, published a lengthy volume consisting of a series of essays on politics and the economy. Prior work had focused on his advocacy of the Constitution. The essays, many of which had been published previously, included views on free trade and paper currency and served as a kind of layman's manual to "the nature and operation of money and finance."[19] Banking, Webster argued, was no longer the purview of the elite; it mirrored the democratic ideal that success in the business world should be available to all, no matter their ancestry or station in life.

* * *

That model lasted until 1810, when rechartering turned into a political hurdle as Nicholas Biddle discovered to his dismay. Before that, the course had been equally problematic. For the first ten years of the First Bank's existence, the Federalists maintained power. With Thomas Jefferson's ascendancy to the presidency in 1801, power shifted. In addition, industrialization had altered the face of American business, redefining alliances. Some commercial interests now desired a closer dependence on local banking and state governments, while agrarian interests looked to protect a stronger federal government. Another chasm was opening, but again the factions were divided into city and country. The Napoleonic Wars also came into play: the impressment of American seamen and the British Orders of Council blockading the northern coast of the European Continent inspired party rivalries. The Federalists tended to side with Great Britain in her war with France; Thomas Jefferson, James Madison, and other Republicans sided with America's former ally, France. Britain owned a large portion of stock in the Bank of the United States. Finger-pointing and blame transcended class, leading to the demise of the national bank in 1811.

The directors requested a two-year period in which to liquidate their stock. The request was refused in less than cordial terms—the reasoning again focusing on the Constitution. According to the naysayers, the Bank of the United States remained unconstitutional, meaning that an extension for liquidation purposes was also unconstitutional. Merchant and financier Stephen Girard, an émigré from France, bought the former temple to finance on Third Street, turning it into a private and very profitable bank.

Then came the Second War of Independence, near the close of which monetary difficulties became so acute that it was impossible to redeem treasury notes in Boston, Philadelphia, or New York. In the western and southern states, banks with sizeable sums on deposit found they were unable to transfer monies, making the deposits all but unusable. At one point, the War Department failed to pay a bill for $3,500, nor could the paymaster settle an invoice for a mere $30. The emergency spawned new interest in a central bank. As with the First Bank of the United States, the issue inspired polarized views: the adherents were convinced that their opinions were indisputable. The detractors were equally certain the notion was impracticable and ill-conceived. The first proposal for a new national bank came as early as January 1814, when the government was desperately trying to fund the war. The opponents pounced, and the measure failed, but in April, a committee was appointed to investigate the matter. That effort also collapsed.

Following the capture of Washington, but less than a month after the capital had been nearly razed, another bank bill was introduced on September 19, 1814. Again, the anti-bank faction took up a hue and cry, accusing its proponents of shoring up the government with the sole purpose of prolonging the war. Debates turned vicious. January 1815 saw the measure rejected, but in March, the pro-bank forces rallied. After peace was declared, the bank issue was dropped until that December when Madison discussed the wisdom of a national bank in his annual speech to Congress. A new bill was put forth in February 1816. Despite the Federalist's attacks on the bank's connection to the government, the amount of its capital, and what they envisioned as the institution's potential for overweening power, the measure passed. On April 16, 1816, with the President's signature, the Second Bank of the United States became official.

* * *

Biddle had followed the battle with keen interest. Since his January 1811 speech in support of the First Bank of the United States, he had understood how vulnerable the nation was without such an institution. As he stated then:

> How could the state banks supersede a national bank? Can the United States place its millions in a bank whose whole capital may not exceed the amount of a single day's deposit, whose affairs they have no right to inspect, over whose operations they have no constitutional control: nay, all whose operations are exclusively controlled by another government. . . . The bank of the United States by means of its branches, is enabled and indeed obliged to place at the disposition of the government, in any part of the union, the whole amount which they have deposited with the bank in any other part of the union, and this with no expense to the government.[20]

Knowing that the nation had been nearly crippled through fiscal incompetence, he believed the creation of a Second Bank of the United States would now rectify those wrongs. He maintained a "Notebook on Currency" in which he examined such subjects as the balance of trade, debt, and world economies.

Another initiative he believed vital to America's growth and stability was transportation. After returning to the State Legislature, he became instrumental in the creation of the Schuylkill Navigation Company in 1815. For Biddle, the nation's prosperity depended upon expediting commerce. As he said in 1811, "A young and vigorous and adventurous people . . . requires some convenient medium of exchanging the fruits of that industry."[21] Navigating the Schuylkill River was a prodigious undertaking, though, requiring a series of canals and slack-water pools, and seventy-two locks, all of which were dug by hand through one hundred eight miles of terrain that was alternatively swampy or rock-hard. The Schuylkill Navigation—its correct name—eventually connected Philadelphia to Port Carbon and the anthracite coalfields.

During 1816 and 1817, Biddle backed additional transportation initiatives, a canal connecting the Delaware River and Chesapeake Bay (and thus Philadelphia with the Susquehanna Valley); and another canal from the upper Susquehanna River to the Great Lakes that would provide a mercantile link between western Pennsylvania and New York. Both measures failed. He made no effort to conceal his impatience with the western representatives who refused to recognize how crucial trade and entrepreneurship were to America's financial growth. Time and again, he found himself at odds with those who espoused the principles laid down by Jefferson. In his opinion, those ideals no longer met the demands of an industrializing country. Adjusting to the constraints of the American political system with its daily compromises and lowered expectations proved difficult. He quit the State Legislature for a second time.

In 1816, he had also been urged to run as a representative from Pennsylvania to the U.S. Congress. However, his prior advocacy of a military draft to protect the state from the British came to haunt him. At that time, he had attacked his opponents as being shortsighted and churlish. "They call it conscription & abuse it in many ways," he complained, adding, "all my political friends have left me except one or two, but I am satisfied with my own course & I shall pursue it."[22] His promotion of a draft angered his foes; they delivered the ultimate insult by damning it as being a "French method of conscription," which lumped the feisty Nicholas with Madison and all the other supposed Francophiles into a pro-Napoleon, war-hawk coven. During the war with Britain, to be accused of embracing anything French was to be accused of being anti-American. At the time, Biddle shot back that he was "too anxious about the defense of the country to care about defending myself."[23] But the damage was done.

A tendency for solitary action aggravated by self-righteousness and intellectual superiority began manifesting itself in Biddle's public life. He may have been justified in his critiques of his fellow legislators, but his high-handedness had repercussions among those who felt themselves belittled. This was especially true of men who lacked his educational advantages or the ability to travel the world. Biddle's behavior could, and would, be construed as elitist. It is doubtful that he would have been surprised by the accusation—or been dismayed by it. He was proud of his family pedigree and took it seriously, recognizing that with it came responsibilities to serve. Accepting his place among the nation's aristocracy, he understood that his duty was to better his country. That sense of old-world noblesse oblige raised the hackles of detractors who considered him a snob.

* * *

From 1815 onward, James Monroe began to play a different role in Biddle's life. As Secretary of State and Secretary of War, he became accustomed to using his former protégé as a sounding board when investigating sensitive, international issues. For a member of Madison's cabinet to reach outside the administration and share restricted or semi-restricted information seems both unorthodox and risky and raises questions about Biddle's function. Was he simply a disinterested observer, residing in far-off Philadelphia, or did the one-time legation secretary have another duty, albeit an unspoken and perhaps clandestine one?

Monroe understood that the perilous waters of Washington politics were full of enemies to the administration. Biddle was someone he could trust to be both discreet and shrewd. In addition, his brothers, Captain James Biddle and Major Thomas Biddle, provided reliable observations regarding global affairs because both had military assignments that took them variously to the West Indies, South America, and the Pacific coast of North America. Biddle's draft letters to Monroe show that he was sensitive to a need for secrecy. He crossed out words and phrases, even entire paragraphs, so the final versions housed in the Library of Congress reveal as little as possible. Except for the dates, and one or two guarded references, there is little to connect Biddle's draft correspondence with the finished letters. Monroe understood Biddle's intent—even to using a single letter in place of a person's name under observation. Although

Monroe's communications were more forthright, the designation "confidential" appeared at the top of each letter.

> (Confidential) Washington May 5, 1815 [I] am much gratified to find that we agree in every circumstance as to the dangers by which we are menac'd by the late events in France, and the precautions we ought to take to avoid them. It would be improper I think to suffer our squadron to sail for the Mediterranean or to disband our army, until we saw more distinctly what were likely to be the consequences of those events, especially as to the U States. It is probable, or rather certain, that Bonaparte will claim to the Rhine; and that will produce a war with England.

Monroe then detailed his fears that a return to hostilities in Europe would again affect America, and concluded with his perceptions of Spain: "Fer^d has cut off the heads of many of those who fought for his restoration; reinstated the inquisition, and revolted the feelings of the whole nation." He also enclosed a copy of a report he had delivered to the Department of War, admitting that he'd encountered "great vehemence."[24] Given Biddle's lack of official status, this decision is curious.

In turn, Nicholas provided information regarding diplomatic affairs, some of it gleaned during his European sojourn, some recently acquired. The American consul at Rome for twenty years, he said, "has been actually residing in New Jersey." He made it clear that the defective organization hampered American mercantile interests. "Over the wide extent of Italy & Sicily & the coasts of Africa & Asia we have a crowd of officers, yet in case of difficulty . . . there was no authority to direct or control them."[25]

One problem with Monroe's reliance on Biddle was that it stymied his ambitions for a diplomatic post, for which his linguistic skills made him an ideal candidate. Although frustrated by the lack of personal advancement, he also felt flattered to be chosen as the Secretary of State's trusted advisor. Ambitious, he desired recognition and fame. When Monroe became president in 1817, Biddle's enthusiasm knew no bounds. "You will have many sincere & warm friends around you on the 4th of March who will mingle their personal congratulations with the general applause of the country, but you will have none in which it excites a sentiment of more pleasure than myself."[26]

Then he returned to the advisory mode when the new president described a proposed national tour to take the country's pulse and assess military fortifications. The former soldier needed to make certain America would be protected in the future. Biddle applauded Monroe's wish "to conciliate parties & to soften the asperities of opposition," but added, "You cannot expect during your administration to walk long on roses."[27] Subsequently, he shared restricted information about the "approach of the Russians"[28] on the Pacific Coast—a report garnered from James, who took possession of the Oregon Territory on behalf of the United States in 1817.

Biddle's unofficial role regarding international affairs expanded in May 1818. Following the Battle of Pensacola (part of the First Seminole War), Andrew Jackson captured the capital of Spanish West Florida. He established a provisional American government in the city and territory. Subsequently, the Florida invasion prompted political finger-pointing. Jackson believed he had Monroe's approval to enter and seize the Spanish territory while pursuing hostile Seminoles and Creeks who found a safe haven there. Naturally, Jackson's occupation infuriated Spain, but the court of Fernando VII was so rife with internecine feuds (which the king encouraged), it was difficult to know what party to trust: the royalists or liberals. Monarch in 1808 and returned to power in 1813, Ferdinand abolished the liberal constitution of 1812. He surrounded himself with sycophants, men as vicious, greedy, and venal as he, making it all but impossible for Monroe to negotiate with him or his government.

The Spanish minister plenipotentiary, Luis de Onís y Gonzalez-Vara, was as unreliable as his master. To Monroe's benefit, Onís resided in Philadelphia. Nicholas knew him well and became Monroe's informant. In Biddle's communications, Onís became "O," and the descriptions of their interactions were abbreviated to a single phrase, or two at the most. The messages were intended to obfuscate.

Onís had arrived in the United States in 1809 to find his status in limbo because of ongoing disputes over the Peninsular Wars and the crown of Spain. By the time he was officially recognized in 1815, he had already established a sort of shadow legation at the Spanish Consulate in Philadelphia. Determined to maintain the boundaries of New Spain and keep America from advancing into East and West Florida and prevent revolutionaries from creating foment in South America, he was rumored to rely on a network of spies.

Biddle had met the diplomat before his acceptance by the American government. Jane's uncle by marriage, Francisco Caballero Sarmiento, a charming but enigmatic and perhaps nefarious Portuguese trader, had made the introduction. Sarmiento had also been a former partner of Peggy's husband, John Craig, and Robert Oliver in a shipping and mercantile concern in Baltimore. At the time, Baltimore had numerous ties to South American businesses, some legitimate, some not. Sarmiento was reputed to have been involved in Venezuela's counterrevolution in 1806-1809, which may or may not have been connected to Onís. Although unproven, it was later said that Sarmiento was assassinated in Spain for his political machinations.

In November 1813, Biddle had approached Onís on behalf of his brother, James, who then commanded the *Hornet*. Needing to resupply his ship, he wanted to enter Spanish ports or West Indian ports controlled by Spain. Biddle sent Onís a confidential letter, stating James's desire for secrecy, as well as an assurance that Spain would not alert England, which might blockade the Americans. He concluded, "If there be any thing in this enquiry on which you are in the slightest degree unwilling to give an opinion you will have the goodness to pardon [me], and I shall consider your silence as a sufficient intimation of your wishes."[29] On behalf of Spain, Onís agreed.

At Monroe's behest, Biddle and Onís repeatedly met in Philadelphia in 1818, with Biddle divulging the substance of those conversations to the President, either in semi-cryptic notes or in person. On January 5, Biddle wrote:

> There are several things which I wish to mention to you. I think
> they may be useful to you & the country. I have determined to go &
> talk them over with you. I shall therefore set off tomorrow morning
> [Tuesday] . . . will be in Washington Thursday night.[30]

That visit led to a subsequent meeting between Monroe, Biddle, and Onís. Nicholas reported back during the return trip to Philadelphia after the Spanish diplomat left him in Baltimore. "On parting with Mr. O last evening I took occasion to express my regret at leaving Washington whilst appearances seemed so favorable to the ~~treaty between our two countries~~ negotiations."

Although striking out the words "treaty between our two countries," he openly discussed measures he believed imperative to American interests, as well as those that would be palatable to Spain. Not only East and West Florida, known then as "the Floridas," but also parts of the Louisiana Purchase were at stake. Monroe sanctioned Nicholas's role as intermediary and agent. Having listened to Onís during the lengthy journey north, he made a list of recommendations on what proposals to offer and what to reject. He concluded by asking Monroe for advice and tools with which to negotiate. "I shall not fail to communicate it."[31]

February 7 brought another communiqué relating to "our affairs." Biddle told Monroe, "the destination of the French officers are known to the Spanish representative (Onís wasn't mentioned by name), but instead of being his agents, it is more probable that their designs have been betrayed to him."[32] This information was especially useful because Monroe had been secretly using the French to infiltrate East and West Florida and wrest them from Spain. However, as Biddle understood, and as he warned Monroe: "O" required cautious handling. That the Spanish minister was playing both sides of the political parties at home became apparent when Biddle learned that another force under Onís's direction was awaiting his orders in the West Indies. Biddle was unable to discover whether Onís had hired them "in favor of the Royalists or in favor of the Patriots,"[33] which aggravated an already convoluted situation.

In addition to this subterfuge, there were the French Brothers Lallemand, the elder a former general who had served in Napoleon's army. Having entered the United States under an assumed name, he intended to create a military colony in Texas, the *Champ d'Asile* (Field of Asylum) for veterans of Bonaparte's *Grande Armée*. The would-be colonists departed from Philadelphia for Galveston in December 1817. Naturally, Spain was hostile to their plans. Biddle kept tabs on the Lallemands as well, garnering most of the information from Onís, though he made clear he mistrusted the "schemes of the L'Allemands [Biddle's spelling] and Onís."[34]

The President forwarded communiqués from Spain as soon as he received them, which Biddle then analyzed. "The intelligence from Madrid," he wrote on March 22, indicated a seismic power shift, producing new personalities to understand and assuage.

"His successor [to Pizarro who'd been dismissed from office] is Mr. Heredia whom you may recollect in Madrid in 1805, brother of the gentleman formerly attached to the legation of Mr. Onís."[35] Because Monroe had acted as Minister Plenipotentiary to Spain in 1804 and England, he understood the turmoil to which Biddle referred. Gossip and backstabbing in Madrid and elsewhere had become endemic. Even the Russians contributed to the intrigues. Nicholas felt Heredia could be trusted but remained uncertain. He ended by indicating that the enclosed was "private information."

Five days later, he sent additional intelligence involving Buenos Aires and the revolutionary government versus the Spanish Royalists. His brother, Thomas, had just received a message dated January 11 from John Mifflin, a Philadelphia trader and merchant, then residing in South America. Biddle told Monroe he could "rely on his statements as facts" and "place full confidence in his conjectures."[36] James Biddle also supplied information from Valparaiso, as well as from an expedition against Chile by Peru. James and Nicholas agreed that recognizing an independent Chile would be advantageous to the United States while also loosening Spain's grip on the subcontinent.

Onís pressured to have the negotiations between Spain and the United States moved from Washington to Madrid; Spain also wanted to put Jackson on trial for seizing Pensacola. Biddle made those demands known to Monroe, but advised against locating a trial in Madrid because of the unstable political climate. He was on the fence about whether it would be diplomatically advisable to accede to Spain's insistence upon a trial. One benefit was that "it will now be evident, that the administration neither authorized the capture, nor the destruction of that post," adding that the invasion of the Floridas was the "personal responsibility of the commanding General [Jackson].[37] We have already enemies enough abroad—people enough to misinterpret our views. . . . The seizure of Pensacola, followed, as it will soon be, by the account from the Columbia River, will furnish the pretext of exaggerated reproaches against our projects of aggrandizement."

He ended with a welcome piece of good news. Again, without providing Onís's name, Biddle explained that the Minister had changed his mind, and "was prepared to cede the Floridas to the U.S. and told me not long since that the proposals he had to make were on the basis which he & I had talked of last winter in Wash^{nt}."[38]

If the about-face seemed abrupt, Monroe accepted it. He jumped at the offer, and Onís returned to Washington to finalize the agreement. Neither Biddle nor Monroe mentioned Pensacola or "O" again. Jackson's proposed trial disappeared. Presumably, he never learned that Biddle and Monroe had pondered making him a scapegoat. Secretary of State, John Quincy Adams, and Luis de Onís y Gonzalez-Vara signed the Adams-Onís Treaty in Washington D. C. on February 22, 1819, establishing new boundaries between Spain and the United States. Spain ceded East and West Florida, but kept Texas as part of the Spanish province of Mexico. The United States' claims through the Rocky Mountains and west to the Pacific were also recognized—in exchange for a payment of $5,000,000 to the Spanish government. Delays in ratification meant the treaty was not proclaimed for two years. By then, Biddle's career had taken a surprising new turn.

* * *

While he worked clandestinely on Monroe's behalf, Biddle's home life appeared deceptively serene and uneventful. He and Jane purchased a home on Chestnut Street, but Andalusia remained Jane's haven, and they spent most of each year there. It was at Andalusia that their three sons, Edward born May 8, 1815, James born July 5, 1817, and Charles born April 30, 1819, could be as boisterous as they wished. They could fish in the Delaware, sail, ride ponies, climb trees, swing on ropes above the barn's hayloft, or race through the big and airy house. Yes, they had their studies, but they were leavened with the rowdiness of boyhood, and Jane did nothing to curtail her sons' play. If anything, she encouraged their games. Essentially a homebody, she considered her upbringing all but perfect and replicated it for her sons, making certain Andalusia was a refuge for her loved ones. John Craig, Jane's younger brother, was also a household member when not away at school, as was family friend, Circé de Ronceray, who had been taken under Peggy's wing and who had known Jane since she was a girl.

Originally from Brittany, the de Ronceray family had global connections, as had Peggy's relatives. Circé would marry Nicholas's older brother, William, in 1820, thereby tightening already close bonds. For Jane, this made a lovely connection between the past and present. A natural matchmaker, she continually strove to find a suitable mate for Nicholas's peripatetic brother, James, who represented American interests in the acquisition of the Oregon Country in 1818, and in 1823 became commodore of the United States Navy's West India Squadron.

At Andalusia, Nicholas devoted himself to farming, experimenting with crop rotation, soil cultivation, and animal husbandry. The same vigor with which he had embraced his prior studies of the Classics, or the economics of Britain's trade, or the complexities of Pennsylvania's inland waterborne commerce, he now applied to agriculture. Nicholas read extensively, filled notebooks with theories and proposals, and queried soil analysis and soil enrichment. His analytical mind made comparisons between ancient and contemporary techniques, leading him to study the systems of Sparta, Athens, and the far-flung regions of the Roman Empire, then compare them to what he'd observed of modern Flemish husbandry or the farms of England's Essex and Sussex counties. He deduced that Italy had a superior method because it maintained the best percentage of population to arable land. "We work badly too much land instead of cultivating well a little," he concluded.[39] He intended to turn Andalusia into a modern farm, using the latest tools and techniques, and expected it to turn a profit.

Much as Nicholas wished to transform himself into a country gentleman, the aftermath of the War of 1812 continued to plague America's economy. Manufacturing stalled or ceased; unemployment rose, especially in the cities where the poor were left homeless and destitute. In Philadelphia, racial tensions exacerbated the plight of impoverished and untrained workers. The Napoleonic Wars had wreaked similar damage in Britain and the Continent, leading to the Panic of 1819 that also afflicted the United States. The central bank's near implosion due to gross and sometimes criminal mismanagement worsened an already dire situation.

The bank's very public plight brought an abrupt change to Nicholas's life. Monroe had another covert job for him. Again, he would be reporting directly to the President. On January 29, Monroe sent Biddle a brief notice of his new intention. Although outwardly an appointment to an illustrious position, it was, in fact, an opportunity for the President to ferret out the central bank's branch managers and directors who'd been accused of fraud—the branch managers in Baltimore being the greatest culprits.

> Without knowing whether it would be agreeable to you to act, I took
> the liberty, a day or two since to nominate you a director of the Bank
> of the U States. I anticipate no oppositions. It makes you better known
> to your country & in that view may be useful. I have a moment only
> to apprise you of this measure & to assure you of my sincere regard.
> Signed, James Monroe.[40]

- CHAPTER EIGHT -

A NEW CAREER

"Department of State. John Quincy Adams to Nicholas Biddle. February 19, 1819. I have the honor to inform you of your appointment on the part of the Government as a Director of the Bank of the United States, and that your commission has been this day forwarded to the President of that Bank of Philadelphia."[1]

Although Monroe had apprised Biddle that he intended to appoint him to the Bank, Nicholas' initial reaction had been tepid. Despite his prior defense of the First Bank of the United States, Biddle explained to the President he had "little concern" with banks and had "hitherto declined sharing in the management of the institution when it was proposed to me by the stockholders." Then, as if persuading himself to accept the position and again become an informant for Monroe, he added, "The truth is, with all its faults, the Bank is of vital importance to the finances of the gov^t. That is has been perverted by selfish purposes cannot be doubted—that it may and must be renovated is equally certain." He ended the letter by admitting he expected to "encounter much hostility."[2]

Hostility was an understatement. Robert Oliver, Biddle's relative by marriage, with whom he and Jane had stayed during their wedding trip, had a long history of mercantile affairs in Baltimore. The city had become the epicenter of a brewing scandal involving greed, graft, and stock manipulation. He intended to gather Oliver's insights into the Baltimore branch's shady practices, making his observations even more beneficial to Monroe. Maryland was not the only culprit. Branch offices in the western states had been no less immune to sloppy, if not criminal, management. The responsibility for this laissez-faire governance rested in William Jones, the Bank of the United States president at its headquarters in Philadelphia. Biddle understood that his role as a director was to be Monroe's eyes and ears, ferreting out the felons, collaborator, and idlers lest the central bank's enemies use Jones's incompetency as an excuse to destroy the institution.

That it had entrenched enemies was obvious. As early as January 4, 1814, a proposal for a new national bank had been put forth in Washington only to be shot down again and again—and again. The anti-war Federalists loathed the idea, believing (correctly) that it would help fund the war. The anti-bank Republicans wanted a different type of national bank. Neither party was interested in reaching across the aisle. Grandstanding on both sides became par for the course, the rhetoric turning increasingly offensive. Debates continued into January and March 1815 when news of the Treaty of Ghent all but closed the matter. However, in December, Madison made the issue part of his annual message to Congress. Discussions began anew in February 1816. This time the measure passed and Madison signed the bill into law on April 10, 1816. He only appointed Republicans as directors, but the stockholders showed more political savvy and added Federalists to the list.

Jones, a former naval officer, merchant, one-term Congressman from Pennsylvania, Secretary of the Navy in 1813, and interim Secretary of the Treasury until February 1814, became the Bank's first president. He had been denounced for his role in burning America's ships moored in Washington lest the attacking British commandeer them; although his reasoning was sound, the loss was crippling. It's hard to imagine a worse candidate for the bank presidency, and all but impossible to understand what kind of favoritism brought about his nomination to this critical position. Philadelphian Stephen Girard, who understood America's economy as well as any man living, and also how precarious it had become due to the war, tried to stop the appointment, but with no success.

Up until then, Jones's mercantile career had been peripatetic. After his single term in the Seventh Congress, he quit America and sailed to India, intending to make his fortune. When that lucrative dream failed to materialize, he returned, poorer but by no means defeated. Then, through personal charm, political connections, and an appearance of reliability, he was appointed Secretary of the Navy. In that position, his financial affairs fell into disarray. By the time he became interim Treasury Secretary, he was bankrupt. His business policies had always been speculative in nature. He carried that risky approach with him into the Second Bank of the United States, permitting a small group of like-minded men to instigate a policy enabling them to borrow $30 million from the bank.

Jones's mismanagement precipitated the Panic of 1819 (beginning in the autumn of 1818), the nation's most severe economic depression to that point. His inability to control paper money issued by branches of the Bank of the United States in the South and West had led to a post-war boom in land speculation that nearly decimated the reserves of specie. Added to the real-estate bubble had been the fiscal euphoria of peacetime. European demand for American tobacco, cotton, and other agricultural products escalated with the return of safely navigable seas. With each auction of a cargo of American produce, welcome infusions of cash came home, resulting in more planting and more spending. Other state banks (not branch banks) and easier credit became necessary to keep pace. It seemed as though the glory days would never end. Instead of reining in the feverish spending and taking steps to regulate the economy, Jones maintained the policy of easy lending.

On August 28, 1818, finally perceiving the coming fiscal storm, he issued an order that the branches must stop receiving notes from other branches, but the measure came too late. By early 1819, credit had become nearly unavailable to the average American. A drop in specie reserves caused state and private banks to fail, dragging local businesses into bankruptcy and creating widespread unemployment. Debtors filled prisons, especially in the cities. Manufacturing stalled. In rural communities, farmers retreated to subsistence living, bartering food for merchandise. At least they had food. Many poor Americans did not.

Reputed to be an alcoholic, Jones was forced to resign in January 1819, but then fought the appointment of his successor, Langdon Cheves, who had served as Speaker of the House during the 2nd Session of the 13th Congress.[3] By the time Cheves became president, the Bank was nearly without specie. It was necessary to clean house. Fourteen (of a total of twenty-five) new directors were appointed in January 1819. Salaries were reduced.

Within this jittery national climate of mistrust, recrimination, and animosity, Biddle began his role as a Government Director of the Second Bank. His first task was to inform Monroe of the actual state of affairs within the Pennsylvania Legislature. The anti-bank party was up in arms; both houses passed an onerous tax on the Bank, which would essentially kill it. "The tax," he told Monroe, "is obviously not a financial measure but designed to expel the Bank from the state [Pennsylvania]. The whole establishment may soon be driven from every part of the Union. The gov^t of the U.S. therefore must now determine whether its powers are to be curtailed & its institution put down at the will of the State Legislature."[4] Biddle ended by asking Monroe for guidance. Having no official position in federal governance but fully cognizant of the anti-bank legislators' vehemence, he felt hamstrung. He could only watch and wait. Given his natural impatience, this was miserable work. Biddle may have confessed himself unfamiliar with a central bank's inner mechanisms, but he believed heart and soul that it was essential to the federal government. As Alexander Dallas had said in December 1815, "[The National Bank] is not an institution created for the purposes of commerce and profit alone, but much more for the purposes of national policy, as an auxiliary in the exercise of some of the highest powers of the Government."[5]

Subsequently, Biddle met with Monroe in Baltimore. As the President had made a point of touring the nation beginning in June 1817, his appearance in the city probably seemed an extension of those visits. The stated purpose was to inspect military installations, fortifications, and coastal and inland defense systems, but his real intent was to connect with citizens throughout the land. He traveled as far north as Portland, Maine, and as far west as Detroit. Aside from its harbor and fort, Baltimore was home of the Second Bank's most egregious transgressors, three men whom Monroe, in a private note to Biddle, called "dark and insidious villains," while admitting that his efforts at cleaning up the mess "have been hitherto thwarted, & may eventually be frustrated."[6]

The triumvirate included branch president, James A. Buchanan, and his cashier, James W. McCullough. Prior to assuming the branch presidency, Buchanan had been one of the city's most influential merchants, a history that should have raised eyebrows in terms of conflict of interest. McCullough had been a lowly clerk; he had no intention of remaining in that abject position long. Together with George Williams, the men formed a company whose sole purpose was to manipulate the Bank's stock prices—thereby making them rich. In addition, Buchanan and Williams were among the directors of the Bank in Philadelphia, allowing for a dangerously incestuous relationship. Jones would profit from their schemes to the tune of $18,000.

From the Bank's first days, Buchanan and his two associates had begun purchasing shares of stocks in bogus names, enabling them to keep voting power in their hands as well as accumulating capital. In April and June 1817, Buchanan and McCullough bought close to 20,000 shares; in December of that year, 12,000. By March 1819, their stocks were worth close to $6,500,000. They financed the purchases by borrowing from the Bank, getting nearly $2,000,000 in Philadelphia, and more than $1,600,000 from the Baltimore branch. They provided no security for the debts, going even further to conceal their schemes in Baltimore by stating that stock loans came under the Bank's executives' exclusive purview and that Jones and his board in Philadelphia had approved the plan. Such machinations required falsifying books, reports, and records, lying when challenged, and then reworking the books with bogus numbers. When Jones resigned, their plot came to light, as did one of McCullough's private ruses; he had been working a scam of which his two partners were unaware. The threesome defaulted on a combined loan of more than $1,400,000.

Although not as felonious as the Baltimore branch leadership, the branches in the South and West had become accustomed to playing fast and loose, making enormous loans on real estate to farmers who had little or no security. The branches in Norfolk, Charleston, Washington, Savannah, Cincinnati, and Lexington had created mini-fiefdoms that had only cursory oversight from Jones and the board in Philadelphia. The Richmond branch president resigned in August 1819; in September 1820, the cashier in the Fayetteville, N.C. also resigned. Both instances involved account deficits. Money had simply vanished. Two state banks in Savannah, the Planters' Bank and the Bank of the State of Georgia, had not even bothered to pay their debts to the Bank of the United States during Jones's tenure. In July 1819, the Bank of Nashville replicated the same high-handed behavior by publicly declaring that the central bank intended to "destroy every state bank." A year later, South Carolina turned equally rebellious when it started plans to print its own paper money. Langdon Cheves would have needed to be a skilled magician to conjure peace and harmony from the fractious branch managers and equally recalcitrant state banks. To say nothing of the politicians and leading citizens who rose in a fury to vilify Philadelphia's leadership. Unfortunately, Cheves had no powers of enchantment.

One of Biddle's earliest undertakings was to prepare a report detailing best practices for the Bank, its directors, and branches, including alterations regarding officers' term limits, branch reports, voting, and proscribing any officer from engaging in share speculation. Additionally, he examined the laws of foreign nations regarding commerce and tariffs. The result was an octavo volume, entitled "The Commercial Digest," which he presented to Cheves, who approved it. Biddle next sent the volume to Monroe on December 9, 1819, saying that Cheves "is desirous that it should appear before the country as explaining the real nature of our operations during the present year."[7]

Whether Cheves understood Biddle's relationship with Monroe is unknown, although the fact that he depended on an outsider and relative newcomer to create this critical document suggests some form of insider knowledge. It's clear that Cheves and Monroe were unacquainted, because Monroe sought, through Biddle, to promote a Dr. Pattison to the branch in Richmond in September 1819, describing him as being "of an unquestionable integrity" and signing himself "your friend" as though the letter came from an anonymous well-wisher. Pattison had been a member of the Virginia State Legislature.[8] In April 1820, Monroe had further suggestions for the branch bank in Lexington. "Being well acquainted with the leading characters of that State . . . I enclose you a note of several who I think very deserving of the appointment. . . . The effect which may be produced, by a judicious selection of persons, for that post in conciliating the public opinion to the institution, you will fully appreciate." He ended the letter with: "I make this communication to you in confidence."[9]

Monroe had begun his first term as America's fifth President in glory. His military prowess and regimental bearing contrasted sharply with Madison's slight and sickly frame. The former President had been blamed for engulfing the United States in a war with Great Britain and censured for fleeing the capital and allowing the British to lay waste to it. Even though the Treaty of Ghent had been signed during his administration, Monroe, the handsome ex-soldier, reaped the benefits. Biddle applauded the President's decision to tour the nation, which enabled him to put his stamp on the executive office while revealing his charm and charisma. Biddle felt the tours would allow Monroe to distance himself from the prior administration, even though he'd served two cabinet positions. Biddle also believed the country hungered for a president who presented an appearance of unassailable power combined with congenial paternity. His former post as Secretary of War lent him the gravitas of experience in defending the nation.

Drafting a letter to Monroe, he wrote:

> Ever since the time of General Washington, the President of the U.S. [Biddle's deletion] has unfortunately appeared to the nation too much like the Chief Clerk of Congress—a cabinet man, stationary at his desk relying exclusively on secretaries, & invisible except to those who seek him. It will, I am persuaded, be highly gratifying to the community to see the Chief Magistrate examining for himself, & taking care that the great operations confided in him are not marred by the negligence or infidelity of agents.[10]

He added the suggestion that his brother, Thomas, then commander of Fort Mifflin south of Philadelphia on the Delaware River, could advise the President on the chain of defenses for Philadelphia.

The tours taken by the "beloved Chief Magistrate" drew crowds of tens of thousands, inspired endless cheering, military parades, artillery salutes, patriotic music, children dressed in special costumes, speeches of public welcome, and festive private and public balls and entertainments. Naturally, the visitor was encouraged to visit every local sight. An exhausting schedule kept him continuously moving: city to village to hamlet, north and west and south. Young and old: all wanted to prove their enthusiasm. Unfailingly courteous and perceptive, Monroe was in his element. Despite his ministries in Europe and his fluency in French, he escaped the damning suspicion of being a Francophile; instead, wherever he went, he was treated like a hero, almost on the scale of Washington with whom he had served. As the last of the patriots of 1776 to attain the presidency, Monroe's old-fashioned costume of buff-colored knee-breeches harkened back to the valiant age of the War for Independence. Like Washington, he rode a white horse, reinforcing the similarity.

The Boston *Columbian Centinel* welcomed Monroe into the state by referring to this hopeful period of political detente as "the era of good feelings" in part because he celebrated Independence Day in the city by joining former political rivals in lauding the nation's birth. Newspapers throughout the nation echoed the sanguine phrase. The optimists hoped that the New England Federalists and southern Republicans would make peace and looked forward to Monroe creating a non-partisan government. In fact, that was what Monroe wanted, which he had proven by asking John Quincy Adams, son of Federalist John Adams, to serve as his Secretary of State. His fellow Republicans began to grumble while some Federalists wondered whether the détente was too good to be true. They reasoned that John Quincy might be a Federalist in name, but as a United States Senator representing Massachusetts from 1803 to 1808, he had voted Republican more often than Federalist.

* * *

The euphoria was short-lived. The flailing economy with its issues of culpability and trustworthiness was too real to ignore. However, the fallout from the Seminole War took precedence over the Recession of 1818-23 during the first half of the year. Although Andrew Jackson's seizure of Pensacola had forced Spain to cede East and West Florida and enter into a beneficial territorial treaty with the

United States, his military leadership came into question, as had his actions in Florida. Jackson insisted that Monroe had sanctioned his attack on Pensacola, when, in fact, Monroe had only approved the general's warfare against marauding Seminoles who preyed upon American settlers and then fled back into the Spanish colony for refuge. Monroe stated that he had explicitly ordered Jackson not to pursue the Seminoles if they fled into a Spanish post. Consulting with Adams, the President had articulated his apprehensions about the allied powers' interference should Jackson pursue a different course.

However, letters between the two men had either gone missing or been ignored, and the truth became difficult to divine. Jackson's status as a hero of the Second War of Independence lent him prestige and influence that no one, including Monroe, could doubt. The situation in which the President found himself demanded tact and diplomacy. One fact was certain; on Jackson's orders, two British subjects, Alexander Arbuthnot and Robert Ambrister, had been executed as spies; they were also accused of inciting the Seminoles against the United States. Their citizenship had the potential of turning their deaths into an international dispute. During months of debates in Congress, Jackson's judgment repeatedly came under fire. Had the men been given a proper trial? Had Jackson acted unilaterally and "without the authority of the law?"[11] The rhetoric from the pro-Jackson senators from the southern states and the anti-Jackson legislators from the North grew ever more rancorous and heated.

Those who applauded the general's behavior compared him to the Marquis de Lafayette and the Barons Steuben and DeKalb and reviled the report delivered by the War Department as "calculated to ruin the reputation of a man who had rendered so signal service to his country."[12] The opposition declared Jackson had been "cruel, and what was worse, vindictive, and such a stain in the character of that officer all the waters of the sweet heaven would not wash out."[13] The southerners insisted he had been following orders from Washington. The northerners repudiated the claim. "*Veni, vidi, vici.* Wonderful energy! Admirable promptitude. Alas! That it had not been an energy and a promptitude within the pale of the Constitution and according to the orders of the Chief Magistrate."[14] When the matter finally began to die in June 1819, Jackson had also been rebuked for "military despotism."[15] Leading the charge against Jackson was Speaker of the House, Henry Clay. Although the senator from Kentucky had never concealed his dislike of Jackson, it was understood that the two men both had presidential ambitions, further complicating the debate.

By then, though, the debacle surrounding the Bank of the United States had grabbed the public's attention. In January 1819, a congressional committee was appointed to examine the central bank's books, dispatching agents to Philadelphia to do so. In February, Congress resolved: "That the Secretary of the Treasury shall cease all public deposits in the Bank of the United States."[16] Jones responded by writing Congress that he had carried out his commission with "the purest motives, and with perfect fidelity, diligence and zeal."[17] No one believed him.

On July 23, the Farmers and Mechanics Bank of Pittsburgh ceased operations; six days later, in Cincinnati, another Farmers and Mechanics Bank suspended specie payment "for the second and probably last time."[18] *Poulson's* opined, "Thus Bank after Bank sinks beneath the waves . . . we shall soon have no banks doing business."[19] At the close of August, there was a run on the State Bank at Trenton. September saw a report that the management of the Farmers' Bank in Reading, Pennsylvania, was under investigation. Mitigating some of the woes was a small ditty mocking the dishonest leadership of the Bank of Washington, Pennsylvania; the president was named Beard. "Some banks have broke by too close *shaving*—but the Washington Bank has broke by keeping a *Beard* too long."[20] Humor spiraled into skepticism and cynicism. Mid-November witnessed a severe run on the Planters' Bank in New Orleans; a rumor that Cashier Bailly Branchard had gone missing after taking his customary afternoon walk incited anxious investors to storm the institution. Unsubstantiated reports that he had sailed for Puerto Rico further stoked fears of malfeasance. Branchard was found drowned, but rumors of suicide kept the public edgy and anxious.

Despite apprehensions about the Bank's accountability and its ongoing efforts to clean house, the institution's new home moved forward as planned. The cornerstone at the property on Chestnut Street between Fifth and Fourth Streets was laid in April. Biddle, John Connelly, James Fischer, and Joshua Lippincott comprised the building committee; William Strickland had been chosen as architect. His renderings were introduced in late May. Biddle's love of ancient Greece held sway; modeling the exterior on the Parthenon in a "Grecian Doric"[21] style, the interior would be graced with Ionic Columns and filled with natural light. The inspiration had been the "Temple of Minerva Polias at Priene."[22] In Philadelphia, at least, an atmosphere of graciousness and calm pervaded. Although even that pleasant bubble was burst with ongoing fulminations from abolitionists who railed against "men stealers kidnapping" freed African Americans because of "great value of negroes to slave planters of south."[23] Philadelphia Quaker and confirmed abolitionist, Anthony Benezet (1713-1784), had been the subject of a recent biography, *Memoirs of the Life of Anthony Benezet*, published in 1817 and written by an equally ardent proponent of abolition, Philadelphia Quaker Roberts Vaux.

* * *

Human bondage became a topic no one could avoid with the introduction of a bill in February 1819 that would allow the people of the Missouri Territory to form a state government, thereby having representatives in Congress. A prolonged and bitter fight over slavery ensued, although it was often clothed as a debate over constitutionality and states' rights. The heart of the issue was whether to permit additional slaves to enter the proposed state or forbid them, free those born into slavery once they had reached twenty-one or twenty-five years of age, or permit free African Americans to enter the state. Many of the Missourians were slave owners; theirs, they vowed, would remain a slave economy. The Southerners felt under attack. The Northerners believed the southern interests had held sway long enough, especially the so-called Virginia Junto. The Junto, in its wrath, came near to denying James Monroe a second term. Arguments questioning the practicality of abolition arose. What if the federal government designated some states slave and some free? Would a white exodus occur, leaving the South the purview of blacks, who would then demand equal representation in Congress?

Congress had never ruled on whether or not slavery could spread west of the Mississippi River, leaving the question of whether Missouri would become a slave or free state without legal antecedents. The southern slave owners vehemently opposed creating a free state; the abolitionists were equally determined to make their case regarding the evils of enslavement. States' rights proponents pitted themselves against the sovereignty of Congress and the federal government. Adding to the rancor was the admission into the Union of Alabama as a slave state in December 1819. The expansionist benefits of the Adams-Onís Treaty that had given the United States Florida and access west through the Oregon Territory to the Pacific became ideological battlegrounds during arguments about how those new lands would be governed. Each was guilty of illiberality and partisanship.

A compromise was reached, but it was hard won and required the enactment of two linked laws. The first was admitting Maine as a free state to balance the admission of Missouri as a slave state (Maine had been part of Massachusetts).

The second excluded free African-Americans from entering Missouri. Under the influence of Speaker of the House, Henry Clay, a promise was wrested from the Missouri state legislature to leave the latter issue on the table.

Augmenting the statehood question was the deeper problem of manumission. Following the war, there had been a boom in the dual slave trades: one, the illegal importation of slaves from Africa; the other, the internal sale of slaves from the Upper South to the cotton frontier in the Lower South. Those trades inspired two unlikely allies to join forces: northern abolitionists who wanted to end the damnable practice and the American Colonization Society in the South, whose mission was to resettle freed slaves to Africa. (Monroe's Secretary of the Treasury, William Crawford, served as the Society's vice president.) Altruism was not the Colonization Society's motivation, nor its genesis; rather, it was self-preservation. In the eyes of the planter class, a free Negro was a dangerous person. Even Monroe mistrusted the freed men and women whom he believed lived by larceny and other criminal activities while poisoning the minds of those still enslaved, which then fostered insurrection. In the spring of 1819, a bill was passed appropriating $100,000 to purchase a colony in Africa, which would become Liberia; the capital would be Monrovia. However, the northern abolitionists and American Colonization Society allies disagreed on the subject of Missouri.

While Clay essayed to soothe the southern legislators' fears regarding Missouri, Monroe worked behind the scenes seeking cooperation and conciliation. Knowing that Biddle had earned the respect of key members of Congress representing Pennsylvania (most of whom were opposed to conceding to southern wishes, but equally impassioned regarding states' rights), he summoned him to Washington. Biddle's assignment was to persuade certain, vocal legislators to change their positions, and, instead, vote in favor of what became known as the Missouri Compromise. William Sergeant held one of those critical votes. Biddle's tact, and perseverance succeeded, but as he wrote Jane on February 12, 1821:

> The great & only business of Wash^n is the vile Missouri question. To-day all the propositions of compromise were rejected & it is supposed that the state of Missouri itself will be rejected. This the southern and western people regard as little short of the dissolution of the union & are this evening in the highest possible state of excitement. To judge from the tone of things here, one would suppose that we in Philadelphia were willing to hazard the peace of the country for the sake of

allowing a parcel of negroes the privilege of settling in Missouri. It is a little less than madness in the manner in which the controversy is conducted.[24]

Boasting that he had been handsomely entertained by the President who asked him to dine with him daily, as well as pass his evenings with the Monroe family and that he also attended state functions at Monroe's and Adams's request, Biddle finally admitted that he missed home. Even his frequent horseback rides with Monroe had begun to pall. "I am tired of Washington & am anxious to leave it," he told Jane, "but there are many things which I must see."[25] Husband and wife communicated daily, Nicholas often several times in one day, while chiding Jane when her letters didn't arrive in a timely fashion. He ended with the injunction to "kiss the dear boys."

Despite this affectionate correspondence, and Biddle's obvious love of his wife and family, he hadn't been truthful about the true purpose of his journey to Washington. Jane had been under the impression that he had some business with the Supreme Court. When she queried him, he obfuscated, telling her she must have misunderstood his intentions. He never mentioned Missouri again.

* * *

Charles Biddle died April 4, 1821, and was buried alongside his father in the family vault at Christ Church. Although he had lived a full long life, beginning in 1819, he had started to fail. He had a difficult time controlling his limbs, and his handwriting had grown shaky enough to require dictation—a situation he loathed. In 1820, a worse calamity ensued; a stroke left him partially paralyzed, forcing him to spend his final months bedridden and in increasing pain and debility. A man who had always been robust, he found the strictures imposed by his situation impossible to bear. He tried to be stoic, but was a poor patient—nor had he ever been a patient person. The household became a giant sickroom, with family, nurses, and physicians kept on constant alert.

For his children, Charles's death brought an end to the era when the United States had been mere colonies, and patriotism had been a physical as well as cerebral undertaking. Demanding and patriarchal, his approbation was valued because it was both rare and honest. His sons understood they were nobler men and more productive citizens because of their father's high expectations of them, his daughters that they should be the helpmeets of respected and industrious husbands.

For Nicholas, however, Charles had always been something of an enigma, the father he had esteemed, but with whom he shared few characteristics. In his letters, Charles praised his son when he believed an action merited it and always signed himself "Yr affectionate father," but in person, he had never been demonstrative like Hannah. There was an awkwardness between the two men, both desiring an intimacy their dual natures could never achieve. Charles felt this lack; as the years passed, he sought additional ways to laud his cerebral son, but the disconnect was more difficult to overcome for Nicholas. Although he grieved for his father, part of him felt a kind of relief. He no longer needed to live under the shadow of past deeds of valor. The memory of Nicholas, the Revolutionary War hero, lay buried with Charles. From that time forward, Biddle had only himself to satisfy.

The following February, Jane and Nicholas's four-year-old son, James, died after a brief illness. Jane escaped the despair she had experienced in 1814, but the household's mood altered to one of apprehension. Although, Jane had never been prone to Peggy's fearful dreams, she had inherited her mother's sensitivities and a predilection for gloomy intuition. Andalusia, the cocoon of family life, and her beloved music became more than ever the source of her moral support.

Even though the city was home to a cultural, political, financial, and mercantile life, Philadelphia could become a dirty, dangerous place where mad dogs roamed the streets attacking children, adults, and other dogs and causing deadly and excruciating hydrophobia, known now as rabies. During the warm spring and summer months, newspapers were filled with warnings about the disease's prevalence. As if the warnings might be ignored, reporters chronicled the ailment's awful and lethal progression. In response to what seemed a daily barrage of disease and suffering, Jane retreated physically and emotionally. She wanted no part of city life.

Nicholas, who had early on assumed the protector's mantle, indulged and may even have encouraged his wife's dependence. When he was away in Harrisburg or Washington, she fretted over various visitors to the couple's house in town. Nicholas urged her to "decide for yourself" and "judge circumstances,"[26] but the tone was parental not that of an equal. Except for the one lapse in which he railed against the machinations surrounding the Missouri Compromise, he focused on family matters, which he thought would appeal to her. Monroe's married daughter was "fat and handsome . . . and soon to be a mama."[27] Or, "I hope you have been to the theatre and the circus as nothing would give me more pleasure that the idea that you are amusing yourself."[28] Or, "Every body has not such a wife & such two children to go to . . ." to which he added, "whom I love more than any thing or any body in the world."[29]

What was Jane's reaction to her husband's patronizing, albeit tender behavior? Her mother had treated her thus. Would she rather have had a partnership with Nicholas, or was she content being petted and called "little Jane?" Did she regard her redoubtable mother-in-law with envy or with awe? Did she wish her husband would embrace her as a helpmeet, or was she too timid or, perhaps, too ambivalent about a changed status to voice her wish? She must have ventured the suggestion on occasion because Nicholas responded. However, her complaints, if they can be called that, were made in writing when her husband was away from home, and she was left feeling forlorn and insignificant. Because Jane destroyed most of her correspondence, we have only Nicholas's letters to her. Although intended to be playful, as was his habit when addressing his wife's worries, most of his messages contain an unsettling air of condescension. On one occasion, he wrote from Washington, "There is nothing new in the political world. If there was I am afraid you would not care much about it."[30] To a woman in the twenty-first century, the assumption of incapacity rankles. How did Jane react to the charge? Given her familial history, how could she react? What would Peggy have answered to such an absurd suggestion? Would she have advised her daughter to dispute the accusation? Or, would she have sided with Nicholas?

* * *

While Jane buried her own needs, Nicholas's ambitions came to fruition. On January 27, 1823, Monroe wrote to him:

> I need not assure you of the great pleasure which I have derived from
> your appointment to the Presidency of the bank of the U States and
> not solely from a thorough conviction that you will discharge the
> duties with great ability & perfect integrity, but in the hope and belief
> that by this opportunity which it will afford, of making known to your
> fellow citizens the great claims which you have to their confidence &
> esteem, lead to other trusts hereafter in which you may be still more
> intensely useful.[31]

Monroe's noble sentiments disregarded the storm clouds that had been gathering over his administration. Facing the conclusion of his two terms as the nation's chief magistrate, he was forced to watch factionalism shred the Era of Good Feelings to near tatters. The issue wasn't domestic or foreign policies; it was Monroe's successor. Five men vied for the position: Andrew Jackson, William Crawford, and Henry Clay: each of whom took every opportunity to snipe at the President; and John Quincy Adams and John Calhoun, who were Monroe adherents and unlikely allies because Adams was a Massachusetts abolitionist, and Calhoun a pro-slavery South Carolinian. Calhoun, as Monroe's Secretary of War, was accused of negligence and profligacy.

In turn, Jackson's ignominious stint as governor of Florida in 1821, and the near calamity he had provoked with Spain over his arrest of the former Spanish governor, haunted him and Monroe. For his part, Jackson never forgave the humiliation he experienced at Monroe's hands. Adams, breaking with the President, believed that Jackson deserved the praise of a grateful nation while at the same time attacking Crawford's overweening ambition (he overlooked Jackson's). Adams accused Crawford of secretly rallying Monroe's foes. John Randolph of Roanoke joined the fray by insinuating that the President had been privately maneuvering to serve a third term. From Monticello, Thomas Jefferson weighed in on the infighting in a letter to Albert Gallatin in October 1822, "the lion and the lamb lie down together in peace. Do not believe a word of it."[32]

No wonder Monroe continued to confide in Biddle. A little over a month after penning the letter congratulating Biddle on his presidency of the Second Bank, he sent him a message regarding troublesome foreign affairs, including battles between Spain and her fractious South American colonies and the Greek fight for independence. He worried that another European war was imminent, and the Continent and Great Britain were slipping back into the bloody enmity of the Napoleonic years.

Monroe had aged while in office. His wife was often too ill to entertain. His bright legacy had dimmed. In addition, he was now facing retirement as a poor man. Again, he sought out Biddle. In a letter dated March 30, 1823, he described numerous personal debts. Although Congress allotted the President living expenses, the amount fell far short of current and past expenditures. Biddle, who had previously represented Monroe in lawsuits over missing funds, was all too aware of the President's fiscal woes, but the style of this particular missive shocked him. Instead of Monroe's habitually forthright penmanship, the writing was cramped; words were excised; repetitions confused the message. It looked like an appeal dispatched by a desperate man.

- CHAPTER NINE -

THE BANK'S PRESIDENT

On December 2, 1823, during his annual message to Congress, Monroe set forth a plan for United States' engagement with foreign powers that would become known as the Monroe Doctrine. The impetus was a total rejection of European and Russian ambitions regarding the nation's territories and fisheries; America had defeated an all-powerful Great Britain; she now deserved and demanded international respect. Monroe also intended that the conflicts between Europe's nations should never again embroil America. The United States had recognized Columbia as a republic in 1822, and in early 1823, the government of Buenos Aires and states of Mexico and Chile. However, the administration was understandably anxious about Spain's future intentions toward her former colonies. In part, the President's message read:

> In the wars of the European powers in matters relating to themselves
> we have never taken any part, nor does it comport with our policy
> to do so. It is only when our rights are invaded or seriously menaced
> that we resent injures or make preparation for our defense. . . . With
> the existing colonies or dependencies of any European power we
> have not interfered and shall not interfere. But with the governments
> who have declared their independence and maintained it, and whose
> independence we have, on great consideration and on just principles,
> acknowledged, we could not view any interposition for the purpose of
> oppressing them, or controlling in any other manner their destiny, by
> any European power, in any other light than as the manifestation of an
> unfriendly disposition toward the United States.

An obvious result of the doctrine, heralded by many, but perplexing to others, would be a tendency toward nationalism and isolationism. At the time, though, the United States' appeal as a sovereign space guiding her destiny without interference or compromise seemed the birthright of the War of Independence and the legacy of the nation's founding fathers. Monroe employed the words "Revolution," "patriotism," and "union" within his speech. On January 1, 1824, *Poulson's* in its annual page-long ode "To the American People—Union, Health, and Happiness" seconded Monroe's declaration:

> We leave thee, *Europe*, to wayward fate,
> And turn awhile to our more happy state –
> Here Freedom strikes her root; her branches spread,
> And Holy Allies give no mortal dread. . . .[1]

Notably, Biddle ignored his mentor's last annual congressional message. His focus was elsewhere. Although he had assumed the Second Bank presidency on January 7, 1823, setting the institution on a proper course required diplomacy and patience—the latter of which had never been his forte. He turned thirty-seven the day following his appointment, but age hadn't tempered his tenacity or habitual need to move quickly. There were members of the board who feared he might become radical in his approach: a man of incisive intellect who acted without sufficient time to ponder or elicit his peers and elders' advice. There were others, like John Jacob Astor of New York, who scoffed at him for being overly interested in "elegant literature" and who critiqued the "suavity of his manners."[2] Biddle proved them wrong. Yes, he was urbane and prided himself on his cosmopolitan demeanor and the refinement of his two homes and their furnishings. Yes, he could gather diverse information rapidly and coalesce it into a cogent approach, but he also understood the need for consensus if a genuine change was to occur. Without forsaking his determination, he practiced self-restraint.

When he became president, the bank's capital was thirty-five million dollars, and its total resources equaled more than fifty-three million. Overseeing eighteen branches required a steady hand because many in the nation continued to view a central bank as oppressive, greedy, singularly untrustworthy, and ruled by conniving men from long-established eastern cities, of which Philadelphia was a perfect example. At the time, recent settlers within the Ohio Valley had accrued large debts while attempting to turn arable, undeveloped land into productive farms. Purchased cheaply, the cost of transforming raw tracts became prohibitive with the necessity of procuring sufficient equipment and livestock to replace the game that had vanished due to overpopulation by humans. The more livestock populated the landscape, the greater the need for tillage and more equipment and labor. Everywhere pioneer communities existed, debt abounded while the newcomers waited to turn a profit or simply survive. In 1818 in Kentucky, forty banks were founded; they failed the following year. The state legislature created the Bank of the Commonwealth of Kentucky in 1820, but it only added to the already prohibitive bank credit. No wonder the western agrarian interests were angry. They thought banks were leeches, and the Bank of the United States the most parasitic of all.

Biddle understood the putative and practical impediments he faced. The first advisors he chose were men experienced and trusted in financial matters: in New York, Robert Lenox, a merchant and director of the first and second banks; from Baltimore, Roswell Colt, and Colt's brother-in-law (and Craig relative), Robert Oliver, as well as John McKim, Jr.: each of whom had helped Biddle untangle the webs of deceit created by Buchanan and his cohorts; in Boston, James Lloyd and Daniel Webster (who would become an especial confidante); in Charleston, Robert Patterson and John Potter.

In order for the Second Bank to execute its duties with reliability and transparency, it needed new rules for supervision, one being that board members would serve three consecutive years. After that time, a necessary rotation occurred. A director could be re-elected at the end of one year's absence. This rule had the effect of removing board members who were ill-equipped or negligent, or those with dubious ethics. Although the worst offenders had been purged, Biddle feared that a tendency toward profligacy might return, especially within formerly insubordinate branches where directors had gotten into the habit of accruing large, unsecured loans. Mandatory rotation ensured compliance with the policy. As he wrote Robert Lenox in February 1823:

> We have had enough, and more than enough of banking in the
> interior. We have been crippled and almost destroyed by it. It is time
> to concentrate our business—to bank where there is some use and
> some profit in it . . . to make at present the large commercial cities the
> principal scene of our operations.[3]

To Lenox and other Biddle advisors who dwelt and conducted businesses in established, thriving cities, this priority made sense. However, the focus would engender future enmity.

Biddle decided that New York, being a growing hub for commerce and trade, should take a larger role. He instructed the office to trade only in Second Bank notes instead of those issued by New York State banks, which drew opposition from local banks. The branch in New Orleans also required strengthening; most of its business was in currency exchange; Biddle intended that that trade become more profitable. Reinvigorating the New Orleans branch had improved operations in the Southwest and West, where the Bank of the United States existed in name only, with little regard for directives from Philadelphia.

These actions Biddle put in place during his first two months in office. Like all wise managers, he believed in astute supervision while encouraging freedom within the branches' daily operations. Electing local cashiers fell under the purview of the central board in Philadelphia, which meant that Biddle handpicked each man, who then took guidance and instructions from Philadelphia. There would henceforth be no more rogue administrations, acting for their benefit and conflicting personal interests.

Choosing new directors for the branch banks also became a personal task. Adapting his role as Monroe's confidant, he picked one or two men to serve as his eyes and ears regarding local branch practices. In addition, he sought counsel within a circle of friends and colleagues when it became necessary to fill a vacating seat on one of the boards and solicited recommendations from the bank presidents and cashiers who understood the intricate daily workings of each institution. Biddle and the central board carefully weighed the names of candidates for each branch board, and although local governance elected its own leadership, names proposed by Philadelphia carried weight. Biddle believed that a symbiotic and mutually respectful relationship was necessary for health and growth. However, he intended that the central board remain the arbiter in all matters, which Jones had spectacularly failed to do and which Cheves had only imperfectly attempted.

Whereas Cheves had created antagonism between state banks and the Second Bank, Biddle promoted collaboration. Local banks met local needs; the national bank reached across state lines and cultural boundaries; loans and solid credit enabled goods to move from one part of the nation to another. Biddle subsequently summed up this theory: "no facilities of traveling and transportation can so completely abridge the wide spaces which separate the parts of this extensive country, as the removal of those barriers which the want of easy commercial exchange interpose to their prosperity."[4] Because he envisioned the central bank as a necessary engine for commerce, he opposed long-term real estate loans that entailed money without creating any means to manufacture goods, saying, "it is entirely inconsistent with its design and its safety that a bank should lend its funds on the security of real estate, should lend on permanent accommodation to parties not in business."[5]

According to every standard, the start of Nicholas Biddle's leadership was a success. He must have relished a sense of triumph in rescuing an institution whose welfare was so intricately entwined with the national good, but understandable pride was leavened with his native wit. In April 1823, responding to a letter from Savannah, he signed his name with a large flourish, then added in small block letters: ["The President of the Bank U States when it fell to almost nothing"].[6]

By the time he had been in office six months, business loans and loans on personal security saw a growth of more than two million dollars. The ability to secure credit increased, bolstering manufacturing, as well as the production and distribution of raw materials, which, in turn, raised business output. Profits grew. The Second Bank, instead of being suspect, met with approval and praise. The public's about-face and evident goodwill resulted in the rise of the bank's stock value. Because the machinery that allowed the currency to circulate between the central and state banks ran smoothly for the first time, state institutions, including remote regions of the West, no longer found fault with unwieldy operations. Although he was describing Philadelphia when he explained the system at the start of his presidency, the practice differed from that in rural areas only in its timing. Rural branches followed the same routine weekly rather than daily.

> Every morning the clerks from this Bank and the State Banks meet and interchange the notes received on the proceeding day. The balances are struck accordingly. But no bank ever calculates on its balances remaining for any length of time and whenever it grows a little too large, no bank ever hesitates to send for ten or fifteen or twenty thousand dollars from its debtor. . . . Thus it goes around no one complains and everyone is satisfied. In truth, it is only when these balances accumulate and remain for any time that they become oppressive to both parties and excite mutual enmity.[7]

Foreign exchange allowed the Second Bank to draw on Baring Brothers in London and Continental bankers; the central bank became the predominant purchaser and seller of foreign trade throughout the country. When European exchange ran low, the bank helped regulate the rate. All these remedies Biddle accomplished, and, as he noted, "with great delicacy."[8] He was determined that the United States and its national bank be subordinate to none.

As a cultural hub, Philadelphia still held sway. Walking to and from the bank's offices, Biddle daily witnessed the fullness of the city's artistic life as expressed through its architecture. William Strickland, who had designed Biddle's parish church, St. Peter's at Third and Pine Streets, in 1761 according to a spare yet fluidly elegant Georgian model, had begun experimenting with new forms of expression. His 1822 design for the new Chestnut Street Theatre melded Palladian with Greek elements and was equipped with gaslighting. The Chestnut Street Theatre, sometimes simply called the New Theatre, rivaled any house in London, and drew the most discerning audiences, offering a different play or opera each day of the week and suiting every taste from Shakespeare's tragedies and comedies to farces like *Fontainbleau: Or, John Bull in France.* Strickland was also commissioned to design the Musical Fund Hall, remodeling a church at 8th and Locust Streets into an odeum lauded for its acoustics. Prior to the recital hall's opening, the public flocked to the Masonic Hall and the city's churches to hear vocal concerts ranging from Mozart to Rossini, Romberg to Kreutzer, and Hayden. Philadelphians' devotion to music made the city a center for piano production and the publication of sheet music.

Strickland's vision for the Second Bank of the United States captured the public's imagination. It stood alone in a white blaze of marble, separated physically and stylistically from other Chestnut Street structures. On both its north and south facades, eight massive Doric columns supported a classical entablature and pediment, the whole clothed in marble. Raised above street level and approached by a double flight of steps that ran the building's width, the bank resembled a Greek temple, which, of course, was the intent: the wisdom of the ancients melded with the can-do spirit of a new nation. Although money wasn't a god, it was a close second. America's rich resources had bought and continued to ensure the country's freedom.

Biddle had taken a keen interest in each detail of Strickland's plans. Watching the craftsmen carve the columns and architrave when he passed the growing structure on his way home from the bank's temporary home on lower Chestnut Street filled him with awe. The ruddy brick of neighboring structures made them seem earthbound and antiquated in comparison. Strickland was so pleased with the work that he commissioned portrait painter John Neagle, Thomas Sully's son-in-law, to use the bank as a backdrop. In 1830, a visiting critic from England wrote that the building "excels in elegance and equals in utility . . . not only the Bank of England, but of any banking house in the world."[9] The interior was equally impressive; the main banking room was surmounted by a barrel vault supported by marble pillars. Light flooded in. The effect produced both the necessary heft that inspired trust and an airy grace indicating flexibility.

Residential architecture for Philadelphia's elite was also undergoing a sea change. Home design for the wealthy began taking its cues from the regency squares in London and Bath and Dublin. Series of uniform, elegant townhouses stretched along entire city blocks. Like their English originals, the interiors had high ceilings and rooms large enough to accommodate dancing parties (Biddle loved throwing balls at his mansion on Spruce Street; less enthusiastic, Jane acquiesced). The brick facades were brightened by local Schuylkill marble. Marble fireplaces and mantels replaced Colonial-era carved wood; chandeliers were now crystal rather than pewter or brass.

Alabaster vases and urns in Grecian or Gothic styles complemented drawing rooms hung with French or satin papers. Decorative statuary filled newly created niches. The French empire style inspired furniture ornamented with *vert antique* gilding; ebony inlays became popular; upholstered couches were intended for reclining instead of sitting stiffly erect—the méridienne being a reminder to rest during the heat of the day. A difference in the American empire version was patriotic symbols, including stars and eagles with outspread wings. Duncan Phyfe, a Scottish émigré, and Charles-Honoré Lannuier, an ébéniste (cabinet maker) from Paris, influenced the vogue in all things French and Renaissance Italian. "A la Raffaele"[10] described the conflation of identities.

In Philadelphia, William and Mary Waln's house designed by Benjamin Latrobe on the corner of 7th and Chestnut Streets predated the vogue, taking it to spectacular heights, even though Waln was a Quaker who should have eschewed all ostentation. Nothing equaled the home's splendor: the receiving rooms painted a rich Etruscan red, offset with black and white; bold frieze images inspired by scenes from the Odyssey circled the walls. The sedate exterior belied its fantastical interior. Winged caryatids supported gilded rosewood or marble-topped tables; gold tassels wrapped in silk threads hung from satin covers adorning chairs inspired by the Greek klismos style, initially wrought in bronze. The couple entertained everyone who was anyone in Philadelphia.

Waln made his fortune in the China trade (or, more precisely, the lucrative market that transported opium to China from India). Though taking its cue from ancient Greek motifs, the decor also reflected the color schemes of the Far East's lacquer work. Waln went bankrupt during the panic of 1819; the home (minus its theatrical furnishings) was sold to the Rosét family in 1821. The Roséts (later Anglicized to Rozet) were of French descent. No longer was it considered un-American to be a Francophile.

French fashions garnered advertising space in the city's newspapers. The owners of each shop assuring their clients that new assortments of cashmere shawls and "blonde" laces, bonnets, and silk flowers had just arrived from Le Havre. If any doubt lingered as to the wares' authenticity, the merchants named the ships in which their goods had traveled. With a nod to the South American nations' fight for liberty, the chicest style of women's hat was dubbed the "Bolivar." Chinese satin damasks, painted muslins, and Moroccan ladies' shoes reflected the public's fascination with all things foreign and rare. One of which was a menagerie of "live animals"[11] on display on lower Market Street, including an African lion, brought to Senegal by Arab traders and thence shipped across the Atlantic, as well as two Arabian camels, two llamas, an elephant, and an orangutan. An Egyptian sarcophagus and mummy rested in solemn grandeur at Earle and Sully's gallery across from the State House. Neoclassicist and French exile, Jacques-Louis David's provocative "Cain Meditating the Death of His Brother Abel" was exhibited at the Masonic Hall. Admission twenty-five cents with half price for children, the artwork was reported to be "superior to any painting introduced in this country."[12]

Augmenting Philadelphian's love of the exotic, one of the most popular books of 1824 was J. E. Worcester's *Sketches of the Earth and its Inhabitants*, containing one hundred engravings depicting the world's chief cities, edifices, and ruins, as well as its natural wonders. Lest anyone fear that their linguistic skills wouldn't permit them to keep pace with a new societal norm, an advertisement in *Poulson's* offered "French Taught in 48 Lessons."

Greece's plight and her struggle for freedom echoed in Americans' memory of their war of independence. The public avidly consumed daily reports of battles won and lost, and established Greek funds and committees to examine the struggle for statehood. Congress routinely discussed the "Greek Question"— which, again, seemed counter to Monroe's precept of America for Americans. Multiculturalism, though, had become intrinsic to city life. In Philadelphia,

Boston, New York, Charleston, Savannah, and New Orleans, commerce and the arts and sciences depended upon an international trade of goods and ideas.

Befitting this world-view, two French émigrés, Joseph Bonaparte (Napoleon's older brother), the former king of Naples and Spain, and now known as the Comte de Survilliers, and his son-in-law, the naturalist, Charles Lucien Bonaparte, became the toasts of Philadelphia. Following the battle of Waterloo, the elder Bonaparte had fled Spain using an assumed name. Initially finding a haven in Switzerland, he had been forced to flee again. He sailed incognito to the United States and disembarked in New York before deciding that the open spaces near Philadelphia offered a better opportunity to create an appropriately princely atmosphere. The city was home to America's French expatriate community, one of whom was financier Stephen (Étienne) Girard. The count chose a 1,700 parcel of land named "Point Breeze" in Bordentown, New Jersey, across the Delaware River from Biddle's Andalusia. Charles Lucien Bonaparte and his wife, Zénaide, lived there, as well, making the estate a haven of old-world Gallicism that somehow managed to deny Napoleon's brutal reign. David had painted a double portrait of Zénaide and her sister, Charlotte, in 1820.

Bonaparte ordered the construction of a man-made lake half a mile long and dotted with ingeniously landscaped islands within a park-like setting. Twelve miles of bridle paths and drives meandered among copses of woods and shrubberies, making the place resemble an imported French chateau. Parterre gardens, graperies, gazebos, fountains, and tame peacocks added to the ambiance. European politics had made Bonaparte cautious; every building on the estate was connected by a series of underground passages, each of which could accommodate a man standing erect. If necessary, the count and his retinue could flee through the passages to a boat he kept moored in the river and that Girard had supplied. Survilliers's apprehensions were well-founded. An earlier version of Point Breeze burned to the ground in 1820, although silver and plate, artwork, crystal chandeliers, gilded mirrors, and library had been rescued. A Russian woman avenging Napoleon's destruction of Moscow was rumored to have started the blaze.

Those precautions and their sense of impermanence aside, the new Point Breeze was designed to garner awe. It housed an art gallery replete with works by Canaletto, da Vinci, Gerard, Murillo, Rembrandt, Rubens, Titian, and Velasquez and a version of David's famed equestrian portrait of Napoleon crossing the Alps. A more titillating piece was a replica of a semi-nude statue of Bonaparte's sister, Pauline, in the guise of Venus Victrix. As worldly as Phila-delphians considered themselves, depictions of nude and semi-nude women challenged a still-inherent Quaker parochialism. Antonio Canova's Venus drew gasps of dismay from the count's female guests. Although John Quincy Adams, Henry Clay, Daniel Webster, and Biddle were guests, Jane seldom accompanied her husband on his frequent visits. However, he liked to entertain on his turf, which allowed Jane to converse with the count either at dinners or balls without glimpsing Pauline's likeness or acknowledging Bonaparte's mistress, Annette Savage. Of course, Jane had had her education in French manners and deport-ment from a family friend, Circé de Ronceray, who had spent most of her time at Andalusia prior to marrying Nicholas's brother, William, in 1820. Jane was delighted to receive the count at her home and converse in his native tongue.

The friendship between Biddle and Bonaparte deepened as the years passed. Formality disappeared, and they called each other by their first names. Often the two men dined alone at Point Breeze, their conversations wide-ranging and involving world affairs past and present. As the former king of Spain, the count's perspective on the Napoleonic era intrigued Biddle. After all, he had witnessed some of those events first hand while serving as secretary to the American min-istry in Paris. At one point, he put precise questions to Napoleon's brother as to specific actions during the Battle of Waterloo, remarking in his journal how forcibly those words from the past struck him. The count returned Biddle's goodwill with gifts, in 1832, a Paul de Vos painting entitled "Wolf Hunt" that had originally hung in the palace in Madrid, and that Survilliers told Biddle "would be well placed in your living room or dining room."[13] Family lore also ascribed a canopied bed to Survilliers's generosity. Of certainty, was a copy of David's equestrian portrait of Napoleon; the count urged Biddle to hire Bass Otis to reproduce the work and place it in Andalusia where it remains.

* * *

Although the Second Bank consumed Biddle's days, his energy and increased prestige gave him a new forum, which he heartily embraced and which, in turn, added to his stature. He and Jane regularly entertained the Peales, Thomas Sully, and other notable painters and the Shakespearean actor, Thomas Apthor-pe Cooper. Washington Irving and James Fenimore Cooper considered Biddle a friend. In addition, he was a founder of the Athenaeum of Philadelphia, a member of the American Philosophical Society, the Pennsylvania Academy of Fine Arts, and the Wistar Association, whose Saturday night meetings revolved around discussions ranging from science to theology, literature, and philosophy. When the Franklin Institute was founded in February 1824, the board sought Biddle's counsel and publicly printed his letter of congratulations on its constitution. The institute, which remains beloved in Philadelphia, was born of populist sentiment, devoted to the "Promotion of the Mechanic Arts" and the "establishment of popular lectures on the sciences connected with them."[14]

Unlike Peale's museum, or the Pennsylvania Academy of Fine Arts, or the Philosophical Society, the Franklin Institute was intended to have broad appeal, crossing socio-economic classes, and raising the study and implementation of mechanical arts such as engineering and metallurgy to the level of the visual and performing arts. Mathew Carey sat on the board, as did Paul Beck, the shot manufacturer, Robert Patterson, president of the United States Mint, and William Strickland, architect and engineer. Biddle commended the effort, calling the enterprise a "union of intellectual and physical labor. . . . It belongs essentially to the institutions of this country, which open all the avenues of power and distinction to every class of citizens, to provide that none may be disenfranchised on account of their ignorance."[15] The emphasis on the sciences changed *Port Folio's* pages too. Reports on "The Geological Survey of the Great Western Canal," a treatise on chemistry, and "useful institutes" accompanied and often outnumbered pages devoted to *belles lettres*.

In this gilded period of public accolades and productive work, Biddle found his days exhilarating and profoundly satisfying. Convinced that a national bank was crucial to his country's welfare, the life-blood that supported the health and vitality of every organ, he kept long but happy hours. His father, uncles, and brothers had believed in their nation's ascendancy to the depth of their souls; Nicholas's implementation of the same belief took a different form, although it was just as potent.

His home life added to his sense of well-being and rightness. Two days after his thirty-seventh birthday and three days after he had been elected president of the Second Bank, he and Jane had had another son. Born January 10, 1823, John Craig Biddle was two weeks overdue. Worry for Jane's health and concern about the baby's birth had undercut a good deal of the pleasure he might have experienced at being chosen for such a position of trust, but those fearful times had now passed. Mother and child were hale and hearty, the baby growing, and Jane shaking free of her maternal anxieties and enjoying life again. The baby was christened at St. Peter's Church on April 10. Although Biddle was an Episcopalian, he had never been much of a religious man. Nonetheless, a sense of divine gratitude imbued his spirit. Despite his prestige, he maintained a boyish wonderment as though surprised by the success of his adult years.

* * *

In August 1824, a frenzy over the American visit of General Lafayette took hold of the nation. In every city and hamlet, committees were formed to welcome him during his year-long progress from Providence, Rhode Island to Boston, from Hartford to New York, Philadelphia, Baltimore, Washington, Alexandria, Yorktown, Norfolk, Fredericksburg, Charleston, and Savannah. A visit to Mt. Vernon was planned. Jewelers cast gold and silver medallions with George Washington's likeness on one side, and Lafayette's on the other; suitably decorated ladies' sashes and waistbands sold out; metal workers advertised they could refurbish and burnish muskets, pistols, and swords at "the shortest notice."[16] Uniforms long unused were taken from storage trunks and boxes and repaired; everyone wanted to look their best for "the Nation's Guest." Lafayette represented all that was noble in America's history. Lest anyone forget, newspapers reprinted personal and official accounts from the Revolutionary War, reminding readers who were too young to remember that the sixty-seven-year-old Frenchman had fought alongside that greatest of heroes, George Washington. In the growing political cynicism and polarity of the United States during the first quarter of the nineteenth century, Lafayette shone a beacon backward to a time when men and women cleaved to a grand ideal.

At least, that was the public sentiment his tour inspired. Thousands lined each of his routes, the women waving white handkerchiefs and openly sobbing; the men were also wiping away tears while shouting continual "Huzzas." Military parades accompanied him from town to town; smartly turned out militias, and mayors and their ladies and other prominent citizens welcomed him at every stop; children, dressed in white, presented flowers, and in Hartford, eight hundred children recited an ode entitled "Nous vous aimons, La Fayette" that concluded with the heartfelt lines:

> When our blooming cheeks shall fade,
> Pale with time, or sorrows' shade;
> When our clustering tresses fair,
> Frosts of wintry age shall wear.
> E'en till memory's sun be set,
> nous vous aimons La Fayette.[17]

In Boston, as in every other place, he and his son and entourage passed, emotions of gratitude and awe gushed out. The mayor there declared, "The citizens of Boston welcome you on your return to the United States; mindful of your early zeal in the cause for American Independence, grateful for your distinguished share in the perils and glories of its achievement."[18]

Lafayette, who spoke perfect, idiomatic English, replied with equal passion. "The emotions of love and gratitude which I have been accustomed to feel on my entering this city, has ever been mingled with a sense of religious reverence for the cradle, and, let us hope it will hereafter be said, of universal liberty."[19]

New York tried to outdo Boston with fireworks over Vauxhall Gardens, a grand *fete* at Castle Garden, evenings at the theater, oratorios written in Lafayette's honor, public balls, and private dinners. Not to be bested by their northern neighbor, Philadelphia arranged processions through every neighborhood, from the Northern Liberties to Southwark. The population was reported to have nearly doubled with residents from the state's western reaches who arrived en masse to see liberty's champion with their own eyes.

Lafayette's approach from Trenton to Princeton and thence south was reported with the same intensity once devoted to Lord Howe's victorious army as it advanced upon a fearful city. Anyone recollecting those long and bitter months found ample cause to weep in thanksgiving. On September 28, at the Frankford Bridge, the general and his suite met a "numerous cavalcade of citizens" who declared in a kind of religious ecstasy, "We have left our ploughs idle in the furrow; we have left the axe in the tree on the hill side. . . ."[20] Naturally, a ball was held in Lafayette's honor, each distinguished guest welcomed with a flourish of trumpets; the city set ablaze with fireworks and artistic illuminations. All the French community in Philadelphia attended the various dinners and receptions, as did Secretary of State, John Quincy Adams, and the DuPont family of Delaware, the general's personal friends. Point Breeze and the count welcomed Lafayette, as a matter of course.

What was Biddle's role in all this heroic fanfare? He had met Lafayette in Paris in 1804, been entertained at his home "La Grange," and developed a friendly rapport while in France. Nicholas's brother, James, had been instrumental in providing safe passage to the United States for Lafayette's friend, Pierre Samuel du Pont de Nemours. Since 1818, Biddle and Lafayette had been in regular communication regarding French merchants and scholars relocating permanently or temporarily to the United States. Lafayette relied upon Biddle to lend whatever aid he could, and Biddle readily complied. The letters from

France also habitually concluded with warm remembrances to Captain Biddle. Starting in January 1825, Nicholas would provide financial advice to Lafayette, initially counseling him on investing $120,000 in American funds. At that time, Biddle confessed that his "connexion [*sic*] with the Bank imposes on me a delicate task." Although proposing an investment in "some National funds such as the share of the Bank of the United States, or the stock of the Government of the United States," he told Lafayette that he should first consult with his board of directors, saying, "Now we are all interested that your fortune should hereafter be subjected to the least possible hazard and that you should be perfectly secure."[21]

James's connection went deeper than the du Pont association; in August, he entertained Lafayette when he first arrived in Boston, providing a quiet, convivial meal, which was one of the few times during his long and grueling journey when he could be a private citizen sitting down to supper with a friend. The two brothers made a good team, one welcoming the illustrious visitor to New England, the other prepared to do the same in Philadelphia, and among a vibrant French community. The State House on Chestnut Street, once the nation's capital, was extensively refurbished and renamed the Hall of Independence in Lafayette's honor. He received guests there during his stay, and the new designation remained, becoming today's Independence Hall.

Understanding Monroe's shrewdness vis-à-vis the political climate, it's entirely possible that Lafayette's visit was orchestrated and that instead of being a spontaneous show of affection and gratitude for past deeds of heroism, the tour was scheduled to coincide with the election of 1824. The dates lend credence to the theory. The election was slated for October 29, and Lafayette's long association with Biddle suggests that Monroe may have been pulling strings to shore up his Secretary of State's campaign. Although Monroe's presumptive heir (Monroe, Madison, and Jefferson had each served in the role before becoming President), Adams faced a strong rival in Andrew Jackson. To his advantage, his official capacity permitted him to accompany "the nation's guest," thereby gaining luster from proximity to a man universally beloved.

The 1824 election was a milestone in the nation's history. It was a choice between the class of men who had always governed and a new type of American leader, the lettered establishment versus the boisterous pioneer. On one side were Adams, William Crawford, and Henry Clay, all career politicians, learned, adept at oratory and the diplomacy necessary for navigating the capital's factionalism. On the other was the charismatic, war-hero Andrew Jackson, champion of the self-made man, and as fond of his unbridled tongue and quick temper as were his followers. The four were members of the Democrat-Republican Party, making the election more a popularity contest than an ideological one. Monroe had straddled the disparate worlds of military and civil service; his own national tour in 1817 had reminded the populace of his Revolutionary War experiences while reassuring them of his rightful place within an impeccable lineage of chief magistrates.

Jackson and his adherents wanted no part of a deferential transference of power. After the hotly contested election, Thomas Jefferson told Daniel Webster that he considered the candidate "dangerous." The occasion for the critique was during Webster's visit to Monticello. Although the conversation's details remained unpublished until 1857, Jefferson's antipathy toward the candidate contrasted markedly with an otherwise philosophical demeanor.

> I feel very much alarmed at the prospect of seeing General Jackson become President. He is one of the most unfit men I know of for such a place. He has very little respect for laws or constitutions. His passions are terrible. When I was President of the Senate he was a Senator; and he could never speak on account of the rashness of his feelings. I have seen him attempt it repeatedly, and as often choke with rage. His passions are no doubt cooler now; he has been much tried since I knew him, but he is a dangerous man.[22]

Adams had an impeccable record—and lest anyone in 1824 forget—was the son of a former President, a former U.S. senator from Massachusetts, and the minister to Great Britain, the Netherlands, Prussia, and Russia. However, his famously bookish tendencies and a proclivity toward formality and reserve made it difficult for him to compete on the same emotional level as the raw-boned hero of the Battle of New Orleans. William Crawford and Henry Clay faced similar obstacles. Crawford, from Georgia, a one-time Secretary of War and present Secretary of the Treasury, had also served as minister to France. Henry Clay, a Kentuckian, who was instrumental in brokering the Missouri Compromise as Speaker of the House, was a southerner like Jackson. Neither Clay nor Crawford had been military men. They represented the status quo while Jackson contrived to mold himself into an outsider despite being a United States senator, offering a bold, new vision: decisiveness rather than concessions, virility instead of palaver. Lafayette, although a candidate for nothing except public goodwill, possessed an aura that went Jackson one better; he had been a confidante and fellow soldier to America's most enshrined hero, George Washington. His history gave him a mythic stature. His visit may not have provided an endorsement for Adams—or Jackson—but it did illuminate core differences between the candidates, as well as hearkening back to nobler times.

On September 5, Biddle wrote Lafayette, who was then in New York, assuring him of the "gratification which it will afford me to see you in Philadelphia" and adding that the tour was "an occasion calculated to awaken the best feelings of our nation."[23] "Calculated" is a strong word, and Biddle never used language lightly or sloppily. Did he mean Lafayette had a role to play that was greater than that of a figurehead?

If Adams, Crawford, and Clay failed to inspire public ardor, Jackson, whose campaign in Florida had been besmirched with accusations of misconduct and even murder, presented a troubling idol. However, his supporters embraced his faults, divining a redeeming grace in his flawed but genuinely human character. While praising him as a born leader, they also hailed him as a man of the people. His detractors, though, saw only arrogance and implacability. In May 1824, Tennessee Senator John Henry Eaton published a biography, *The Life of General Jackson*, in which he extolled the general's war record, his valorous battle against the Creek Nation, and the conflicts in the South that had terminated in the decisive defeat of the British in New Orleans. Accompanying the book was an "elegant likeness" of Jackson.[24] Jackson's supporters were encouraged to purchase the book post haste, as supplies of the finer editions were certain to sell out.

Timing was everything. By early August, plans for Lafayette's imminent arrival had eclipsed Eaton's literary efforts and appeared to have squelched Jackson's candidacy, too.

* * *

The Jacksonians persevered. When results of the October 29 election started slowly coming in from Pennsylvania's western counties, readers perusing *Poulson's* daily newspaper must have wondered if Philadelphia shared any traits in common with the hinterlands. As of November 5, Jackson had received 780 votes in Cumberland County and 536 in Lebanon County; Adams was awarded 180 and a mere 2, respectively. On November 9, Jackson's numbers continued to rise: Columbia County – 507 versus 8; Lehigh County – 753 versus 5; Allegheny County – 386 versus 19. The next day, Adams received his cruelest blow; Beaver County awarded him no votes; Jackson got 465. The ballots from

Ohio came on November 24. Clay received 17,290 votes, Jackson, 16,735, and Adams only 12,112.

Reading those numbers, Biddle must have recalled the stunning defeat the central bank had encountered in 1811. Here was the same ideological and cultural rift opening again. From his cosmopolitan sanctuary, he could only hope that rational deliberation would prevail.

- CHAPTER TEN -

A LIFE'S WORK

Andrew Jackson won the popular vote, defeating Adams by a handy margin. Crawford and Clay limped in in third and fourth place, respectively. However, Jackson failed to win the majority of the electoral votes, which threw the contest into a tailspin of suspicion, name-calling, and intolerance. Adams was labeled a "Tory;" Crawford, a "giant intriguer;" and Jackson, a "murderer."[1] Even the press was attacked for trading in "falsehood" and "truth according to the object in view."[2] Because this was the first time in the nation's history that the popular vote had been reported, Jackson's supporters felt justifiable anger that their individual ballots were being discounted. They expected him to take his rightful place as President, not wait for the House of Representatives to decide who would govern the country, as was mandated by the terms of the Twelfth Amendment.

For them, the situation looked rigged, especially considering Jackson's numbers: 151,271 popular votes, and 99 electoral votes as opposed to Adams, who won 113,122 popular, and 84 electoral votes. Crawford received 41 electoral votes, and Clay 37. A majority of 131 was necessary for victory. Like Pennsylvania, the populace was divided between rural and urban areas and between southern, northern, and western interests, each had coalesced into an almost inflexible ideology. Philadelphia and Philadelphia County, supposedly bastions of satisfied laborers with cosmopolitan tastes, voted for Jackson by a sizeable margin, which shocked the city's governing classes.

However, the Depression of 1816-1823 still rankled among those who felt ignored by their elected officials. So did the machinations surrounding the Missouri Compromise, which further widened the gulf between the slave and free states. Jackson appealed to the disenfranchised in the deep South, the

West, and parts of the mid-Atlantic. Anxious for change and disgusted by what they conceived as a political aristocracy who disregarded their needs, they gave him Louisiana, Mississippi, Alabama, Tennessee, North and South Carolina, Indiana, Illinois, Pennsylvania, New Jersey, Delaware, and Maryland. Clay also made a strong showing in the West, winning Missouri, Kentucky, and Ohio. Adams's base was solidly New England, winning critical electoral votes in those geographically small but populous states, even though it was reported that voters in Connecticut "confidant in the success of the Adams ticket were careless about attending the polls."[3] Crawford took Georgia and Virginia.

The Twelfth Amendment gave the House of Representatives the right to decide between three of the strongest candidates. As fourth in the race, Clay was disqualified, but he remained in a powerful position as Speaker of the House. Having made no secret of his dislike of Jackson as a person and potential chief magistrate (Clay derided him as a mere "military chieftain"), he used his seasoned abilities of persuasion to garner support for Adams. On February 9, 1825, two months after the election results had been published, Adams won the House's election on the first ballot, taking 13 states: Louisiana, Missouri, Illinois, Kentucky, Ohio, Maryland, and all New England. Jackson maintained his hold on Pennsylvania, which had 25 electoral votes, the most of any state, and New Jersey, Indiana, South Carolina, Tennessee, Mississippi, and Alabama. Crawford came in a distant third.

Throughout the nation, the politicking before the House vote was fraught with incivility if not outright slander. In Boston, a broadside extolled Adams as the candidate "most experienced, best qualified and in every respect most worthy" compared to Jackson, who was portrayed as evil incarnate "a man who has disobeyed the divine command do thou no murder."[4]

The Jacksonians castigated Adams by insisting he had laid bogus claims to his participation in the nation's fight for freedom because he "never raised a sword to achieve that Independence."[5] They repudiated his scholasticism with its aura of elitism and insisted that Thomas Jefferson had lost confidence in Adams, recalling him from Prussia despite his ministerial posts. "This is a strong proof of his being unworthy of *his* confidence and that of the nation."[6] If those arguments weren't convincing enough, Adams's father's presidency was maligned as a time when "corruption began to rear its head." Jackson, meanwhile, was portrayed as a "magnanimous and generous soul" and "unparalleled hero," who, during the Indian wars, had urged his soldiers to "put your trust in God, and confide in me."[7] The writer of that broadside awarded Jackson additional saintly qualities, saying that during the latest war with England when Baltimore came under attack, "he was made the instrument by Heaven to check and punish that reptile and barbarous foe." God's support was obviously up for grabs.

On February 8, one day before the House vote, Thomas Hart Benton, the sharp-tongued senator from Missouri, rebuked a colleague who threatened to cast his ballot for Adams, warning him that the "vote is not your own. It belongs to the people of the state of Missouri. They are against Mr. Adams." Winding up for the punch, Benton declared, "Tomorrow is the day of your self-immolation. If you have an enemy, he may go and feed his eyes upon the scene, your former friend will shun the afflicting spectacle."[8]

Political cartoonists had a field day. David Claypoole Johnson's "A footrace" depicted the candidates in ungainly attitudes as they fought to outmaneuver each other while the crowd cheered on their favorites and jeered the opposition. A fat purse sat on "the Presidential chair."[9]

"Caucus curs in full yelp" by James Akin was nastier. Jackson, dressed in full uniform, held a sword emblazoned with Julius Caesar's famed "Veni, Vidi, Vici" as he stood, valiant and huge, among a pack of snarling, mangy dogs. Each mongrel bore the name of a newspaper hostile to the candidate. Financial bribes were bandied back and forth, as did a bribe of rum for an Indian who begged, "Rum for de baby." A naked black boy rode and whipped a cringing dog named "Richmond Whig," scoffing at his mount as a "jew."[10]

Poor Adams, in his inaugural address on March 4, 1825, admitted that "the peculiar circumstances of the recent election" had rendered him "less possessed of your confidence, in advance, that any one of my predecessors" adding, "I am deeply conscious that I shall stand, more and oftener, in need of your indulgence."[11] After the ceremony, Jackson was one of the first to shake the new President's hand. But when Adams named Clay as his secretary of state on March 7, Jackson's ire could not be contained. He and his supporters considered the appointment treacherous and conniving, a back-room deal whereby Adams, in return for Clay's electoral votes, granted him power in the present administration as well as a probable future presidency. The Jacksonians likened "the friends of Clay" to "the Swiss" who "fight for those who pay best."[12] It was rumored that Clay's supporters had also approached "the friends of Jackson," promising, "they would close with them" if offered "the same price."[13]

No wonder Jackson felt abused. Having positioned himself as an outsider to Washington's intrigues and infighting, he had been cut out altogether.

Throughout the nation, his supporters experienced their own sense of abasement at the maneuverings of the "unholy coalition."[14] They admired Jackson for being like them: plainspoken, unequivocal, wary of chicanery, and belligerent when aggression was needed. Not for them, drawing rooms and dancing masters, or ambiguous language couched in courteous phrases. That behavior smacked of the Old World nobility, and the Jacksonians would have none of it. They felt as cheated by their hero's loss as "Old Hickory" did. Although he appeared to take the high ground with Adams, he reviled Clay with his "selfish motives" and "secret conclaves."[15] Comparing his own patriotism, "I contributed my mite to shake off the yoke of tyranny, and to build the fabric of free government," Jackson cast a military man's ultimate scorn on Clay, whom he declared, "has never yet risked himself for his country."[16]

The sparring continued well into the spring with Clay impugning Jackson's intelligence "General Jackson fights better than he reasons" and asserting he had never engaged in cabals. Private letters became fodder for the press, but the authenticity of the remarks drew skepticism. A private (and published) letter, supposedly written by Jackson, claimed he had never wished to run because he felt unqualified, proved to be planted by the opposition. In state after state, mistrust escalated as supporters of "the hero of New Orleans" challenged the election's legitimacy. "It is not Jackson that has been defeated or Tennessee that has been overlooked—It is the sovereign will of the people. . . . The political assassin has stabbed at the vitals of the constitution, and the life's blood of the blood of the republic flows through the wound."[17]

Thus was born the "Corrupt Bargain," which term stuck to Adams's presidency for the ensuing four years.

* * *

Andrew Jackson was an idol for a new America. Tall, slender to the point of gauntness, his carriage ramrod straight, and blue eyes that could blaze with rage or patriotic zeal, he inspired fierce admiration among those who revered him. With scant formal education and a flair for ignoring all spelling, syntax, and grammar rules, he made it clear that courage under fire was more valuable than erudition and that candor eclipsed pretty phrases. His father, Andrew, and mother, Elizabeth, with two young sons, Hugh and Robert, had emigrated from Northern Ireland in 1765. Andrew, named for his father, was March 15, 1767, mere weeks after the elder Jackson's death. Even in America, the family remained Scots-Irish to the core, carrying with them into the sparsely populated

Waxhaw region of western North Carolina a tendency toward clannishness, and the knowledge that since time immemorial, the English had been enemy and oppressor. William Wallace, dead for more than four hundred years, was a hero, god, and martyr to the cause of freedom.

Young Andrew, whose widowed mother found a home and work with wealthier relations, loathed living off their largesse. His sense of honor was easily damaged; combativeness and a reckless disregard for society's strictures became his defenses. He was a bully, swore as fiercely as any adult, and learned that his explosive rage could be a useful tool—a means to achieving respect and approbation. Within his querulous nature, he also evinced manifestations of leadership. Even at his most bellicose, he found admirers and followers. He was only thirteen when Charleston fell to the British on May 12, 1780. He lost his eldest brother, Hugh, to the war soon after. When the British savaged the Waxhaw region, he and his brother, Robert, joined the fight. After being taken prisoner, his insubordination earned him a lashing with a sword, which scar he carried for the rest of his life. He survived smallpox, though Robert did not. Orphaned as a young teen, he found his way to Charleston, where he became a rakehell, squandering a small inheritance with gambling and hard living that garnered the esteem of other young bucks who had survived the war. While they lauded his cock of the walk attitude, the respectable citizens and their equally respectable daughters snubbed the offensive young man with his intemperate ways. Because he secretly yearned to be considered a gentleman himself, he felt doubly pained by the rebuffs, although, of course, he was the cause of his undoing. Jackson never forgot personal sleights.

He studied law, began practicing, grew bored, then moved west, eventually settling in Nashville in 1788, which was then little more than a town. Local tribal peoples hated the interloping whites—and with good cause. The settlers' other enemy was Spain; the nation controlled commerce on the Mississippi and inspired the tribes in their battles against the advancing Americans. Jackson learned to abhor Spain as much as he did the indigenous peoples. He took lodgings with the Widow Donelson, whose married daughter, Rachel Robards, became the love of his life. The controversial and contested dates of her divorce and remarriage to Jackson would have sent the couple spiraling out of polite society in Charleston. However, they lived on the frontier, where unconventionality was praiseworthy.

When Tennessee became a state, Jackson, then twenty-nine, became its first congressman, traveling to Philadelphia in the fall of 1796, where he soon achieved notoriety for repudiating the nation's exemplar of gallantry and states-manship, George Washington. Jackson voted against a tribute to Washington, citing the recent Jay Treaty with Great Britain (The Treaty of Amity, Commerce, and Navigation, Between His Britannic Majesty and the United States of America), which fostered trade with Great Britain, as well as Washington's seeming indifference to the Indian massacres in the frontier regions. The unpopular stance drew ire, but Jackson was his own man.

In 1797, he returned to the capital, this time as a senator, but found the place and his fellow legislators as incompatible as before. Nothing in his background prepared him for Philadelphia's studied refinements, nor did he want to adapt. He was also in debt, and Philadelphia, home to the Bank of the United States, must have felt like salt rubbed in a wound. Jefferson, who served as John Adams's vice president, would later recall the novice senator's inchoate rages.

Ill-suited though Jackson was for the strictures of late eighteenth-century etiquette, he was wholly at home within a military environment. Victories over the Creeks at Tallushatchee, Talladega, and Horseshoe Bend in 1812, aided by the Cherokees fighting alongside him, cemented a reputation for daring, ruthlessness, and perseverance. Despite a penchant for lethal duels, his prowess as a soldier grew. His leadership and decisions as a general could be problematic, as revealed in Pensacola, but notoriety brought fame. In 1815, after the long, depressing war, Jackson's crushing defeat of the British at New Orleans enshrined him in the popular imagination. Those who supported him in the election of 1824 embraced his unorthodoxy, seeing heroism that had its origin in the stony soil of the frontier. His successes were not derived from family connections or ancestral privilege or the halls of academe. He had made his own destiny. For his adherents, he became a singular model for American virtue.

As the year 1825 drew to a close, rage over Jackson's shabby treatment escalated rather than dissipated. Everywhere he traveled, throngs of impassioned Jacksonians rushed to greet him, making speeches in which his valor became the stuff of legend. "At a period when the American military character was depressed and sunk by the misfortunes of our arms, you called into action the patriotism of your neighbors and friends."[18] A recurring theme was his compassion for his troops. "They have seen you distributing your last morsel of bread to your famished soldiers."[19] It was natural that the man who had been the "choice of a majority of the people"[20] and "the great, the fearless and incorruptible soldier and politician"[21] should find himself nominated by the upper and lower Tennessee houses to run for President in 1828.

On November 5, 1825, he accepted the nomination, telling his supporters that "The world cannot remain at peace. Human nature is restless—and man as he ever has been, is ambitious."[22] The words and their underlying sentiment impressed. Those who listened were also restless, ambitious men, who understood that no matter how much the politicians in Washington could prattle on about amity and accord, peace on the nation's frontiers and peace between the laboring and ruling classes were nonexistent. When Jackson continued, warning his audience about "intrigue, ambition, cunning" and saying that "the mere form and ceremony in the guidance of our affairs can avail but little,"[23] the message needed no decoding. For the Jacksonians, the tenure of John Quincy Adams was as good as over.

* * *

Perhaps as a respite from partisan politics, or because he needed an outlet in which to express his dismay at finding himself, his family, friends, and acquaintances derided as an old-fashioned, foppish haut monde, Biddle commenced writing a novel soon after the 1824 Adams/Jackson contest concluded. Attempting a bantering air a la Jane Austen, he never completed the work, which was just as well. Any Jacksonian who considered reading it would have deemed it a trifling and inconsequential thing. Even the author's friends might have agreed.

> I had a cold last winter which kept me at home in the evenings. So I determined to write a novel. The cold left me and I incline to suspect has gone into the novel. But the fact is that there are many useful truths which our countrymen ought to hear—and as they would not listen to them in the form of a grave rebuke[,] the attempt to treat lightly topics of a really serious interest may not be wholly unavailing. We shall see.[24]

Biddle's opinions regarding the entitlements of the elite versus the moral obligation of honest labor turned the piece into a disquisition during which "Julia" (a stand-in for Jane) organized a formal entertainment for one hundred friends, and ridiculed "the follies which we have inherited from England:"[25] inclusion or exclusion from the guest list by dint of social connection. Completing the family portrait, "the Colonel" was Major Thomas Biddle, "the Commodore," James. Nicholas appeared as the nameless husband. As if the moral of the tale—that of coequality—might be more palatable when presented by a woman, Nicholas gave Julia the lion's share of the dialogue.

> Distinctions in society you must have because wealth, beauty, noto-
> riety, family connexions create them—different circles in society you
> must have because no individual can be acquainted with everybody &
> our assemblies must conform to our houses. But it is against the absurd
> pretension of being the first society—against the exclusion from your
> circle of acquaintance of persons fitted to adorn it because the pursuits
> of their fathers & brothers is not what is absurdly called genteel, it is
> against this that I must protest.[26]

Although he believed himself to be an egalitarian, Biddle was unable to escape his heredity. It's tempting to imagine him meeting Jackson on Chestnut Street in front of the capitol in 1797: the precocious boy already devoted to a life of the mind and the tough frontiersman who had experienced enough turmoil to last several lives. How could they not have regarded each other with perplexity and even condemnation?

Biddle's faith in his egalitarianism also slammed hard into the reality of rampant poverty in Philadelphia. Accustomed to dine with the city's wealthiest individuals in homes that bespoke luxury and exclusivity, he also witnessed large numbers of poor Blacks and Whites attempting to eke out meager livings. Because of the metropolis's increasing congestion, which was exacerbated by the migration of free Blacks from the South, and unskilled Irish laborers, the down-trodden's presence became inescapable within every section of the city. Racism increased when Whites competed with Blacks for the same ill-paying jobs.

Authors of fiction in the style known as Philadelphia Gothic, Charles Brockden Brown and Rebecca Rush—and later Robert Montgomery Bird and George Lippard—depicted the city as a cesspit of crime, disease, and vice instigated by poverty; in their works, the rich were perpetually venal, the downtrodden mercilessly brutalized. The odious term "worthy poor" separated those whom society deemed responsible from the "unworthy poor" who were reviled as profligate, felonious, and drunkards, to boot. Those worthless paupers were dispatched to the Bettering House (Spruce to Pine and 10th to 11th Streets), where they endured punishments intended to cure their intemperate ways and religious instruction to heal their wayward souls. Biddle lived at 8th and Spruce. Although a wall and wrought iron gates enclosed the Bettering House, as if it were a garden instead of a place of incarceration, passersby could easily see its residents.

There were rays of hope in this misery: wealthy black entrepreneurs like James Forten, the sail maker, and caterer Robert Bogle, who worked out of his residence on Eighth and Sansom Streets, three blocks from Nicholas and Jane's home. Bogle was ubiquitous on the social scene, providing food and drink from every type of gathering from balls to christenings and funerals, and, naturally, the Biddles' numerous entertainments. In his humorous "Ode to Bogle," Nicholas called the man a "Lover of pomps!

> Before his stride the town gives way;
> Beggars and Belles confess his sway;
> Drays, prudes, and sweeps, a startled mass,
> Rein up to let his cortege pass.[27]

Biddle's paean notwithstanding, it's hard to tell how affected emotionally he was by the plight of those of different races and classes, or whether his financial insulation and predilection toward optimism blinded him.

* * *

Jackson's candidacy encouraged the cultural and racial divide already inherent in America. Within polarized political affiliations lay a festering stew of bigotry and prejudice masquerading as justification or even morality, the polarization often abetted for personal or corporate economic gain. In 1822, a freed African American, Denmark Vesey, had allegedly conspired to create a slave uprising in South Carolina with the intention of capturing Charleston and terminating the institution of slavery. He, his son, and other co-conspirators were executed in July 1822, but their deaths failed to assuage White fears that other Blacks were poised to rebel. On December 20, 1824, the South Carolina state legislature passed an act that made it legal to seize and incarcerate free African Americans entering the state; they were then sold as slaves. If freed men came into a port while laboring on a merchant vessel, the owners were obliged to pay a fine, as well as fees accrued for the detention of their sailors. That done, the men were released to their employers. If the employers chose not to pay, the men were sold. Free women were also placed into bondage.

Draconian measures extended beyond slavery. Broken treaties with the tribal peoples became commonplace. On February 5, *Niles' Weekly Register*:

The Past—The Present—For the Future published a comprehensive list of tribes "now remaining within the limits of several states and territories, and the quantity of land claimed by them respectively."[28] The tally was an invitation to reevaluate tribal allotments, which the government had begun already. In his farewell message to Congress on December 7, 1824, Monroe had told the members:

> The condition of the aborigines within our limits, and especially those who are within the limits of any of the states, merits likewise particular attention. Experience has shown, that unless the tribes be civilized, they can never be incorporated into our system in any form whatsoever.[29]

The "removal of the Indians,"[30] thereby "extinguishing their title to the lands occupied by them,"[31] delineated a new white supremacy strategy. In a prelude to the "Trail of Tears" in 1837, the Creeks were forced to cede all land in Georgia in 1825 and relocate west of the Mississippi "for the better protection and security of said tribes, and for their improvement in civilization."[32] Gone were the days when Madison, as President, had assured tribal deputies visiting him in Washington City that "The red people who live in the same great island with the white people of the eighteen fires, are made by the same Great Spirit out of the same earth . . . differing in color, only."[33]

As if the election had not created enough discord and disunity, the panic of 1825 further exacerbated class divisions, pitting the Jacksonians with their historical aversion to a central bank against the establishment. One of the causes for the alarm, which started in London, was a scheme that involved brazen deceit, a swindle so inventive that even the most jaded British baronet found himself fleeced. In 1822, a Scottish adventurer and charlatan by the name of Gregor MacGregor, who had fought on the side of Venezuela during its war of independence from Spain, charmed wealthy London with his tales of heroism and a righteous battle against oppressive and venal Spanish rule. He became immensely popular in the peerage drawing rooms, persuading enrapt audiences that a new Central American nation of Poyais desperately needed their help to develop an infrastructure and exploit its natural resources.

MacGregor promised enormous returns on the investments and could point to the bona fide mining firm, Anglo Mexican, whose shares had increased in value from £33 to £158 in a single month. Poyais was nonexistent, but no one questioned the validity of MacGregor's claims. If they did, he could show them a newly published book about the nation, *Sketch of the Mosquito Shore, including the Territory of Poyais,* written by an equally fictitious Captain Thomas Strangeways, Captain 1st Native Poyer Regiment. The tome was dedicated to MacGregor, who styled himself as the Cacique (Prince) of Poyais. Strangeways signed himself as "His Highness's Most Devoted and Most Humble Servant." Printed in Edinburgh, the book bore a likeness of MacGregor wearing military garb. He looked like an actor dressed in stage-gilded epaulets and medals to play a plum role.

For three-hundred-eighty-nine pages, the glories of Poyais were extolled, a land of untapped wealth that already had the beginnings of government, commerce, and a tidy town (in fact, several squalid huts amid dense jungle and noxious swamp). MacGregor knighted himself so that he could be addressed Prince and Sir; he insisted the former "king" of Poyais had elevated his status before granting him ownership of the country. To maintain the fiction, Spanish names like the mountains, Sierras de la Cruz, were rechristened "Poyer Hill."[34] "The great salubrity of the air of this delightful and most valuable country supplies a constant fund of health and activity to the European settler, a blessing which is seldom enjoyed in the same degree in any other part of either North or South America."[35] Gold, silver, lapis calaminaris, mahogany, cedar (with cheap labor to harvest the valuable trees) were there for the taking, as were acre upon acre of arable land in which to grow profitable cotton and tobacco crops; happy natives were supposedly eager for employment. The book included charts indicating how a "clear profit"[36] could be had, lest an earl or viscount was slow on the uptake.

The more detailed and outrageous his claims for the mythical country's topography, the more eager his dupes became, permitting MacGregor to float a large bond issue on the London Stock Exchange. Those without the financial wherewithal to invest were advised to emigrate. He created a currency (with an impressive emblem), sold land, ranks in a bogus military, and positions working for his fake government. Two hundred forty settlers sailed for the phony Principality; sixty survived. When those who opted to return to London arrived home, the scheme fell apart. MacGregor fled to France, where he was arrested on December 7, 1825.

MacGregor's scam might not have been the genesis of the Panic of 1825, but it served as a famous example of unchecked greed and authority gone to the dogs. Centered in London, which had succeeded Amsterdam as Europe's financial capital, it involved a bond and stock market crash in April. The prior year, credit had been cheap, and speculation soared, especially in commodities of the emergent Latin American nations. The price of Brazilian and American cotton nearly doubled by May 1825. Fighting this threat to their livelihoods, the spinners and loom owners in Manchester, England, refused to buy the raw material at grossly inflated new prices, causing importers to dump their goods at a loss and default on loans. In addition, the value of all bonds in Latin America plummeted (not only the bogus Poyais shares), increasing banks' debts and resulting in runs on British banks in December when it was discovered that there wasn't enough cash to go around. One hundred four banks failed, their liabilities more than nineteen million pounds. Latin American joint-stock companies, English railroads, and companies dependent upon them foundered, and individuals faced sudden bankruptcy.

Biddle watched from afar as the Bank of England attempted but failed to rectify the situation. He feared "wild and exaggerated speculation"[37] would erupt in America, too. An unnamed and terrified director in Philadelphia went so far as to advise publicly "suspending specie payment."[38] Instead, Biddle chose caution and a soothing touch, quietly substituting paper for specie in New York, where foreign commercial trade had created the greatest pressure. Rather than decrease loans there, he increased them to $50,000, which had the effect of calming nervous investors who began to believe that Britain's travails might not cross the Atlantic, after all. Shrewdness and an appearance of confidence became Biddle's bywords. As he wrote to Isaac Lawrence, president of the branch bank in New York on April 22:

> In the midst of the speculations which are abroad, combined with
> the demand for specie, prudence requires that we should keep within
> reasonable limits, and that under all circumstances, and at all hazards
> the Bank should keep itself secure and strong. . . . In the present
> state of the office the true course I think is, to turn over as quietly as
> possible to the other Banks, any demand which you cannot supply—to
> let the diminutions of your discounts, and the public revenue as it
> accumulates turn the scale in your favor. . . .

He also cautioned against making "sudden or very rigid demands."[39]

However, the Poyais scandal exacerbated the fears of those wary of a central bank and the bankers they felt were no better than puppet masters pulling strings to deceive the gullible. *Poulson's*, though, sang Biddle's praise following a stockholders' meeting during which he gave an account of his leadership. "The luminous and masterly statement of the present flourishing condition of the affairs of the Bank, presented by the President, was received with feelings of the strongest and most universal satisfaction."[40] In November, Hezekiah Niles reported that "the alarm has subsided in New York" and "a spirit of accommodation is abroad, and confidence has increased." But on December 6, the branch in New Orleans fired Charles West, a cashier who had defaulted on a loan of $24,000 in addition to a theft of $20,000. Biddle had suspended him in October, pending an investigation into wrongdoing. Rumored to have speculated in cotton, West disappeared, justifying the naysayers' forebodings.

* * *

Biddle and the Bank of the United States weathered the storm. He prided himself for his perspicacity, although he had to keep those feelings private. Letting the public know that America had come close to following Britain's example would undercut trust and could easily precipitate another panic. Only well after the fact did he describe the Bank's stabilizing influence, writing in a memorandum:

> [it] accomplishes all the purposes of its creation. It furnishes a universal & equal circulating medium, it performs the domestic exchanges for the interior trade—the foreign exchange for the external trade. . . . It may be said without presumption, that for many years the country has enjoyed a system of currency & exchange such as no other nation possesses.[41]

Calling the Bank "the experiment," he added, "it cost several years of gradual development & the establishment of several new Branches to complete the circle of internal communications throughout the union."

Commerce, Biddle understood, was the nation's lifeblood; the central bank, as America's largest corporation (and one of the largest globally), was integral to economic stability. The free movement of goods from one part of the country to another created employment and steady livelihoods. Imports and exports brought wealth not only to port cities but inland where the products of the soil were harvested or natural resources utilized. He saw his legacy as promoting equality through the aegis of a central bank. By building symbiotic relationships among branch offices, cities in the North and South would gain mutual respect;

and investors in all parts of the country would embrace their interdependence no matter their family backgrounds or politics.

In 1828, he stated his philosophy thus:

> We believe the prosperity of the Bank & its usefulness to the country depend on its being entirely free from the control of the officers of the Govt, a control fatal to every Bank. In order to preserve that independence it must never connect itself with any administration—& never become a partizan of any set of politicians. In this respect I believe all the officers of the institution have been exemplary. The truth is that, with us, it is considered that we have no concern with politics. Dean Swift said . . . that money is neither Whig nor Tory, and we say with equal truth that the Bank is neither a Jackson nor an Adams man, it is only a bank.[42]

Of course, the institution was not "only a bank." It was anything but, and Biddle was at pains to make certain it acted the part of a powerful agency in which the federal and state governments and their citizens put their trust. The Second Bank enabled the seamless movement of money from one part of the nation to another. Also, it served as a repository for government funds from tariff receipts and the sale of federal lands. Additionally, the branch system helped regulate the flow of money, expanding or contracting supply as necessary to balance the demand for specie. If Biddle felt a state bank was engaging in risky behavior: making speculative loans or overissuing banknotes, the Bank of the United States could pull its notes and leave the vault of the offending institution empty.

The measure diminished his popularity with critics who accused him of being tyrannical, but it did produce the fiscal stability the nation needed. Biddle referred to his system as "mild and gentle" in a letter written in April 1826. No one agreed with that nurturing assessment, but they had to admit that his stated purposes of enlarging the portfolio of business paper, increasing dealings in domestic and foreign exchange, and retaining the bank's capital had succeeded. The bank was precisely what a central bank should have been. "The Bank of the United States," Biddle had written in 1826, "was established for the purpose of restoring the currency. It went into operation amidst a great number of institutions whose movements it was necessary to control and often to restrict, and it has succeeded in keeping in check many institutions which might otherwise have been tempted into extravagant and ruinous excesses."[43]

The sanguine tone belied ongoing difficulties: appointing trustworthy and knowledgeable branch officers and directors who weren't also borrowers. Because directors served only three-year terms, this made for a continuous search for qualified candidates. Additionally, Biddle relied upon branch cashiers whom he used as confidential agents, just as Monroe had first utilized his services. He instructed branch cashiers to report directly to the board in Philadelphia. Despite delays in communication with the farthest offices, Biddle kept up a steady correspondence with these men in the field, making certain the branches and their officers and directors followed his directives.

* * *

As Nicholas concentrated on what he understood was his life's work, Jane focused on her children and household. Home and hearth gave her more pleasure than dinners and balls, although she acquiesced to her husband's constant desire to be out and about in society because she knew how much pleasure it gave him. Among a large sphere of friends and acquaintances, he was universally admired. Jane recognized that public acclaim was as necessary to him as breathing. His vanity was also at stake; he liked wearing his hair long, with his chestnut-colored curls framing his patrician face. Jane, sweet and retiring in appearance and temperament, was his opposite. No longer did she feel inconsequential, though. She had come to realize that her life's work was to nurture: her children, of course, but her husband, too. Self-assured as he was, Nicholas required cosseting, which Jane, in her quiet way, undertook. It is doubtful he appreciated or even perceived the extent of her solicitude. The prodigy had never lost the need for adulation.

Another aspect of his nature was a childlike quality that she encouraged because it had echoes in her own guilelessness. In his dealings with his sons, he often seemed their peer rather than an exacting elder. As a father, Nicholas was determined not to model himself after Charles. A letter he wrote in 1824 to Edward, who was then nine and who was traveling through New England with his mother and five-year-old brother Charles, shows this playful proclivity.

> My dear Edward, I received your letter from New York, and your
> postscript from Albany, but nothing since. Why is this? Has the pencil
> I gave you worn out? You have seen so much by this time that I would
> think you had a great many things to tell me about New York &

Albany & Boston. . . . Write descriptions of them. When you become a man you will be very glad to see them yourself.

Biddle shared news from home, told Edward that all his friends were well, briefly described Lafayette's visit, and asked his son to "Kiss—mother—for me." The letter ended with words that must have made the older brother laugh, as well as do his share of gloating. "Tell your brother Charles I hope he looks people in the face like a gentleman, not like a toad, and talks to everybody."[44] It's easy to imagine that word "toad" being bandied about until Jane put her foot down and reminded her sons that they were supposed to be "gentlemen." It's also compelling to envision Nicholas egging them when they returned home. Despite the pressures of the office, he was a doting parent.

Margaret Craig Biddle was born on June 16, 1825. "Meta", the first girl in the family, quickly became her father's darling. When she was four, her father dedicated his "Ode to Bogle" to her "with permission and a piece of mint-stick." As usual, he chose rhyming couplets:

> Meta, thy riper years may know
> More of this world's fantastic show,
> In thy time, as in mine, shall be,
> Burials and poundcake, beaux and tea;
> Rooms shall be hot and ices cold,
> And flirts be both as 'twas of old.
> Love, too, and mint-stick shall be made,
> Some dearly bought, some lightly weighed. . . .[45]

* * *

Biddle's prominence as the nation's foremost banker entailed a good deal of travel, both to the nation's capital and to the branch offices, which created understandable tension at home. Jane may have indulged him, but she disliked being a grass widow, and Nicholas was continually at pains to soften her frustrations at his protracted absences. As the years went by, she increasingly politicked for his retirement from such a demanding position. But her husband had too much energy to remain still for long, and travel being as arduous and unreliable as it was, a visit to Washington, thence south to Branch offices in Virginia or North Carolina could consume a month or more. As a hands-on manager, Biddle felt it necessary not to merely dispatch directives but to inspect each office. He missed Jane, "I became homesick & am now on my way to embrace you,"[46] but understood that leadership required diligence. "I told you that circumstances might detain me from home for a month."[47]

When Adams became President, he and Biddle developed a friendship that superseded any professional affiliation between the nation's chief magistrate and its banker. Alike in their love of literature and the classics, they shared quotations from Cicero, as well as scholarly queries. It was clear they considered themselves intellectual brothers. Their relationship would deepen as time passed, and Adams was no longer President but Biddle's champion and advocate in the House of Representatives. Adams's wife, Louisa, welcomed Biddle on his frequent visits to Washington; they also developed a friendship. Where Adams sent Biddle orations in their original Greek and Latin, Louisa dashed off songs translated from French. Born in England, she was a cosmopolitan woman who had accompanied her husband on his various European missions. Her skills at diplomacy and her Continental élan had helped Adams win the presidency. Although her husband preferred acting with gravity and was prone to be ponderous, she was impulsive. Louisa understood how and when to flatter.

In October 1826, Biddle traveled with Adams to Boston to visit public schools and bestow medals on deserving scholars during a celebration at Faneuil Hall. John Adams had died July 4, and the President acknowledged the personal and public loss, making the event more subdued than usual. For Biddle, though, the journey provided an unanticipated boon: the opportunity to study changes in national transportation—an issue dear to Adams's heart and one he had spoken of during his inaugural when he proposed the Federal Government build a network of canals and roadways. Biddle had joined Mathew Carey on a committee to study the Commonwealth of Pennsylvania's internal improvements, which resulted in commissioning William Strickland in 1825 to visit Britain and write a report on "Canals, Railways, Roads and other Subjects."[48]

The published document listed subscribers ranging from the Military College at West Point (four copies) to the U.S. House of Representatives (twenty-five copies) to Duke Barnard of Saxe-Weimar, the governor of Louisiana (four copies), the College of South Carolina (two copies) the War Department (three copies). Strickland wrote, "The superiority of England in her public works, is principally attributable to her unlimited command of pecuniary means."[49] As a civil engineer and architect, his study was exhaustive as he traversed England and Scotland, then sailed to Dublin in July 1825 to examine the breakwater and harbor. The locks of Prince's Dock in Liverpool, he declared, "much superior" as they were built of stone blocks measuring 6-8' in length, with a width of 4' and height of 2'. The stone had been quarried eighteen miles from the site. Strickland inspected aqueducts, embankments, tunnels, turnpike roads, iron and steel manufacturing, collieries, blast furnaces, cast-iron boilers, and quarry cranes and pipes for conducting gas to supply gas lighting. His report included costs for labor, materials, and maintenance. The plates accompanying the text revealed modernity in all its wonders, especially George Stephenson's locomotive engine "Locomotion," which "when lightly loaded travels 10 miles an hour, and does the work of 16 horses in 12 hours." Nothing rivaling it could be found in the United States. The Society members were agog.

Biddle believed that improved transportation throughout the nation would end political and geographical divisions. The Chesapeake and Delaware Canal opening on October 19, 1829, allowed him to give voice to that opinion. One of the most expensive canals to date, it had required thousands of laborers working by hand and years of toil and redesign and altered routing to link the Chesapeake and Delaware Bays. Fourteen miles long with four locks, it permitted schooners and sloops to navigate its waters carrying grain, coal, lumber, and iron. Mule and horse teams paced the canal's banks pulling barges for passengers and freight. Sixty-six feet wide at the waterline, the canal flowed like a broad and mighty stream as it reached the Elk River and Back Branch, where they emptied into the Chesapeake Bay. In his official speech at the canal's opening, Biddle called it "the triumph of genius over nature; the triumph of resolute industry over obstacles deemed insuperable."[50]

Standing beside waters that reflected the burnished blue of an autumnal sky, his excitement mounting with each word, he said:

> This work, therefore, while it benefits Philadelphia, will be useful to Baltimore and to Norfolk and ultimately to New York. In truth, every mile of the railroad westward, every section of a canal in the remotest part of the Union, is serviceable to all the American cities. They add to the movement and the mass of the nation's wealth and industry; they can develop its resources; and the share of these advantages which each can obtain is a fit subject of generous competition not of querulous rivalry. [It is] the great channel for the movements of free men and the diffusion of free institutions. . . .

> While men are insulated at remote distances, their views are readily
> misconstrued, their interests misunderstood, and difference of opinion,
> at first easily explicable, ripen into causes for deep hostility. It is thus
> that national prejudices spring up for want of knowledge, and become
> hereditary for want of intercourse. . . . All these disappear when men
> come to approach and understand each other.

He believed that an enhanced, enlightened patriotism would result.

* * *

Biddle's speech took place in the aftermath of the election of 1828 in which
John Quincy Adams had been unceremoniously ousted, and Andrew Jackson
welcomed into the national bosom as an agent of change and hope. Eight
months after the inauguration, old-guard Washington remained anxious, as did
America's established business interests, but Biddle believed partisan enmity
could and would be overcome. He had learned of Jackson's amicable intentions
in two communications from the new President's trusted advisor, William B.
Lewis, in November 1829. During the War of 1812 and the Indian Wars, Lewis
had served with Jackson, giving him a long history as confidante and counselor.
"Say to Mr Biddle the Prs much gratified with the report I have made him upon
the subject of the Bank, all things with regard to it will be well." Two days later,
the news seemed even brighter.

> If you see Mr-Biddle say to him the President would be glad to see his
> proposition for sinking or paying off the three per cent Stock. He had
> better write to me when his leisure will permit & I will submit it to the
> General. I think he will find the *old fellow* will do justice to the Bank
> in his message for the handsome manner in which it assisted the Gov^t
> in paying the last instalment [*sic*] of the national debt.[51]

CHAPTER ELEVEN

ANDREW JACKSON BECOMES PRESIDENT

The "old fellow," as William Lewis referred to the new President, hardly considered himself old, although ancient war and dueling wounds kept him in nearly constant pain. Nor was he as malleable as Lewis suggested, especially when it concerned financial matters and "ragg money," which was Jackson's derogatory term for paper currency—a thing he considered as untrustworthy as banking itself. Yes, he had surrounded himself with clever men like Martin Van Buren, but his nature remained as implacable and independent as ever. Ever on the lookout for treachery, there was no changing his opinion if he suspected someone was his enemy.

Preparations for the election 1828 had begun almost immediately following the election of 1824 when Jackson and his supporters swore they would never be cheated out of the presidency again. After resigning his office as Tennessee's senator and allying himself with South Carolina's John Calhoun, a pro-slavery man and Adams's vice president, Jackson began a tactical attack on Congress and the Administration. Promising to rebuild the federal government, cleanse it from presumed corruption and inefficiency, and make it representative of the people it served rather than a greedy aristocracy, his watchwords became reform and liberty. The fight turned into a moral battle: the good, hard-working folk taking on the venal powers that had ruled America for far too long, as exemplified in one man whom they felt had all but inherited the presidency, as well as the candidate for Vice President, Richard Rush, Secretary of the Treasury, Philadelphia blue-blood and son of Benjamin Rush, one of the signers of the Declaration of Independence. The two were the antithesis of self-made men. Even Adams's proposal for internal improvements came under fire. Who would benefit from constructing new roads and railways and canals if not the nation's wealthy commercial interests—and their bankers? Shouldn't each state be permitted to decide if and where it wanted to build?

On July 4, 1828, Adams broke ground for the new Chesapeake and Ohio Canal. It was an august occasion, replete with a sumptuous repast, and elegant speeches; the President was accompanied by the Secretaries for War and Treasury, Members of Congress, the Commander of the Army, foreign ministers representing Great Britain, Russia, the Netherlands, Sweden, Brazil and France, and two surviving officers who had served in the War of Independence. Adams's speech was typically intellectual, although he tempered it with an appeal to the common man. He referred to the ancient civilizations of Assyria, Persia, Greece, and Rome, saying they were "empires of conquest, dominions of man over man" as opposed to America, an "empire of learning and the arts, the dominion of man over himself," then added, "Let us not forget that the spirit of Internal Improvement is catholic and liberal. We hope and believe that its practical advantages will be extended to every individual in our Union."[1] Those earnest sentiments were well and good, but when it came time for Adams to put his spade into the earth, it hit a tree root, and he was forced to pull off his jacket and toil in the heat to fork out a handful of dirt. The effort elicited cheers, but his huddled figure invited comparisons to Jackson's more authoritative mien.

Targeting newspaper editors friendly to the general's cause, the new Democratic Party started a strategic campaign. Van Buren, believing that a two-party system (instead of the former coalition Democratic-Republican Party that had elected Adams) would be the nation's salvation, built an alliance of influential editors from New York (his home state) to Virginia. Born in 1782 near Albany in Kinderhook, his parents kept a tavern, which kept him busy attending to customers during his youth. Van Buren had little formal education, which made his subsequent embrace of the Jacksonian democratic ideal seem like a foregone conclusion. Later known as the Little Magician due to his relatively small size and an ability to conjure political advantages from potential fiascos, Van Buren, as a senator from New York, had sided with Adams during the 1824 election before switching his allegiance to the man who won the popular vote.

The Jacksonians organized public fetes and parades to celebrate their candidate's heroism and formed local Hickory Clubs to spread the word of his prowess and self-sacrifice. Hurra Boys distributed hickory canes and brooms (presumably to sweep clean the Administration's house) and planted hickory trees in town squares. Printed and verbal propaganda depicted the fight between

Jackson and Adams as akin to a holy war: Liberty, unfettered and brave, scaling the corrupt walls of Power and Patronage. It was the old argument between a Republican (Jeffersonian) and a Federalist (Hamiltonian) ideal remade into a battle between honest labor and the rapacious rich.

An ode entitled "The Grumblers, Or Some of the Bad Effects of the Present Administration" mocked Adams.

> Ah me! how bad the times are growing!
> All, all is to destruction going;
> All kinds of evil threat the nation,
> The Devil take the Administration.
> No—Patriots! No! this ne'er will answer,
> Adams no more must be our man, Sir!
> Too tame—to oust him we must muster,
> And get a man of storm and bluster.
> We want a man of fire and fury,
> Who'll hang men without judge or jury . . .
> When we have got our hickory king up,
> Then halcyon days again may spring up."[2]

The other side countered with its ditty:

> General Jackson, I've been told,
> In battle bore the sway;
> He bravely fought the British bold,
> And drove them quite away . . ."

But the bit of doggerel couldn't compete with the hickory king's "fire" and ended with a limp whine:

> Why should a man be called so great;
> Though he a battle won;
> And he be made to rule our State,
> If that's all the good he's done.[3]

The backlash to the Jacksonian boosterism was found in the candidate's history. Which of his naysayers could forget the man's repudiation of the great

George Washington, or the execution of six militiamen during the Creek War? Or the British subjects, Ambrister and Arbuthnot, who'd been executed as spies in Florida, and whose deaths nearly caused an international incident? Or the cruelties visited upon the tribal peoples? "We shot them like dogs" had never been a metaphor, but a boast among the general's ardent Indian haters. A popular handbill framed in mourning black with six black coffins propped up under the heading: "Some Account of some of the Bloody Deeds of Gen. Jackson," cataloged atrocities attributed to him. The placement of seventeen additional coffins made the page look like an image found in contemporary books on the slave trade: the interior of a slaver with bodies stacked for maximum space usage and profit.

A letter repudiating Jackson was reprinted in *Poulson's* on September 2. Written by James Madison when he was Secretary of War in 1815, the topic was Jackson's unlawful arrest and imprisonment of a Louisiana legislator and a judge in March 1815, which had resulted in the notorious trial *United States v. Major General Andrew Jackson*. In his letter, Madison accused Jackson of ignoring the United States' judicial powers and suspending the liberty of the press.

Intending to aid the administration, *Poulson's* praised Adams for his "remarkably laborious habits," extolling an "extremely elaborate report on the intricate state of weights and measures."[4] That report had been completed when Adams was Secretary of State. Although weights and measures were critical for the sale and purchase of liquid and dry goods, and therefore a necessity of everyday life, the establishment of common measurement standards could hardly compete with a military hero's swagger.

Jackson and his supporters ignored the insults. Should the frontier settlers be forced to live in fear of Indian massacres? Should mutinous troops go unpunished, or traitors avoid execution? "Usurper," they scoffed at the President. At the same time, pro-Adams forces drew themselves up in a self-righteous rage, accusing the Jacksonians of being "foes to our government and disturbers to our peace . . . Mr. Adams is our rightful President, which none but those who are destitute of honour and honesty will pretend to deny."[5]

The accusations made no dent in the Jacksonians' zeal. Nor did it affect the candidate. Despite the quickness with which he took offense, he relished a good fight. However, the slander leveled at his wife, Rachel, nearly broke him. She was accused of adultery and bigamy; every aspect of her character, from her first, abusive marriage to the conflicting dates of her divorce and remarriage, came under the withering glare of the pro-Adams press. She was deemed unfit to be called a lady, a person of loose morals who had the temerity to imagine she would be worthy of being elevated to the first lady of the land.

Shielded from the accusations lobbed at her, Rachel discovered them by happenstance in early December while reading campaign literature defending her honor. Shock and horror overwhelmed her. She collapsed and was taken home to the Hermitage. There she rallied physically but not emotionally. On December 18, she suffered a heart attack, and on December 22 at nine o'clock at night, she suffered a second one and died. Jackson was beside himself with grief.

* * *

The Hero of New Orleans won the popular and electoral vote, taking 647,276 popular and 178 electoral votes as compared to Adams's 508,064 and 83. Despite last-minute get-out-the-vote announcements warning of "every Jackson man at his post, and many of us absent. . . ."[6] Adams simply could not compete with Jackson's charisma or dodge the attacks on him and his Administration. According to the editor, Hezekiah Niles, a supporter of the opposition, a "triumphant majority" paved the way for building a new nation. Adams's camp looked upon the election as a dangerous revolution, an annihilation of wisdom and order. After the last ballots were counted, and it became certain that Andrew Jackson would occupy the White House, and that the cultured sophistication of Louisa and John Quincy Adams had come to an end, there were worries that the Jacksonians would desecrate the "palace," as the President's house had come to be known.

Adams's final speech to Congress delivered on December 2, had a weary tone. Like a man hoping to find hope, he referenced God, giving thanks for the "never failing mercies of Him who ruleth over all. He has again favored us with healthful seasons and abundant harvest, He has sustained us in peace with foreign countries, and in tranquility within our borders. . . ."[7] It was clear he wanted to go home to Massachusetts and be done with the politics of factionalism and rage. As if released from a heavy burden, he became chatty and affable at several soirees he and Louisa held prior to leaving Washington. At the conclusion of the last levee on Wednesday, January 28, the weather was bitterly cold, and the ground was covered with snow. Inside, the East Room and ground floor reception area were thronged with well-wishers. Again, Adams broke character; habitually reticent in mixed company, he proved a loquacious host. At the end of the evening, the band played "Home—Sweet Home."

That bittersweet air must have provided the revelers with momentary solace, but the sentiment competed with the realities of the election's aftermath.

As early as October 8, the *United States Gazette* had reported that the "majority of the south is infected with a resolution to dissolve the union."[8] Two months later, on December 8, the *Gazette* reverted to the subject of disunion in an article entitled "Feelings of the South." These were expressed in a published letter that had been addressed to the U.S. Congress:

> We can no longer look for protection. Congress itself is the invader.
> The states must shield themselves and meet the invader foot to
> foot. . . . If resistance proves disunion, let disunion come. . . . But
> place before me union on the terms of the manufacturers, and coloni-
> zation and abolition societies of the north, and I will spurn it.[9]

Such was the mood of angry provocation that Jackson had engendered.

* * *

On January 19, 1829, the President-elect left the Hermitage on a journey to Washington that would require over three weeks. Because of Rachel's death, he was in deep mourning, dictating no displays of exuberance along his route. His nephew and adopted son, Andrew Jackson Donelson, who served as his private secretary, told the press that the general didn't intend to visit friends on his way to Washington and that he would "decline the acceptance of any mark of public respect whilst on the journey."[10] Arriving at Cincinnati on January 24, the only expression of celebration was found in hickory brooms lashed to the flagstaffs of all the steamboats in the river. His detractors remained intransigent. *Poulson's* printed a letter to the editor on February 9 entitled "The Duelist" and signed by an "Old Soldier." Although Jackson was unnamed, it was clear he was the subject. "Let him look at the mother or widow of the son or husband murdered by his hand. Let him look at the orphans. . . . He sallies forth in the majesty of heroic honor" to "storm Hell and take damnation by force."[11]

A wait-and-see mood pervaded Washington, as Daniel Webster explained to his brother, Ezekiel, on January 17. Webster would become a staunch ally of the Second Bank and friend and confidante to Biddle.

> Nobody knows what he will do when he comes. Many letters are
> sent to him; he answers none of them. His friends here pretend to be
> very knowing; but be assured, not one of them has any confidential
> communication from him. Nobody is authorized to say, whether he

intends to retire after one term of service. Who will form his cabinet is as well known at Boston as at Washington. The apparent calm is a suspension of action, a sort of syncope, arising from ignorance of the views of the President elect. My opinion is, that when he comes he will bring a breeze with him. Which way it will blow, I cannot tell. . . . My fear is stronger than my hope.[12]

On February 11, Jackson arrived in Washington and immediately went to Congress for the official counting of the votes. With him was his trusted friend, Tennessee Senator John Eaton, in whose carriage they rode. Eaton had authored Jackson's laudatory 1824 biography. Establishing a cabinet was the President elect's first piece of business. Martin Van Buren became his Secretary of State, which angered Vice President Calhoun, who saw himself next in line for the presidency. Pennsylvania Congressman Samuel D. Ingham was named Secretary of the Treasury, a nod to Pennsylvania's longtime support of Jackson; the appointment also ensured that the Treasury remain in the Democratic fold. Eaton became Secretary of War. Georgian John MacPherson Berrien, a states-right proponent and advocate for Indian Removal, became Attorney General. Prior to the inaugural Wednesday, March 4, Jackson made a point of snubbing Adams—a thing never done by an incoming President who considered a visit to the outgoing chief magistrate pro forma. He blamed Adams and the pro-Administration newspapers for Rachel's death. Unaware of the motive behind the discourtesy, Adams retaliated by being equally impolite; he refused to attend his successor's inauguration.

Eaton was Jackson's first political liability. On January 1, 1829, the widower had married Margaret (Peggy) O'Neal Timberlake, a recent widow. Peggy was the daughter of a Washington innkeeper. She liked power, loved to flirt, and was considered a beauty; the latter two didn't recommend her to the capital's dignified matrons. Additionally, her first husband, a naval lieutenant, had died under mysterious circumstances, which some rumored had been suicide. Some believed she had been Eaton's mistress before their marriage and even before her husband's death. It was bruited about that she had enjoyed other lovers and even had an abortion. The wives of Jackson's cabinet secretaries rebelled at the notion of socializing with her. Floride Calhoun, the vice president's wife, led the insurrection. Complicating the problem was a rivalry between Calhoun and Van Buren, both of whom had presidential ambitions. It was assumed that Calhoun would become the next chief magistrate. However, he had criticized

Jackson during his invasion of Florida during the Seminole War, and the general could not forget nor forgive the rebuke.

The internecine wars were abetted by the President's family and friends, all of whom lived in the White House: Rachel's nephew, Andrew Jackson Donelson and his wife, Emily, and their three year old son, and, of course, William Lewis. Forming a cocoon around the President, they allowed or encouraged him to underestimate Peggy Eaton's detractors. He defended her as he had defended Rachel. If he heard language impugning Peggy's morals, his wrath became ungovernable, but the wives of his cabinet members remained obdurate.

Faced with internal rebellion, Jackson persevered. He was determined to embark on his campaign promise of government reform. On December 7, 1829, he delivered his first State of the Nation Address to the Senate and House of Representatives. In fact, the message was delivered by Andrew Jackson Donelson, not by the President. After referring to the "Federal Legislature of 24 sovereign States and 12,000,000 happy people" and "the most friendly footing" with European powers and Russia, with which "the United States have always found a steadfast friend," the speech got down to brass tacks.

First was the electoral process, which Jackson intended to change by amending the Constitution. Next, he assailed the chicanery and ineptitude of the previous administration, fraudulence in the Treasury Department, and a bloated federal government. Then came "Indian removal"—for their own good, naturally.

> I informed the Indians inhabiting parts of Georgia and Alabama that
> their attempt to establish an independent government would not be
> countenanced by the Executive of the United States, and advised them
> to emigrate beyond the Mississippi or submit to the laws of those
> States. . . .

However, it was a brief critique of the central bank that would change Nicholas Biddle's life.

> The charter of the Bank of the United States expires in 1836, and its
> stock holders will most probably apply for a renewal of their privileges.
> In order to avoid the evils resulting from precipitancy in a measure
> involving such important principles and such deep pecuniary interests,
> I feel that I cannot, in justice to the parties interested, too soon present

it to the deliberate consideration of the Legislature and the people. Both the constitutionality and the expediency of the law creating this bank are well questioned by a large portion of our fellow citizens, and it must be admitted by all that it has failed in the great end of establishing an uniform and sound currency.[13]

* * *

That Jackson distrusted banking and the Second Bank of the United States, in particular, was a given, but he found a ready ally in Van Buren. The "Little Magician" used his humble origins to prove himself worthy of the President's trust while at the same time privately recognizing the intertwined relationship between the federal government and financial institutions. His motive in encouraging Jackson's eventual battle with Biddle was less the central bank's death than its removal from Philadelphia to the place he believed should be its natural home—New York. As a U.S. Senator beginning in 1821, he kept a low profile during the contested election of 1824. However, he sided with Jackson thereafter, utilizing the finesse and dexterity he had honed as a one-time leader of the Albany Regency (as the politicians who controlled New York State were known) to help garner votes for his candidate. In 1828, Van Buren was elected governor of New York; in 1829, Jackson made him Secretary of State.

Despite Jackson's best efforts, the "Petticoat Affair," as the Peggy Eaton scandal came to be known, dominated Washington politics for over a year. Eaton proved to be as pugnacious as the President. On June 17, 1831, Eaton sent a snarling letter to Secretary of the Treasury Ingham, demanding whether a story about the Attorney General and Secretaries of the Treasury and Navy refusal to associate with Peggy was true. He insisted upon an "immediate answer." When that message failed to rouse the Pennsylvanian, Eaton sent another furious missive. "I demand of you satisfaction [Eaton's underlining]. . . . Your answer must determine whether you are so far entitled to the name and character of a gentleman, or to be able to act like one."[14] He was so enraged, his handwriting shook. The word "satisfaction" could only mean one thing; he was threatening Ingham with a duel. More violence ensued when an Eaton brother-in-law accosted Ingham in his office.

As a result of this brouhaha, Eaton resigned from the cabinet; Van Buren, hoping a clean slate would settle the issue and calm Washington's nerves, did, too. The cabinet dissolved, but Ingham dug in his heels until Jackson forced him to resign on June 21. The chest-thumping was far from over. Eaton's brother-in-law was accused of lurking at the corner of Pennsylvania Avenue and 15th Street, while Eaton waited nearby at a grocery shop on F Street. The two men planned to attack Ingham, whom Eaton threatened to kill.

That Ingham became the lighting rod, rather than Calhoun, shows decided favoritism for the South. A Pennsylvanian from New Hope, north of Philadelphia, a former member of the Pennsylvania State Legislature, and a United States Congressman before being tapped for Treasury, his appointment had been thrust upon Jackson by state delegates who had supported the President's campaign. After banishing Ingham from Washington, Jackson derided him as a "Judas."[15]

* * *

Despite Jackson's message to Congress during which he critiqued the Second Bank of the United States and the bellicose sensibility that reigned in Washington, Biddle initially found little cause for alarm. Instead, the President's and his cabinet's theatrics had a farcical air that made anxiety seem absurd. Biddle knew he had a stalwart ally in Calhoun who had long been a central bank champion, responsible for its charter in 1816 and advocating for the institution during Monroe's administration. Ingham and Berrien also supported the Bank. Van Buren, whom Biddle considered a personal friend, was assumed to be in the same camp. So, although the President might mistrust the central bank, Biddle believed that the Washington professionals would prevail and that the upheavals caused by the populist posturing would subside. In this, he was naïve.

Nor did he fully appreciate the factionalism that had been inherent within the Jackson administration from the beginning. Van Buren was a wily politician; he almost met his match in James A. Hamilton, Alexander Hamilton's third son, who hitched his star to that of the Secretary of State, becoming his aide, and acting on his behalf before Van Buren resigned from his position as New York's governor to move to Washington. He gained the President's trust, although he deemed him "wholly uneducated and without talent" while also conceding that "his intentions were upright, his integrity unquestionable."[16] Hamilton believed that Jackson had been "elected only because he had been a successful soldier."

"The General's misfortune is, that his confidence is reposed in men in no degree equal to him in natural parts, but who have been of use to him heretofore in covering his very lamentable defects of education; and as he is unwilling to make these defects known to any others, he is compelled to keep these gentlemen about him."[17] Those negative traits hardly diminished Hamilton's desire to make his reputation within the new government.

While Van Buren bided his time in Albany, watching which way the wind blew, Hamilton supposedly became his man on the scene. He had no respect for the Magician's education and intellect.

> Mr. Van Buren was certainly not eminently fitted for the State Department, by his knowledge of public affairs, by his education, which was very limited, or his intellectual endowments. In the preparation of his first report as secretary, he required a friend to revise and correct that document. Indeed all his public papers required the assistance of a friend.[18]

Outwardly, though, Hamilton seemed faithfulness, itself; and Van Buren repeatedly asked him to suggest various measures to Jackson, but to do it on the q.t. lest Lewis or Donelson become suspicious of maneuverings to cut them out of the equation.

The President, who had intended to surround himself with loyal friends, had inadvertently encouraged envy, competition, and scheming among those closest to him. Hamilton, to whom Jackson confided, "I want you to be near me,"[19] prided himself at being able to manipulate the chief magistrate. He encouraged Ingham's ouster and lobbied to remove Berrien. But the central bank drew his especial ire, the "hydra of corruption,"[20] as Jackson styled it, putting Hamilton at odds with his father's legacy.

* * *

As palace intrigues continued to roil through Washington, Biddle attended to the needs of the Bank. It must have appeared to him as though a second Jackson term were well nigh impossible, and that when the nation returned to judicious leadership, institutions like the Second Bank of the United States would be necessary to correct the country's course. Biddle was then a leading member of the city's most notable private institutions: the Philosophical Society, founded by Franklin in1743; the Athenaeum, founded in 1814 whose stated purpose was the gathering of materials "connected with the history and antiquities of America, and the useful arts, and generally to disseminate useful knowledge"; the Philadelphia Society for Promoting Agricultural; the Historical Society of Pennsylvania; the Pennsylvania Society for Internal Improvements, that Biddle had helped to organize; and the Franklin Institute of the State of Pennsylvania for the Promotion of the Mechanic Arts, among others. The latter three had been founded in 1824, a benchmark year in the city's cultural history, and, of course, the date of Jackson's first defeat. The intellectual divide between Philadelphia's scholars, practical scientists and authors, and the Jacksonians were very great, and the follies of Washington almost too infantile to believe.

On April 11, 1827, when the shift to a populist administration remained uncertain (though dreaded), the leading lights of Philadelphia's intellectual community gathered to laud a founding father and a scientist whom they considered one of their own. Biddle delivered a "Eulogium on Thomas Jefferson" to the Philosophical Society. Every detail of Jefferson's history was well known to the members, of which he had served as president. Biddle's accolades, which ran to a forty-seven subsequently printed pages, reminded his listeners just how different the "Sage of Monticello" and "Old Hickory" were. Referring to Jefferson as a "scholar and a statesman,"[21] Biddle said that "All his actions [were] imbued by learning,"[22] adding that he was "fearless in temper, fertile in resources, prompt in pouring out the stores of his accumulated knowledge. . . . The declaration of independence is among the noblest productions of the human intellect. . . . It seems like the gushing out of an oppressed but still unconquered spirit."[23] Cataloging the former President's accomplishments even up until the time of his death, Biddle compared them to the present time and present generation. "The passions which have agitated our life disturb our latest hour; and men go down to the tomb, like the sun into the ocean, with no gentle and gradual withdrawing of the light of life back to the source which gave it, but sullen in its beamless descent."[24]

But it was toward the conclusion of the address that Biddle gave a hint of his own personality. Although describing Jefferson when he said, "It is this exhaustless love of study which enables the finer intellects to sustain the burthen of public duties,"[25] the words carried a prescient ring as if he had a glimpse of his own future battles.

- CHAPTER TWELVE -

FOR JACKSON OR THE BANK

Jackson's antipathy to the Second Bank eclipsed even James Hamilton's scheming. The institution had come to embody his long-held dread of economic instability because it represented a personal, historical reality, as well as his fear for the nation's future financial health. During a private interview with Biddle in 1829, he had been blunt.

> I would have no difficulty in recommending it (the recharter) to Congress, but I think it right to be perfectly frank with you—I do not think that Congress has a right to create a corporation out of the ten mile square. I do not dislike your bank any more than all banks. But ever since I read the history of the South Sea Bubble, I have been afraid of banks.[1]

As if that response might appear irrational, he sought to justify himself:

> I have read the opinion of John Marshall who I believe was a great & pure mind—and could not agree with him—though if he had said that as it was necessary for the purpose of the national government there ought to be a national bank I should have been disposed to concur. . . . I feel very sensibly the services rendered by the Bank at the last payment of the national debt & shall take an opportunity of declaring it publicly in my message to Congress.

Jackson also stated that he "had every reason to be satisfied with the Parent Board."[2]

Subsequently, though, Biddle received conflicting opinions about the President's intentions, in part generated by a continual jockeying for power among his advisors. On May 8, 1830, he sent William Lewis a letter marked "private" in which he worried whether or not the President was:

> satisfied that the powers of the Bank have not been abused for political purposes, & and that towards him & his administration, the Bank has acted frankly, fairly & cordially . . . it would be exceedingly gratifying to know the feelings of the President towards the Bank at the present moment, because some of his injudicious friends & many of his opponents seek to make an impression that such is his rooted dislike to the Institution, that he would refuse his sanction to a Continuance of the Bank. . . .[3]

On May 25, Lewis provided an answer. His opinion ran counter to Jackson's own words.

> Before closing this letter permit me to say one word in reference to a subject mentioned in your last letter to me—I mean the information you recd of the President's having declared that if Congress should pass a law renewing the Charter in the U.S. Bank he would put his veto on it. I told you in Phila when you first mentioned the thing to me, that there must be some mistake, because the report was at variance with what *I* had heard him say on the subject. . . .[4]

* * *

As Jackson's first term progressed, it continued sending mixed signals regarding the Bank. Where Van Buren stood on the question was a matter of debate. Both sides of the issue viewed him with mistrust, but Biddle respected the man's tactical skills and assumed, mistakenly, that he was above pouring poison in Jackson's ear. Although the charter would not expire until 1836, Biddle began advocating for an early renewal; he believed the institution had solid friends in Congress and the Secretary of the Treasury, Louis McLane. However, other forces were at work over which he had no control and little ken.

In June 1830, Henry Clay, who had been biding his time after serving as Secretary of State during Adams's administration, wrote Biddle that he had learned "from one of the most intelligent citizens of Virginia" (who remained anonymous in the correspondence) that the administration intended "to make the destruction of the Bank the basis for the next Presidential Election."[5] In September, Clay was more specific with his warning, naming

> a strong party, headed by Mr. V. Buren, some Virginia politicians and the Richmond Enquirer. . . . I now entertain no doubt of their purpose. I have seen many evidences of it. The Editors of certain papers have received their orders to that effect, and embrace every occasion to act in conformity with them. . . . If you apply at the next Session of Congress [for re-charter] you will play into the hands of that party.[6]

He prefaced his remarks by telling Biddle, "It may be assumed, as indisputable, that the renewal of the charter can never take place, as the Constitution now stands, against the opinion and wishes of the President of the U.S. . . ."[7]

Unwilling to accept failure or the fact that partisan politics could wield such destruction, Biddle refused to heed Clay's advice. He sought alternate opinions, delaying his response until November when he informed Clay that the timing for renewing the charter was "inexpedient."[8] Tempting as Biddle felt the application for renewal was, he told Clay that he feared Congress' "dread of responsibility" and "love of postponement"[9] would defeat the measure and "that nothing but a certainty of success should induce an application now."[10]

Certainty, though, was impossible; nobody knew which way Jackson would eventually turn. Confidential letters to and from Biddle's allies pondered the question, but no one agreed. Then, on December 7, 1830, the truth was revealed during the President's message to Congress. He made it clear he intended to eviscerate the Bank of the United States. "Nothing has occurred to lessen, in any degree, the dangers which many of our citizens apprehend from that institution, as at present organized. . . ." While admitting that, "It is thought practical to organize such a bank," the principal theme of the announcement was that state institutions should dominate the system, thereby reducing all operating powers of a central bank.

> Not being a corporate body, having no stockholders, debtors, or property, and but few officers, it would not be obnoxious to the constitutional objections which are urged against the present bank, and having no means to operate on the hopes, fears, or interests of large masses of the community it would be shorn of the influence, which makes that

bank formidable. The states would be strengthened by having in their hands the means of furnishing the local paper currency through their own banks. . . .

The present "system cannot continue to exist in its preset form," was the conclusion.[11]

Biddle finally understood that the tides had changed and that Jackson meant to make the topic central to his campaign for reelection. In addition, his words would inspire individual states to strengthen their banks by hoarding currency and insisting that their Congressional delegates oppose the Second Bank's re-charter. Again, letters between him and his advisors concerning the advisability of immediately asking Congress to vote on the matter circulated daily. Determined, Biddle grew belligerent, and with his belligerence came foolhardiness. He became overly confident that wisdom would prevail and that Jackson's antipathy was simply posturing for political gain. By then, Van Buren had also shown his hand as being a foe of the Bank.

"In respect to Gen[l] Jackson & Mr. Van Buren," wrote Biddle on December 20, 1830:

> I have not the slightest fear of either of them, or both of them. Our country-men are not naturally disposed to cut their own throats to please any body, & I have so perfect a reliance on the spirit & sense of the nation, that I think we can defend the institution from much strong enemies than they are. In doing this we must endeavour to reach the understandings of our fellow citizens by the diffusion of correct views of a subject which is much misunderstood. . . .[12]

A year later, Biddle maintained his opinion that the Bank would survive even though the political waters had grown more treacherous. Van Buren was now at odds with Calhoun. Despite those inconstant alliances as well as his allegiance to Clay, Biddle declared in a personal memorandum that, "The Pres[t] is now perfectly confident of his election—the only question is the greater or the less majority, but he is sure of success & wishes to succeed by a greater vote than at the first election." Further pondering Jackson's character, he wondered whether self-confidence might make the President veto the bank bill "as if dared to do it," or whether a position of accepted power would make him magnanimous. "I think he would be more disposed to yield when he is strong than when he is in danger."[13] Nonetheless, he was beginning to prepare for the worst.

> What I can do and will do is this. It is obvious that a great effort will be made to array the influence of the Executive & all his party against the Bank. It is not less evident that our most effectual resistance is the dissemination of useful knowledge among the people, and accordingly I am endeavoring to convey to all classes real & positive information in regard to the working of the institution & its beneficial influence on the prosperity of the nation. To do this newspapers must be used, not for their influence, but merely as channels of communication with the people.[14]

"I believe," he subsequently stated, "that nine tenths of the errors of men arise from their ignorance—and that the great security of all our institutions is in the power, the irresistible power, of truth."

Recalling his first battle over the issue of a central bank in 1811, he said, "I have lived to see the very individuals the most zealous in the work of destruction, candidly confess, as they have grown older and wiser, that they did not properly appreciate the organization."[15] To combat that ignorance, he reached out to every editor he knew.

* * *

After Henry Clay resumed his place in the Senate, he changed his mind about an early renewal of the Bank's charter and advocated that Biddle quickly act lest Jackson win a second term. Daniel Webster agreed, saying,

> it is expedient for the Bank to apply for the renewal of its charter without delay. I do not meet a Gentleman, hardly of another opinion; & the little incidents & anecdotes, that occur & circulate among us, all tend to strengthen the impression. Indeed, I am now a good deal inclined to think, that after Gen¹ Jackson's re-election there would be a poor chance for the Bank.

Describing the President's "old opinions" as "unchangeable," Webster told Biddle:

the best advice I could give you, is, that you come down here, yourself, & survey the ground. You will have access to men of all parties, & can digest your information, compare opinions, & judge discreetly upon the whole matter. In my judgment, this is your true course, & ought to be immediately followed.[16]

Secretary of the Treasury, Louis McLane, counseled patience. Through an intermediary, he advised, "if time be given to the P^t to convince himself of the Error into which opinion long formed (prejudice if you pleased) had committed him," he was certain Jackson would come round. "If pressed into a *Corner*," the results could prove disastrous.[17]

All the while, Jackson's advisors continued plotting against one another, but it was the Nullification Crisis that ultimately destroyed Calhoun's trustworthiness in the President's eyes. Supporting South Carolina's right as a state to declare federal tariffs of 1828 and 1832 unconstitutional, Calhoun resigned his post to return to the Senate and fight the hated measures that imposed heavy taxes on raw materials or cheaply imported goods. To the Southerners, it became known as the Tariff of Abominations because it raised the prices paid for goods the South did not produce while simultaneously reducing British imports made with southern cotton, which naturally reduced market value for the commodity. The 1828 tariff, of which Van Buren had been one of the authors, appealed to the middle and west of the nation. Naturally, it put Jackson's two most visible advisors at odds with each other, creating high drama not only for Washington's gossips but for those who hoped a new administration would bring back stability within the government. In a January 1831 message, Biddle's old friend, Roswell Colt, told him:

> Tis said that Van Buren & Calhoun have kissed & made up their dispute—it is a fact that Calhoun has dined with Mr Van Buren—and now the Secretarys [*sic*] party are crowing under the idea, that Calhoun is courting the favor & forbearance of Mr V B—at which it is said that Mr C. (Clay) is not a little vexed. If Jackson determines to run again for the Presidency, & Calhoun does the Same, as he says he will, then Van B. & his party will denounce Calhoun & throw him off. . . . The Clay party are trying to get Calhoun to separate himself from Jackson. . . .[18]

Those maneuverings came to naught. With Calhoun leading the charge, South Carolina threatened to secede from the Union; and Van Buren was chosen as a candidate for Vice President in 1832.

As before, Van Buren sought out James Hamilton, turning him into a sounding board and political operative. On August 5, 1832, he communicated that, "Pennsylvania is as safe as Tennessee,"[19] but urged vigilance lest the votes for Jackson slip away from want of attention. Both men were playing their own game. Hamilton wanted power and prestige, which Van Buren's continued ascendancy denied. Finally, he turned against his former mentor, writing to the banished Ingham from Pennyworth Island in the Savannah River on January 1, 1833: "The declaration of war of the Despot (the once-revered Jackson) against South Carolina has done more for our cause, than even his support could have benefitted us." Hamilton then proceeded to refer to the President as "old Dionysius," or "The King." Van Buren, he called the "little knave." So much for loyalty.

Despite his double-dealing, when Jackson eventually won his second term, Hamilton angled to become Secretary of State. After that gambit failed, he told Jackson, "If I can be of any use to you, in any, even the most subordinate, situation, I will immediately repair to Washington. . . ."[20]

Although he eventually fell from grace, Hamilton's prestige in the President's eye continued into early 1832. The Bank issue became his constant focus, and he was at pains to inform Jackson of what he perceived as Biddle and his allies' stratagems. Jackson took the bait. On March 28, he wrote Hamilton, "The affairs of the Bank I anticipated to be precisely such as you have intimated. When fully disclosed, and the branches looked into, it will be seen that its corrupting influence has been extended everywhere that could add to its strength and secure its recharter."[21]

* * *

During July of that election year, a bill for the recharter of the Bank came before Congress. The proposal had been drawn up by Biddle and his directors in January, after which he worked mightily to obtain the necessary votes, reaching out to the bank branches to encourage local voters to petition their lawmakers. He also applied to the press, especially newspapers who believed in the necessity of a central bank: the *National* (Philadelphia) *Gazette*, the *New York American*, and the *National Intelligencer*. All that propaganda cost money, which was paid by the Bank of the United States to the tune of $14 378.14; the amount included expenditures from January 1830 through the end of June 1831.[22]

The lead-up to the vote had seen more advice—pro and con—circulating among Biddle's allies, one being Charles F. Mercer, a representative to the House from Virginia, and fellow Princeton graduate.

> Genl Jackson's popularity has declined much more among men of intelligence than with the great body of the people. It has especially declined in Congress. But his election is as certain as his life. He hates your Bank and had reason enough to do so. His silly notions respecting it have been exposed with your approbation, and he is mortified or vexed as well as angry. . . . Calhoun is friendly to your bank and he will certainly not be again Vice President. He has little influence, but where it exists it is powerful and it exists among your enemies to the South. . . .[23]

Clay and Webster agreed with Mercer that a bill to renew the Bank's charter should be submitted without delay. Webster went so far as to suggest that Jackson's reelection might render the effort hopeless. Colleagues tallied up votes for the proposed measure as belonging in two camps: Jackson and anti-Jackson votes. As might be expected, the Bank's proponents included members of the nation's leading families: Senator Nathaniel Silsbee of Massachusetts; Horace Binney of Philadelphia (subsequently a Congressman), Philadelphia attorney, legislator, and author; Charles Jared Ingersoll; and General Thomas Cadwalader, who was descended from the Van Courtlandts and Schuylers of New York and related by marriage to James Monroe. Former President John Quincy Adams and Richard Rush, his running mate in 1828, were among the list. Biddle listened to advice regarding making the Bank's structure more palatable to the President and tried to maintain a tranquil demeanor. However, his hackles were rising, and he found it difficult to control his frustration at objections he considered obsolete and anachronistic.

> Here am I, who have taken a fancy to this Bank & having built it up with infinite care am striving to keep it from being destroyed to the infinite wrong as I most sincerely & conscientiously believe of the whole country. To me all other considerations are insignificant—I mean to stand by it & defend it with all the small faculties which Providence

has assigned to me. I care for no party in politics or religion—have no sympathy with Mr Jackson or Mr Clay or Mr Wirt or Mr Calhoun or Mr Ellmaker or Mr Van Buren. I am for the Bank & the Bank alone. Well then, here comes Mr Jackson who takes it into his head to declare that the Bank had failed & and that it ought to be superseded by some rickety machinery of his own contrivance. . . . I suppose the President has been made to believe that the bank is busy in hostility to him— you know how wholly unfounded this is. For myself I do not care a straw for him or his rivals—I covet neither his man servant, nor even his maid servant, his ox nor any of his asses. . . .[24]

The letter ended with a threat that Biddle and his allies intended to fight if Jackson "means to wage war upon the Bank."

The threat appeared unwarranted. On Tuesday, July 3, came welcome news:

The Bank Bill has passed both houses of congress with handsome majorities. Whether the wishes of the representatives of the people, and of the states, is to be confirmed or *nullified* by the President, seems even yet doubtful. Though this is a question about which the executive will seemed made up about three years and a half ago.[25]

That report appeared in *Niles' Register* on July 7, 1832. Biddle was present for the passage, as he had been during the lead-up to the vote: assuaging, persuading, and politicking. From his communications to Jane, it is clear that he breathed a sigh of relief that the nation's legislators recognized the necessity of a central bank. There was vindication, too, and a sense that the federal government would maintain an even keel despite Jackson's opinions. A veto was possible, but Biddle could not bring himself to believe that Jackson would run counter to what he perceived as the nation's wishes.

Biddle's confidence aside, no one knew which way the wind blew. Every time the President's secretary, Andrew Jackson Donelson, appeared in the Senate chambers, all heads turned to watch him in hopes of learning the chief magistrate's views. As a political strategy, Donelson's uncommunicative presence served to keep the Bank's supporters on edge. *Poulson's* ascribed Jackson's indecision to a "struggle between two cabinets, the cabinet proper supporting, and the cabinet private [the ridiculed "kitchen cabinet"] opposing the bank. The latter has more of his confidence; the former more of the people. It may be, however, that he will finally be governed by neither, his guide, philosopher and friend, Martin Van Buren having just arrived in time to decide all doubts."[26]

Poulson's was correct; Van Buren had been in a sort of self-imposed exile acting as Jackson's minister to Great Britain, while the Peggy Eaton affair blew over. His return presaged ill for the Bank's proponents. When he arrived in Washington on July 8, the President greeted him with the cry, "The bank, Mr. Van Buren is trying to kill me, but I will kill it!"[27] Old Hickory was true to his word. On July 10, he sent his veto to Congress.

Niles' Register reported the news on July 14. "The veto of the bank bill seems to have occasioned a great shock at Philadelphia, for it was not expected by many of the friends of the present administration. They held out to the last that the bill would be approved."[28]

Delivered by Donelson, the message accompanying the veto required an hour to read to the gathered legislators. *Niles'* reprinted the "BANK OF THE UNITED STATES (THE VETO)" in full: from allegations ranging from "opulent citizens" controlling the institution to the Bank being "a monopoly of the foreign and domestic exchange" that made "The American people debtors to aliens."[29] Too blunt-spoken for creating a long and cadenced speech, Jackson allowed the Bank's bitterest foes, Roger Taney and publisher Amos Kendall, to write the message. Taney would become Secretary of the Treasury in 1833 and Chief Justice of the Supreme Court in 1836. A diehard Jacksonian, he wrote the majority opinion in the Dred Scott ruling of 1857 that declared that African Americans could not be considered citizens of the United States. Taney and Kendall laced the document with inflammatory language, intimations of serial mismanagement, profiteering, and even accusations of treason.

Essentially a political manifesto aimed at furthering Jackson's appeal and his power, the veto hearkened back to every historical fear regarding a central bank. It blamed the Second Bank for manipulating an unfair distribution of wealth between its branches and making "the rich richer, and the potent more powerful,"[30] raised the specter of rapacious foreign investors preying upon innocent, hardworking Americans, invoked the Jacksonians' anxieties of sacrificing states' rights to a strong federal government, but saved its most damning language for a charge of treason.

> Is there no danger to our liberty and independence in a bank, that in
> its nature has so little to bind it to our country? The president of the
> bank has told us, that most of the state banks exist by its forbearance.

Should its influence become concentered, as it may, under the operation of such an act as this in the hands of a self elected directory, whose
interests are identified with those of the foreign stockholder, will there
not be a cause to tremble for the purity of our elections in peace, and
for the independence of our country in war?[31]

If the threat of treason were not bad enough, Taney's contribution to the veto
also questioned the Bank's constitutionality.

As a piece of partisan propaganda, it was sublime, pitting Biddle and the
venal rich against every patriotic, honest toiler of the soil. As Donelson read:

There are no necessary evils in government. Its evils exist only in its
abuses. If it would confine itself to equal protection, and, as heaven
does its rains, shower its favors alike on the high and the low, the rich
and the poor; it would be an unqualified blessing. In the act before me,
there seems to be a wide and unnecessary departure from these just
principles.[32]

* * *

The next day, Daniel Webster rose to his feet in the Senate to attack Jackson in
a thunderous speech. Because Webster's eloquence was legendary and the issue
incendiary, the gallery was packed. "According to the doctrines put forth by the
President, although Congress may have passed a law, and although the Supreme
Court may have declared in constitutional, yet it is, nevertheless, no law at all, if
he, in his good pleasure, sees fit to deny it effect; in other words, to repeal or an-
nul it." Webster further castigated Jackson for what he called "despotic power."[33]
In an oration that took over two hours, Henry Clay concurred in equally strong
language, accusing the President of a "perversion of the veto power."[34]

Never one to avoid a battle, Missouri's Thomas Hart Benton entered the
fray, too, and in a "violent rage" shouted a denial to the charge that he had
once loathed Old Hickory. Equally loud, his detractors jeered and heckled him.
Benton attempted to silence his opponents, but the fight lasted until day's end,
adding fodder to newspaper reports, both pro and anti-Bank.

Biddle also lashed out in a fury. His behavior was ill-advised, but he viewed
Jackson and his coterie as obtuse, uncomprehending, and reactionary. He believed that their period of power would end and was itching for a fight. He
wrote angrily to Clay on August 1st.

You ask what is the effect of the Veto. My impression is that it is working as well as the friends of the Bank and of the country could desire. I
have always deplored making the Bank a party question, but since the
President will have it so, he must pay the penalty of his own rashness.
As to the veto message I am delighted with it. It has all the fury of a
chained panther biting the bars of his cage. It is really a manifesto of
anarchy—such as Marat or Robespierre might have issued to the mob
at the faubourg St Antoine: and my hope is that it will contribute to
relieve the country from the dominion of these miserable people.[35]

After that, he tried to calm down but with little success. Then he returned
to systematically educating everyone he could reach that a central bank was
indispensable to the common good. He failed to recognize that by pushing for
the bank's re-charter, he had permitted and even encouraged Jackson to use it
as a campaign issue. He even ordered fifty copies of the President's veto in both
English and German for distribution among the Bank branches.

But Biddle had begun a fight for which his upbringing had ill equipped
him. He had never challenged a man to a duel, would have sidestepped a
street brawl had he happened upon it; nor would he have considered starting
one. Dignity was a guiding principle. Jackson's supporters, however, relished a
good public scuffle, and the more provocative, the better. Following the veto,
a populist image appeared in New York in the form of a political cartoon entitled "Old Jack, the famous New Orleans mouser, clearing Uncle Sam's Barn
of Bank and Clay Rats, which had burrew'd through to get into his capital
Corn Crib." In the gleefully partisan image, a huge cat with a "Kilkenny tail"
(a reference to Jackson's Scots-Irish heritage) chased down and killed rats with
human faces—Clay's and Biddle's being discernable. The animal's tail had the
letters VETO stamped into the fur. "Uncle Sam and his active laborers" happily
watched the carnage. One fellow jeered, "How he nicks them."[36] What Biddle,
who would also be derided as "Old Nick" or "Czar Nick," made of the jest he
never recorded.

By then, Jackson had left Washington for the Hermitage, leaving behind
Van Buren and the Kitchen Cabinet to pick up the pieces. In his wake, the war-
fare continued. Jurist and author Henry Brackenridge in an open letter to the
President published in *Poulson's*, reviled his "ungovernable temper, consummate
deceit and hypocrisy," his "insatiate revenge" and "unbounded lust for power."[37]
Brackenridge knew whence he spoke. He had served under Jackson as a U.S.

judge in western Florida starting in 1821. Old Hickory's supposed friendship with the laborer was equally repudiated. "He employs no white laborer on his Hermitage plantation, with the exception of his overseer."[38] The fight cut across class. Laborers who had supported Jackson during his previous campaign and who were naturalized citizens of Irish descent came under verbal and physical assault, taunted with being "coarse, vulgar . . . brutal and ferocious."[39]

* * *

The Presidential campaign ran from November 2 to December 5. As Henry Clay had feared and as he'd intimated to Biddle in June 1830, the focus of Jackson's campaign became the Bank's destruction. For old Hickory, this was a struggle of good versus evil. He believed he had been chosen as the people's champion in order to to rescue them from the clutches of Mammon. Biddle, rather than candidate Clay or William Wirt, who was running on a third party Anti-Mason ticket (Jackson was a Mason, as was Clay), drew the ire of the President and his followers. "Old Nick" was portrayed as the devil incarnate and the Bank as a den of iniquity, corruption, and greed. The Jacksonians saw the choice between democracy and a rapacious aristocracy intent on keeping the common man in its thrall.

The President had confided in Van Buren in 1830, "you know, I never despair. I have confidence in the virtue and good sense of the people,"[40] which aura he radiated wherever he went. His followers were reluctant to disappoint the faith entrusted to them by the Hero of New Orleans. Van Buren agreed with Jackson's single-issue tactic, saying, "the Veto is popular (in NY) beyond my most sanguine expectations. I have not heard of a single case where it has driven a friend from us."[41] Previously, he had told Hamilton that Jackson's veto was "destined to be the most popular act of his life."[42] The endlessly repeated phrase "Bank or no Bank" epitomized the fight.

Without possessing Jackson's clear call to arms, Clay's campaign floundered. Although the Bank of the United States lavished money on Clay's efforts, spending upward of $42,000.00 to reprint and circulate speeches of Clay and Webster, as well as Jackson's veto, and other literature promoting its cause, the effort appeared suspect to those who mistrusted any large and moneyed institution. Amos Kendall, the pro-Jackson publisher, insisted that his rival journalists were being "bribed" by the Bank. A letter written by Samuel Ingham, Jackson's deposed Secretary of the Treasury, appeared in *Niles'* November 3. In it, Ingham repudiated his former boss, insisting he had never understood the intricacies of finance, and the necessity of foreign investors, without whom "we ought to expunge off our loans, demolish our public works, and abandon all the improvements in which foreign capital in employed . . . I deplore the evils which his re-election must fix upon our country. . . ." The word TYRANNY appeared in boldface.[43]

For the anti-Jackson contingent, Ingham's accusation made perfect sense; for the Jacksonians, the message was yet another spurious attack from a man they considered to be a disgraced public servant. *Niles'* condemned the election rhetoric of both sides: "In this ardent controversy, which has cast out, we think, a larger amount of gross and rude, and strange and curious matter than any previous one. . . ."[44] The weekly was hardly unbiased; it had condemned Jackson's veto, saying that the President had "cast himself upon the support of the people against the acts of both houses of congress."[45]

On November 6, the *New York Sentinel* ran a sizeable pro-Clay announcement, "THE GREAT CONTEST IS AT HAND!" that urged folks to get out and vote.

> Will you remain at home and suffer a tyrannical rule still to exist
> that strikes at the very root of our independence and prosperity. . . .
> Should Jackson be re-elected, we are to expect: The Destruction of
> the Supreme Court; the Constitution to be a dead letter; The Laws to
> be binding or not, as the President pleases; The Indians to be driven,
> in spite of Laws and Treaties, into the wilderness; the United States
> Bank and its safe notes to be destroyed. . . . An avowed and systematic
> corruption of the Press.[46]

Meanwhile, the Jacksonians invested in exuberant and wildly popular public spectacles: barbecues, picnics, fireworks, and free hickory brooms. Flag-waving was de rigueur. Being against Jackson, the savior of New Orleans, was akin to being a traitor. "Hunters of Kentucky," a song celebrating the New Orleans victory and made popular during the 1828 campaign, found new enthusiasts. One lyric, "We are a hardy, free-born race," became emblematic of an iconoclastic, frontier spirit that refused to be intimidated or defeated. A Jackson poster, "The Union must be Preserved," cast potential voters in the roles of the nation's saviors. Another displayed Old Hickory in military garb, looking eagle-eyed and formidable. Beneath his portrait, cannons, swords, and pistols were arrayed; above him perched an eagle whose protective wings shielded the candidate from harm.

Jackson's opponents played into their hands, signing stinging letters to the Editor with donnish names like "Civis" and "Quaerist" and "Pro Bono Publico," which fed the Jacksonians' mistrust of all things foreign and elite. Both factions fueled the class war, creating a chasm impossible to bridge, although no one felt inclined to do so. In some instances, voters were assaulted and beaten while going to the polls. The pro-Jackson and pro-Clay presses screamed for justice. Whether intentionally or unwittingly, Nicholas Biddle, in his efforts to ensure the future of a central bank, had unleashed a firestorm no one seemed inclined to suppress. He and the Second Bank would suffer.

* * *

Jackson's State of the Union address on December 4, 1832, made it clear he believed he had a mandate to battle with the Bank. Delivered, as usual, by Donelson, the message stated:

> It is my duty to acquaint you with an arrangement made by the Bank of the United States with a portion of the holders of the 3% stock, by which the Government will be deprived of the use of the public funds longer than was anticipated. By this arrangement, which will be particularly explained by the Secretary of the Treasury, a surrender of the certificates of this stock may be postponed until [1833 October], and thus may be continued by the failure of the bank to perform its duties.
>
> Such measures as are within the reach of the Secretary of the Treasury have been taken to enable him to judge whether the public deposits in that institution may be regarded as entirely safe; but as his limited power may prove inadequate to this object, I recommend the subject to the attention of Congress, under the firm belief that it is worthy of their serious investigation. An inquiry into the transactions of the institution, embracing the branches as well as the principal bank, seems called for by the credit which is given throughout the country to many serious charges impeaching its character, and which if true may justly excite the apprehension that it is no longer a safe depository of the money of the people."[47]

In addition, a national bank flew in the face of Jackson's intention "of reducing the General Government to that simple machine which the Constitution created."

Niles' Register reported the President's words on December 8. However, the weekly devoted more space to the South Carolina convention that began November 19 in Columbia, and whose priority was overturning the hated tariff. James Calhoun served as a member of the central committee. While Jackson focused on the Bank, the ongoing removal of Indians, foreign affairs, and fiscal prudence, the people assembled in Columbia were on fire.

> We the people of South Carolina, assembled in convention, have solemnly and deliberately declared, in our paramount sovereign capacity, that the act of congress approved 19th day of May, 1828, and the act approved the 14th of July, 1832, altering and amending the several acts imposing duties on imports, are unconstitutional and therefore absolutely void, and of no binding force within the limits of this state.[48]

Words like "oppression" and "tyranny" rattled like gunfire. "CONSTITUTIONAL LIBERTY"[49] (in capital letters) became a battle cry. The federal government was accused of attempting "to reduce the plantation states to poverty and utter desolation."

Thomas Jefferson and his legacy were hailed as exemplifying a perfect doctrine of states' rights. Although the representatives recognized that the "separation of South Carolina would inevitably produce a general dissolution of the union,"[50] they were prepared to secede. "Of all the governments on the face of the earth," they bellowed, "the federal government has the least shadow of a constitutional right to exercise such a power."[51] Georgia's Anti-Tariff Convention commenced December 1.

While Jackson's campaign continued on its almost exclusively anti-Bank platform, the secessionists in South Carolina and their sympathizers in Georgia waged a separate war. In the Ordinance of November 24, the tariffs of 1828 and 1832 were declared unconstitutional and unenforceable. Any attempt to collect them after February 1, 1833, would lead to the state seceding from the Union. Mobs of armed men had already been roving the streets before the Ordinance; riots had become commonplace. Jackson's reaction to the perilous situation remained a closely guarded secret. Daniel Webster attacked his lack of direction during a speech at the National Republican Convention in Worcester, Massachusetts on October 12:

[The] Administration keeps itself in profound silence, but its friends have spoken for it. We are told . . . that the President will immediately employ a military force and at once blockade Charleston. The President has no authority to blockade Charleston; the President has no authority to employ military force, till he be duly required to do so by law, and by the civil authorities.

Webster further urged the electors to "relieve the country from an administration which denies to the Constitution those powers which are the breath of its life."[52]

James Hamilton, Jr, Governor of South Carolina (no relation to Jackson's confidante), made plans to defend his state from the possibility of attack, calling for a militia of 2,000 volunteers to muster in Charleston and another 10,000 statewide. He insisted that U.S. troops be withdrawn from the state citadel in Charleston and declared his intention of "repelling force by force."[53] More belligerent oratory followed; the Carolinians demanded to know whether they were "Russian serfs or slaves of a [Turkish] Divan?"[54] Clearly, the irony was lost on them. Slave owners themselves, the white electorate, objected to becoming enslaved.

Simultaneously, Jackson gave orders to his Secretaries of War and Navy, telling them to be on guard lest southern officers attempt to capture Charleston harbor and other areas of defense. Additional orders organized a 10,000-man militia to march on the state if the crisis couldn't be averted by negotiation. The President said he was prepared to "crush and hang" the traitors.

Watching the melee from afar, the British concluded that America was "fast going to pieces" and that the "whole country [was] sinking into decay. . . . The Southern States of Carolina have virtually declared war against those of New England, and are resolved to throw off the yoke of the Federative Union." The opinion further quoted the South Carolinians as declaring that "when they moved the slave question . . . they from the south would meet it . . . where powder and cannon would be their orators, and their arguments lead and steel."[55]

- CHAPTER THIRTEEN -

SAVING THE BANK

Although Andrew Jackson led in votes tallied, and his and Martin Van Buren's victories appeared all but assured, nullification continued to dominate the news throughout the month of December 1832. The dissolution of the union appeared ever more probable as South Carolina and Georgia held anti-tariff conventions. Emotions reached fever pitch. States Rights became a rallying cry, especially among the people of South Carolina:

> We have, therefore, deliberately and unalterably resolved, that we will no longer submit to a system of oppression, which reduces us to the degrading condition of tributary vassals; and which would reduce our posterity, in a few generations, to a state of poverty. . . . We believe the federal government has no shadow of right or authority, to act against a sovereign state of the confederacy, in any form, much less to coerce it, by military power.

That declaration concluded with a warning that the citizens would fight until only the slaves remained.

> We would infinitely prefer that the territory of the state should be the cemetery of freemen, than the habitation of slaves. Actuated by these principles, and animated by these sentiments, we will cling to the pillars of the temple of our liberties, and if it must fall, we will perish amidst the ruins.[1]

On December 10, a proclamation issued by the newly-reelected President warned of the consequences of this rebellious behavior, which he declared was "a direct violation of their duty as citizens of the United States, contrary to the laws of their country, subversive of its constitution, and having for its object the destruction of the union."[2]

The South Carolinians referred to the proclamation as "THE DECLARATION OF WAR, made by ANDREW JACKSON," further stating, "If not execrated from Maine to Mexico, the union is not worth preserving, and will not be preserved."[3] They demanded to know who had written the proclamation, insisting it was "some intriguer behind the dictator's throne,"[4] and compared Jackson to Caesar, Cromwell, and Bonaparte, adding the slur that he was inferior to all three men in both intellect and spirit.

The President countered by moving cannons, light arms, ammunition, troops, and military stores toward Charleston. The month's end saw meetings supporting the union and old Hickory erupting in Boston and New York. Union demonstrators took to the streets throughout the north, but South Carolina remained defiant, claiming there was a "Holy zeal in a good cause, which is the best safeguard of our rights and liberties."[5] Counties in Georgia shared the grievances and planned to raise troops to help their neighboring state. "General Jackson is therefore warned not to rely upon Georgia for any assistance against South Carolina."[6]

The fight became personal during a brutal attack on December 24 by General James Blair, a member of Congress from South Carolina, on the publisher Duff Green. Reports worried whether Green had been "maimed for life."[7] Green, owner and editor of *The United States Telegraph*, had helped Jackson defeat Adams, becoming one of the President's closest advisors and a kitchen cabinet member. The *Telegraph* was decidedly in Jackson's camp, but an about-face put Green on Calhoun's side. While the editor was recovering, Blair entered a Washington theatre armed with "four pistols and two dirks"[8] shot randomly at the stage before being forcibly restrained and dragged outside. In April, he committed suicide, so the attack on Green could have been politically motivated, as most assumed, or an aberration that resulted from an overabundance of nerve-jangling news. Mary Shelley's *Frankenstein; or, the Modern Prometheus* saw American publication the same month, the novel finding an audience both fascinated and appalled by demons come to life.

The "Great Debate" over the tariff took center stage throughout January and February. On January 16, the President's message to Congress focused almost exclusively on South Carolina. Although he had won the election by a considerable margin: 219 electoral votes as opposed to only 40 for Henry Clay, the threat of secession had become a thorn in his side from which there appeared to be no escape. Outraged, he lashed out at the people who had deprived him of the joy of victory in defeating Clay so soundly.

> Aggressions upon the authority of congress, and subversive of the
> supremacy of the laws and the integrity of the union. . . . The right of
> a single state to absolve themselves at will, and without the consent of
> the other states, from their most solemn obligations, and hazard the
> liberties and happiness of the millions composing this union, cannot
> be acknowledged.[9]

Back in Washington, Calhoun, looking pale, sickly, and exhausted insisted that, "South Carolina never intended resistance by violence."[10] No one believed that bogus claim. Webster, formidable with his jet-black hair and impenetrable mien, challenged the South Carolinian, showing himself to be firmly on the side of the union and administration. Hailed as a hero in the debates, or the "War of the Giants," many wondered whether Webster would be rewarded with a cabinet position. Even the ever-eccentric John Randolph of Roanoke weighed in, arriving with a stable full of horses and a pack of hounds to add his denunciation of South Carolina. So did John Quincy Adams, stating that the union was "tottering to its foundations," and quoting an ode of Horace that praised tenacity in the fight for justice while deploring the clamor of the mob and the threats of a tyrant. Rumors that tens of thousands of people were quitting South Carolina over the danger of secession added to the national sense of dislocation.

When Clay's bill modifying the tariff was read, the hall was packed with onlookers. Every man and woman present was silent until Calhoun gave his approval, then the chambers burst into applause. For all in attendance, it seemed as though the near catastrophe had been averted, although even after the bill passed on March 2, the national mood remained tense. A much read speech of Webster's referred to "the friends of nullification" as "the architects of ruin."[11]

The drama appeared to bode well for Biddle and the Bank, however. Rumors in Washington pointed to a more lenient Jackson and a probable re-charter. It was said that government deposits in the Bank would "be safely continued."[12]

* * *

On January 8, 1833, Biddle was reappointed as a director of the bank of the United States for the term of one year (as was customary) and re-elected as president. John Sergeant, Henry Clay's running mate, and former Congressman from Pennsylvania, was also elected to the Bank's board for a one-year term. On March 2, Sergeant communicated his hopes to Biddle that the South's crisis might work in the Bank's favor.

> The new state of parties will be founded upon a combination of the South, and the leaders of it (the Southern party) are friends of the Bank upon principle, and will be more so from opposition to Jackson. If they succeed in their first object, of uniting the South, they will carry the whole of it in favor of the Bank, either actively or passively. . . . In the middle and Northern States, and in the West too, their view as to the Bank question will be an argument to gain friends for their party. Against a combination which threatens to be so powerful, Van Buren will have to look for alliances in the North, I think, and in so doing will be obliged to give up his hostility to the Bank. . . . In the meantime, Jackson's influence will be diminishing, and his personal feelings will be no means have the same weight as before. And, besides, I think he will be pressed by so powerful an opposition, that even he will be obliged to behave himself with some decency.[13]

Sergeant further "hinted" that the present Congress would evince "less ferocity" toward the Bank.

In February, Biddle was named a director of the new Girard College in Philadelphia, an institution whose founding tenet was the education of poor white male orphans. The French-born Stephan Girard had been reared for a life at sea; his formal education had been negligible. While engaged in a successful maritime trade between New York, New Orleans, and Port au Prince, the British fleet forced his ship to take shelter in Philadelphia in 1776, and there he remained. Subsequently, he became a citizen. Girard continued his maritime trade, purchased the building that had housed the first Bank of the United States, and opened his own bank. By the time of his death in December 1831, his fortune was unsurpassed. One of the stipulations of his will forbade clergy from participating in the students' education and life. After Biddle was elected president of the college's board, he expressed his "conviction that every citizen owes to his country his services, however, humble, wherever they may be deemed useful. . . ."[14]

Despite this buoyant public persona, Biddle still mourned the death of his dashing and handsome younger brother, Thomas, who had perished in August 1831 in a duel on St. Louis's aptly named Bloody Island. A paymaster in the United States Army, Major Biddle had been stationed at St. Louis, although he dearly missed Philadelphia. His duties made it impossible for him to return even for a brief visit. Nearsighted and indifferent to scholarly pursuits, he had chosen a military career during the War of 1812, fighting on the Northern Frontiers, and seeing action at the capture of Fort George and the siege of Fort Erie.

Despite his preference for action over erudition, he was a voracious reader and, like Nicholas, a Classics lover. Subscriptions to Philadelphia newspapers made his home seem less distant. He complained that he was growing uncouth and unmannerly and feared he would never be fit for polite society again. In 1823, he married the Kentucky native, Ann Mullanphy, whose father was purported to be the wealthiest man west of the Mississippi. Having been schooled in New Orleans and France, Ann helped her husband learn French. Under her genteel guidance, the couple imported furniture from Philadelphia, which lessened the place's wildness, but Thomas still pined for the city of his youth.

Because his interests also included political economy and history, Major Biddle aided his brother by establishing a branch of the Second Bank of the United States in St. Louis, of which he became a director. In 1828, he took an anti-Jackson stand and ran for Congress in opposition to Old Hickory and his party. Failing election, he aimed for the Senate in 1830. By then, he had become vehemently opposed to everything Jackson stood for. In print and private, Thomas voiced his outrage over Jackson's treatment of the Bank and his brother, Nicholas, which drew the ire of Spencer Pettis, who was then running for re-election to Congress on the Jackson presidential ticket. Congressman Pettis had a quick temper; Biddle did, too.

Verbal attacks escalated. Because Thomas considered the congressman less than a gentleman, he entered the tavern where Pettis dwelled, intending to give him a thorough whipping as a punishment for maligning Nicholas. Pettis brandished a sword, and the major was arrested. The feud intensified, although the two men might have retreated had it not been for external forces urging them to challenge each other. On both sides, the cause of Jackson or the Bank had reached fervid proportions. Although Thomas kept the duel a secret from Ann, he was not about to permit Pettis to spread calumnies about his beloved older brother.

On August 26, 1831, at the appointed hour, Biddle and Pettis faced each other. The distance had been set at a mere five feet owing to Biddle's myopia. Both men died from their wounds, Pettis the following afternoon, and Biddle lingering for five agonizing days. The nearly inarticulate message sent from Ann's father announcing the awful news stunned Nicholas. At first, he couldn't believe it was true.

> Oh my god what dreadful news to communicate to you, your good
> your worthy & noble Brother, is no more; he died about six o'clock
> this morning of a wound he rec'd in a duel with Mr. Pettis on Friday
> last. . . . His death is owing to his active vigilance in the Bank business
> at this place.[15]

Ann journeyed east that winter and stayed with Mary Biddle before returning to St. Louis. She never complained that family devotion had cost her husband his life, but every Biddle felt that this was so, and Nicholas especially. Guilt and sorrow oppressed him; he understood that the Bank and the partisan frenzy it had induced had caused his brother's death.

* * *

Politics, Biddle had always believed, should have no sway over fiscal matters. He had early rejected the idea that the Bank's boards be balanced as to parties. However, over time, there had been constant pressure to put Jackson men on the boards, which Biddle did in Baltimore, New York, New Orleans, Portsmouth, Nashville, Lexington, and Utica. In addition, he allowed Lewis to name the majority of the members in Nashville; Lewis attempted to do the same in Louisville. The result was that the parent board was kept free from political bias, but the branch boards were not, which led to charges of corruption. It mattered little that Biddle had declared that the Bank should never participate in the 1832 campaign. In the estimation of many Americans, it already occupied that partisan position.

Its critics continued to accuse it of currying favor with congress members by extending credit to them that ordinary citizens couldn't access. The Bank provided drafts on congressmen's salaries without charging interest even when the amount was payable at a site distant from the nation's capital. The institution also made loans on easy terms, leading to allegations of indirect bribery. Those charges, such as paying exorbitant legal fees, making political contributions from Bank funds, or buying the allegiances of newspaper editors, were never proven. However, they dogged Biddle and the Bank when Jackson's second term began on March 4, 1833.

One of the President's first official acts was to veto Clay's Land Bill, which elicited the expected hue and cry. *Poulson's* called the President a "supreme Dictator, more absolute that the Autocrat of all Russias."[16] Despite Jackson's show of strength, insiders in Washington murmured that Van Buren was the "President de facto"[17] and that no official "appointments will be made but with his approbation and consent."[18] A widespread belief existed that Van Buren intended to take the Bank from Biddle's hands (and Philadelphia's) and move it to New York City's Wall Street, where, as an arm of the Treasury, it would put "an incalculable amount of influence into the hands of corrupt men," allowing them to "control elections and subvert states."[19] Capricious as always, John Randolph of Roanoke changed his opinion about the Bank of the United States, declaring that the proposal to create a Treasury Bank would benefit only "little Martin."

Van Buren's agenda of forming a Treasury Bank and moving it to Wall Street had vocal supporters among New York bankers who were tired of playing second fiddle to Chestnut Street in Philadelphia. They felt that Penn's "greene countrie town" had become antiquated, stuck revering the past while New York was a metropolis on the ascendancy. Envy also played a part. The Second Bank's extensive branch system from Maine to Kentucky, and Louisiana to Ohio kept Wall Street in a lesser, defensive position. Van Buren, who intended to succeed Jackson as President in 1836, needed Wall Street's discontents, climbers, and arrivistes on his side to win the election. Relocating the Bank would ensure his popularity because Wall Street, rather than Chestnut Street, would have access to the federal government's deposits, eclipsing Philadelphia as a financial hub. Board members of the Manhattan and Mechanics Bank were already in the Jackson/Van Buren fold. New Yorker Jabez Delano Hammond, a former member of the U.S. Congress and the New York State Senate, declared:

> The local state banks, anxious to enjoy the golden harvest growing out
> of the use of national deposits, could not wait patiently for the death

of their great rival for the fruition of their hopes, but availed themselves of the indignant feelings of General Jackson toward Mr. Biddle
and the managers of the national bank. . . .[20]

Wall Street likened the Second Bank to a monopoly, which was like calling it
the Devil incarnate. In reality, the New York bankers wanted that monopoly
under their control. Stoking fears and making promises, Van Buren secured
Wall Street's allegiance.

* * *

In the spring of 1833, Jackson embarked on a victory tour through the north-
eastern states. Van Buren never left his side. As Old Hickory's heir-apparent, it
was natural for the Vice President to take advantage of the President's popularity, but Van Buren's critics knew better. They carped that "the most cunning
man in the union . . . does not dare trust his master out of his sight."[21] Con-
spiracies among Jackson's inner circle were still rampant. As early as March 3,
Daniel Webster's name had been proposed as a candidate in 1836, stoking fears
in both the "kitchen" and "parlor" cabinets.

While Jackson's "Eastern Progress" moved from Philadelphia, where he attended Sunday services at the First Presbyterian Church on June 10 (the sermon
was taken from Daniel 4 and King Nebuchadnezzar's humbling by God), to
New York and Boston and towns in between, Webster made a similar journey.
Pointedly, he went west, keeping out of range of Jackson's entourage. At each
stop, from Buffalo to Cleveland (where he arrived on the steamboat "Daniel
Webster") to Columbus and Cincinnati, enthusiastic crowds pressed close to
shake his hand. At the same time, during a parade in Boston on June 24, Van
Buren was lampooned for riding a "non-committal" horse that refused to trot
in a straight line, instead dodging sideways, which inspired more gibes about
the Little Magician's mendacity. The tour's hectic pace also affected Jackson's
health, so the triumphal time was less jubilant than planned.

One perplexing aspect of the President's journey was the addition of two
captive Sauk chiefs. Black Hawk and his adopted son, the Prophet Napope,
traveled in Old Hickory's wake. The chiefs never appeared with Jackson in public, but arrived under guard in each city a day or two later, and were then put
on display as a reminder of America's military prowess during the Black Hawk
War. The conflict began in April 1832 when an alliance of Sauks, Kickapoos,
and Meskwakis crossed the Mississippi River into Illinois to settle on tribal

lands. Mistaking the motive as hostile, government forces attacked and finally defeated the tribes in August.

In May 1833, Black Hawk and Napope were brought in chains to Washington, where Black Hawk protested that his people had only wanted to protect the food supply for their women and children. He expressed concern over the Sauk peoples' welfare in his absence. Jackson ignored the chief's peaceable overture and instead used the tribes' defeat as additional motivation for Indian removal. In June 1833, amid the tour, he made a show of meeting with Black Hawk, saying,

> My Children, - When I saw you in Washington, I told you that you had behaved very badly in raising the tomahawk against the White people and killing men, women and children on the frontier. Your conduct last year compelled me to send my warriors against you, and your people were defeated with great loss, and your men surrendered, to be kept, until I should be satisfied that you would not try to do any more injury.[22]

Not everyone agreed with Jackson's position regarding the tribal peoples. A month prior, the artist, George Catlin, had returned from a long sojourn west; among other subjects, he'd painted Black Hawk and the Prophet whom he viewed as embattled and heroic. "Lo, the Poor Indian!" *Poulson's* had entitled the report on Catlin's works. On July 20, 1833, *Niles' Register* compared them to ancient heroes who "have come down to us immortalized in the records of patriotism and philanthropy" and then quoted from Horace: "Dulce et decorum est, pro patria mori."[23] As a political stunt, Jackson's showmanship and the abject state of the two Sauk chiefs might have appealed to the frontier states, but it made the North squirm.

* * *

While Jackson continued his celebratory tour, Biddle focused on saving the Bank. The ongoing rivalries between the President's advisors both helped and hindered him. Hamilton maintained his role as a favorite, using the issue of the Second Bank as a way to garner political clout. Whether his revelations were substantiated or not, he kept the institution at the forefront of Jackson's worries. In February 1833, he had told the President,

> I am informed by a gentleman whose knowledge of the United States
> Bank is only second to that of its President, and therefore repeat to you
> (with the assurance that you may rely upon it), that the bank counts
> upon being rechartered. Its purpose is for the next two years to fortify
> itself beyond all hazard by calling in its responsibilities gradually, to an
> amount at which they will be entirely manageable, and also by secur-
> ing its debts. This operation will be performed under the avowed idea
> that it is necessary and preliminary to winding up its concerns.[24]

Using the incriminating phrase "it is believed," Hamilton made a case against
Biddle's Bank with its "large credit in London," its exportation of specie, which
he averred would cause a run on all "moneyed institutions." The document
served Jackson as a handy reference on the evils of abundant money, excessive
trading, and rising prices leading to a sharp reaction. "The serpent is scotched,
not killed," Hamilton concluded. "It has power as long as it can wind and move
its immeasurable length along. Its exertions will be violent. . . . The reputation
of your Administration may not escape unquestioned."[25]

Unfortunately, Jackson never saw Hamilton's letter "To a Discreet Friend"
dated March 19, 1833; it might have made him query his informant's motives.
"I am up to my eyes in business. Enjoying all the confidence of the President
and the gentlemen around him . . . there is an excitement in this large game
which is most congenial with my feelings and temperament."[26]

Regrettably, Biddle was also unaware of Hamilton's machinations. If so, he
might have been better prepared for Jackson's subsequent decision to withhold
government deposits from the Bank and distribute them to state and private
banks instead. The President had become convinced the deposits were unsafe
in Biddle's hands. He also suspected that they would be used to bribe congressmen to vote for re-charter—despite the veto. "I've no hesitation to say if they
can recharter the bank, with this hydra of corruption they will rule the nation,
and its charter will be perpetual, and its corrupting influence destroy the liberty
of our country."[27] Turning to Hamilton again, he asked him to write a history
of banking, and in particular, of Biddle and the Second Bank. The result was
a lengthy, biased narrative whose tone was nothing if not condescending. As
Hamilton later recalled, he prepared the "brief history of Banking and Bills of
Exchange" because "it was believed that [Jackson] had very little knowledge
of the subject."[28] Biddle's Bank was repeatedly likened to a "monster" with
"strength and inclination to do mischief."[29]

Armed with this spurious document, Jackson presented a "manifesto" to the cabinet on September 18, 1833. In it, he accused the Bank of having attempted to sway the election. Having won, he believed he had been returned to office to kill the "unconstitutional"[30] Bank.

His campaign against Biddle continued when he dismissed Secretary of the Treasury, William Duane. Duane had protested Jackson's order to remove government deposits from the Bank of the United States and place them in state banks friendly to the administration—soon dubbed "pet banks." Legally, Duane was within his right; the removal fell under the purview of the Treasury Department. Enraged, Jackson insisted the secretary retire. Duane refused, placing Jackson in a difficult position because Cabinet positions required Senate confirmation. Undaunted, the President sacked Duane and replaced him with Roger Taney, who vowed to carry out Jackson's orders, which plunged the Bank's stock down by 1½ percent. The date set for the removal was October 1. Although the deposits remained in situ, no one seemed to notice. The slogan "Removal of the deposits" became a call to arms. For Old Hickory, a retreat was impossible.

For Biddle, a retreat was equally unthinkable. "The fact is that the real sin of the Bank in the eyes of the Executive is, that it is refractory & unmanageable," he seethed.

> When these people first came into power on a current of overwhelming popularity, to which they thought ever thing should yield, they considered the Bank a part of the spoil, and one of their first efforts was to possess themselves of the institution for the benefit of their partizans. . . . From that time they resolved, that as they could not bend it, they would break it.

Biddle accused Jackson of intending to dole out "Directorships to worthy friends who have no character and no money."[31] He also recognized the Little Magician and "political gamblers" at work. "The truth is, that the question is no longer between this Bank & no Bank. It is a mere contest between Mr. Van Buren's Government Bank and the present institution—between Chestnut St. and Wall St."[32]

However much he raged, Biddle knew that Jackson and his supporters held the Bank's future in their grip. After the President's September "manifesto," he had appointed a committee of seven people to create a plan for the Bank's management. One of its orders was that state branches could no longer accept notes outside of their home cities. An unintended result was that money became scarce. Throughout the nation, private and state banks experienced runs or failed. Laborers were laid off. Public works projects and manufactories discharged workers for lack of sufficient capital. In Lancaster County, Pennsylvania, Philadelphia's breadbasket, prices for oats, corn, rye, and wheat tumbled. Farmers and merchants alike felt they were facing ruin.

Similar reports of loss and fear were heard throughout the country. *Niles'* called the situation "THE PUBLIC DISTRESS"[33] Unrest and anxiety brought together large groups of people supporting the Bank's retention of government deposits, or those virulently opposed to it. The clamor was heard on both sides of the argument from Ohio to Louisiana, from New Hampshire to Kentucky. Newspapers, pro and con, augmented the fury. As *Niles'* editorialized, "It was hoped we might work through it [the affairs of the bank]—but that hope is now given way to despair."[34] Banks in Ohio were supposedly "tottering" in March 1834;[35] in Washington, a district bank failed in April, the result of which was that no banks would accept district notes. The Bank of Alexandria failed the same month. The Second Bank was pilloried as a "reptile to be crushed at will," and Biddle as a "money-king."[36]

Outrage fractured the populace into two camps whose rhetoric further divided it. On one side were the laboring classes emboldened by a President who had their primary interests at heart; they knew that a conniving aristocracy had always attempted to cheat them. The Democrats pandered to their indignation and fears. On the other side were men who thought Jackson was a despot and reviled his adherents as willing dupes of a power-mad regime. A moral imperative propped up both arguments.

The angst drove some people to consider desperate acts. On February 22, 1834, *Niles'* published one of several anonymous letters threatening Jackson's life.

> To gen. ANDREW JACKSON, president of the United States of
> America: I am very sorry to inform you that if the deposites [*sic*] are
> not replaced, and the bank of the United States is not rechartered
> the 4th of March next, you will be a dead man by the 15th of March
> next. . . . Your humble servant, A DEMOCRAT[37]

The writer was supposedly a Jacksonian, making the motive behind his revelation unclear. Had he uncovered a plot to kill the President, or had he become disenchanted enough to carry out the deed himself? Or, as a cynic might posit, was the threat a political ploy? One thing was certain. The populace was angry.

Eleven months later, the warning turned into action when Richard Lawrence, who worked as a house painter in Georgetown, fired a pistol at the President following a funeral at the capitol in February 1835. When his first weapon misfired, Lawrence took another pistol from his pocket and shot again. Jackson rushed at him, brandishing his cane, while those nearest leaped upon the would-be murderer. Although denounced as a madman, Lawrence's landlord spoke well of him, insisting he was "sober and industrious."[38] Before the assassination attempt, though, he had been observed frequenting the capitol rotunda enough times to arouse suspicion. Whatever the truth: a deranged man or sane person who'd grown violent through desperation, it rattled an already polarized nation.

Throughout, Biddle retained a sanguine pose as if he believed that unity and cooperation would return; inwardly, he remained vigilant and resolute. On July 4, 1833, he had addressed the crowd gathered for the laying of the cornerstone of Girard College in Philadelphia. Speaking of the necessity of education, his private fears regarding the country's political strife surfaced. The words could have been leveled at a mob screaming for the Bank's destruction, instead of a group of civic-minded folk celebrating financier Stephen Girard's legacy in an institution of learning.

> Our general equality of rights would be unavailing without the intelligence to understand and to defend them—our general equality of power would be dangerous, if it enabled an ignorant mass to triumph by numerical force over the superior force which it envied—our universal right to political distinction, unless the people are qualified for it by education, becomes a mere abstraction, exciting only an abortive ambition.[39]

* * *

By early 1834, all of Washington had become embroiled in the Bank issue. Even Hamilton started cautioning restraint, but Old Hickory would have none of the advice. "There is no real general distress. It is only with those who live by borrowing, trade on loans, and the gamblers in stocks. It would be a godsend to society if all such were put down."[40]

Although still playing his own game, Hamilton began to worry. He had resigned his position of New York's District Attorney to make himself available whenever Old Hickory wished, but what if the President's efforts were to fail? In his journal, Hamilton confided that the "efforts to enlighten the President, made at his request, were wholly unavailing. He had determined, before he came to Washington, to destroy the Bank of the United States. . . ."[41]

At the same time, Lewis encouraged him:

> Your services are due to the Old Chief, who has *always* been your friend, if not to others. This is his last and greatest struggle, and we should neither desert him, nor even be lukewarm in this, his greatest need. If he succeeds—and I have *now* no doubt of it—in prostrating the Bank, and overthrowing his enemies, his evening sun will be brighter and more glorious than his morning sun. Things are looking well to the South. Virginia, I feel confident, will be regenerated and redeemed. The opposition in the Senate are cast down and look desponding. Clay's last speech upon his resolutions, was considered a failure by his own friends. . . .[42]

As the financial panic spread, Biddle and the Bank bore the brunt of the blame for its lack of leniency in lending practices, leading to conjecture that its policy was politically motivated. The institution's detractors believed that the Bank could push for—and win—recharter by forcing the nation to its knees. There was truth to the allegation. As Biddle stated in January 1834:

> The ties of party allegiance can only be broken by the actual conviction of existing distress in the community. Nothing but the evidence of suffering abroad will produce any effect in Congress. If the Bank remains strong and quiet, the force of events will save the Bank and save all the institutions of the country which are now in great peril. But if, from too great a sensitiveness—from the fear of offending or the desire of conciliating, the Bank permits itself to be frightened or coaxed into any relaxation of its present measures, the relief will itself be cited as the evidence that the measures of the Govt. are not injurious or oppressive. . . . Our only safety is in pursuing a steady course of firm restriction—and I have no doubt that such a course will

ultimately lead to a restoration of the currency and the recharter of the Bank.[43]

Daniel Webster disagreed with this stringent measure and said so, advising a gradual easement of the lending policy. Otherwise, as he cautioned, the government would undoubtedly use the Bank's intransigence against it, but Biddle remained obdurate. Convinced the panic would finally compel Congress to recognize the necessity of a central bank, he held to his course.

That decision played into Jackson's hand because the economy continued to weaken. Having painted the Bank as an enemy of the common people and himself as an avenging angel, the President used the question of the removal of deposits to consolidate his base. If Congressional members of his Democratic party didn't support him, they were repudiated as untrustworthy renegades. The moral outrage of the disenfranchised silenced those on the fence. The opposition was attacked as being controlled by the Bank, or the nation's money powers, or foreign investors—all of whom the Jacksonians regarded with suspicion. The President also began pillorying Biddle personally, falsely insisting he had amassed vast amounts of specie in the Bank's vaults and, like Mammon, intended to hoard it while the country starved. The rhetoric further inflamed Jackson's supporters.

Pushing back against Old Hickory's imperious style, a new political party began to coalesce in the early spring of 1834. Although the wounds from recent confrontations were still fresh, nullifiers joined National Republicans; Bank men made peace with States' Rights supporters, and those espousing internal improvements. All who were anti-Jackson for whatever reason drew together under the banner of "Whig," a name that had anti-monarchy associations in contemporary British politics, as well as being a potent reminder of American's fight for freedom during the Revolutionary War. The Whigs girded themselves to battle the "Tories," as they referred to the Jacksonians, and their leader, King Andrew. They further resolved to publicly rebuke Jackson for removing government deposits from the Bank, insisting that his action was unconstitutional. On March 28, 1834, the Senate voted to censure the President of the United States by 26 to 20.

Henry Clay added his condemnation of the President's tactics on April 14, 1834, in a speech that started in a deceptively equable tone, then categorically began destroying Jackson's ideological position:

And what is the state of the public treasury? The President, not
satisfied with the seizure of it, more than two months before the commencement of the session, appointed a second secretary of the treasury. . . . We are now in the fifth month of the session; and in defiance
of the sense of the country, and in contempt of the participation of
the senate in the appointing power, the President has not yet deigned
to submit the nomination of his secretary to the consideration of the
senate. . . . The partisans of the present executive sustain his power in
the most boundless extent. They claim for him all executive authority.
They make his sole will the governing power. Every officer concerned
in the administration, from the highest to the lowest, is to conform
to his mandates. Even the public treasury, hitherto regarded as sacred,
and beyond his reach, is placed by them under his entire direction and
control.

Clay ended with a call to arms:

Senators! We have a highly responsible and arduous position; but the
people are with us, and the path of duty lies clearly marked before us.
Let us be firm, persevering and unmoved. Let us perform our duty in a
manner worthy of our ancestors—worthy of American senators—worthy of the sovereign states that we represent—above all, worthy of the
name of American freemen! Let us 'pledge our lives, our fortunes, and
our sacred honor,' to rescue our beloved country from all impending
dangers. And, amidst the general gloom and darkness which prevail, let
us continue to present one unextinguished light, steadily burning, in
the cause of the people, of the constitution, and of civil liberty.[44]

Jackson flew into a rage, and three days later, sent a rambling message to
Congress that required more than an hour to read. He insisted that he and
the Legislature shared equal rights, but that the President had full authority
to choose all government officers (except judges and court officers) with or
without the consent of Congress. He further declared that the Treasury Department, as a custodian of public monies, was solely responsible to the executive
branch, and the Senate had "no right to interfere."[45] Even though he claimed he
acted as a servant and disciple to the American people, his ego could not allow
Congress members a similar position. Calling upon "the Almighty Being who

has hitherto sustained and protected me,"[46] he cast himself as a Moses rescuing his flock from Pharaoh and Pharaoh's minions.

As might have been expected, the communication provoked an uproar. The Senate resolved, "That the communication of a paper of such a character, with the declarations that accompanied it, is a plan, an open breach of the constitutional rights and privileges of the senate."[47] The body debated whether or not to refuse officially receiving the President's letter. Even Jackson's supporters understood he intended to undermine all power but his own.

On April 21, addressing the Senate, Webster leveled a critique at Jackson's message, calling it "one of the most important and ominous occurrences of these extraordinary times. . . . The President denies that this house, or indeed either house of congress has any right to express any opinion upon his conduct, except by way of impeachment." Citing the communication's unconstitutionality, Webster queried who had produced the document and advised Jackson to send it. It was generally accepted that the President could not have been the author.

> Whoever he was . . . the President of the United States has been
> misled. He is uninformed, or misinformed, as to the real state of
> opinion in this country. I fear there are those who share his confidence,
> and who present to his view only one side of things. . . . The whole
> measure is of an alarming character. It attempts one great stride toward
> the accumulations of all power in executive hands.

Webster concluded by declaring that the Senate would resist Jackson's dictatorial actions, and "that resistance will be supported by the country."[48]

Calhoun, now Jackson's sworn enemy, also rebuked him, accusing the President of making:

> His declaration of war against the senate. . . . He first seized upon the
> public money, took it from the custody of the law, and placed it in his
> own possession, as much so as if placed in his own pocket. The senate
> disapproves of the act, and opposes the only obstacle, that prevents
> him form becoming completely master of the public treasury. To crush
> the resistance which they interpose to his will, he seeks a quarrel with
> them. . . . Since, then, hostilities are intended, it is time that we should
> deliberate how we ought to act; how the assaults upon our constitu-
> tional rights and privileges ought to be met.[49]

Jackson's reaction to the angry clamor was to re-nominate directors to the Bank of the United States that the Senate had already rejected. The Senate defied him, voting against the appointments 30 to 11. Perhaps, his maneuver had the outcome he intended because the Bank then had no government directors for the coming year, which Jackson was quick to point out to the recalcitrant legislators.

All the while, Biddle had been toiling mightily to save the Bank. As he explained privately and publically, without government deposits the Second Bank of the United States was powerless. Without a national bank, local banks would continue to founder, and private and corporate debts increase. "Real and permanent stability to the currency is in fact the question of the recharter of the Bank,"[50] he wrote to Kentucky lawmaker John S. Smith on May 9, 1834. He knew that time was of the essence. As Biddle said, "before long the evils will grow entirely out of our control."[51] His determination and his hope for a good outcome were tempered by his understanding that Jackson loathed both him and the Second Bank.

Implacable, Jackson continued his assault. On May 13, 1834, he nominated another group to become Banks directors (three from Philadelphia, one from New York, and one from Baltimore). It was anti-Bank to a man. *Niles'* editorialized whether they would "sit there as spies?"[52]

- CHAPTER FOURTEEN -

"THE PUBLIC TREASURE – WHERE IS IT?"

"This worthy President thinks that because he has scalped Indians and imprisoned Judges, he is to have his way with the Bank. He is mistaken—and he may as well send at once and engage lodgings in Arabia."[1] So wrote Nicholas Biddle to his friend, Joseph Hopkinson, in February 1834. Hopkinson, a Philadelphian, had been a member of the U.S. House of Representatives; since 1829, he had served as a federal judge. Like Biddle, he was drawn to the literary arts and had composed the lyrics to "Hail Columbia," which served as a national anthem. The letter was in response to queries Hopkinson had posed regarding Jackson's demands that the Bank ease lending to relieve the Panic of 1833. Biddle's impatience was reaching a breaking point, and he stated in exact and angry words that the Bank "will be neither frightened nor cajoled from its duty." He blamed the President for ordering the removal of the government deposits and "the miserable people" who concurred with him.

Clay had believed that the Bank's re-charter in 1836 would become a *fait accompli*, because the Panic would force pro-Jackson legislators to reject the President's wishes. Biddle was informed that the Cabinet was meeting daily to discuss the financial depression. Calhoun suspected the members were plotting to create a new government bank. There were even rumors that Taney might be forced out of the Treasury, heightening anxiety that the Bank's end was nigh.

By mid-February 1834, when hope faded that the depression would revive the Second Bank's necessity, Clay, Webster, and Calhoun started making plans for a bill to re-charter it even though the twenty-year charter didn't expire until January 1836. The problem was that the three men disagreed on a time limit.

Webster espoused a period of six years; Calhoun favored twelve; both began to ignore Clay and object to his leadership. Biddle preferred Webster's proposal but understood the necessity of bringing Calhoun and Clay into an alliance. At that point, the two were plotting their futures. Calhoun made it no secret that he believed the administration's power was waning and that action should be taken quickly, while Clay cautioned delaying until May to take action.

"Let us go for the practical," Biddle advised on March 11. "If we can get a permanent charter, let us do so—if not, let us take the temporary & make it permanent thereafter. Above all, let us do something soon. The country wants something to rally to—it requires some point on which to concentrate its thoughts."[2] His advice was ignored.

Webster outlined his proposed bill on March 18; three days later, Calhoun made his objections known by presenting his own bill. Clay supported neither. Complexities within the various arguments were beginning to take their toll. Voters found themselves confused rather than reassured. They wanted precise, uncomplicated explanations instead of lengthy fiscal and legal jargon, which they construed as obfuscation. Even Hezekiah Niles, long a Bank supporter, expressed his frustrations:

> Whether the location of a renewed bank shall be at Philadelphia or
> New York, is of little moment to the people, as large; but a plan could
> be easily devised (as I think), by which all reasonable cause for local
> jealousies, or interferences with local concerns, might be relieved. . . .
> In the existing state of parties, I think that a spirit of accommodation
> ought to prevail. THE NATION STANDS ON THE VERY BRINK
> OF A HORRIBLE PRECIPICE.[3]

The defections included Governor George Wolf of Pennsylvania, who had also been a Bank supporter. "All confidence in the currency of the country is said to be destroyed," he told a joint session of the state legislature on February 26. Referring to the Bank as "a powerful moneyed institution," he accused it of using its considerable resources and equally influential friends to defeat Jackson "and to frustrate his designs in relation to it."[4]

Following Wolf's lead, the state's Democratic party turned against the Bank. Blaming it for the state's insolvency, the Commonwealth's Senate passed resolutions opposing re-charter. Pennsylvania's two United States senators also turned their backs on the Bank, as did nearly all the state's representatives to the House. Although Biddle had had ample experience with Pennsylvania's antipathy to a central bank, the condemnation felt like a betrayal. All the more so, because immediately before delivering his message, Wolf had given the impression that he continued to be "decidedly friendly to the Bank."[5] Biddle retaliated in a private letter in which he accused Wolf of a lack of "patriotism."[6] More than ever, he believed that a national bank was crucial to America's financial health. With banks imploding or failing to meet commitments, "the only security," he said, "is the Bank of the U.S. It holds its power as a trust for the ultimate protection of the banking system."[7]

April brought Biddle more dire news. Led by Tennessee's James Knox Polk, who chaired the House Committee of Ways and Means, and who was an ardent Democrat and Jackson protégée, the committee brought the Bank's recharter to a vote on April 4, 1834. The Democratic majority in the House successfully pushed through Jackson's agenda. It was resolved not to re-charter the Bank by a vote of 134 to 82, and not restore the public deposits by a vote of 118 to 103. The state banks (the pets) were permitted to continue holding government deposits by a vote of 117 to 105.

The same day a Congressional subcommittee was convened to investigate the Bank for malfeasance. It was tasked with visiting the principal bank in Philadelphia and its branch offices and examining all books and correspondence. Although stating that "The bank of the United States was chartered for great public purposes, as an agent, deemed necessary to the federal government, in the efficient exercise of its high prerogative, to fix the value of money, and thereby secure the benefits of a sound circulating medium to the confederacy"[8] accusations had been leveled against the Bank that its charter had been violated by interfering in politics, influencing elections, controlling the press, and contributing to the nation's financial distress.

Similar arguments had surfaced before, but this time Polk's maneuverings forced the House to act. Although the four Congressional decisions provoked cries of partisanship and the willful destruction of the Bank by the president and his kitchen cabinet, the damage was done both in Washington and the greater populace's estimation. For them, Polk's purported scheming had to be weighed with the possibility that the Bank was, in fact, corrupt. The ongoing depression did nothing to aid the institution's cause. The average voter—even those who believed in a central bank—understood that the nation was suffering, and it was all too easy to persuade them that the Bank of the United States was to blame.

Congressional committee members arrived in Philadelphia and interviewed Biddle on April 23. The following day, they returned to Chestnut Street's offices but found the directors assembled and waiting for them. Searching through the Bank's books and the president's and directors' correspondence in private became impossible. Committee members feared their investigation was being purposely obstructed. They retreated to the North American Hotel and requested that the books be sent there. Biddle and the board refused.

On May 5, the committee returned to the Bank; Biddle again denied the members access to Bank materials unless the request was delivered in writing. He demanded that if the intention was "to establish a violation of the charter, then to state specifically in writing, what the alleged or supposed violations [were]."[9] At that point, the committee's opinion was "that the charter of the bank was violated, and a contempt of the authority of the house of representatives committed."[10]

A marshal summoned Biddle and thirteen board members to appear before the committee at the North American Hotel on May 10. They arrived with written testimony but again refused to supply the necessary items. "I have not the custody of, nor control over, the books and papers mentioned in the resolution," Biddle told them. It was a last ditch effort to protect investors and borrowers' confidentiality, but the statement struck everyone present as a lie. Committee members were now convinced that Biddle and his board were involved in deceit, collusion, and corruption.[11]

The committee had no choice but to quit Philadelphia and return to Washington, where it delivered a full report to the House on May 22. It was then resolved to arrest Biddle for contempt of authority and compel him and the thirteen directors to stand before the House for questioning. All individual loans dating from January 1, 1829, would further be examined. Supporters of the Bank suspected partisan politics, but Biddle's actions did nothing to allay suspicions. Instead, his stonewalling made him look guilty. For those who believed the Bank was involved in criminal activity, its president's behavior confirmed the opinion.

Biddle had enough friends in Congress (members who had received favorable loans, as well as southern anti-Jackson Democrats and Whigs) to prevent being hauled down to Washington. However, his reprieve raises questions about both parties' intentions. Would a witch-hunt have damaged the Jacksonians in Congress and out? Did they fear that too much public pillorying would have an adverse effect? Finally, what did the Whigs have to gain? 1834 was a mid-term election year. Did they intend to ride out the Bank problem, hoping that the balance of power would shift? Or did they make a covert deal with the Democrats? If so, what would have been gained—unless both parties decided the Bank was a political liability?

Endeavoring to discern the truth, *Poulson's* published an article entitled "The Plot Thickens."[12] In it, the committee was accused of pandering to Amos Kendall's wishes, a Jackson henchman, who followed his own agenda and didn't mind stabbing fellow Jacksonians in the back. Positing a malevolent mystery, *Poulson's* opined that if Biddle and his board journeyed to Washington, Kendall and his associates would travel to Philadelphia and rob the Bank.

Biddle reacted as if he had won a major battle. The country's anti-Jackson merchant class abetted this crowing response. They blamed the administration for the financial chaos. They denounced the so-called "pet" banks in which the administration had placed the government deposits because they'd failed to correct the nation's financial distress. However, the pet banks lacked the central bank's extensive infrastructure and were overwhelmed by the enormity of the task they'd been given. Biddle had foreseen the problem, but he had no intention of being humble or forgiving.

Instead of expressing fear or shame, Biddle called the Congressional actions "deliberate efforts to destroy the Bank,"[13] and went on the attack. Perhaps it was delusional that he believed he could defeat a sitting President, or maybe it was stubbornness, which was a recognized trait. Or, his behavior could have been due to heredity of valor under fire, as well as familial competitiveness. Maybe it was his outsized ego or even elitism. Whatever the motive or motives, he remained at his post, reaching out to influential friends and colleagues who informed him of the state of affairs in Washington. He redoubled his efforts to protect the Bank at all costs. Hindsight might have enabled him to recognize that the fight was between Jacksonians and anti-Jacksonians and that the Bank issue was a pretext—useful to both sides, but not the point. However, hindsight was a luxury Biddle lacked. Nor did he discern the virulence of partisan politics within weeks of Congressional debate over "bribery, wanton extravagance and wanton corruption"[14] within the Post Office—another example of Whig attacking Democrat.

The Anglo-American economist, Thomas Cooper, a nullifier from South Carolina, provided only a small hint that the Bank debate might be a feint. "The talking will go on in Congress till nothing is done and the members and the public grow weary. . . . If Jackson obtains controul [*sic*] of the revenue we are defeated, and nothing but extensive bloodshed will preserve us. . . ." Describing the difficulties of aligning Webster-led representatives from the North with Calhoun adherents, Cooper concluded:

> If Jackson seizes the revenue in spite of the Senate, and in defiance of a rejection of the appropriation bill, the game is up, for he has the means and the inclination of buying up not merely political but military adherents; and half measures will only plunge us deeper into the whirlpool destined to absorb what little of freedom remains.[15]

Calhoun also persisted in his war against Jackson, accusing him of endeavoring:

> to excite the sympathy of the people, whom he seeks to make his allies in the contest. He tells them of his wounds—wounds received in the war of the revolution—of his patriotism; of his disinterestedness; of his freedom from avarice or ambition; of his advanced age, and finally, of his religion; of his indifference to the affairs of this life, and of his solicitude about that which is to come. Can we mistake the object? Who does not see what is intended . . . ? He has proclaimed in advance, that the right to interfere, involves the right to make that interference *effectual*. To make it so, force only is wanting.[16]

As compelling as those and other speeches were, the "old tactician,"[17] as Calhoun called the President, continued to stymy his opponents.

The situation suited Old Hickory perfectly. Without waiting for the Congressional committee's written report, Jackson proposed measures to begin reforming United States banking. On June 28, 1834, just before Congress's recess, he signed the Coinage Act, which was intended to regulate gold coins, replacing paper with hard currency. Defining coin weights, the act also devalued overvalued silver coins. (It was subsequently known as the "Gold Coin Laws.") The House, largely Jacksonian, passed the bill by a significant margin. The Senate, although mostly anti-Jackson, approved the measure, as well. The act had its detractors, though, who viewed it as another attack on the Bank. Governor Samuel Foot of Connecticut (a former member of Congress) in his message to the state's legislature scoffed at the measure:

The idea, that a commercial country of such vast extent, and great resources as our own, should ever return to a metallic medium, after the long and extensive use of a paper currency, is too absurd and preposterous to require refutation. The necessity of transmitting the vast sums of money required in our ordinary commercial transactions, though this extensive and flourishing country; and the collection and disbursement of the revenue in the whole extent of the union, must shew [*sic*] the impracticality of such a visionary project." He called the "openly avowed hostility to the bank . . . truly alarming.[18]

By then, Treasury Secretary Taney had found himself in an untenable position. Because he was a Jackson favorite, the Senate, still smarting from the President's attack, refused to confirm his continuation as Secretary of the Treasury. He resigned. The President thanked him in a published letter that adroitly positioned Taney as being the author of the Bank's woes while simultaneously decrying the Bank's supporters as immoral and persecutory:

The plan of financial policy which you have initiated by your acts, and developed in your official reports, and which has thus far received the full approbation of the representatives of he people, will, ultimately, I trust, be carried into complete operation; and its beneficial effects on the currency of the country, and the best interests of society, will be, in all future time, more than an adequate compensation for the momentary injustice to which you have now been subjected. And as it is the martyrs in any cause, whose memory is held most sacred; so the victims in the great struggle to redeem our republic from the corrupting domination of a great moneyed power, will be remembered and honored, in proportion to their services and sacrifices.[19]

As expected, the sentiment drew outrage from Jackson's opponents, who pointed out that the President, not Taney, was to blame. Van Buren and Polk came under attack, too. The "little magician" became the brunt of a series of lampooning "Jackson Currency" advertising cards: "Pay My People in Glory [a reference to the General's "blaze of glory"]. The Glory Bank in Washington promises to pay five dollars in GLORY to MARTIN VAN BUREN, or the Bearer, on Demand. Signed, Andrew Jackson, President. Amos Kendall, Cashier."[20] Old Hickory's foes also critiqued his unstable cabinet. During his five years in office, he had had four secretaries of state, five treasury secretaries, two war, three navy, and three attorneys general; unprecedented upheavals in any administration. Even the Jacksonians agreed with the prognosis.

The day prior to the signing of the Coinage Act, Daniel Webster's Senate Committee on Finance made its final report for the session. Harking back to the removal of deposits from the Bank of the United States, he announced, "the senate has decided, by a clear and unequivocal majority, that they are unsatisfactory and insufficient." He closed his argument with the Committee's recommendation:

> That all deposites [sic] of money of the United States which may accrue, or be received on or after the 1st day of August, A.D. 1834, shall be made with the bank of the United States and its branches, in conformity with the provisions of the act entitled 'an act to incorporate the subscribers of the bank of the United States,' approved 10th April, 1816.[21]

As Thomas Cooper had predicted, neither side had advanced. However, a great deal of energy and verbiage had been expended during the so-called "Panic Session," in which Congress had attempted unsuccessfully to rectify the nation's financial distress. Democrat and Whig alike had hurled loud partisan charges of "traitor" and "tyrant" at either Biddle or Jackson, and the President shouted during a twenty-minute rant in February that he "would rather undergo the tortures of ten Spanish inquisitions" than yield.[22]

Opponents insisted that he was nothing but a "dotard despot who imbibes adulation till his weak mind is swollen almost to bursting."[23] They claimed that the Kitchen Cabinet was sheltering and manipulating him to work their schemes—Van Buren, being cited as the worst conniver. So violent had tempers become that the two men received anonymous threats of assassination. In the end, though, nothing had been decided. Leaving the Bank's future in the balance, Congress adjourned.

* * *

Jackson quit the capital for the Hermitage in Tennessee, where he planned to remain until October. Rumors spread that he might resign. Clay, journeying home, was injured when the stage in which he traveled overturned on the road to Winchester in the Shenandoah Valley. He was urged to recover in that

crossroads town but declined all invitations and pressed on. His physical injuri-
ous were superficial, but he was tired. The Bank debate had taken its toll. On
June 30, 1834, the last day of the congressional session, Senator Thomas Hart
Benton had proposed eliminating from the record the resolution to censure
Jackson. The suggestion roused the wrath of his fellow senators, who roundly
rejected it. Benton retaliated by declaring that he planned to reintroduce his
proposal at the beginning of the next session, which prolonged the hostilities
between Democrats and Whigs.

Biddle also showed signs of fatigue. Jane proposed taking the European
journey he had promised her after the deaths of her mother and the couple's first
child. She was eager to pull Nicholas away from the Bank, away from Philadelphia, and even Andalusia, and return to a time when public acclaim had been
less important to her husband than his cozy family circle. That period in Nicholas's life—if there ever had been one—had vanished. He had become a political
animal, and Jane was unable to recall him to the carefree years of their courtship
and early marriage. He now moved in a sphere that she didn't fully comprehend
or even wish to understand. Being the wife of a public figure had never been her
intention or desire, and the threats on his life terrified her continually.

Nicholas listened to his wife's suggestion, but being Jane, she couched
her appeal quietly and with little hope of success. The couple's marriage was
suffering from their disparate interests. Jane misconstrued her husband's all-
consuming focus on business affairs. He felt perplexed by her disinterest. His
one-time role as a gentleman farmer now seemed misguided and amateurish.
He countered Jane's plea to travel to Europe by saying that he could not absent
himself from the Bank for months. Instead, he proposed sailing to the new
seaside town of Newport and then traveling inland to Niagara. They would
return home in September. Relieved at having her husband to herself even if the
time was far shorter than she had hoped, Jane acquiesced. At least, the banking
house would be left behind. Or so she hoped. With their four children and two
nurses, they left Philadelphia on July 11.

The day of the family's departure, Biddle responded to a letter he had received from a committee of New York merchants who wrote him July 10 to
express their "opinion that the time has now arrived when the United States
bank, in safety beyond all contingency, with resources abundant, and increasing
beyond all example, can, and ought, to come forward to the relief and support
of the commercial interests of the country."[24] The merchants requested a "free
and useful enlargement of its loans."

Biddle thanked the committee for its diligence, cited Congress's adjournment "without adopting any measures, either of redress to the bank, or of relief to the community,"[25] and apprised the committee's members that his board of directors had partially adopted the plan they requested. Praising "the long experience and the sagacity in business for which so many of you, gentlemen, are distinguished," he described a proposal "to increase the loans cautiously at those points which require the most relief."[26] *Niles'* published both letters on July 19, and commended the Bank's "promptness" in attempting to accommodate "the great body of merchants and traders in shaping their future business."[27]

By then, Biddle was in Newport. The report in *Niles'* followed him, enhancing the esteem with which the northern Whigs greeted him, but hardly comforting Jane. In Boston, on the anniversary of the nation's birth, a figurehead of Andrew Jackson, newly placed on the frigate *Constitution*, was decapitated. A reward of $1,000 was offered for information on the culprit or culprits, but the symbolic act engendered more humor than outrage.

> Thus nobly suicidal, went
> ANDREW, by handsaw, to his rest –
> Self-immolating President! –
> Of Blockheads 'greatest and the best'.[28]

The warfare between the anti-bank and pro-bank factions dogged Biddle as he traveled with his family. In August, a writer in *Niles'* accused him of "criminal hypocrisy," insisting that rather than save the American people, he'd been "sending funds to the great bankers in Europe. . . . Let those who have been deceived by the cant of the bank, reflect on this fact, and judge of Biddle's sincerity."[29]

At the same time, George Dallas of Philadelphia, formerly a United States senator, Biddle confidante, and "zealous advocate" of the Bank, turned against him and the institution for which he'd voted. Dallas chaired the Democratic party of Philadelphia that passed a resolution, declaring, "the contest at present waged by the bank of the United States and its friends is from first to last a war against the rights and liberties of the people, waged to revive the prostrated pretensions of wealth and aristocracy."[30] Biddle had believed Dallas was both friend and ally; now, he wondered what enmity his once supportive colleagues might harbor. Beleaguered, anxious, and uncertain how to defend himself, he and Jane and the children continued their supposedly restful holiday. No pleasant letters to family members at home survive if any existed. Stoic Jane must have attempted a cheery aspect which her husband was incapable of mirroring.

At the Hermitage, Jackson also received criticism. Before leaving Washington, he sent Donelson to the "pet" Metropolitan Bank for money to defray traveling expenses. He had instructed his relative and aide to request notes on the Bank of the United States because they were safer and more efficiently utilized. The fact that the President insisted on payment in what was popularly referred to as "Nicholas Biddle's paper"[31] inspired nationwide ridicule.

Meanwhile, the gold debate versus "wretched paper currency" continued throughout the nation: "Gold instead of Paper"[32] became a popular slogan. It soon became apparent, however, that the coins could be counterfeited as easily as paper notes. They soon bore derisive nicknames like "Benton's Yellow Jackets"—as a nod to Benton's slavish devotion to the President—or "Andrew d'or," which hearkened to France and King Louis d'or, or, worse, Napoleon d'or.

* * *

With Congress adjourned for the summer and America's fiscal woes refusing to abate, the populace's mood turned truculent. Poverty and heat exacerbated racial hostilities. Race riots, also called anti-abolition riots, broke out in New York in early July, subsequently in Newark, New Jersey, and Norwich, Connecticut, and in Philadelphia in mid-August. Poor Whites targeted both wealthy and poor Blacks, burning churches and homes, breaking precious glass windows, and savagely attacking anyone within—even corpses awaiting burial. In one particularly horrifying instance in Philadelphia, a grieving Black mother begged the mob to spare her dead child in his coffin. In response, they clubbed her and dumped the deceased baby onto the pavement. They did the same with the corpse of an elderly man.

The carnage among people and property was absolute: furnishings stolen or tossed into the streets and set ablaze. Those fires kindled fresh fires, especially along roads where the housing was wood. In each city, militias attempted to stem the riots, but they were overwhelmed, and the destruction of people and homes and places of worship and business lasted for days. In every area, homeowners feared that their neighborhoods would become targets for the mobs. In Philadelphia, a former servant (perhaps slave) to George Washington was murdered. His was not the only death.

The anti-abolition riots had their political equivalents in the 1834 elections. Jacksonians threatened and attacked Whig voters and candidates. "Liberty" poles (as opposed to the "Hickory" poles of the 1832 election) were burned by mobs, which no amount of policing could control. Fire brigades, racing to arson scenes, found access to the conflagrations blocked, and their men threatened with knives and pelted with bricks and rocks. Violence between groups and individuals was suddenly everywhere. Philadelphia, home to successful black entrepreneurs like Forten and Bogle, the American Anti-Slavery Society (founded in 1833), institutions of learning and erudition like the American Philosophical Society, and a predominantly white workforce in increasing poverty, now exemplified the nation's schism. The ugliness and viciousness of racial hatred and its underlying socio-economic disparity swept through the city. Nothing and no one seemed capable of restoring peace and hope.

Fearful for his family's safety, Biddle sent Jane and their children to Andalusia in October. He remained behind, hiring armed men and equipping them with muskets and bayonets to protect both his house and the Bank while the election fury reached its peak.

The national chaos came to represent a Democratic campaign that set the White working poor against the rich: the poor always depicted as the county's moral backbone, and the rich as parasites and worse. In the Senate, Webster was falsely accused of stating, "Let Congress Take Care of the Rich, and the Rich Will Take Care of the Poor."[33] The fact that this was a calumny and that Webster repeatedly disavowed the damning words meant little. The Jacksonians believed the statement. They labeled Webster a "pensioner of the Bank," which made him an enemy of the people.

During Webster's appeals to his fellow Whigs, he reminded them in ardent terms of America's fight for liberty in 1776. He asserted that Jackson's war on the Bank was merely one example of his rapacious desire for power, rather than an election issue. However, the "Jackson men" or "Jackson candidates" denied all allegations that the President had been guided by personal animosity instead of policy. Instead, they bruited about a rumor that their hero intended to run for a third term in order "to save the country."[34]

Concerned Whigs began to worry that Old Hickory would target the Judiciary next. Voting along party lines became imperative to save the "American system," but the Jacksonians decried the system as profligate (pro tariff, a central bank, and internal improvements). Whigs accused Democrats of buying votes with gold coins: "Turn for Jackson and your pockets will be lined with gold."[35] Newspapers daily reported the latest results of each state's staggered elections, making readers of both parties seesaw between jubilation and terror.

· * * *

The Democrats won. When the 24th Congress convened on March 4, 1835, the Senate and House were both pro-Jackson. Theirs would be a difficult task because the 23rd Congress had left two significant business pieces unfinished. One was Biddle's Bank; the other was the President's sudden threat of war against France. The latter became a frightening focal point during the first half of 1835, consuming both public and private individuals who worried that "bloodshed and devastation"[36] were soon to engulf America. Even devoted Jacksonites queried the advisability of provoking the nation's former ally.

In his annual message to Congress, delivered by Donelson on December 2, 1834, Jackson had referred to happy relations with all foreign nations except France, which he attacked for its "history" of "unprovoked aggressions upon our commerce."[37] He insisted that France owed money to the United States for former "unlawful seizures, captures, sequestrations, confiscation or destruction"[38] of American vessels. The sum presented was twenty-five million francs. A treaty, ratified on July 4, 1831, in Paris and on February 2, 1832, in Washington, had established a schedule of payments. The vagaries of French politics had, as yet, prevented the French from complying. Rather than seek redress through diplomatic channels, Jackson demanded immediate satisfaction. "It is my conviction," his speech read, "that the United States ought to insist on a prompt execution of the treaty, and in case it be refused, or longer delayed, take redress into their own hands. . . . Every day's delay on our part will be a stain upon our national honor."[39]

Having made known his enmity toward France, Jackson then turned his sights on the Bank, calling it "the scourge of the people." He also used the incendiary descriptions "anarchy and violence" about its practices, blamed it for the nation's fiscal distress, which it "wantonly produced," and for destroying "the confidence of mankind in popular governments."[40] Jackson urged Congress to guard "against an evil of such magnitude"[41] by passing a law "authorizing the sale of the [Bank's] public stock" and suspending its charter. As with his bellicose communiqué regarding France, "honor" and "power" were bywords.

The timing for the French attack was odd. On December 31, Congress planned to devote an entire day to commemorate Lafayette's life, who had died on May 20 and been awarded public memorial services and eulogies extolling his heroism throughout the nation. Jackson had even written to Lafayette's son, commending his father as a great man. As a result of the President's proposed "fight, for fighting's sake,"[42] as *Niles'* subsequently labeled the saber-rattling, the French minister withdrew from Washington.

"Our Relations with France" became the focus of daily newspaper articles. On January 2, Senator David Crockett of Tennessee published a letter to the editor asking how the United States intended to pay for a war, now that the President had eviscerated the Bank. He accused Jackson of making his speech for "popular effect,"[43] and worse, being beguiled into doing so. "The war-whoop was sounded from the Kitchen"[44] referred to the machinations of the President's Kitchen Cabinet, but no one understood what had motivated the most likely conniver, Van Buren.

The Senate moved quickly to curtail the president's combative posturing. The entire front page of *Poulson's* January 14th edition was devoted to a report from the Foreign Relations Committee, during which it cited Jackson's "limited view of the subject" and resolved: "Not to allow the President authority for making reprisals upon French property."[45] Jackson held his ground and insisted France make good its promise. If not, he intended to seize whatever French property he could.

The French Press vilified him, referring to the "ill humor of the President"[46] and calling him "mistaken and unskillful (*et une faute et une maladresse*)."[47] The *Journal du Commerce* stated:

> We do not hesitate to say that of all the wars practible or possible for France, the most foolish, the most *gauche*, the most impolitic, that would cause the loudest laughter at St. Petersburg, Berlin and The Hague, and would most afflict all the friends of liberty in Europe would be a war between France and the United States.[48]

In case Jackson had forgotten, the *Journal* reminded him of America's debt to France during the War of Independence.

"Suppressed letters"[49] were next exposed, revealing ongoing diplomatic negotiations that Jackson had either ignored or purposely concealed. He was ridiculed for misinterpreting the French verb "*demander*" as demand, rather than ask. The new Congress attempted to make sense of reams of documents between America's minister to France and the French government. The correspondence made its way into newspapers, begging the question of which individual had made the letters public and to what purpose. There were theories that Jackson or one of his advisors had released the correspondence intending to blame the contretemps on the United States minister's bungling rather than on the President.

* * *

Biddle and the Bank were drawn into the fracas when the new Secretary of the Treasury, Levi Woodbury, demanded an accounting of a bill of exchange on France and accused Biddle of "ardent defense of a foreign nation."[50] Woodbury was fierce. In all matters, both national and international, he blamed the Bank for malfeasance, obstructionism, and in the case of the "protested French bill,"[51] abetting a hostile government. It was clear he was speaking for Jackson. Defending the institution, Biddle chose equability and pragmatism, but the simplicity of his language further enflamed Woodbury, who believed Biddle was patronizing him. Siding with Woodbury, Polk declared his intention to open a new Congressional investigation into the Bank's affairs. The House voted down the motion 111 to 90. However, Polk, stayed staunch in his belief that the Bank had committed multiple crimes, despite Clay's efforts to persuade him otherwise.

Throughout the country, it was a jittery time. Added to the mood of insecurity and trepidation was the assassination attempt on Jackson on January 30. The question of war with France hung in the balance. By mid-March, attempting to assuage America's fears, Daniel Webster, by then an acknowledged candidate for the presidency, stated that there would be no conflict, unless "the President in his own folly and rashness provokes France to declare war upon us. Congress," he said, "will not declare [it.]"[52]

Jackson refused to concede. Nor would he apologize to France for his impolitic verbiage. By coincidence, *The Democracy of the United States* by Alexis de Tocqueville made its American debut in May, which prompted further mockery of the President. He ignored the taunts and turned his attention to the future Presidential election, announcing that he had chosen Van Buren his "legitimate successor."[53]

"The Crown is to descend from King Andrew to King Martin," hooted *Poulson's*, adding that the choice was "in character with all the outrageous and uncontrollable acts of the present administration."[54] Some queried whether the Little Magician had penned Jackson's letter appointing him. A jest made the rounds that the "Slippery Elm" was soon to replace the "Hickory Tree."[55]

Senator Crockett also made his disgust with Jackson known, writing a letter that was published widely: "The truth is, I do believe he is determined to expend every dollar of the Treasury. . . . In fact, I see no hope. The people have almost given up to a Dictator." Revealing that the Democrats had begun making it a habit of paying $25 per vote, he concluded, "I do believe Santa Ana's kingdom will be a paradise compared with this, in a few years."[56]

Political infighting and a refractory Jackson caused the worldview of America to deteriorate. "The French Question" became a recurring newspaper report. The President made no further threats against the nation, but he maintained his aggressive stance. In August, Canada lambasted "Andrew Jackson's damnable principle of democracy." Citing the President's oft-repeated words: "I take the responsibility. I construe of the Constitution as I understand it," the Canadians called him "the monarch of this country disguised as a republican."[57]

In America, the partisan battles impacted Biddle's extended family. In late summer 1835, William Biddle Shepherd, of North Carolina (related through Hannah Shepherd, Nicholas's mother), was attacked and brutally beaten. The reason an assailant gave was that Shepherd was known to be "a blood relation of President Biddle."[58] The assault badly frightened Jane.

A change was necessary if the nation hoped to regain an even course. In September, a candidacy for William Henry Harrison appeared to offer that hope. Although Webster had been considered the most likely Presidential candidate for 1836, Harrison, as a former general, governor of Indiana Territory, congressman and senator representing Ohio, offered a combination of local and national political leadership. Harrison also had a military history that would appeal to the Jacksonites who had begun to lose confidence in Van Buren. "Tippecanoe," who had once served as aide-de-camp for "Mad Anthony Wayne," was the antithesis of Van Buren with his penchant for visiting fashionable watering holes and riding in splendid carriages equipped with liveried servants.

Webster also labored under considerable misconceptions regarding his character. He was wrongly accused of being: "an old Federalist" and "opposed to the War" and having "favored the Hartford Convention," but perhaps the most damaging of all, a "friend of the Bank."[59]

* * *

The nation's unsettled financial future intensified. On November 30, *Poulson's* accused Jackson of illicitly taking "3 millions, at least, of the people's money" and giving it "to the shavers in Wall Street."[60] The following day, a headline ran: "THE PUBLIC TREASURE—WHERE IS IT?" "The public treasure has not been provided for by law. It is deposited in institutions not known to the law, under regulations not imposed by lay, or recognized by law."[61]

The attacks did not affect Jackson. During his yearly message to Congress on December 7, 1835, a full third of his written oration (again delivered by Donelson) revolved around his confrontation with France. He insisted that he had no intention of revoking his prior condemnation of the nation, declaring, "The honour of my country will never be stained by an apology by me. . . . This determination will, I am confident, be approved by my constituents." Almost as an afterthought, the President boasted, "The condition of the Public Finances was never more flattering that at the present period."[62]

By that time, it was widely believed that Amos Kendall had become the only man capable of controlling Jackson.

Whether Kendall had that much power was a moot point. Jackson's harangue had the immediate result of ruining any remaining goodwill with the French *Chargé d'Affaires*. He said that his nation had no intention of living up to the 1831-31 treaty until Jackson was out of office. "He has insulted France, and we do not desire to give him the triumph of saying he brought France to terms."[63]

* * *

Biddle felt dispirited. He had also suffered another private loss in late May 1835 when his elder brother, William, died. Retired from the practice of law, he had recently begun devoting himself to literary studies. Unfailingly kind, he was the pillar of an extended family, which turned to him for quiet counsel and his generosity of spirit. After William married Jane's childhood companion, Circé de Ronceray, the two couples' lives had grown intertwined.

In mid-December, Nicholas became ill. He paid no heed to the physician's recommendations, nor Jane's, with the result that his ailment grew worse until he was confined to his room under strict supervision while the year drew to a close. It ended on an equally sour, personal note. Maryland's Roger Brooke Taney, who had served as Jackson's Secretary of the Treasury, and in 1833, precipitated removing the government deposits from the Bank of the United States, acceded to a far loftier position on December 31, 1835. Jackson nominated him to be the fifth Chief Justice of the Supreme Court. For Biddle, it looked as though all three government branches were now the exclusive domain of Old Hickory and his cohorts.

- CHAPTER FIFTEEN -

THE DEATH OF ONE BANK, THE BIRTH OF ANOTHER

In anticipation of losing the charter of the Second Bank of the United States on March 3, 1836, Biddle had begun shutting branch offices while also attempting to care for the officers who had served it so faithfully. Writing to the cashier in Buffalo, he suggested a move to Maryland to apply for the same position in the Bank of Baltimore; he did the same with the presidency of the North Carolina State Bank's branch at Fayetteville. His eyes and ears were everywhere as he made long-distance introductions and wrote recommendations, intending to both aid the Bank's stewards and bring stability and experience to local banks, which would come under duress once a central bank ceased to exist. The deadline for concluding the Bank's affairs was 1838.

He still hoped that the election of 1836 might alter the institution's future, and that he could induce either Van Buren or a Whig rival to recharter the Second Bank, or, at least, charter another national bank. So, while Biddle appeared to systematically dissolve the Bank's business, he spent an equal amount of time privately devising alternative means of formulating a new central bank. He believed that the health of America's economy rested on a sound national currency, the regulation of foreign and domestic exchanges, an institution independent of the federal government that could protect and direct other banks, keep safe the Treasury funds, and monitor and manage internal and external pressures. Jackson, he thought, apprehended nothing of the complexity of America's financial enterprises. Biddle had no intention of giving up the fight.

"My theory in regard to the present condition of the country is in a few words this. For the last few years the Executive power of the Gov^t has been wielded by a mere gang of banditte [*sic*]," he wrote to the Bank's agent, Herman Cope, in August 1835.

> I know these people perfectly—keep the police on them constantly—
> and in my deliberate judgment, there is not on the face of the earth
> a more profligate crew than those who now govern the President.
> The question is how to expel them. . . . As yet the opinions of the
> opposition are unformed. No man as yet can combine them: they are
> not fixed on any one man. But they are fixed on several men who are
> acceptable to various sections. . . . I have said again and again to my
> friends, I have said it this very morning, 'This disease is to be treated
> as a local disorder—apply local remedies—if Genl Harrison will run
> better than any body else in Pennsa, by all means unite upon him.'
> That as far as I understand the case, is the feeling very generally of the
> opposition & Genl Harrison must not suppose that there is in this
> quarter any unwillingness to give him fair play. On the contrary, he
> is very much respected, and if our friends are satisfied that he can get
> more votes in Pennsa than any other candidate of the opposition they
> will take him up cheerfully & and support him cordially.
>
> I have but one remark more to make. If Genl Harrison is taken up
> as a candidate, it will be on account of the past, not the future. Let
> him rely entirely on the past. Let him say not one single word about
> his principles, or his creed—let him say nothing, promise nothing. . . .
> Genl Harrison can speak well & write well—but on this occasion he
> should neither speak nor write—but be silent—absolutely and inflex-
> ibly silent. . . ."[1]

There was political acumen in this counsel. Van Buren was glib-tongued, his policies malleable; Harrison, the soldier, would appeal by being the opposite.

While pondering the national election, Biddle simultaneously focused on his home state. If the U.S. Congress failed to recharter of Bank of the United States, he began making plans for a replacement: a national bank chartered in Pennsylvania that would exist outside of the purview of Jackson and his "gang of banditte." The decision was both bold and chancy. Biddle knew the obstacles, and knew, too, that such an institution might be short-lived—a stop-gap measure until sanity returned to Washington. He was confident that the merits would be obvious for the legislature in Harrisburg: Pennsylvania would become more prosperous than New York. Conversely, if the state lacked the fortitude to create a new national bank, Wall Street and New York State would become America's financial seat. There were other considerations: foreign investors, which Pennsylvania already had owing to internal improvements, plus a sizeable loss of capital if the Bank were to relocate. Having served on the state legislature, Biddle understood the dual appeals of pocketbook and state rivalry.

Applying for a charter as a Pennsylvanian who was "devotedly attached to her interests and fame,"[2] Biddle found support within the leadership of both parties. When news reached Washington of his intention, Democrats there balked, sending word to their Pennsylvania cohort that supporting a new national bank would "break the President's heart."[3] Though Jackson's tenure would soon be ending, his fellow party members had begun to test other waters. Van Buren also got wind of the arrangement, but he understood he'd lose crucial Pennsylvania votes if he intervened. The little magician could only work so many miracles on behalf of Wall Street.

Biddle had a powerful friend in Thaddeus Stevens, then a Pennsylvania state legislator. Stevens had the useful distinction of being "perfectly reckless of [his] popularity,"[4] which permitted him to leap in where others might fear to tread. Stevens agreed to throw his full support into aiding the creation of a national bank in Pennsylvania. Biddle also employed lobbyists whose methods were often as questionable then as they can be now. Biddle recognized that his efforts were for the nation's strength and betterment and knowingly turned a blind eye to their tactics. Even a Democratic legislator's demand for a branch bank in his home county met with accord—the cost of doing business. Shrewdly, Biddle kept all records of his various intrigues within his private papers rather than at the Second Bank offices. When allegations of bribery arose—and they did—the Bank produced clean books and ledgers.

Biddle's machinations progressed beyond lobbyists and mercenary legislators; he used charm, powers of persuasion, undated letters marked confidential, and threats. He brooked no amendments to his proposal. If Pennsylvania chose not to charter a national bank, he intimated that that he would approach the legislature of New York, or Maryland, or Delaware. When those state legislators learned about his proposal and wrote to offer their states as home to a new national bank, Biddle made a point of revealing the overtures. He knew he was playing a dangerous game, but the prize was worth every risk. He also understood that the venture would be pricey. Two million dollars was paid to the state for the charter, plus an additional six million dollars in loans for completing and creating infrastructure, but once chartered, the new national bank would be impervious to attacks from Jackson's or any future administration.

In January 1836, a bill was introduced entitled "An Act to Repeal the State Tax on Real & Personal Property and to continue & extend the improvements of the State by Railroads & Canals, and to charter a state bank to be called the United States Bank." The fact that the Bank's charter appeared ancillary to tax alterations and central improvements fooled no one. Opposition came immediately. *Niles' Register* reported that the *Pennsylvanian* decried the bill:

> The moment is fast approaching when it will be in the power of this body to acquire imperishable honor, and entitle itself to the enduring gratitude of the state. It is reserved to the senate of Pennsylvania to strangle the bank of the United States in its last and most insidious attack, and to finish the work commenced by Andrew Jackson.[5]

Niles' then offered its home state of Maryland as a better home to Biddle's new bank. "We'll give the bank a charter 'in less than no time,' and relieve the 'democrats' of Pennsylvania of their 'awful fears.'"[6]

Biddle and the pro-state bank faction pressed ahead. On January 29, the bill passed its first reading in the House by a vote of 57 to 30, moving it to the State Senate, where it seemed to languish. One of the most outspoken enemies was Dallas. New Yorkers were quick to insist that their state, not Pennsylvania, should take the honor of becoming home to the new bank. They insisted that it would increase capital on Wall Street, attract more merchants, businessmen, and investors, augment the state's ability to build canals and railroads, and grow the maritime trade. Rumors also flew that members of the Kitchen Cabinet were outraged at Pennsylvania's temerity, as was the President, who furiously denounced both the state and the notion of the Pennsylvania bank.

On February 5th, a Biddle confidant who was on the scene told him, "Yesterday and to day [*sic*] has been spent in Skirmishing—the troops raw thay [*sic*] could not be brought to close action—a counsel of war has been held and it has been resolved to force the matter tomorrow."[7] A charge of corruption nearly killed the bill when Henry Krebs, an elderly senator, admitted being offered "large sums of money"[8] to vote pro-bank. Then it was disclosed that the offer had not been made by Biddle, but by a Jacksonite from Schuylkill County, Henry Conrad, one of the "most foul mouthed and violent opposers"[9] of a national bank.

Despite the efforts to kill it, the bill succeeded, passing the Pennsylvania Senate on February 13 by a vote of 19 to 12. The governor signed The United States Bank of Pennsylvania into existence on February 18, which was the date of the final meeting of the trustees of the Bank of the United States in Philadelphia. The charter was to last thirty years, until March 3, 1866.

The wild fluctuations of public favor were beginning to tell on Biddle's equanimity. He was angry and had reason to be. Jackson's annual address to Congress in December 1835 had accused the Bank of the United States of waging war against the government. He insisted that it followed a "fundamental principle of which is a distrust of the popular will as a safe regulator of political power"[10] while intending to accrue all authority into its own hands. "Despotism" and "great moneyed monopoly" were terms leveled at the Bank's management.

During a speech at Princeton's commencement the September prior, Biddle had warned his audience about tyrannies past and present, differentiating between "true statesmen" and "temporary favorites." It was obvious that he was describing Jackson, Van Buren, and their cohorts.

> Their knowledge of themselves inspires low estimates of others . . .
> their theory is to have no principles and to give no opinions, never
> to do any thing so marked as to be inconsistent with doing the direct
> reverse—and never to say any thing not capable of contradictory
> explanation. . . . Accordingly they worship cunning, which is only the
> counterfeit of wisdom, and deem themselves sagacious only because
> they are selfish. They believe that all generous sentiments of love of
> country, for which they feel no sympathy in their breasts, are hol-
> low pretenses in others—that public life is a game in which success
> depends upon dexterity—and that all government is a mere struggle
> for place. . . . Such persons may rise to great official stations, for high
> offices are like the tops of pyramids, which reptiles can reach as well as
> eagles. . . .

He concluded with an exhortation he might have been delivering to himself.

> Never desert the country—never despond over its fortunes. Confront
> its betrayers. They will denounce you. Disregard their outcries—They
> will seek to destroy you. Rejoice that your country's enemies are yours.

> The avenging hour will at last come. It cannot be that our free nation
> can long endure the vulgar dominion of ignorance and profligacy. You
> will live to see the laws reestablished.[11]

Pushed to the limit, Biddle stayed resolute even though he had started having doubts about whether Van Buren could be defeated. Having devoted years to developing and maintaining a national banking system, he was adamant in his intention to combat Jackson or Van Buren's efforts to destroy it. The United States Bank of Pennsylvania was now a reality. The next step was to turn it into something more significant than a commercial bank and imbue it with a central bank's similar powers and services.

* * *

Working against him was a national economy facing severe money pressure. In mid-March, the Washington *Globe*, a Jacksonite newspaper, predicted that a "scene of unparalleled distress is at hand."[12] Other pro-Democrat newspapers like the *Richmond Enquirer*, *Boston Morning Post*, and *Albany Argus* echoed the warning. However, there were rumors that the Kitchen Cabinet, motivated by its hatred of Biddle, was manipulating forces to create a panic, or else deceive the public into believing one was at hand. "Treasury in Danger" ran a *Poulson's* headline on March 19, 1836. During his annual message to Congress in December 1835, Jackson had extolled the sales of public lands as swelling the Treasury's coffers "to the unexpected sum of $11,000,000."[13] Now, the much-heralded surplus was no more. Or was it? More rumors flew. Did the President believe, as he later claimed, that the money had vanished? Or, had a cadre of insiders lied to him? Such was the state of the nation that the truth became challenging to ascertain. The Jacksonites insisted they were correct in every allegation. The anti-Jackson, anti-Van Buren party said the same.

The possibility of a war with France continued to bedevil the populace. In early January 1836, Senator Benton proposed devoting the Treasury surplus in its entirety to the military, making the threat seem even more imminent and drawing rebukes from those seeking a peaceable settlement. Are we to "plant the stars and stripes upon the walls of Paris?"[14] was a query that appeared in *Poulson's*. Although an agreement had been reached whereby the Rothschild banking house in Paris could receive and transmit payments contractually owed the United States, the treaty debacle remained. The French accused Jackson of "irresponsibility" and "offensive language."[15] He refused to soften his stance.

In February, Great Britain offered to intervene and mediate. Some blamed the Kitchen Cabinet for fabricating the drama to keep the Whigs out of the White House.

In addition to the French question was an on-going Congressional dispute regarding sales of public lands. The policy, which entailed selling parts of reservations belonging by treaty to the Creek, Choctaw, and Chickasaw tribes and public lands, had been rife with fraudulent practices and had inspired a lengthy investigation led by a Senate Committee. The committee learned that many of the speculators were elected officials or else possessed sufficient "wealth and influence" to purchase tracts of properties at reduced rates or buy them on credit.[16] Accusations ran from the corruption of public officials to the attempted murder of one of the investigators. Violence had been commonplace throughout the inquiry, and the instances of criminal practices in Alabama, Mississippi, and Louisiana the most egregious.

Van Buren came under attack for enabling wealthy investors in New York and New England to buy up large tracts of public lands, thereby shutting out the individual settler whom the act had been intended to benefit. The pet banks were charged with making illicit loans to Congress members to do the same, but the lack of transparency in their books made proof difficult, engendering the derogatory sneer that they'd become "secret societies."[17] In an act of nepotism that surprised no one, Jackson appointed his adopted son, Andrew Jackson, Jr., to the General Land Office.

Increasing public anxiety were reports of massacres by the Seminoles in Florida and Santa Anna's storming of the Alamo on March 6, 1836, and Col. David Crockett's death. The news didn't reach the eastern states until May, further stoking fears about what other horrors might be revealed. The general's initial claim of having "buried six hundred foreigners"[18] in ditches was subsequently debunked, but Americans worried. Were they weaker and more vulnerable than they believed? John Quincy Adams, writing to Biddle, was blunt: "If we take Texas, John Bull will take Cuba." He believed Jackson intended to "plunge us into a war with Mexico for the conquest of Texas and the restoration of slavery."[19]

While the nation peered into the uncertain future of another presidential election, Biddle focused on the work he knew best: strengthening the nation's economy. Adams, serving in the House of Representatives, became a constant confidant, warning Biddle of the political winds in Washington. Simultaneously, Biddle made plans for branch offices of the new Bank of the United States of Pennsylvania throughout the country, concentrating first on established commercial metropolises. Adding resident foreign agents in London and Paris became another crucial endeavor. Once he'd built a reliable network, merchants dealing in national and international trade could utilize any branch office or its agents to buy and sell bills of exchange. The strategy for a global system was more expansive in scope than the former national bank. He believed that it would establish the United States Bank of Pennsylvania as an equal to the houses in Europe. Heretofore, a European having money in the United States (Lafayette, for instance) had been forced to engage in a complex series of exchanges that depended upon an individual in Europe who owned American funds providing personal credit. Those payments, in turn, depended upon the willingness of European institutions to approve drafts drawn in the United States.

In late March 1836, Biddle dispatched Samuel Jaudon, the head cashier in Philadelphia, to begin implementing the new methodology. Both the Bank of England and the Bank of France refused to participate. The system seemed too daring; besides, it would put The United States Bank of Pennsylvania on an equal footing as those time-honored institutions. Jaudon, whom Biddle had invested with full authority, then negotiated with Baring Brothers in London and Hottinguer in Paris, who became the American bank's foreign agents. Loans arranged by him gave Biddle's new bank working capital.

In May came the news that New York requested the aid of Biddle's new bank, which was especially galling to Van Buren. Biddle explained that the Pennsylvania-chartered bank was no longer a national institution, but complied with a request that had stated: "It is believed by many to be in the power of the Bank of the United States to restore the money market to a more sound and healthy state."[20] Boston also approached Biddle to establish a branch bank in the city, complaining that: "circumstances unconnected with the business operations of the country have produced a scarcity of money."[21] Pittsburgh followed suit. Bills on the Bank of the United States of Pennsylvania were now at a premium in Jackson's home state of Tennessee. Biddle's success undermined Van Buren's prospects because it raised the question of why the administration had waged war on a national bank in the first place.

At the final meeting of the Second Bank of the United States' stockholders on February 20, 1836, Biddle accepted the praise due to him during which his thirteen years of leadership. Director, John Sergeant, began his remarks by insisting he hadn't intended to make a speech but proceeded to do so:

> When danger threatened; when credit was trembling; when confidence was shaken; whenever, in a word, a revulsion was threatened, with its disastrous train of consequences, this bank, strong in its power, stronger in its inclination to do good, anticipated and averted the crisis. By judicious liberality, it prevented or relieved the pressure, it encouraged by its example and support, it cheered by its countenance.

Continuing, he described Biddle's habits and methods of leadership.

> I have seen him assailed with menaces, enough to cause alarm and despondency. But I never saw him irritated, and I never saw him dismayed. When those who were about him yielded to indignant feeling, he calmed and tranquilized them by his cheerful good humor. When they were almost ready to despair, he animated and assured them by his undaunted firmness. However the storm might rage without, there was peace and order within the institution.

Sergeant concluded by saying he hoped his ["testimony"] "will be to him and to his descendants a grateful trophy of a victory won at last by integrity and truth. . . ."[22]

* * *

The United States Congress adjourned July 4, 1836—the longest session since 1815. Jackson had intended to spend the national day of celebration in Harrisburg, encouraging his stalwarts to assure Van Buren's presidency. The bank bill had shown that the state might be vulnerable to a Whig election. With thirty electors (second to New York's forty-two), it was imperative to have Pennsylvania vote for the Democrats. Michigan and Arkansas, with three electors apiece, were the newest states. Jackson's departure from Washington City left a skeleton Kitchen Cabinet. It was bruited about that Amos Kendall ran the government in the president's absence, which immediately drew critiques from the Whigs.

News of the ongoing wars: in Texas, against the Seminoles in Florida, and the Creeks in Georgia, as well as a fresh spate of anti-abolition mobs and riots, dominated the public imagination throughout the summer and into the autumn. Abolitionists accused slave owners of dragging the United States into a war with Mexico to procure a new slave state—Texas. Even while volunteers aided the rebelling "Texians" in their fight against Mexican President Santa

Anna's absolutist regime, and he vowed to crush the revolt and retake Texas for Mexico, American citizens questioned the war's constitutionality. Because Congress had adjourned before the war's onset, was it legal? Henry Clay, who had already indicated his intention of retiring from the Senate, made no secret of his dismay over the nation's health.

"One rash, lawless and crude experiment succeeds another,"[23] he said at a public dinner in Kentucky. Among his targets were public land sales. Clay also castigated the administration for its treatment of tribal peoples. In August, *Niles' Register* published a list of tribes that had "emigrated" to the west of the Mississippi and those already "resident." [24] Eighteen thousand members of the Creek nation moved west "free, for a while, from the avarice and cupidity of the white man,"[25] as a letter to *Poulson's* declared. Clay foresaw increased friction over land: tribe fighting tribe amid a constant wave of white settlers driving the tribal peoples' further and further west. He believed they would face extermination.

Unwilling to relinquish the fight over the Bank of the United States of Pennsylvania, or permit the institution to flourish, in July, George Mifflin Dallas had suggested annulling its charter according to constitutional provisions. He accused his fellow Democrats in Pennsylvania's state legislature of fatal divisions within their ranks. The letter containing his recommendations was sent to Jackson, Van Buren, and Thomas Hart Benton. "The 'calamity, gentlemen,'" he stated, "is the more poignant, because we could and should have avoided it by concentrating against the common foe the assaults we made upon each other."[26] It was clear that he was rallying fellow Pennsylvania Democrats to band together. Perhaps, they couldn't abolish the new bank—though Dallas wanted to try—but they could elect Van Buren as president. He indicated that he had "pledged to become an implacable opponent"[27] of the bank.

The Whig backlash was swift, pronouncing that Dallas's present stance ran counter to his beliefs four years prior when he'd declared his support on the floor of the United States Senate. "The committee did not entertain the slightest suspicions of any misconduct on then part of the president [Biddle], the directors, or those entrusted with the management of the bank, or that they had, in any way, abused their charter."[28]

What had changed? Was it "insanity"[29] or "decayed morality?"[30] Or, had the "ultra nullifier"[31] been motivated by expediency and personal gain? The known facts were that Dallas had praised the Second Bank of the United States, then recanted his position less than two weeks later, following Jackson's disastrous veto of the measure.

Throughout September 1836, Dallas's popularity plummeted while the press pilloried him. Letters to the editor in *Poulson's* warned him about currying favor with Van Buren. At that point, Jackson's chosen successor's ascendency seemed unlikely. The journey to Harrisburg that the President had planned for July, then altered due to Congress' late adjournment, was rearranged to take place on his return trip to Washington City. The political ramifications were understood. "He will not go out of his way for nothing,"[32] a writer to *Poulson's* observed. Again, Biddle's bank was ancillary to the argument of who should lead the nation and how.

The Jacksonites stayed true to their hero even when he exploded in rage at the Mexican minister in October, which caused the man to demand the return of his passport and arrange to quit the country, leaving the two nations with no diplomatic means of making peace. Or, perhaps, the oaths and antagonism toward America's perceived enemies maintained the popularity of the "old chief." Van Buren sought to mimic the president's bellicose manner, jeering that all Whigs were the "bank aristocracy."[33]

For their part, the Whigs lost no opportunity of ridiculing Jackson's erratic syntax, sloppy spelling, and primitive writing skills, depicting him as a country bumpkin whose speeches were always composed by members of his Kitchen Cabinet. However, the derision became a badge of honor in a class war that showed no signs of abating.

"IRISHMEN! LOOK AT THIS—GENERAL HARRISON IS YOUR FRIEND,"[34] and other populist appeals tried to counter the misapprehension that the Whigs were elitists, and Van Buren a Democrat of the blunt-spoken Jackson school. A second Whig candidate, Judge Hugh Lawson White, a United States senator representing Tennessee and former Jackson ally who had distanced himself from the President, added confusion to the race. Jackson considered him a traitor to the Democratic party. Whigs, Daniel Webster, and North Carolina Senator Willie Person Mangum also ran, each appealing to a different geographical and ideological constituency. The four candidates effectively split the party, although for the month of October and into early November, official and unofficial tallies of returns showed Harrison defeating Van Buren.

Those initial tallies proved false when voting concluded on December 7, 1836. Van Buren took 170 electoral votes, Harrison 73; the other three candidates split 51 between them.

The same month, emboldened by Van Buren's win, the governors of Arkansas, Mississippi, and Virginia revealed plans to create state banks that would replace the former Second Bank of the United States' shuttered branch offices. It was difficult to ascertain Van Buren's intentions as President regarding the new Bank of the United States of Pennsylvania. Would he continue in Jackson's footsteps as he had promised to the party convention in Baltimore when declaring himself: "happy if I shall be able to perfect the work which he has so gloriously begun?" Or would he equivocate, as had been his established pattern, appealing to one group and then another? One fact was certain, despite Pennsylvania Governor Joseph Ritner's year-end message on December 6, 1836, during which he praised the new bank, Biddle's foes in the state legislature were on the attack again. They proposed an investigation into the passage of the bank bill, claiming that it had been too hasty, voted into existence by a minority, and that a full review of the conduct of the stockholders and leadership had become a necessity.

* * *

Jackson's final annual address to Congress coincided with Ritner's message. Although about to leave office, Old Hickory persisted in his hostility toward Biddle. He wanted the Van Buren administration to take up the cudgel he was now forced to relinquish. It mattered not whether Biddle's institution was the defunct Second Bank of the United States or the new Pennsylvania-chartered national bank. Damning "the dangerous power wielded by the bank of the United States, and its repugnance to our constitution," Jackson insisted he had been "induced to exert the power conferred upon me by the American people, to prevent the continuation of that institution."[35]

Biddle's outrage at Jackson's incomprehension of basic economics burst forth in two published letters to John Quincy Adams:

> The whole pecuniary system of this country, that to which, next to its freedom, it owes its prosperity, is the system of credit. Our ancestors came here with no money—but with far better things—with courage and industry—and the want of capital was supplied by their mutual confidence. This is the basis of our whole commercial and internal industry. The people of the United States through their representatives recharted that institution (the Second Bank). But the executive . . . rejected the act of congress—and the favorite topic of declamation was, that the states would make banks, and that these banks could create a better system of currency and exchanges. And what is the consequence?

The bank of the United States has not ceased to exist more than seven months, and already the whole currency and exchanges are running into inextricable confusion.[36]

Counting upon Adams to hear him and provide counsel, Biddle argued, correctly, that the sales of public lands had had a deleterious effect on local banks nearest the transactions, which then impacted institutions and merchants. Commercial intercourse had reached a standstill; interest on loans had risen sharply; transmitting funds from the west and southwest cost five or six times what it had a year past. Calling the Democrat leadership "demagogues" and "rash and ignorant politicians with no guides but their own passions and interests," he added,

> For the last six years the country had been nearly convulsed by efforts to break the mutual dependence of all classes of citizens—to make the laborer regard his employer as his enemy, and to array the poor against the rich. These trashy declaimers have ended by bringing the country into a condition where its whole industry is subject far more than it ever was before, to the control of large capitalists—and where every step tends inevitably to make the rich richer, and the poor poorer.[37]

The communications appeared in abbreviated form as a front-page in *Poulson's* on December 14 and in full in two installments of *Niles' Register*, December 10 and 17. Written more than a month prior, Biddle prevailed upon his publishing friends to print the letters to combat Jackson's ongoing attack.

Old Hickory rose to the occasion. He continued pillorying Biddle in his farewell speech during Van Buren's inauguration on Saturday, March 4, 1837. On a sunny, dry day with the snowfall of Thursday still clinging to the ground, Jackson and the new president rode together in a carriage fashioned from timbers of the famed frigate *Constitution*. Onlookers thronged the streets during the ceremonial procession. They admitted that Jackson looked gaunt and feeble. His physical appearance belied his inner strength.

Employing tactical phrases, he made his personal fight sound like a battle against a foe supplied with superior resources. The language hearkened back to the colonies' struggle for independence from a cruel, usurious monarchy. Biddle and the Second Bank had "waged war upon the people, in order to compel them to submit to its demands." It was "ruthless and unsparing" and willfully left in its wake "individuals impoverished and ruined. . . . If such was its power in a time of peace, what would it not have been in a season of war?" Jackson demanded, returning to the necessity of "eternal vigilance" to guard against future incursions from Biddle and the new Bank of the United States of Pennsylvania. "Defeated in the general government, the same class of intriguers and politicians will now resort to the states."[38] The former President may have been in failing health, but he remained vindictive against perceived enemies. He could not eliminate Nicholas Biddle from his thoughts.

But neither could Biddle forego the fight. Like Jackson's, his personality had also intensified with age. His position as a man of power who had experienced the plaudits and execration of being in the public eye accentuated a hereditary nature that could turn vehement and combative. He believed he was justified in all his business dealings and that his critics were uninformed, unwise, and insular. A portrait painted in 1836 by Rembrandt Peale shows the sitter as proud, successful, and defiant. The eyes are steely, the lips pinch, the jaw clenches.

- CHAPTER SIXTEEN -

"A GREAT DISASTER HAS BEFALLEN THE COUNTRY"

Van Buren was sworn in as President on March 4, 1837, and Richard Johnson of Kentucky became Vice President; the Democratic Party controlled the Senate by 34 to 18, which should have empowered the new chief magistrate. The inaugural speech, though, was acknowledged to have "disappointed both friends and foes."[1] Lacking Jackson's military bearing and history, Van Buren kept one hand in his pocket while delivering his oration. This personal habit looked out of place with the momentousness of the occasion. He also hedged his bets with flowery but noncommittal language. He fawned over the man who'd chosen him to inherit the President's mantle, hoping that he "may yet long live to enjoy the brilliant evening of his well-spent life."[2] One of Van Buren's first appointments was sending George Mifflin Dallas as minister plenipotentiary to Russia. The clever ploy rewarded Dallas for his loyalty while also removing him from national politics. Van Buren preferred temporizing over confrontation and was wily enough to understand infighting such as Jackson's kitchen cabinet had engaged in might become his undoing. Biddle was happy to see Dallas go, but he misinterpreted the new President's intentions as potentially pro-national bank.

Unfortunately, Old Hickory's ghost continued to hover. He had vowed to veto the new Treasury Bill if it reached him before March 3, frustrating the Whigs who desperately wanted to see the nation on a firmer financial footing. They worried that another crusade against the new U.S. Bank might be at hand. They were correct in their fears because Amos Kendall held a pivotal role in Van Buren's administration and cabinet. In early April, Kendall journeyed to the Hermitage to confer with Jackson, presumably with the object of creating a Benton/Kendall ticket. Old Hickory was still rewarding his favorites.

The January before the inauguration, Benton had insisted on expunging from the public record the 1834 Congressional Resolution rebuking Jackson. Sneering that the prior Senate had been "ruled by the Bank,"[3] he demanded to be heard. However, owing to a Senate investigation into corruption by the Treasury and the state pet banks, Benton's mulish defense of Old Hickory caused the gallery to erupt in jeers and hisses.

Benton's attack on the former Second Bank—and by extension the U.S. Bank of Pennsylvania—could not have been timed more poorly. February 1837 had witnessed a series of bread riots in New York City. "BREAD, MEAT, RENT, FUEL—THEIR PRICES MUST COME DOWN"[4] had been posted as handbills, enkindling long-simmering public frustrations with rising prices. The militia, muskets loaded, had been mustered. No lives had been lost, but property had been damaged and arrests made. The Loco-Foco Party had a loud and conspicuous presence before and during the riots. Born in New York City and popular among the poorer wards, the Loco-Focos' precept was "to bring back the Democratic party to the principles upon which it was originally founded." Members called their work the "Loco-Foco Revolution."[5] Mostly laboring-class men, they suspected all banks, despised paper money, taxes, tariffs, and anything that reeked of monopoly or aristocracy. They reveled in being outspoken and anti-establishment, reviling any connection between government and banking, and insisting that all public office candidates adhere to their principles. Jackson had been their hero. As yet, they were undecided about his successor. The Loco-Focos' critics accused them of being ignorant, uncouth, and easily manipulated.

In early spring, Webster embarked on a lengthy tour of western and eastern cities to promote rechartering a new national bank (to replace the Bank of the U.S of Pennsylvania). He reminded his audiences that the exigencies following the War of 1812 had necessitated the creation of the Second Bank of the United States and that the country was currently undergoing a similar financial depression. The crowds attending his orations were eager to hear the message and to encourage their representatives to act upon it, too. At that point, the sole issue the Whigs and Democrats could agree upon was that the economy was in peril. Both parties blamed the other.

Under the new administration, America's money markets continued to weaken. They had grown so depressed that the cost of a slave in Mississippi had fallen from $1,200 to between $150 and $300. Tobacco and cotton, vital to the southern economy, had also plummeted in value. In April 1837, the failure of

St. John & Co. in New York City, large dealers in Southern Exchange, wiped out fifteen other houses on Pearl Street. New York had already experienced other failures: five foreign and exchange brokers, twenty dry goods jobbers, twenty-eight real estate speculators, and six stockbrokers. New Orleans reported closures of businesses on prestigious Chartres Street because cotton prices had bankrupted them. Plummeting cotton prices also caused failures in Natchez, Mississippi, and throughout Alabama. In Maine, lumber sales stagnated because of a dearth in demand for new construction. Massachusetts reported that paper and textile mills were in the process of turning off machinery and dismissing employees; the town of Lowell, nicknamed the "city of spindles," had grown in population from less than 1,000 to more than 20,000; jobs, food, clothing, and shelter depended upon the mills remaining open. The Depression of 1837 was starting to paralyze the country.

In April 1837, Biddle visited Van Buren to offer his aid and counsel. However, the President, as *Niles'* reported, "remained profoundly silent"[6] throughout the interview, and Biddle left without achieving his goal. Lacking Jackson's charisma, Van Buren appeared haughty and unsympathetic as if the ordinary citizen's plight were of no concern.

* * *

The same month, during this economic free fall, Nicholas Biddle received an odd bit of unsolicited advice from Thomas Cooper of Columbia, South Carolina. An educator born in England, Cooper had served as chair of chemistry at the University of Pennsylvania before moving south, where he became president of South Carolina College in Columbia. He was the author of *Lectures on the Elements of Political Economy*, in which he discussed the balance of trade, circulating medium, banks, banknotes, paper money, and bills of exchange. Cooper suggested that Biddle run for President of the United States in 1840.

> I enter upon my 79th Year, next October. By the time Mr. Van
> Beuren's [*sic*] first period has expired, I shall be superannuated. I can
> have therefore no selfish motive in my present proposal. The tide is
> turning strongly agst [*sic*] the measures of the last and present Ad-
> ministration. The poor now groan under the financial follies of Gen.
> Jackson as well as the rich. To be sure, over trading and gambling
> speculation will account for three fourths of the present distress, but
> no one can be blind to the effects produced by the desperate ignorance

of the last President. . . . Can your name be brought forward at a time more advantageous than the present? You are rising, your opponents are falling: strike the ball on the rebound, and I think this is the moment.[7]

Biddle replied May 8, a lapse given how promptly he usually responded. He had spent time considering Cooper's proposal, which soothed his battered ego while raising the possibility that the idea might catch fire. He purposely alluded to Jackson and Van Buren when he answered: "I have been for years in the daily exercise of more personal authority that any President habitually enjoys. But I stand ready for the country's service. If therefore you think that my name can be productive of good, I am content to place it—as I now do, at your disposal."[8]

Cooper's enthusiastic answer came a short six days later. He listed Biddle's potential competitors (Calhoun, being one), but said, "these gentlemen are like me, Nullifiers. They could not be sustained out of the State." Cooper then focused on Webster, although he believed that the South wouldn't accept him.

> Webster has a character for talent, but he is not qualified for a leader.
> He has no personal friends. He is a good partisan parliamentary
> debater, but he cannot trace out the plan of a political Campain [sic],
> nor is he fit to be the head of it. I see no fearful competitor at present,
> or in prospect.[9]

On May 24, Cooper provided additional advice "All to whom I have guardedly spoken, agree with me in opinion, decidedly."[10] On July 1, he made further suggestions. "The time has not yet arrived for the direct nomination of any man as future president. But all secondary means and appliances may be usefully brought forward, and should be so."

He concluded by saying, "I see no serious obstacle to the success of my proposal."[11]

While engaged with this flattering notion, Biddle received an anxious appeal from the secretary of war, Joel Roberts Poinsett. "Can you not in your financial knowledge and experience devise some plan by which a wholesome control may be exercised over bank issues and exchanges be brought back to which they were before the destruction of the Bank?"[12] The request was unusual. Was Poinsett acting on his own or on behalf of the President? If so, why had Van Buren chosen an intermediary?

Biddle responded with two letters on May 8, the first declaring:

> I have always thought that the best thing which Mr. Van Buren
> could do in reference to himself personally, as well as to his political
> party, would be to make peace with the Bank—and the present state
> of things furnishes an admirable opportunity of accomplishing that
> object. . . . The way therefore would be open for a general amnesty—
> which for the sake of the country I am willing to consent to—and I do
> believe that just now the effect would be electric and decisive. [13]

The second missive provided technical means for the U.S. Treasury and Bank of the United States of Pennsylvania to resume a working relationship. Biddle suggested making the Bank of the United States of Pennsylvania the depository of the public funds, utilizing the Bank's paper for debts owed to the government. "I am perfectly willing to forget all quarrels with the last administration, which neither party would desire to have perpetuated,"[14] he told Poinsett while authorizing him to approach the President and cabinet. Biddle also approached General Robert Patterson, a mill owner and president of the Pennsylvania electoral college that had cast its vote for Van Buren:

> I submit all these matters to you, and if, as I trust, you will see them
> in the same light, I would ask you immediate concurrence in carrying
> it into effect. I care not how it begins, or who proposes it, but if it be
> necessary for me to commence, I am agreed. I am too proud to think
> my step humiliating which may benefit this poor bleeding country of
> ours.[15]

Patterson wasted no time. He saw Van Buren that very day, but the President, although acknowledging the nation's financial woes, felt unable to do anything that might diminish his predecessor's legacy. By this time, Van Buren had acquired the unfortunate nickname "the Flying Dutchman,"[16] which produced numerous allusions, none of which were flattering or pleasant.

* * *

Biddle's advice to Poinsett and Patterson came to naught. In early May, state banks began suspending species payments: The Planters' and Agricultural Banks in Natchez on May 4, the State Bank in Montgomery, Alabama on May

9, New York City banks May 10, Hartford, Albany, New Haven, Baltimore and Providence May 11, Boston and Mobile May 12, six banks in New Orleans May 13, the Bank of Washington and the Metropolis Bank May 15, Charleston and Cincinnati May 17, the State Bank of North Carolina and its branches May 18, Savannah and Augusta May 19. The Dry Dock Bank of New York declared insolvency in May, as well.

A delegation of mercantile leaders from New York journeyed to Washington in early May 1837 to meet with the President and try to persuade him to repeal the Specie Circular, which left specie piling up in the West and Southwest, thereby disrupting or destroying the flow of credit between the western and eastern states, and, in turn, devastating the cotton market. As he had done during his interview with Biddle, Van Buren remained silent while his visitors stated their case. Without revealing his thoughts, he then asked the delegation to put their request in writing. A day after receiving the document, he also responded in writing, saying, "I have not been able to satisfy myself that I ought, under existing circumstances, to interfere."[17] He refused to accede to their demand to convene an extra session of Congress.

Frustrated by the chief executive's inaction, Biddle wrote a third (published) letter to John Quincy Adams on May 13, 1837. "All the deposite [sic] banks of the government of the United States in the city of New York suspended specie payment this week—the deposite banks elsewhere have followed their example." Detailing the pecuniary difficulties faced by "merchants and manufacturers and mechanics" as well as America's foreign debtors, he railed that "The result of the whole, is that a great disaster has befallen the country."[18] With customary determination and more than a little hubris, Biddle concluded, "I shall now strive to repair it."

Meanwhile, Jackson, ensconced in the Hermitage, dispatched two letters to the Washington *Globe* in July, further lambasting Biddle as the cause of the nation's fiscal "explosion." His obsession made his enemies shake their heads. They understood that Van Buren remained under Old Hickory's thrall. Although the Democrats now possessed the majority, it seemed doubtful they would alter "the headstrong and ruinous policy which originated with President Jackson."[19] James Hamilton, Jr., the former Governor of South Carolina, wrote Nicholas Biddle on May 18 to suggest he convene a meeting of the nation's banking leaders in Philadelphia. *Niles'* published it on July 15. "In the work of remedy and conciliation, your institution may be made the rallying point—Let us then leave no effort untried to accomplish this result. On it depend the public credit, honor, peace and prosperity of our country."[20]

The bank foes remained obdurate. They held an Anti-Bank Convention in Harrisburg beginning on July 4. Claiming to eschew "partisan rivalry" and "bias," they described "the deserted streets of our cities" and the "smaller towns, and the country at large, what do we behold but business interrupted, merchants and mechanics idle, all the necessities of life exorbitantly high, the means to purchase them straitened. Creditors pressing their demands, and debtors unable to pay. . . ."

At fault, they believed, was Biddle and his old and new Banks. Despite the claim at nonpartisanship, the three-day Convention concluded with a call to arms.

> There are but two parties in this conflict—those who will correct, and those who will perpetuate the evils you endure. . . . Go to the polls, then, not as partisans, but as Americans. . . . Let your watch-words be *reform of the rotten banking system, and immediate resumption of specie payment. . . .*

Like Jackson, they advocated for "the constitutional currency of gold and silver."[21] Naturally, the Convention also recommended repealing the charter of the Bank of the United States of Pennsylvania.

The same month, Jackson raged against the pet state banks he'd created:

> Now is the time to separate the government from all banks, receive and disburse the revenue in nothing but gold and silver coin. . . . The history of the world never has recorded such base treachery and perfidy, as has been committed by the deposit banks against the government, and purely with the view of gratifying Biddle.[22]

Biddle feigned indifference, but in a speech celebrating the opening of the Philadelphia, Wilmington, and Baltimore Railroad, he retaliated by denouncing Jackson's revisionist faith in a metal currency. Toasting "The rail roads of the United States—A firm metallic basis of circulation—the best metallic conductors in political storms,"[23] he drew guffaws by equating railroads to the gold and silver coin touted by Jackson and his anti-bank adherents. It was also an allusion to both the former Bank and the new Bank's large and tensile reach. American expansionism had been furthered by Biddle's policies that set monies in motion to aid individuals purchasing federal lands on which to settle and made loans to farmers and businesses, enabling them to bring their products to distant markets.

* * *

Van Buren finally assembled a special session of Congress on September 4. His critics expected his customary non-committal palaver during his address to the joint houses, but his recommendations regarding the nation's economy were clear. He proposed a Treasury Bank that would replace any other national bank, whether the former Second Bank of the United States that had another year to wind up its business or Biddle's new Bank chartered in Pennsylvania. In 7½ columns reprinted in *Poulson's*, he suggested, appealed, wheedled, and argued against a central bank, "I felt it due to the people to apprise them distinctly that in the event of my election I would not be able to cooperate in the reestablishment of a national bank." Insisting that a national bank would favor a "moneyed power . . . threatening the permanency of our republican institutions," he stated and restated his belief that only a Treasury bank was safe. The argument verged on the simplistic. "Surely banks are not more able than the Government to secure the money in their possession against accident, violence, or fraud. The President also chose states' rights as a subtext: "to leave every citizen and every interest to reap under its benign protection the rewards of virtue, industry, and prudence."

Van Buren was being politically expedient. He needed Calhoun and other states' rights advocates to change allegiances. The speech, which was the opposite of Jackson's pugnacity, did contain a rebuke for the "luxurious habits founded too often on merely fancied wealth, and detrimental alike to the industry, the resources, and the morals of our people."

As was typical of Van Buren, he concluded on a conciliatory note, as if the problems facing the country had no bearing upon his predecessor (or his own administration) but had been Biddle's fault all along. "I deeply regret that events have occurred which require me to ask your consideration of such serious topics. I could have wished that in making my first communication to the assembled representatives of my country I had nothing to dwell upon but the history of her unalloyed prosperity."[24]

One wag observed of the Treasury Bank suggestion: "The [Washington] *Globe* says Mr. Van Buren has proposed a plan by which the Government can dispense entirely with the use of banks. Would it not be well if the President could devise some plan by which the Government could dispense with the use of the People entirely? They are likely to be more annoying to the money projects than the banks have been."[25]

Van Buren urged a quick vote on the "sub-treasury scheme" (creating sub-treasuries in Boston, Charleston, New York, St. Louis, a mint in Philadelphia, and a branch mint in New Orleans). However, despite Webster's advice that it was time to put partisan politics behind for the nation's good, the measure languished. By early 1838, no more movement had been made. On February 3, Biddle wrote a confidential letter to Clay.

> You can readily suppose that we are not idle while this insane Sub Treasury scheme is urged forward to break down all the great interests of the country—and preparations are made to obtain from our legislature at Harrisburg instructions to our representatives in Congress to oppose it. . . . I lose no time therefore in suggesting that you would keep up the debate in the Senate for a few days until the resolutions can reach you. I attach great importance to this measure as separating our State from those desperadoes.[26]

* * *

By this time, Calhoun had become one of Biddle's "desperadoes." In late December 1837, a proposal to abolish slavery in the District of Columbia had engendered a noisy backlash among the southern states' rights bloc. Calhoun used the Sub-Treasury measure to rally southern votes to protect slavery in the District of Columbia, while opposing northern interference, whether on the slave issue or northern commercial interests—Biddle's Bank of the United States of Pennsylvania, being paramount. In addition, it behooved Calhoun to have a Sub-Treasury established in Charleston. Webster contacted Biddle regarding efforts to alter Calhoun's position, sending an unsigned letter with the heading "Private as murder," and concluding, "Burn this—as it is libellous [*sic*] in the extreme."[27] Calhoun quit the Whig party and became a Democrat.

Instead of damaging Biddle's chances, Calhoun's defection to the anti-Bank party proved an unexpected boon. Still, there were concerns, which Biddle and

Clay shared. "I have a thousand things to say to you," Clay wrote him on April 30, 1838, "most of them good, a few otherwise. . . ."[28] The "few otherwise" changed their opinions due to tireless cajoling and politicking on the part of both men. On May 31, Biddle told Jaudon:

> The tide now has begun to turn, and the Bank has received today a triumph such as it never enjoyed in any part of its career. You know that the stand taken by the Bank was, that it would not resume until the Gov^t changed its course, as there could be no security for specie payments while the Gov^t itself made the distinction between specie & notes. Accordingly the contest has literally been between the Bank and the Executive. With what result you will see by the proceedings of yesterday when on the very same day the Specie circular was repealed in the Senate by a vote of 34 to 9, and in the House by 154 to 29. I have immediately endeavoured [sic] to justify the confidence of the country by issuing a note to Mr Adams in which suppressing all feelings of triumph, I merely announced the fact that we should now proceed to take measures for resumption.[29]

Biddle went on to assure Jaudon, who remained in London, that the new Bank had not only survived but prevailed, and that investors in Great Britain and the Continent should take heart in the "civil revolution on the side of the Bank." He also explained that he intended to "yield to our New York friends" by creating a New York branch and commencing plans for doing the same in the "South & West." Biddle may have claimed that he had no intention of crowing over his victory, but a letter to Adams reiterating those proposals saw publication in *Niles'* on April 14 and May 31, 1838.

Biddle was right to worry because the anti-Bank Pennsylvanians refused to relinquish the fight. They had an ally in Calhoun, but Biddle had as fierce a supporter in abolitionist Thaddeus Stevens, who endangered his career by defying the Loco Focos in his home county (Adams), and who subsequently—and unsuccessfully—sought to unseat him from the Pennsylvania State Legislature.

A tense month ensued during which the Bank opponents rallied their forces. Biddle made private appeals to ambivalent members from Pennsylvania, explaining the wisdom and necessity "that the business of the country & the public revenue shall pass through Banks—and not thro' mere receivers."[30]

Stevens also cajoled, as well as harangued. The vote to reopen the measure ended in defeat: 205 to 21. Biddle had won. The nation had won, too.

On July 10, Pennsylvania's governor, in consultation with Biddle, issued a proclamation that required all Commonwealth banks to resume redeeming "notes, bills, and other obligations in gold and silver"[31] by August 13, 1838. Banks throughout the country, except those in the southwest, immediately followed suit. Those interior banks required additional time to resume specie payments and began the first Monday of January 1839. Throughout the remainder of 1838, the federal government and Biddle worked together to rescue the country from financial disaster. As he said, the action "brought the government into efficient cooperation for the re-establishment of the currency."[32] Rightfully, Biddle crowed, "The repeal of the specie circular and the defeat of the subtreasury are the results, exclusively, of the course pursued by the Bank of the United States (of Pennsylvania). I took a deliberate stand against the administration, determined to do nothing until they were defeated, and I know this opposition caused their defeat."[33]

Biddle's policies, which had become both Banks' policies, had endeavored to form a symbiotic relationship with the federal government whereby government and individual funds could move quickly from place to place. As he had expressed to Francis Hopkinson in November 1830 when describing "one of the most beautiful of our operations," the (Second) Bank addressed the needs of "a pay day of six or seven millions of dollars without the slightest change in its daily business or the least shock to the business of the country."[34]

* * *

In July 1838, Biddle, using his political acumen, had told his supporters in New York (via the Bank's counsel, Richard Milford Blatchford) that, rather than exult over "the termination of the war,"[35] they should "avoid anything like exultation," and instead extoll the Van Buren administration's timely sagacity. As a friend to Webster and Adams, Blatchford recognized the diplomatic expediency in the request. He immediately contacted every New York state newspaper friendly to the Bank, ensuring a "proper tone"[36] for all communications.

If Biddle avoided the appearance of "exultation" in public, he experienced it in private, sending his son, Edward, who was then in Liverpool, a gleeful account of his and the Bank's vindication. Biddle's enthusiast, Thomas Cooper, contacted him in October with additional advice about the banker's future role in national government. Examining probable candidates for the 1840 election, he dismissed Harrison as "out of the question," adding, "So is that very able man Webster."[37] Clay seemed the obvious choice for the Whigs, and who better to serve as Secretary of the Treasury than Biddle? Cooper indicated that he was ready to perform whatever service necessary to ensure that result. Cooper, by then eighty, stated, "it will be your own fault, if you do not make the next step into the chair which you ought to occupy."[38]

Peace between Biddle, the new Bank, and Van Buren seemed finally secured when the President invited the financier to be a guest of honor at the White House on February 26, 1839. By then, they had an enemy in common—Calhoun. Both men wanted to see the country regain its financial footing and economic vigor, and Calhoun had become an obstructionist, insisting that the Sub Treasury proposal be revived. James Hamilton was among the company and dismayed to find Biddle not only present but apparently in his element. As "the most distinguished gentleman," of non-official rank [Van Buren's words] Biddle accompanied Hamilton's wife to the dinner table, which elicited a private protest from her husband, who believed the pairing was due to his father's legacy as the originator of the national bank. Irritated by this perceived slight to his reputation, Hamilton groused that, "This dinner went off very well, Biddle evidently feeling as the conqueror. He was facetious and in intimate conversation with the President."[39]

* * *

Despite his ascendency and success in reviving the nation's economy, Biddle resigned as president of the Bank a month later, on March 28, 1839. The news came as a surprise to all but his closest confidants. At the close of a meeting during which he and the directors had discussed ordinary business, he said he had "long meditated" such an action, reminding them—although it scarcely needed stating—that he had served both the new and old Banks for over twenty years.

After that, he briefly detailed the position of strength that he now believed the institution faced:

> All the political dissensions connected with the Bank for the last ten years have passed; all its extraordinary exertions for the protection of our national interests are happily ended, and the Bank has returned to its accustomed channels of business in peace. . . . I leave the affairs of

the Institution in a state of great prosperity, and in the hands of able Directors and Officers.

He concluded on a rare, melancholy note, saying, "This separation from friends with whom I have been so long agreeably associated is among the most painful acts of my life, and I pray you to accept at parting, my sincere wishes for the personal welfare of you all."[40]

Unaccustomed as all the Biddles were to public displays of grief, he immediately left the building whose design and construction he had overseen and the offices he'd inhabited for as many, if not more, hours than he had his home. Quitting the city as abruptly as he had exited the Bank, he traveled by coach to Andalusia. There, he spent several days in "absolute solitude," writing sparingly in his journal as he pondered the momentousness of his decision. His desertion must have hurt Jane, but Nicholas, husband, father, a man of affairs, and a person for whom social intercourse was as necessary as breath, required silence and the solace it might bring.

The weather was mild and pleasant. After a changeable beginning to the month, spring had begun in earnest, and the fields, orchards, and flower gardens of the country estate showed plentiful signs of rebirth. Shad were starting to run in the river. Everywhere he looked, he witnessed abundance and fruitfulness and hope. Still, he needed time to acclimate himself to allow the busyness, rancor, triumphs, and reverses of the last two decades to begin fading into a distant memory. For the first time in his life, he had no grand plans for the future.

On January 8, 1839, he'd penned in his diary:

> Today is my birthday. Born in 1786, I am now 53 years of age. I
> know this & yet as I write down the number of years it seems strange
> to me. I feel that, so to speak, I have earned my age for I began life
> very early—have seen it in all its varieties . . . and I have not the least
> unwillingness to grow old or to be old.

Admitting that his childhood been an awkward time, he reflected that his years at college had been relatively friendless, too, and then marveled that the last decade or so seemed to have been the time "in which I have most enjoyed myself." He added a rueful, "I have been the object of the most violent warfare by a political party of great power and great malignity." Nicholas had come to know himself and his emotional life very well.

The very opposition of a whole popular party led only by a popular chief piqued my pride & I was resolved not to be conquered, but to beat them—and so I think it has ended. I feel deeply grateful to God therefore for having permitted me to have gone thus far on my way thro' life with little comparative suffering and with many sources of happiness for which I am in truth profoundly sensible.[41]

In March, he took up his pen again, and expressed what had seemed unthinkable:

March 28th, 1839. I resigned the Presidency of the Bank of the United States. I wished before I died to have a few years of quiet rather than drag on till I fell like those worn out horses in the street with my harness on. . . . The change was as strange as it was delightful, simply to walk about—to breathe the fresh air—at those hours in which I had been surrounded by business . . . and I absolutely bathed my heart as it were in this delicious coolness. May this feeling last during my life.[42]

What he never described in writing or in person was the fame he had gar-nered in Europe and Great Britain, where he, rather than the Second Bank or the Bank of the United States of Pennsylvania, had come to represent the ambitious robustness of America's thriving, growing economy. True, there had been financial depressions, but in each instance, America seemed to rebound stronger and more prosperous than before.

To foreign investors, Nicholas Biddle was alike in stature, vision, and ex-pertise to the Rothschilds and Barings who guided their nations' prosperity, and whose reputations as fiscal wizards brought them wealth, power, and adulation akin to a king's.

Biddle, a descendant of Revolutionary War patriots, cleaved to a more egalitarian ideal. He wanted to create an America where laborers, farmers, and large and small manufacturers had parity in their financial transactions:

to make the currency as sound and the exchanges as equal over this immense territory as it was in the smallest and richest kingdom in Europe. My purpose was that in every section however remote of this nation every citizen should have his industry rewarded in what was equivalent to gold and silver, and if he exchanged the fruits of that industry with his most distant countryman, he should do it at less expense than the cost of transmitting that gold and silver.[43]

By the late 1830s, the value of annual regional trade was estimated at approximately $16 million. Biddle recognized the necessity of keeping that money in motion.

- CHAPTER SEVENTEEN -

DEFEAT

Although Biddle had retired and had been covered with accolades, there were those who suspected he had no intention of whiling away the remainder of his life as a country farmer. As early as April 3, 1839, rumors were already circulating that he had retired to set his sights on a cabinet ministry, Secretary of the Treasury, perhaps, or maybe Minister to England, if Treasury didn't suit. Thomas Cooper continued to tell Biddle to aim for higher office, or, at least, leave retirement behind and again become the face of a national bank. Simultaneously, the Loco Focos kept a weather eye on the financier; even humorous letters to *Poulson's* made them fear that Biddle intended to supervise the U.S. Bank of Pennsylvania in the same manner that Jackson kept manipulating Van Buren and his cabinet. In fact, Jackson overshadowed his successor. His graphic phraseology still found its way into the press. That same April, *Poulson's* quoting "the old General" referred to Andrew Stevenson, Van Buren's Minister to Great Britain, as "not worth the powder and ball necessary to kill him off."[1]

Biddle disregarded Jackson's dogged shade, ignored the Loco Focos, placated Cooper, begged off of a celebratory dinner proposed in his honor, and tried to avoid all public notice, which made the rumor mills turn faster. He was reported in the Democratic press to be in the "field" again,[2] to which one wit responded that the man was now a farmer. Where else should he be but attending to his crops?

The publisher, Hezekiah Niles, who had been supportive of Biddle and both the Second Bank and U.S. Bank of Pennsylvania, died on April 3, following a long bout of declining health. The *Register* was now offered for sale. In the same month, Van Buren's presidential tour was deferred owing to his lack of popularity; when it resumed, the sparse crowds disappointed him. Webster, elected that winter to another Senate term and now bruited about as a candidate for vice president under Harrison, sailed for England aboard the steamer *Liverpool* on May 18. Biddle, for whom each of those events would have had importance, now merely read about them in the newspapers. He intended to make Andalusia his true home. There, he marked the river's tides, strolled the lawns, and consulted with gardeners about graperies and hothouses. Unlike the hero of Lamartine's *Le Lac*, he had come to rest.

> Ainsi toujours poussés vers de nouveaux rivages,
> Dans la nuit éternelle emportés sans retour,
> Ne pourrons-nous jamais sur l'océan des ages
> Jeter l'ancre un seul jour?
> [So driven toward new shores forever,
> Into night eternal swept away without return,
> Can we never upon the sea of time
> Drop anchor for a single day?]

In this muted mood, he made journal entries, considered his work with Girard College, and pondered and wrote about Napoleon's exploits, whose coronation ticket he had kept.

* * *

As spring gave way to summer, Samuel Jaudon found himself in an untenable situation in London. In August 1839, he could not persuade Baring Brothers to continue using the Bank as its agent, because they believed the institution had, or would soon, become insolvent. They knew little of Biddle's successor, Thomas Dunlap, and feared that without the storied financier at the helm, American politics would again topple the country's economy. Deeming the Bank too big to fail, Rothschild and Son rescued it with sizeable loans, but the problems at home and in England escalated.

Blame circled back to Biddle and Jackson as partisan politics continued to widen an already significant chasm. Van Buren was regarded as a dupe who merely did the ex-president's bidding; the Loco Focos, sworn enemies of all banks, created their own brand of chaos. In September, *Niles' Register* reported that the British stock market was falling and that bankruptcies were anticipated in the manufacturing cities of Manchester and Liverpool. The price and availability of cotton were the culprits, tying the deep South to Britain's monetary malaise. With the advent of steamships, news traveled quickly across the Atlantic (an average of sixteen days west and 13 days east). Panic set in.

On October 9, in Philadelphia, directors of the Bank of the United States of Pennsylvania and private banks, met and decided on a grave step. They suspended specie payments. Hard currency would no longer be available for redemption. Vaults were locked as a precaution. The financiers declared that "They had no course left but to ruin many of their customers, and oppress the whole mercantile community, or suspend specie payments and throw themselves on the mercy of the legislature."[3] Rumors circulated that the Bank of England might also be driven to suspension. Biddle was accused of having abandoned the Bank because he had anticipated the disaster. Banks in other cities followed suit: Baltimore and all of Delaware on October 10, Washington, Norfolk, Virginia, and banks in the Pennsylvania interior on October 12, and Tennessee on October 19. Similar actions were taken in the southern planting states and western farming states.

On Tuesday, October 23, 1839, *Poulson's* reprinted Daniel Webster's 1834 speech in which he had forewarned the Senate about the disastrous consequences of the removal of deposits: "As surely as you sit in that chair, or I stand here, our tendencies at the present moment, are strong toward disorganization, to the time of state securities, bills of credit, separate state currencies and paper money—and if those tendencies be not seasonably addressed, they will make a shipwreck of our highest interests."[4] By then, the government had also suspended specie payments.

Van Buren, the supposed advocate of the common man, but who had an estimated worth of $600,000 and drew a salary of $25,000, came under attack. "Confidence is dead," the press bellowed about his and Jackson's "experiment" with hard currency, "public credit is degraded, private capital is destroyed."[5] A writer in *Poulson's* proffered a lugubrious bromide: "Grain grows rich when armies bleed and die."[6] When Andrew Jackson was rumored to have died in early November, would-be humorists suggested that it had been an honest mistake. The "monster is dead"[7] had been taken to refer to the former President, rather than Biddle's Bank. By then, failures in manufactories were occurring in Massachusetts and Rhode Island. The only persons seemingly impervious to the national disaster were Thomas Hart Benton and the Loco Focos, who regarded the calamity with contempt.

* * *

The 1st Session of the 26th Congress found both houses in disarray. The Whigs detested the Van Burenites; the Loco Focos despised both parties; fraud was alleged in the New Jersey elections. The nation looked to its leadership for aid, but no help was forthcoming. Van Buren's annual address to Congress in March 1839 had either ignored the economy's disarray by positing putative success stories, or scolded about "gigantic banking institutions," or "splendid but profitless railroads and canals." He asserted that "Indebtedness cannot be lessened by borrowing more money, or by changing the form of the debt. The balance of trade is not to be turned in our favor by creating new demands abroad."

The President had refused to bear any blame, either for his own or Jackson's administration. At fault were the financiers who had mismanaged the nation's money, and a populace all too eager to overextend itself.

> It is only by retrenchment and reform, by curtailing public and private expenditures, by paying our debts, and by reforming our banking system, that we are to expect effectual relief . . . a chain of dependence which leads all classes to look to privileged associations for the means of speculation and extravagance—to nourish, in preference to the manly virtues that give dignity to human nature, a craving desire for luxurious enjoyment and sudden wealth, which renders those who seek them dependent on those who supply them—to substitute for republican simplicity and economical habits a sickly appetite for effeminate indulgence, and an imitation of that reckless extravagance which impoverished and enslaved the industrious people of foreign lands. . . .

All this misconduct and wickedness, he insisted, had been carried out "by partial legislation," meaning that the Bank of the United States of Pennsylvania had never been a bona fide institution. He demanded the Sub Treasury scheme be revived, reviled all use of paper money as well as credit, and urged each state to regulate its own banking system, which wooed the states' rights' advocates. In an appeal to the Loco Focos, Van Buren pointedly used the word "revolution."[8]

* * *

Having forfeited his public platform as president of the Bank, Biddle could only respond locally, which he did during a speech in Pottsville, Pennsylvania, in January 1840, and subsequently in June at the opening of the Tidewater Canal on the Susquehanna River. In the first instance, he spoke of Americans' courage, tenacity, resourcefulness, and vigor. In the second, while acknowledging the state's debt of thirty-two million dollars, he enthused about the possibilities such debts and investments engendered by creating a robust infrastructure—the very canals and railroads Van Buren had decried. With that investment would come prosperity. The development of Pennsylvania's interior natural resources and transportation to the marketplace would create wealth in the hinterlands and the eastern cities. Both themes were similar: hope for the future and a government led by bold and honest men, rather than by self-serving demagogues who complained about cost rather than acting with vision and confidence. He avoided mentioning Van Buren by name, but his audiences understood the reference when he said, "These are the maudlin lamentations of men unfit to lead a great nation."[9] Biddle continued to believe that credit was the foundation of a robust economy.

Biddle's quiet life as a private citizen soon palled. There were only so many convivial dinners with friends to enjoy, only so many pleasant hours at home with his family, only so much private correspondence, or educational reading with which to fill the hours. In March 1839, he commissioned a study of his "cerebral development," supposedly a science. Some of the results of his emotional state were unsurprising, but two showed him markedly different from the man he'd been fifteen years prior. His "love of approbation" was "very large;" his "self-esteem" was "large;" his "combativeness" as well as his "wit" both "large and unequal," but "hope" was only "moderate," and "cautiousness" deemed "large."

Philadelphian Sidney George Fisher, who later became noted for keeping a series of diaries chronicling the 1830s through 1860s and penning a proslavery tract *The Laws of Race*, marked Biddle's fall with a habitual sneer. Fisher abhorred a "vulgar crowd" or "detestable" company, Jacksonians, Van Burenites, or any political activity that smacked of the slightest Democratic-leaning. He was caustic even toward friends.

> Biddle, once the idol, the God of Philad: upon whom for years every species of flattery & attention was lavished, & whom not to speak of as the greatest man of these latter times, was regarded as flat blasphemy. . . . The embarrassment of business, the distress of the community, the dangerous position of the banks, all are attributed to him, and he is called a knave & a fool by the very men, who a year ago joined in the chorus of servile adulation.[10]

Admitting that he had never liked or admired the man (Fisher reserved his adulation for the "divine Fanny" [Kemble]), he grudgingly referred to the financier as "able, brilliant, agreeable, plausible, cultivated"[11] while repeating the rumor that Biddle "got out of the scrape just in time."[12]

Fisher, a guest at most gatherings to which Biddle was invited, and among the company at musical evenings provided by Jane—and where Fanny sang and performed, reminded the financier of how low his estate had fallen. Proud of his acid tongue, Fisher was expressing what others whispered behind closed doors, or when Biddle's back was turned.

Additional fodder for the critics was his replacement at the Bank of the United States: Thomas Dunlap, married to Anne Wilkinson Biddle, Clement Biddle's daughter, which made her Nicholas's second cousin. The family connection inspired suspicions that the former president had never intended to relinquish power. Fisher claimed the appointment had "sprung upon the board in the absence of some of its most influential members."[13] Despite the "immense fortune" Fisher believed the banker possessed, and his current ability to "let those laugh who win,"[14] Biddle's days and nights were spent trying to discern real friends from false while simultaneously watching the nation's economy continue to flounder. A change of scene became imperative.

On December 13, 1840, he took pen in hand and appealed to Daniel Webster for aid. He wanted a ministerial position in Europe. Using the excuse that his family desired to travel abroad, he explained in an unusually formal tone—this was Webster with whom he had enjoyed a decades-long relationship—that "travelling in Europe as a mere private gentleman is a dull business. If a man had a high public station & higher public fame, as you had, he gets along well, but a private gentleman delivering cold letters of introduction & making his way into what is called society has a task extremely repugnant to his pride."[15]

Declaring he was "too old for that" and that any proffered positions in London, Paris, or St. Petersburg would hamper his and his family's movements (in fact, those prized spots had already been claimed), he suggested that Vienna would be ideal. He then provided his resume dating from his position as Legation secretary in London and Paris. He indicated that Madison had intended to send him as Minister to London in 1815, but his lack of credentials as a legislator had prevented the appointment. The appeal was bald, bold, and, in many ways, desperate. The concluding paragraph showed the pain Biddle felt at being sidelined: a proud man, begging while attempting a modicum of light-hearted humor. "And now my story is told. . . . Now tell me what you think of all this? Is it a reasonable thing? Is it a probable thing?"

Although Webster declared that "Nob'y could be better for the Country—& nothn would be more agreeable to me" he couldn't help. He gave politics as the reason; the "Tobacco men" had Austria in their pocket.[16] Disappointed, Biddle dropped his appeal, but not his efforts to maintain a comradely relationship with Webster and appear savvier to the ways of Washington than he was rapidly becoming. On February 2, 1841, he told Webster that a colleague from Cincinnati had informed him that Harrison (elected in 1840) was considering creating a new national bank, because of the imminent repeal of the Sub Treasury bill. If so, might the President name him to a position of authority—perhaps Secretary of the Treasury, as he alluded to Webster, who became Secretary of State.

Harrison made clear his intentions regarding instituting another central bank during his two-hour inaugural speech on March 4, 1841. Those plans died with him when he succumbed on April 4. The cause was blamed on pneumonia having taken chill during the cold, wet inaugural ceremony. Vice President John Tyler, a Democrat turned Whig and staunch espouser of states' rights, was sworn into office two days later. Whig loyalists jeered at him as "His Accidency."

By then, the Bank of the United States of Pennsylvania had shuttered its doors. Fisher had been partially correct in his assessment of Dunlap's ascendancy. However, he was unaware of deeper divisions among the directors; a cadre determined to remove all future and past allegiances to their former leader. Some of the animosity was due to investments in the Schuylkill Navigation Company and stockholders and board members with conflicts of interest. Some of the reaction was due to personal antipathy. Biddle had been in place long enough to inspire both envy and mistrust. Now that his star was setting, it became easier to debunk him. If Fisher could say, "He was in no possible sense a great man, & had no greatness about him, either of mind or character,"[17] others could and would, as well.

Internal disarray within the Bank stoked public fears. On January 14, 1841, the Bank had learned that on January 15, it would be forced to meet specie demands valued at two and a half million dollars. Despite striving to meet those demands, the Bank was soon reputed to have become insolvent, which produced a panic. Biddle, who had wanted Jaudon, rather than Dunlap to replace him, blamed management. Dunlap accused former directors, especially Biddle. Even though Pennsylvania's legislature passed a bill (over the Governor's previous April 8 veto) lifting penalties for banks that failed to pay specie, the directors closed the institution.

* * *

Biddle's reputation was ruined. He tried to keep his head up, but the weight of public opinion bore down upon him. A handsome gift of a coin silver service that had crowned his departure from the Bank had to be melted to pay bills. The horrors of his father's early memories of poverty made this sad act a double burden. Nicholas appeared stoic when outside of Andalusia's confines, but his psyche cringed.

In April 1841, to explain his and the institution's activities and redeem his former position, he published a series of lengthy letters that appeared on the front pages of national newspapers. They may have been fair and reasonable in their finger-pointing "It is the vengeance of the Schuylkill Navigation Company against the Bank of the United States for lending money to the Reading Railroad,"[18] or name-calling: Manuel Eyre's dismay at being removed from the Board; or Joshua Lippincott's double-dealing; or that the accusations were produced by "miserable intriguers,"[19] but the missives were prolix and overly laden with the minutia of annual investment accountings, board resolutions, and votes counted.

Biddle's stated purpose: "I am about to explain to you some singular details of what would otherwise be unintelligible—the origin and nature of the late proceedings touching the Bank of the United States"[20] were sadly *unintelligible* to anyone hoping to gain clarity into the institution's history, glory days, and subsequent demise. The complexity of his theses, the digressive process whereby he reasoned, and his often-truculent tone harmed his prospects rather than gained adherents. The fourth letter supplied written testimony taken from Board proceedings that supposedly implicated Biddle's wrongdoers within the Bank (Eyre and Lippincott); the fifth letter defended Samuel Jaudon:

> To see such a man denounced and vilified by those professing to
> represent the institution which he had served and saved—to see such
> a man stabbed behind his back the moment when he was laboring to
> protect the Bank, and when all his talents and character were needed
> in its service, is an act not merely of injustice to him, but of insanity as
> respects the Bank itself.[21]

No one reading that passage could have failed to insert Biddle's name for Jaudon's.

He also tried unsuccessfully to explain a ruinous cotton exchange and trade the Bank had devised to shore up its failing resources. Edward Biddle, Nicholas's and Jane's eldest son, then residing in Liverpool, had helped broker the sale, which raised suspicions of wrongdoing. The investment in cotton had been one of the Bank's investment strategies; unfortunately, it had allied the institution with the fluctuating southern economy and long-term credit, which Biddle had perceived as beneficial in uniting diverse segments of the country and its merchant and planter classes. Biddle had also personally invested heavily in cotton, making his explanations appear questionable at best. The more the financier aimed for transparency and made assurances of honesty and probity, the murkier the tale seemed, and the more dubious it sounded. Knowing that he was an honorable man, descended from decent men, he failed to comprehend that his own words would hurt him. Even his most loyal supporters must have wished they could have wrestled the pen from his hand as he sat writing in his library at Andalusia.

Worse was to come. Biddle was informed that he must pay $320,000 to settle stockholders' claims. He did so but refused to retaliate by blaming the political forces that had challenged and stymied the Bank's effectiveness. His fortune obliterated, he spent the remainder of his life dependent on Jane's inheritance. Though they lived in comfort at Andalusia, he was, in the parlance of the time, "unmanned."

In June 1841, the stockholders sued for $1,000,000 more. The amount was reduced to $240,000 in September, begging the question of whence the higher number had come and why it was so drastically lowered. If Biddle understood the cause, he made no reference to it. By then, his abasement had become a matter of course.

On January 6, 1842, he, Dunlap, Jaudon, Joseph Cowperthwaite (cashier), and John Andrews (assistant cashier) were arrested at three o'clock in the afternoon and charged with a "conspiracy to defraud the stockholders of the Bank of the United States."[22] Appearing with counsel, they made bail of $10,000 each and were told to present themselves at the Court of General Sessions to stand trial. Taking the high road, Biddle's attorney declared that all parties were "anxious to proceed with the investigation," lending a false air of gentlemanly misunderstanding to the proceedings. However, the headline in *Niles' Weekly Register* read "U.S. Bank Officers Arrested," and the court was crammed with people eager to witness the "former distinguished 'lions' of the Bank of the United States" laid low.[23]

The weather in Philadelphia that January was deceptively mild, the thermometer registering 55 or 60 degrees, and the skies often a benign and spring-like blue, but the nation's financial news verged on the catastrophic. A teller in Boston's City Bank was arrested for embezzlement mid-month; at the same time, bank riots occurred in Cincinnati with mobs looting specie and stuffing the pilfered money into hats and handkerchiefs. On January 27, the Girard Bank failed; threatening crowds gathered outside its locked doors, necessitating a police presence. Saturday, January 29, there were reports of runs on the Bank of Pennsylvania and the Chesapeake Bank in Baltimore. It was also rumored that the United States Treasury had become nearly insolvent.

Throughout the month, Biddle made no appeals to friends or former colleagues. Instead, he remained silent, neither defending himself nor attacking perceived or genuine enemies. Reading the newspaper reports of Daniel Webster's festive party as Secretary of State must have pained him: "one of the most splendid and tasteful soirées that this capital has seen for many years."[24] At another time in his life, Biddle would have been one of the notables among the happy throng.

Charles Dickens was then touring America and being mobbed in every city; when he arrived in Philadelphia March 6, Parkinson's Ice Cream Palace on Chestnut Street, one of the most fashionable places in the city, created a "Temple to Boz." Biddle would undoubtedly have entertained the author as he had other visiting literary and theatrical stars. He also would have been quoted regarding the construction of the Athenaeum of Philadelphia, the private library he had espoused. Instead, all he wanted was to keep his name out of the newspapers.

When Judge Josiah Randall announced that Samuel Jaudon was to be discharged, Democrats attacked the jurist, insisting he "appeared rather as advocate than Judge,"[25] which stirred up a hornet's nest of abuse, even after Randall wrote a letter in his defense. Randall's opinion ran for two and three-fourth columns starting on the front page of the Democrat-leaning *Pennsylvanian*. An announcement that Van Buren (in superb health) had passed through Philadelphia on his way to visit the party's god, Jackson, glared across the page in reproof. The anti-bank believers were quick to harken back to early warnings about the folly of depending on "ragg money," which they reviled as a "worthless pile of trash."[26]

Amos Kendall, one of the architects of the Bank's demise, bought a farm of one hundred acres near Washington, where he was said to be "cultivating potatoes and politics." He was coy in describing his retirement, leaving it open to conjecture that he might jump at the chance of returning to the halls of power. The Bank trial kept the Jacksonians fuming while they anticipated vengeance. In early March, when Dunlap was "released from responsibility under the criminal process,"[27] it seemed their hopes might be dashed. Still, the Democratic press kept up their battles against "Whiggery," insisting that President Tyler's March message to Congress was too lenient on the Bank that had "turned all its immense weight and influence on the government."[28] Tyler had equivocated, espousing neither party nor laying blame despite stating that he recognized the financial emergency and the government's deficit of $14,000,000.

> If the credit of the country be exposed to question—if the public defenses be broken down or weakened—if the whole administration of public affairs be embarrassed for want of necessary means for conducting them with vigor and effect, I trust that the Department of the Government will be found to have done all that was in its power to avert such evils, and will be acquitted of all just blame on account of them."[29]

No wonder he was accused of being a "President without a party."[30]

The "broken banks" list in Philadelphia numbered the Schuylkill, Moyamensing, Girard, Pennsylvania, Penn Township, Mechanics, and Manufacturers. The Bank of the United States' assets had been $35,000,000. New Jersey counted the Hamburg Bank, Franklin, Monmouth, Weehawk, and Bank of New Jersey among "Broken and Defunct Banks."[31] Bankruptcies appeared in newspapers daily: cabinet makers, pump makers, omnibus proprietors, millers, farriers, coach makers, coopers, cane and whip makers; every walk of life suffered while the Democrats and Whigs pointed fingers at each other. Biddle was caught in a maelstrom of public loathing: one side defending his actions, the other lambasting him. Pennsylvania Democrat, James Buchanan, on the Senate floor, posited a biting, "The Whig party has succeeded a thrifty old gentleman in the management of a trust estate, who had always used the utmost prudence and economy in his expenditures."[32] Buchanan never identified the "thrifty old gentleman" as Jackson or Van Buren, but his partisan message was plain. Whiggery (and Biddle) were at fault.

By this time, Nicholas Biddle became so demonized that Thaddeus Stevens felt impelled to defend him before the Harrisburg legislature, ferociously denouncing the financier's "former friends and enthusiasts" as being sycophants who had curried the man's favor out of rank opportunism during his prosperous years, but who now found it expedient to revile him. "He may have his faults, and I will not palliate them; but I believe him to possess a nobler mind and purer soul than the whole jackal tribe prowling around him and haunting his retirement." Describing the "bitter pangs of ingratitude and infidelity" Biddle was currently experiencing, Stevens railed at his audience. "He has lived long enough . . . to have realized, as we shall all sooner or later realize, the truth of the remark, 'that he is a happy man who has one true friend, but he is more truly happy who never has need of a friend.'"[33]

Friends and foes notwithstanding, Biddle's case riveted the nation. In Philadelphia, the trial consumed every edition of every newspaper. No one could anticipate the outcome, so speculation kept gossip alive. Was Nicholas Biddle an honest man or a thief? Was the trial justified or driven by revenge? As the days dragged on, tension mounted, and conclusions solidified. Everybody was convinced theirs was the correct opinion.

When Biddle was acquitted on April 26, 1842, another avalanche of angry Democratic responses greeted the news. The *Pennsylvanian* vilified the "abuses practiced by a vicious banking system"[34] and accused the trial of being a "defect in the administration of justice."[35] The Whigs insisted he had been "unjustly held responsible."[36] Battered, Biddle crept home to Andalusia.

* * *

On June 25, 1842, a notice appeared in *Niles' Register*: "*The U. states bank for sale*. Sheriff Morris, of Philadelphia, advertises that the splendid building of the U.S. bank, and the lot upon which it stands, will be sold at auction the 2nd of July."[37] Biddle's Bank, the marble-clad temple to national and international finance, was no more. Although exonerated from criminal activity, a part of the population continued to condemn him, as perhaps was natural given the raw and growing wounds of the country's fiscal lacerations. In George Lippard's potboiler murder mystery, *The Quaker City, or The Monks of Monk Hall*, he was given a new identity and the sobriquet "old Snatch and Grab." The novel wasn't published until 1845 when Biddle was already dead, but he heard similar scurrilous nicknames during his final years.

The "orphans and widows" his policies had supposedly beggared found him an easy target; so did the nativists who from America's birth had mistrusted any foreign interference or influence, and who therefore denounced the international banking model Biddle had espoused. At the height of his fame as a financier, his counterparts in Europe hailed him for his boldness, vision, and audacity. To the Rothschilds, Barings, and others, he symbolized an American ideal, personifying the nation's limitless possibilities and a land of vast, untapped resources. They embraced him and the commercial wealth they perceived he represented. Parochialism had no place in their firmaments. They found his fall from grace inconceivable and shocking.

But Biddle also mirrored an Old-World ideal; he was an aristocrat, and proud of it. Although innocent of charges that he had attempted to defraud the Bank's stockholders, he was guilty of many other corporate and personal flaws: impracticality, careless bookkeeping, errors in judgments large and small, misplaced trust, a naïve dearth of diplomacy, and above all, hubris. As he had early admitted, he'd never trained to become a banker; instead, he believed philosophy and intellect and a steadfast desire to do his duty could carry the day. Baser instincts had always been foreign to him, even the simplest need for food and shelter.

As a banker, he had not fully appreciated the institution's need for profit. The organization he entered at Monroe's behest had been formed on a Hamiltonian ideal: a central bank to serve the federal government rather than a profit-making business. The loss of its charter, the fight for re-charter, its evolution as a state bank with a national name and reputation created a hybrid, which Biddle misjudged—just as he failed to embrace the rise of the self-made man.

The efforts he made for Girard College also came crashing down on his head when he was accused of having spent too much money on a building not yet completed. The mayor and aldermen of Philadelphia, who were trustees of the college, removed him as chair and board member. The good he had intended to do by providing education to indigent boys continued, but without his participation.

Nicholas Biddle, in his prime, had soared. He had great plans for the nation's financial health and stability, which he devoutly believed must come from a national bank. Abased, he plummeted.

* * *

Andalusia was sold at a public auction. Biddle had mortgaged it to pay his debts to the Bank. Jane's trustees quietly repurchased the estate, which had been originally put in trust to her and her brothers in accordance with her father's will. The couple continued to dwell there, provoking more accusations of chicanery and double-dealing. Biddle's foes wanted to see him suffer, or, if prevented from witnessing his misery, at least to know of his distress.

By then, the mood of the city and nation had reached a nadir. As Sidney George Fisher wrote on July 15, 1842:

> Everybody has become poor & the calamities of the times have not only broken up the gay establishments & put an end to social intercourse, but seem to have covered the place with a settled gloom. The streets seem deserted—the largest houses are shut up and to rent—there is no business—there is no money—no confidence and little hope. Property is sold every day by the sheriff at a 4th of the estimated value of a few years ago—nobody can pay debts—the miseries of poverty are felt both by rich & poor—everyone you see looks careworn & haggard.

From 1838 through 1844, the "Great Depression" (in fact, an international depression) inspired anti-abolition Riots, Workers' Rights riots, and anti-Catholic riots that turned Philadelphia into a tempest of unrest and rage. Unemployment soared; spiritualism and mesmerism became a popular, if useless, panacea. An offshoot of the period's pernicious racism was the advent of the Minstrel Show in 1842. Billy Whitlock, dressed in black face, starred in the nation's first such "entertainment" at the Walnut Street Theater.

Despite his diminished state, Biddle persisted in believing that the only means to rescue the nation financially was to expand credit and currency instead of contracting. He desperately wanted to be heard. When Tyler became President, Biddle sent suggestions regarding the tariff and a revenue bill. When Webster proposed resigning as Secretary of State, he was appalled. "You can do nothing abroad which you cannot do better while you remain here & speak thro your agents—as Secretary you are the Govt—as Minister you are the Government's agent. Then if you go who is to take your place? Some transcendentalist—some cobweb spinner?"[38] His friendship with John Quincy Adams continued as strong as ever, with Adams joining the Biddles at Andalusia for family dinners. However, everyone, including Biddle, understood that his status had eroded. The days of Fanny Kemble and her husband, Pierce Butler, inviting the Biddles to "a riotous sleigh party"[39] were gone, just as were the financier's official sojourns in Washington, or Boston, or New York.

* * *

In March 1843, Nicholas Biddle was forced to relinquish the home on Spruce Street, where he and Jane had entertained the leading lights of the city and nation. By then, anxiety and a lifelong disdain for physical exercise had told on his health. He realized he was becoming "corpulent," but either refused or was incapable of altering his habits. In October 1843, he wrote to Roswell Colt, his friend, as well as relative through marriage, "I have been very sick—and what is harder—very much doctored."[40] Biddle described treatments of "sulphur baths, a horrid wash called Dulcamara, and calomel powder."[41] He also admitted that he was being dosed with digitalis and laudanum. Shortness of breath prevented him from walking his property, which, in turn, exacerbated his weight gain. He managed to assuage Jane's fears, however (or believed he had), by insisting his weakness was due to bronchitis, or influenza, or ordinary fatigue. He was a terrible patient.

Ill but resolved not to allow his symptoms to defeat him, he began spending most of his waking hours in his library among his treasured books. The works of Dryden, Milton, and Pope were at his elbow. So were volumes of Tacitus, Plinius, Plautus, Suetonius, and the *Opere di Metastasi* and *di Machiaveli*, and Adam Smith's *The Wealth of Nations*. A fireplace kept the room cozy and warm; the view of the Delaware was ever-present, brightening his sanctuary with sunny benignity or shrouding it in the silver-gray of reverie. Two pictures of Napoleon hung on the walls; one of the Emperor as a doting father, and the other of Bonaparte in exile, standing on a rocky summit, staring out to sea.

Within this cloistered space, Biddle started compiling a scrapbook. Covered in green and russet-colored marbleized paper with a spine of green leather, it began to fill with newspaper clippings he had saved. Most of the articles dealt with banks and banking, with commerce, foreign stocks, mining in the United States and Mexico, the tariff laws, statistics on the cotton trade and agriculture, specie drains, South American debts, and tobacco production in Maryland and Ohio—all the forces that had driven and continued to drive America's economy. The publications had been gathered from across the nation: Boston, Albany, Savannah, Cincinnati, Charleston, New York, Philadelphia; even the anti-bank *Globe* was represented, which derided the *National Intelligencer*, also a Washington newspaper, as "the Bank Organ in the city."[42]

He also included lists of members of Congressional sessions and two articles in which he was featured. One had been published in the *Franklin Gazette* in

October 1818, extolling Biddle as a candidate for "The Democratic Congressional Ticket." Stating that "the political virtues" he possessed "shone with a distinct and determined character in the late war." The article further applauded him, "In the Senate of Pennsylvania he manifested the same honorable zeal to uphold and to contribute to the glory of our arms, as did his three brothers, in the army and navy of the United States."[43] His orations were compared to the poems of Pope.

The second article spoke to Biddle's philosophy and sense of self. The words were taken from his dedication at the laying of Girard College's cornerstone in July 1833. "We dedicate it to the cause of Education, which gives to human life its value, to the cause of Morals, without which knowledge were worse than unavailable; and finally to the cause of our Country, which service is the noblest object to which knowledge and morals can be devoted."[44]

Biddle never completed the scrapbook. He died early in the morning on February 27, 1844, leaving it as a work in progress. He was fifty-eight. Knowing the end was near, his children Edward, Charles, Craig, Adele, Meta, and Jane were in the house, as was Edward's wife, the former Jane Josephine Sarmiento, and of course, Nicholas's wife, Jane.

EPILOGUE

I have reason to believe that I am the first person since Nicholas Biddle's death to read his unfinished scrapbook. His grandson, Edward, took it upon himself to catalog Biddle's effects, sending collections of papers to the Library of Congress, the Historical Society of Pennsylvania, and Princeton University. Some correspondence remained at Andalusia; some found its way into other descendants' homes—the draft letters to Monroe being the latest discovery. The scrapbook, though, sat unregarded, wrapped in archival paper, tied with string, forgotten. If Edward perused it, he made no note of doing so.

The discovery of that incomplete volume allowed me to envision Biddle's final days. Ailing in body and soul, prematurely aged, he gathered the pieces of his story. The inclusion of the two brief articles describing his Congressional aspirations and his speech at Girard College, I found profoundly moving. Not quite centered, they manifest a physical effort in his work as if overcome by frailty or emotion. Full accounts of his orations had appeared in numerous newspapers over the decades, but these two small stories clearly held a special place in his heart. I felt as though I were watching him reread them, reliving each long-gone moment before taking up the glue pot and pressing the brittle paper into the blank pages. Duty to his country, morality, and knowledge were the words he chose for his private epitaph.

* * *

Jane finally got her chance to visit Europe in late March 1845—not as the wife of a great man, nor as a diplomat's helpmeet and partner, but as kindly, undemanding Jane. Grief had eroded her health after Nicholas's untimely death, and her children and brother-in-law, James, had prevailed upon her to leave behind Andalusia with its bittersweet memories and Philadelphia with its still-vituperative press.

Jane's son, Craig, and the three girls accompanied her on a tour to her mother's ancestral homeland of Ireland. They were also able to visit Scotland, England, and the Continent. Commodore James Biddle had intended to join the party but had been called to Canton to exchange ratifications for the first American treaty with Imperial China, the Treaty of Wanghia.

By that time, Meta, who was twenty, and to whom her father had dedicated his humorous "Ode to Bogle" was engaged to her cousin, another James Biddle. Adele, three years younger than Meta, was then seventeen. Jane, fifteen, kept a sketchbook, which she soon relinquished in favor of purchased prints of the chief sights the family visited. While perusing the sketches, it's easy to imagine her leaving girlhood behind and becoming impatient with her artistic skills as well as with the bucolic scenes of rural Ireland that must have seemed as sleepy as Andalusia. London, Venice, Pisa, Pompeii, Herculaneum dazzled her. She had grown up dreaming of those places while flitting in and out of her father's library. He had been there, too.

CORDELIA FRANCES BIDDLE
PHILADELPHIA

NOTES

PROLOGUE : MARCH 7, 1778

1. "'murdering' his time." Clark, William Bell, *Captain Dauntless: The Story of Nicholas Biddle and the Continental Navy*, (Louisiana State University Press, 1949), 46.

2. "I did not apprehend danger," Biddle said of the experience. Ibid., 68.

3. "little brig" *Andrea Doria*. Cooper, James Fenimore, *History of the Navy of the United States of America*, in two volumes (Philadelphia: Lea and Blanchard, 1840), 1:87.

4. "The very best vessel for sailing that I ever knew," Biddle boasted of her. Clark, *Captain Dauntless*, 175.

5. "I am much more afraid of doing a foolish thing than losing my life." Ibid., 2.

6. "There is little question that Nicholas Biddle would have risen to high rank." Cooper, *History of the Navy of the United States of America*, 121.

CHAPTER ONE : AN AMERICAN FAMILY

1. Biddle, C. Miller, M.D., *William and Sarah Biddle, 1633–1711: Planting a Seed of Democracy in America* (Privately Printed. Saline, MI: McNaughton & Gunn, Inc., 2012), 8.

2. Biddle, Charles, *Autobiography of Charles Biddle, Vice President of the Supreme Executive Council of Pennsylvania 1745-1821* (Privately Printed. Philadelphia: E. Claxton and Company, 1883), 2.

3. "he had ruined me and his children." Ibid., 2.

4. "As pickled a rascal as ever was hanged." Ibid., 45.

5. "as great a ruffian as ever was hanged." Ibid., 92.

6. Ibid., 5.

7. Ibid., 5.

8. "My going to sea was the best thing I could have done," Charles said. Ibid., 6.

9. "I got severely beaten." Ibid., 16.

10. "as to give great offence." Ibid., 43.

11. "I will tomahawk you." Ibid., 144–45.

12. "courted Danger for her sake." Andalusia, Biddle Papers, Autograph Letters, Bound vol. A-K, no. 61, 24 April 1760, no. 46.

13. "on a unanimous vote." Ibid., no. 76, 77.

14. Ibid., 72.

15. "before the dispute was settled." Biddle, *Autobiography of Charles Biddle*, 74.

16. "next in command to General Washington." Ibid., 74.

17. "Before this he was never sick." Ibid., 75.

18. "join the army." Ibid., 75.

19. Ibid., 87.

20. "As my brig was armed . . ." Ibid., 101–102.

21. "most happy circumstance of his life." Biddle, *Autobiography of Charles Biddle*, 116.
22. "the cause of America." Ibid., 146.
23. "or any other country." Ibid., 217.
24. "with great contempt." Ibid., 219.
25. "this I adhered to." Ibid., 194.
26. "ardently affectionate." Ibid., 241–42.
27. "three miles from town" Ibid., 275.
28. "I hardly ever remember him out of temper." Ibid., 267.
29. "the only man in whose presence he felt any awe." Ibid., 284.

CHAPTER TWO : THE CHILD PRODIGY

1. Govan, Thomas. "Nicholas Biddle at Princeton" Princeton University Library Chronicle, vol. 9, no. 2 (February 1948), 52.
2. "the constitution either of body or of mind." Biddle, Nicholas. Journals Europe 1804–1807 Call 2146, box 15, The Historical Society of Pennsylvania.
3. "your minds are too noble to disobey her call." Govan, "Nicholas Biddle at Princeton" Princeton University Library Chronicle, 53.
4. "Favorable to Virtue." Nicholas Biddle Personal Letters (Collection 2039), 1:40, The Historical Society of Pennsylvania.
5. "On the Study of Dead Languages." Ibid., 11.
6. "The Civilized and Savage State." Ibid., 38.
7. "Strong Government." Ibid., 15.
8. "To the King of the Russian Empire." Ibid., 19.
9. "rather wild." Govan, Thomas Payne. *Nicholas Biddle, Nationalist and Public Banker 1786–1844* (Chicago: The University of Chicago Press, 1959), 6.
10. "his mind is highly improved." Nicholas Biddle Personal Letters (Collection 2039), 1:44, The Historical Society of Pennsylvania.
11. "a 'brilliant mathematician.'" Biddle, *Autobiography of Charles Biddle*, 287.
12. "excessively hot" Ibid., 287.
13. "I ever made." Ibid., 286.
14. "A thousand melancholy reflections filled my mind." Ibid., 286.
15. "fast-sailing vessel." Biddle, *Autobiography of Charles Biddle*, 300.
16. "a berth for your son." Andalusia: Nicholas Biddle, Jr. Collection, box 6, no. 2, 31 July 1804.
17. "the greatest pleasures of my life." Nicholas Biddle Personal Letters (Collection 2039), 1:48, The Historical Society of Pennsylvania.
18. "walk every day half hour or hour." Ibid., 46.
19. Govan, *Nicholas Biddle*, 11.

CHAPTER THREE : THE ADVENTURER

1. Ninety-two volumes of Voltaire, Andalusia, Biddle Papers, Nicholas Biddle Letters, no. 73, 9 September 1802.
2. *Secretaire de la Légation*. Nicholas Biddle Personal Letters (Collection 2039), 3:126, The Historical Society of Pennsylvania.
3. *N BIDDLE 1804*. Biddle, Nicholas. Journals Europe 1804–1807 Call 2146, box 15, October 13, 1804 – December 27, 1804, The Historical Society of Pennsylvania.
4. "*Parlez un peu*," Lafayette replied. Ibid.

5. "I had not yet reached my nineteenth year." Ibid.

6. "private audience with the Emperor." Ibid.

7. "the Emperor did not smile." Ibid.

8. "*Le Gauche du Trone, Pour un Homme.*" Andalusia, Biddle Papers, Autograph Letters, Bound vol. A-K, no. 90, Ticket to Bonaparte's coronation.

9. "What a sight was this for a philosopher." Biddle, Nicholas. Journals Europe 1804–1807 Call 2146, box 15, October 13, 1804 – December 27, 1804, The Historical Society of Pennsylvania.

10. "nothing new." Ibid.

11. "lady whom I most esteem." Ibid., Journals Europe 1804–1807, August – September 1805, vol. 1, Switzerland.

12. "you will not perhaps be displeased at a romantic note." Ibid., August 1805, Austria, Switzerland.

13. "Dear Rebecca, I have just come into my bedroom . . ." Ibid., Journals Europe 1804–1807, August – September 1805, vol. 1, Switzerland.

14. "1 towel, 1 pillowcase, 1 fork" Ibid., Ship Passage to Europe.

15. "at once sublime, terrible and enchanting." Ibid., August – September 1805, vol. 1, Switzerland.

16. "with headlong fury." Ibid., Austria, Switzerland.

17. "constantly quarreling with his son and his wife." Journals Europe 1804–1807, Metaphysical Meditations, December 1806 (also notes on Rhine).

18. "Every monarch in Europe is interested in the fall of America." Ibid.

19. "circumspect people hold the head higher." Ibid.

20. "I attend to nothing else." Ibid.

21. "All is melancholy, wild & dreary." Ibid., Journey Towards Rome September – December 1805.

22. "a sad monument to human frailty." Ibid.

23. "the French who were so anxious to collect the monuments of the arts." Ibid.

24. "no man can look with indifference on the Palais Riccardi." Ibid.

25. "I danced very badly." Ibid.

26. "Memorial Lines." Andalusia, Nicholas Biddle Papers, gift of Charlotte Biddle.

27. "their valor are still the same . . ." R. A. McNeal, ed., *Nicholas Biddle in Greece: The Journals and Letters of 1806* (University Park, PA: the Pennsylvania State University Press, 1993), 49–50.

28. "being useful to my country" Ibid., 193.

29. "The conquest would be easy." Ibid., 225.

30. "set him on fire" Ibid., 203.

31. "neutral officer" Ibid., 203.

32. "where all my hopes & my ambitions tend." Ibid., 54.

33. "I die of hunger assails a stranger at every avenue." Ibid., 58.

34. "The govt has been particularly favorable to America." Ibid., 61.

35. "he spoke with frankness on all the concerns of the navy." Ibid., 71.

36. "The port is very secure." Ibid., 67.

37. "opening some channels of commerce." Ibid., 86.

38. "every man in his kingdom." Ibid., 158.

39. "drove him before him like a dog." Ibid., 102.

40. "holy soil of Greece." Ibid., 88.

41. "Yet I have seen few ruins so noble." Ibid., 97.

42. "the mistress of the world." Ibid., 111.

43. "Elgin robbed for gold." Ibid., 230.

44. "recollections of former times." Ibid., 224.

45. "dignity of my pursuit & the labors thro' which it must lead me." Ibid., 180.

46. "I have many duties to perform to my family, my profession & my country." Ibid., 193.

47. "As early as convenient." Andalusia: Nicholas Biddle, Jr. Collection, box 1, folder 5.

48. "I do not know what to say on it." Nicholas Biddle, Jr. Collection, box 1, folder 6, 21 July 1807.

49. "equally fond of flattery." Ibid., 27 June 1807.

50. "very little to recommend them." Ibid.

51. "the noise of the gallery is brutal." Ibid.

52. "dependable men of the country." Biddle, Nicholas. Journals Europe 1804–1807 Call 2146, box 15, Diary June 1807, England, The Historical Society of Pennsylvania.

53. "to get money into his own hands." Ibid.

54. "our political distinction." Andalusia, Biddle Papers, Nicholas Biddle Letters, box 1, folder 9, no. 2.

CHAPTER FOUR : THE YOUNG LAWYER

1. "You are performing a public duty." Nicholas Biddle Personal Letters (Collection 2039), vol. 4, no. 124, letter from William, 27 September 1807, The Historical Society of Pennsylvania.

2. "Journey to Monticello." Ibid.

3. UNMERITED OUTRAGE." *Poulson's American Daily Advertiser* (Philadelphia: Printed by Zachariah Poulson, N. 106 Chestnut Street), 29 June 1807.

4. "purchased with their blood." Ibid., 30 June 1807.

5. "several shots fired at her." Ibid., 4 July 1807.

6. "National wrongs require national redress." Ibid.

7. "without any delay to depart from the scene." Ibid., 6 July 1807.

8. "the British 'navy is particularly anxious for war.'" Biddle, Nicholas. Journals Europe 1804–1807 Call 2146, box 15, Diary, June 1807, England, The Historical Society of Pennsylvania.

9. "Nothing material has occurred since my return with regard to that business." Andalusia: Nicholas Biddle, Jr. Collection, box 1, folder 9, no. 3.

10. "the present session of Congress." Andalusia: Nicholas Biddle, Jr. Collection, box 1, folder 9, no. 3.

11. "somewhat inauspiciously." Andalusia: Nicholas Biddle, Jr. Collection, box 1, folder 10, no. 1, 2 April 1808.

12. "God bless you ever. A Burr." Andalusia, The Papers of Charles Biddle 1793–1817, 7 December 1802.

13. "Your very affectionate friend Aaron Burr." Ibid., letter from New York, 21 April 1793.

14. "I took a large dose of opium." Ibid., 28 September 1784.

15. Vice-President of the United States." Biddle, *Autobiography of Charles Biddle*, 289.

16. "I am ashamed to trouble you with these trifles." Andalusia, The Papers of Charles Biddle 1793–1817, 23 July 1804.

17. "I never knew Colonel Burr speak ill of any man." Ibid., 303.

18. "Hamilton did not act as a saint in accepting it." Ibid., 305.

19. "He will inform you of the state of things in the U.S." Andalusia, Biddle Papers, Autograph Letters, Bound vol. A-K, no. 98, 30 July 1804, Introduction to William T. Boone in Paris by Aaron Burr – written from Philadelphia.

20. "he would have been elected Governor of New York." Biddle, *Autobiography*, 309.

21. "would make the fortunes of all those concerned in revolutionizing the country." Ibid., 313.

22. "a better opinion of him than he deserved." Ibid., 318.

23. "immense concourse of citizens from various parts of the Union." *Poulson's*, 30 May 1807.

24. "Wilkinson would go almost all lengths to hang Col. Burr" Ibid., 26 June 1807.

25. "'I was intimate with them all,' was Charles's weary assessment." Biddle, Charles. *Autobiography*, 316.

26. "the richest treasures ever conferred on me." Andalusia: The Papers of Charles Biddle 1793–1817, 27 June 1807.

27. "knaves, swindlers, gamblers, drunkards, villains." Ibid., 2 June 1815.

28. "the occasion of his asking my assistance." Andalusia: Nicholas Biddle, Jr. Collection, box 1, folder 10, no. 1, 2 April 1808.

29. "he had ended his sufferings with a pistol." Biddle, *Autobiography*, 322.

30. "merits rather the name of a cabbin [*sic*] than a cottage." Andalusia: Nicholas Biddle, Jr. Collection, folder 2 1808-11, no. 1, 28 March 1808.

31. "intellectual eminence." *Port Folio*, new series, vol. 1 (1808), by Oliver Oldschool, Esq. Printed and Published for the Ed., by Smith & Maxwell, no. 28, North Second Street.

32. "Genius, Science, and Art." *Port Folio*, vol. 1 (1809).

33. "The common soldier's blood makes the general a great man." Ibid., vol. 2, no. 4 (1809).

34. "not a 'despot in politics.'" Ibid., vol. 1 (1809).

35. "They know only to go forwards, but never backwards." Ibid., vol. 1 (1809).

36. "probability of war appeared to thicken upon us every day." *Poulson's*, 6 January 1809.

37. "Buonarte [*sic*] about to let slip the dogs of war against Spain." Ibid., 17 January 1809.

38. "In our Imperial Camp at Madrid 7th of December. (signed) Napoleon." Ibid., 21 March 1809.

39. "Holy Bible Explained" Ibid., 14 January 1809.

40. "A likely Black boy who have five years to serve" Ibid., 1 June 1809.

41. "100 Dollars Reward." Ibid., February 28, 1809.

42. "Street dirt at auction 7th and Vine." Ibid., 5 April 1809.

43. "Black Italian Crape", Ibid., April 14.

44. "Vive La Plume – Metallic Pen Manufactory" Ibid., September 9.

45. "renewable" after June 10 of that year. Ibid., 25 May 1809.

46. "insecurity of our commerce." Ibid., November 29.

47. "Your union with Austria is the source of all your misfortunes." Ibid., July 28.

48. "peoples among whom they would dwell. "Customs of the Creek Indians" by Col. Benjamin Hawkins, Agent for Indian Affairs of the United States, south of the Ohio." Ibid., July 13.

49. "lands ceded to the United States by the Cherokee and Chickasaw Indians" Ibid., June 19.

50. "born on the 18th of August, 1774." *The Journals of the Expedition Under the Command of Capt.¹ Lewis and Clark*, Letter of Thomas Jefferson reflecting on Capt. Meriwether Lewis.

51. "I could have no hesitation in confiding the enterprise to him." Ibid.

52. "panting for some new enterprise." Ibid.

53. "penetrate to and through, that to the United States." Ibid.

54. "left to himself." Ibid.

55. "the nearest river to the Pacific." Ibid.

56. "the geography of his route." Ibid.

57. "direction of the enterprise" Ibid.

58. "I will happily join you." William Clark to Meriwether Lewis, Clarksville, 18 July 1803, William Clark Papers, Library of Congress.

59. "this vast enterprise." William Clark to Thomas Jefferson, Clarksville, 24 July 1803, Library of Congress.

60. "for your own perusal" William Clark to Thomas Jefferson, Fort Mandan, 3 April 1805, Library of Congress.

61. "5 Elephant Teeth." William Clark to Thomas Jefferson, 10 October 1807, Library of Congress.

62. "Mastodont" owing to the formation of its teeth. Thomas Jefferson to William Clark, Monticello, 10 September 1809, Library of Congress.

63. "symptoms of derangement." *The Journals of the Expedition* . . . Letter of Thomas Jefferson reflecting on Capt. Meriwether Lewis.

64. "publisher is prepared to print it." Letter from Biddle to William Clark, Philadelphia, 17 March 1810, Nicholas Biddle Papers, Library of Congress.

65. "For rural peace & meek sequestered life." Biddle Family Papers, Nicholas Biddle Journals Call 2146, box 15, Virginia Diary 1810, The Historical Society of Pennsylvania.

66. "laws, customs, and dispositions" *The Journals of the Expedition* . . . Letter of Thomas Jefferson reflecting on Capt. Meriwether Lewis.

67. "highly spoken of by his acquaintances." Nicholas Biddle Papers, vols 1–2; 1775–1812 William Clark to Nicholas Biddle, 22 May 1810, Library of Congress.

68. "honorable respectable living." Ibid.

69. "catechism of inquiries." Nicholas Biddle Papers, vols. 1–2; 1775–1812 Letter to William Clark, Philadelphia, 7 July 1810, Library of Congress.

70. "mahopah." Nicholas Biddle Papers, vols. 1–2; 1775–1812 William Clark to Nicholas Biddle, St. Louis, 7 December 1810, Library of Congress.

71. "mentioning the Commission at all." Ibid., William Clark to Nicholas Biddle.

72. "an event so remarkable and important in the annals of our country." Andalusia: Nicholas Biddle, Jr. Collection, box 1, folder 2, James Monroe to Nicholas Biddle.

73. "assurance of my sentiments of high esteem and respect." Andalusia, Biddle Papers, Autograph Letters, Bound vol. A–K.

CHAPTER FIVE : "PRAY GOD FOR A LUCID INTERVAL"

1. "poor may be taught gratis" Govan, *Nicholas Biddle*, 25.

2. "before the Legislature this session." Biddle, *Autobiography*, 331.

3. "to prevent the charter of the bank of the United States from being renewed," Debate in the House of Representatives of Pennsylvania, on Mr. Holgate's resolutions relative to the Bank of the United States, January 1811. Reported by W. Hamilton. Printed by the Reporter. Td+ v.1. 1811. 96p. [Session 1810-11] p. 8. Library Company of Philadelphia.

4. "betray their country." Ibid., 7.

5. "love of pomp and splendor." Ibid., 7.

6. "a rod of iron." Ibid., 7.

7. "congress of the United States." Ibid., 8.

8. "you are wrong." Ibid., 9.

9. "that we employ for our own?" Ibid., 11.

10. "something like a national character . . ." Ibid., 16.

11. "no security for their stability?" Ibid., 17.

12. "his immediate wants." Ibid., 28.

13. "a most extraordinary deficiency of the precious metals." Ibid., 30.

14. "held by citizens of this state." Ibid., 31.

15. "such indignation." Ibid., 33.

16. "desperate experiments?" Ibid., 35.

17. "Pray God for a lucid interval." Nicholas Biddle Papers, vols. 1–2; 1775–1812, notes for Central Bank Speech, January 1811, Library of Congress.

18. "the paper of a country bank." Debate in the House, etc., 61.

19. "almost all the specie of the state." Ibid., 61.

20. "lest we should be taken by surprise." Ibid., 90.

21. "commanding energy and firmness of mind" Biddle and Craig Family Papers, box 1, folder 6, Margaret Craig obituary, The Historical Society of Pennsylvania.

22. "came from the heart." Biddle and Craig Family Papers, Biddle and Craig Family Papers, box 1, folder 6, Margaret Craig obituary, The Historical Society of Pennsylvania.

23. "the abbreviated 'Dal.'" Biddle and Craig Family Papers (Collection 1451B), box 1, folder 4, The Historical Society of Pennsylvania.

24. "a penitent offender" Ibid.

25. "beloved husband" The Historical Society of Pennsylvania (Collection 1451B), box 1, Margaret M. Craig Pocket Almanacs 1805, 1807, 1812.

26. "toujours votre fidele J. Craig." Biddle and Craig Family Papers (Collection 1451A), box 1, folder 5, Correspondence of John Craig and Margaret Craig, The Historical Society of Pennsylvania.

27. "Yes or no will do." Ibid.

28. "taken from the world" Biddle and Craig Family Papers (Collection 1451B), box 1, printed material, prayer book, 24 November 1796, The Historical Society of Pennsylvania.

29. "pleasure to me and their father." Biddle and Craig Family Papers (Collection 1451A), box 1, folder 5, Correspondence of John Craig and Margaret Craig, The Historical Society of Pennsylvania.

30. "left me a wretched widow . . ." was all she wrote. Ibid., (Collection 1451B), box 1, Margaret M. Craig Pocket Almanacs 1805, 1807, 1812.

31. "the best, the most virtuous of men." Biddle and Craig Family Papers, box 1, folder 12, Memorandum Book, The Historical Society of Pennsylvania.

32. "my Adored Children I live but for you." Biddle and Craig Family Papers (Collection 1451B, 1451A), box 1, folder 5, Correspondence from Margaret Craig to Jane Craig Biddle and Nicholas Biddle, The Historical Society of Pennsylvania.

33. "tenderest affection." Ibid.

34. "warm hearted Irish woman." Ibid.

35. "exhausted by tears and perspiration." Ibid.

36. "my beloved girl, in her old days." Ibid., 2 November 1811.

37. "many enquiring after you." Ibid., 25 October 1811.

38. "The warm cordial heart of your own dear Nicholas." Ibid., 18 September 1812.

CHAPTER SIX : A SECOND WAR OF INDEPENDENCE

1. "foreigners" Biddle, *Autobiography,* 331.

2. "hardy, warlike race" Ibid., 261.

3. "did not stop to calculate the dangers of defending their freedom." Oration Delivered before the Pennsylvania State Society of Cincinnati on the Fourth of July 1811 by Nicholas

Biddle, Esq. Published at the request of the Society, (Philadelphia: C. and A. Conrad and Co., 1811), 7.

4. "the gallant patriotism of our country." Ibid., 8.

5. "sacrificed in foreign wars." Ibid., 13.

6. "blest" Ibid., 15.

7. "Around us all is prosperity and peace," Ibid., 17.

8. "our manhood may defy the world." Ibid., 27.

9. "to fight on Napoleon's 'behalf.'" *Poulson's*, 19 June 1812.

10. "the people of the United States." Ibid., 13 July 1812.

11. "FRIENDS OF PEACE" vs "ADVOCATES OF WAR" Ibid., 19 August 1812.

12. "Her Yankee thunders roar" Ibid., 12 September 1812.

13. "smashed to atoms" Ibid., 23 September 1812, report of hurricane in New Orleans.

14. "queue wrapped in yards of black silk." Oberholtzer, Ellis Paxson. *The Literary History of Philadelphia* (Philadelphia: George W. Jacobs & Co. 1906), 183.

15. "1,000 literary schemes and projects." Andalusia: Nicholas Biddle, Jr. Collection, box 2, folder 22, Final Days of Joseph Dennie written in 1812.

16. "face could scarcely be recognized." Ibid.

17. "that there may be a change in our situation." Andalusia: Nicholas Biddle, Jr. Collection, box 1, folder 14, 1, 30 January 1812, Honorable James Monroe, Secretary of State, Washington.

18. "it's best to let everything take its natural course." Biddle and Craig Family Papers (Collection 1451A), box 1, folder 13, letter to Miss Montgomery, 16 November 1813, The Historical Society of Pennsylvania.

19. Andalusia Letters of Commodore James Biddle, vol. 1, 1798–1813 (August 23– Demember 4. 85.), 2589. November 27, 1811 to Lieutenant James Biddle from Paul Hamilton, Navy Dept. "Sir: M. Dupont de Nemours of Paris having expressed a desire of being conveyed to the United States in one of our public vessels, and the President being disposed to gratify him, on your arrival in Paris you will communicate with him, and offer him a passage on the *Hornet*."

20. "rapid and extensive" Ibid., 91., 2596 & 2597 May 1812. "U.S. Ship Hornet, At Sea, May 1812 My dear N . . . Lewis and Clarke's work is looked for enthusiastically in Paris, & a translation will be undertaken the moment a copy reaches Paris . . . sales will be "rapid and extensive. I was in the practice while at Paris of keeping my newspapers . . . for the Port Folio."

21. "Bearer of dispatches to France" Nicholas Biddle Personal Letters (Collection 2039), 5:1–10, The Historical Society of Pennsylvania.

22. "lustre on our arms." Andalusia: Nicholas Biddle, Jr. Collection, box 1, folder 15A, no. 3, 31 October 1812, Nicholas Biddle to Monroe.

23. "VOTE WAR TICKET" *Poulson's*, 30 October 1812.

24. Interpreted as 666. Ibid., 21 November 1812.

25. "*Moscou n'existe plus.*" Private collection, Christian Braun Dietrich.

26. "We are all very proud of their gallant actions." Andalusia: Nicholas Biddle, Jr. Collection, box 1, folder 15A, no. 5, 29 November 1812.

27. "Jane is fat and hearty and much improved in her looks." Biddle and Craig Family Papers (Collection 1451A), box 1, folder 13, letter to Miss Montgomery, 16 November 1813, The Historical Society of Pennsylvania.

28. "my books, my family, my son." Andalusia: Nicholas Biddle, Jr. Collection, box 1, folder 16, Biddle to Monroe.

29. I am fairly nailed down." Andalusia, Letters of Commodore James Biddle, vol. 1–16, 151, 2684, Philadelphia, 5 November 1813, Nicholas Biddle to James Biddle.

30. "Peace has left us not to return." *Poulson's*, 5 January 1813.

31. "public calamity and private grief" Ibid., 10 March 1813.

32. "must a nation's blood in rivers flow?" Ibid., 15 December 1813.

33. You see how naughty it is to let such feelings take a hold of you." Biddle and Craig Family Papers (Collection 1451A), box 4, folder 5, 5 November 1811, Jane writes MC.

34. "most anxious affection of his parents . . ." Ibid., box 2, folder 6, letter from Dr. James Abercrombie, 26 February 1814.

35. "others vibrate and tremble also." Ibid.

36. "their late Domestic afflictions . . ." Biddle and Craig Family Papers (Collection 1451B, 1451A), John Vaughan to Thomas Jefferson, 28 May 1814.

37. "lolling on the bed and reading." Biddle and Craig Family Papers (Collection 1451A), The Historical Society of Pennsylvania, box 4, folder 1, Sweet Springs, 17 August 1814, Jane to Mary Biddle.

38. "eleven million dollars" *Poulson's*, 29 June 1812, Secretary of Treasury Albert Gallatin advertises war loans "subscriptions."

39. "At the present moment when we are all occupied in preparing to repel the enemy." Andalusia: Nicholas Biddle, Jr. Collection, box 1, folder 4, 14 September 1814, To James Monroe.

CHAPTER SEVEN : MONROE AND BIDDLE

1. "an unlimited armistice than a peace." *The War of 1812*. Hickey, Donald R., ed. (New York: Literary Classics of the United States, 2013), 631.

2. "the northern part of Maine," Ibid., 633.

3. "decidedly in our favor." Ibid., 632.

4. "hostilities are not to cease until ratified by the President." *Poulson's*, 14 February 1815.

5. "unjust and ruinous wars." *The War of 1812*, 650.

6. "nor shall the President be elected from the same state two terms in succession." *Poulson's*, 2 February 1815.

7. "having fully discharged your duty." Andalusia: Nicholas Biddle, Jr. Collection, box. 1, folder 4, 19 February 1815, Biddle to Monroe.

8. "the carnage was 'immense.'" *The War of 1812*, 680.

9. "upwards of an hour." Numbers of slain. *Poulson's*, 8 February 1815.

10. "vital to the freedom and greatness of the nation." Govan, *Nicholas Biddle*, 47.

11. "highest powers of government." Ibid., 50.

12. "happiest engines that ever were invented for advancing trade." Hammond, Bray, *Banks and Politics in America: From the Revolution to the Civil War* (Princeton: Princeton University Press, 1957), 36.

13. "shall die abhorring." Ibid., 36.

14. "mischievous" Wilson, Janet, "The Bank of North America and Pennsylvania Politics: 1781–1787," *The Pennsylvania Magazine of History and Biography* 66.1 (1942), 6.

15. "monopoly" and "aristocracy" Wilson, 21.

16. "more delicacy were observed" Ibid., 21

17. "An Act to revive the incorporation of the subscribers of the Bank of North America." Ibid., 28.

18. "ecclesiastical corporations and perpetual monarchies of England and Scotland." Hammond, *Banks and Politics in America*, 116.

19. "the nature and operation of money and finance." Webster, Pelatiah. *Political Essay on the Nature and Operation of Money, Public Finances and Other Subjects*, 1791, Preface.

20. "with no expense to the government." Debate in the House of Representatives of Pennsylvania, on Mr. Holgate's resolutions relative to the Bank of the United States. January 1811. Reported by W. Hamilton. Printed by the Reporter. Td+ v.1. 1811. 96p. [Session 1810-11] p. 17.

21. "some convenient medium of exchanging the fruits of that industry." Ibid., 31.

22. "I am satisfied with my own course & I shall pursue it." Biddle and Craig Family Papers (Collection 1451A), box 4, folder 1, The Historical Society of Pennsylvania.

23. "too anxious about the defense of the country to care about defending myself." Andalusia: Nicholas Biddle, Jr. Collection, Pamphlets, folder 2.

24. "great vehemence." Andalusia: Nicholas Biddle Jr. Collection, box 1, folder 5, Monroe to Biddle, 5 May 1815.

25. "there was no authority to direct or control them." Ibid., folder 18, Harrisburg, 7 March 1816, Biddle to Monroe.

26. "in which it excites a sentiment of more pleasure than myself." Ibid., 28 February 1817, Biddle to Monroe.

27. "You cannot expect during your administration to walk long on roses." Ibid., 31 May 1817, Biddle to Monroe.

28. "approach of the Russians" Ibid., 11 December 1817, Biddle to Monroe.

29. "intimation of your wishes." Nicholas Biddle Papers (Collection 2039), 2:21–30, The Historical Society of Pennsylvania.

30. "will be in Washington Thursday night." Ibid., folder 19, Philadelphia, 5 January 1818, Biddle to Monroe.

31. "I shall not fail to communicate it." Ibid., 28 January 1818, Biddle to Monroe.

32. "their designs have been betrayed to him." Ibid., 7 February 1818, Biddle to Monroe.

33. "in favor of the Royalists or in favor of the Patriots" Ibid., Philadelphia, 5 March 1818, Biddle to Monroe.

34. "schemes of L'Allemands and Onís." Ibid., folder 19, 5 March 1818, Biddle to Monroe.

35. "attached to the legation of Mr. Onís." Ibid., folder 20, 22 March 1818, Biddle to Monroe.

36. "place full confidence in his conjectures." Ibid., 27 March 1818, re letter from Major Biddle – Rio de la Plata, Biddle to Monroe.

37. "personal responsibility of the commanding General." Ibid., folder 21, 30 July 1818, Biddle to Monroe.

38. "which he & I had talked of last winter in Washnt." Ibid.

39. "instead of cultivating well a little," Andalusia: Nicholas Biddle, Jr. Collection, Pamphlets, folder 4, Address Delivered Before the Philadelphia Society for Promoting Agriculture, Annual Meeting, 15 January 1822.

40. "assure you of my sincere regard." Signed, James Monroe. Biddle Papers Autograph Letters, vol. 2 L-W, 175, Andalusia.

CHAPTER EIGHT : A NEW CAREER

1. John Quincy Adams to Nicholas Biddle, Biddle Papers, Autograph Letters, vol, 1 A-K, Andalusia.

2. "encounter much hostility." Andalusia: Nicholas Biddle Jr. Collection, box 1, folder 22, 31 January 1819, Biddle to Monroe.

3. Jones, William, DuVal Edward W., and Redlich Fritz. "William Jones' Resignation from the Presidency of the Second Bank of the United States." *The Pennsylvania Magazine of History and Biography* 71, no. 3 (1947), 223–41.

4. "at the will of the State Legislature." Andalusia: Nicholas Biddle Jr. Collection, box 1, folder 22, Biddle to Monroe, 7 February 1819.

5. Catterall, Ralph Charles Henry. *The Second Bank of the United States* (Chicago: University of Chicago Press, 1903), 19. Dallas to Calhoun, 28 December 1815.

6. "eventually be frustrated." Andalusia: Nicholas Biddle Jr. Collection, box 1, folder 5, Monroe to Biddle, 27 September 1819, re Bank branch in Baltimore.

7. "operations during the present year." Andalusia: Nicholas Biddle Jr. Collection, box 1, folder 22, Biddle to Monroe, 9 December 1819.

8. Andalusia: Nicholas Biddle Jr. Collection. box 1, folder 5, Monroe to Biddle, 27 September 1819.

9. "communication to you in confidence." Ibid., Monroe to Biddle, 11 April 1820.

10. Ibid., folder 18, Biddle to Monroe, 10 April 1817.

11. "without the authority of the law?" *Poulson's*, 3 February 1819.

12. "signal service to his country." Ibid.

13. "sweet heaven would not wash out." Ibid.

14. "orders of the Chief Magistrate." Ibid., 4 February 1819.

15. "military despotism." Ibid., June 8.

16. "public deposits in the Bank of the United States." Ibid., 4 February 1819.

17. "diligence and zeal." Ibid., February 12.

18. "for the second and probably last time." Ibid., August 18.

19. "no banks doing business." Ibid.

20. "by keeping a *Beard* too long." Ibid., September 22.

21. "Grecian Doric" style Ibid., May 27.

22. "Temple of Minerva Polias at Priene." Ibid.

23. "great value of negroes to slave planters of south." Ibid., May 5.

24. "the controversy is conducted." Biddle and Craig Family Papers (Collection 1451A), box 4, folder 2, Biddle to Jane Biddle, Washington, 13 February 1821, The Historical Society of Pennsylvania.

25. "but there are many things which I must see." Ibid.

26. "judge circumstances" Ibid.

27. "soon to be a mama." Ibid.

28. "you are amusing yourself." Ibid., 11 December 1816, Written from Harrisburg.

29. "whom I love more than any thing or any body in the world." Ibid., n. d.

30. "you would not care much about it." Ibid., n. d.

31. "still more intensely useful." Andalusia: Nicholas Biddle Jr. Collection, box 1, folder 8, Washington, 27 January 1823, Monroe to Biddle.

32. "Do not believe a word of it." Ammon, Harry. *James Monroe: The Quest for National Identity* (Charlottesville: University of Virginia Press, 1990), 509.

CHAPTER NINE : THE BANK'S PRESIDENT

1. "And Holy Allies give no mortal dread . . ." *Poulson's*, 1 January 1824.

2. "suavity of his manners." Govan, *Nicholas Biddle*, 81.

3. "the principal scene of our operations." Catterall, *The Second Bank of the United States*, 95.

4. "commercial exchange interpose to their prosperity." Govan, 86.

5. "accommodation to parties not in business." Govan, 88.

6. "when it fell to almost nothing"] Nicholas Biddle Personal Letters (Collection 2039), 2:91–100, N. Biddle to John Cummings, Esq, Savannah, 22 April 1823, The Historical Society of Pennsylvania.

7. "excite mutual enmity." Govan, 86.

8. "with great delicacy." Govan, 87, Biddle to DeGrand, 27 April 1827.

9. "any banking house in the world." Russell F. Weigley, ed., *Philadelphia: A Three-Hundred Year History* (New York: W. W. Norton, 1982), 253.

10. "A la Raffaele." Freeman and Son, advertising card, *Poulson's*, 16 April 1824.

11. "live animals" Ibid., 20 January 1824.

12. "superior to any painting introduced in this country." Ibid., February 18.

13. "would be well placed in your living room or dining room." Andalusia, Miscellaneous Documents, Jane B Lewis, Auction, Letter accompanying painting, 15 July 1832.

14. "establishment of popular lectures on the sciences connected with them." *Poulson's*, 9 February 1824.

15. "disenfranchised on account of their ignorance." Ibid.

16. "the shortest notice." *Poulson's*, 3 September 1824.

17. "*nous vous aimons La Fayette.*" Ibid., 8 September 1824.

18. "glories of its achievement." Ibid., 30 August 1824.

19. "universal liberty." Ibid.

20. "left the axe in the tree on the hill side . . ." Ibid., 5 October 1824.

21. "you should be perfectly secure." Andalusia, Biddle Papers, Autograph Letters, vol. 2 L-W, Biddle to Lafayette, 2 letters, 15 January 1824 and 18 January 1824.

22. "he is a dangerous man." Ibid., 371.

23. "calculated to awaken the best feelings of our nation." Andalusia, Biddle Papers, Autograph Letters, vol. 2. L-W, Biddle to Lafayette, 5 September 1824.

24. "elegant likeness" of Jackson. *Poulson's*, 12 May 1824.

CHAPTER TEN : A LIFE'S WORK

1. "murder." *Niles'*, 27:385, 19 February 1825.

2. "truth according to the object in view." Ibid.

3. "careless about attending the polls." *Niles'*, 27:215, 4 December 1824.

4. "Do thou no murder." *[To Electors of Boston- To the polls then on Monday - one and all, and give our voices and your ballots for the Adams Ticket. Boston 1824]*. Boston. Retrieved from the Library of Congress.

5. "never raised a sword to achieve that Independence." Brown, W. (1824) *To the voters of Baltimore County. Fellow Citizens. Having been announced as an elector of President and Vice-President of the United States . . .* Retrieved from the Library of Congress.

6. "and that of the nation." Ibid.

7. "put your trust in God, and confide in me." Ibid.

8. "shun the afflicting spectacle." *Niles'*, 28:51, 26 March 1825.

9. "the Presidential chair. . . . A foot-race" LOC Prints and Photographs Division.

10. "a sick man's appetite." James Akin. "Caucus curs in full yell, or a war whoop, to saddle on the people, a pappoose president." LOC.

11. "in need of your indulgence." *Niles'*, 28:10.

12. "fight for those who pay best." Ibid., 27:353, 5 February 1825.

13. "the same price." Ibid.

14. "unholy coalition." Ibid., 374, 12 February 1825.

15. "secret conclaves." *Niles'*, 28:20, Letter to Samuel Swartwout, 23 February 1825.

16. "has never yet risked himself for his country." Ibid., 20.

17. "flows through the wound." *Niles'*, 28:205, 25 May 1825.

18. "your neighbors and friends." Ibid., 185, 21 May 1825.

19. "famished soldiers." Ibid., 185.

20. "choice of a majority of the people" Ibid., 206, May 25.

21. "incorruptible soldier and politician" *Niles'*, 29:65, 1 October 1825.

22. "man as he ever has been, is ambitious." *Niles'*, 29:45, 5 November 1825.

23. "can avail but little." Ibid., 45.

24. "We shall see." "An Unfinished Novel by Nicholas Biddle" – with an introduction by Thomas. P. Govan – Princeton University Library Chronicle, vol. 10, no. 3 (April 1949), 125.

25. "we have inherited from England" Ibid., 132.

26. "I must protest." Ibid., 133.

27. Biddle, Nicholas, *Ode to Bogle* (Philadelphia: Privately Printed for Ferdinand J. Dreer, 1865).

28. "land claimed by them respectively." *Niles'*, 27:353, 5 February 1825.

29. "any form whatsoever." Ibid., 237, 11 December 1824.

30. "removal of the Indians" Ibid., 405, 26 February 1825.

31. "lands occupied by them" Ibid., 405.

32. "their improvement in civilization." *Niles'*, 28:63, 26 March 1825.

33. "differing in color, only." Ibid., 175, May 14, 1825, James Madison's 1812 speech to deputies from tribal nations traveling with General Clarke.

34. "Poyer Hill." Strangeways, Thomas. *Sketch of the Mosquito Shore, including the Territory of Poyais* (Edinburgh: Sold by William Blackwood, 1822), 53.

35. "either North or South America." Ibid., 54.

36. "clear profit" Ibid., 313.

37. "wild and exaggerated speculation" Catterall, 107.

38. "suspending specie payment." Ibid., 107.

39. "sudden or very rigid demands." Biddle, Nicholas. *The Correspondence of Nicholas Biddle Dealing with National Affairs, 1807–1844*, ed. Reginald G. McGrane (Boston: Houghton Mifflin, 1919), 35–36. Biddle to Isaac Lawrence, president of the New York branch, 22 April 1825.

40. "most universal satisfaction." *Philadelphia: A Three-Hundred Year History*, Wainright, Nicholas B. "The Age of Nicholas Biddle, 261.

41. "such as no other nation possesses." Ferdinand J. Dreer Collection (Coll. 175), The Historical Society of Pennsylvania, box 288, folder 45, Memorandum, n. d.

42. "it is only a bank." McGrane, 63, Biddle to Samuel Smith, 29 December 1828.

43. "extravagant and ruinous excesses." Hammond, Bray. *Banks and Politics*, etc. (Princeton: Princeton University Press, 1957), 306–307.

44. "talks to everybody." Biddle and Craig Family Papers (Collection 1451A), The Historical Society of Pennsylvania, box 4, folder 2, Biddle to son, Edward, 22 August 1824.

45. Some dearly bought, some lightly weighed . . ." Biddle, Nicholas. "An Ode to Bogle." (Philadelphia: Privately printed for Ferdinand J. Dreer, 1865), Author's collection.

46. "on my way to embrace you" Biddle-Craig Family Papers (Collection 1451 A), box 4, folder 2, n. d.

47. "might detain me from home for a month." Ibid., 28 January 1827, Washington, Biddle to Jane.

48. "Canals, Railways, Roads and other Subjects." Strickland, W. *Reports on Canals, Railways, Roads, etc. Made to "The Pennsylvania Society For The Promotion of Internal Improvement"* (Philadelphia: Carey & Lea. 1826).

49. "unlimited command of pecuniary means." Ibid., 1.

50. "over obstacles deemed insuperable." *United States Gazette*, Philadelphia, 20 October 1829.

51. "the national debt." McGrane, 84–85, Letters from William B. Lewis to Henry Toland, 9 November and 11 November 1829.

CHAPTER ELEVEN : ANDREW JACKSON BECOMES PRESIDENT

1. "every individual in our Union." *Poulson's*, 9 July 1828.
2. "Then halcyon days again may spring up." Ibid., July 10.
3. "If that's all the good he's done." Ibid., July 29.
4. "intricate state of weights and measures." Ibid., 5 September 1828.
5. "honour and honesty will pretend to deny." Ibid., 12 September 1828.
6. "many of us absent . . ." *Poulson's*, 10 October 1828.
7. "tranquility within our borders . . ." *Poulson's*, 4 December 1828.
8. "dissolve the union." *United States Gazette* (Philadelphia: Hart & Chandler), 6 October 1828.
9. "I will spurn it." Ibid., 8 December 1828.
10. "whilst on the journey." *Poulson's*, 14 January 1829.
11. "take damnation by force." Ibid., 9 February 1829.
12. "My fear is stronger than my hope." *Private Correspondence of Daniel Webster* (Cambridge: Houghton and Co. 1856), 467, to Ezekiel Webster, Washington, 17 January 1829.
13. "uniform and sound currency." *Niles'*, 37:37, 12 December 1829, Address to Congress, 7 December 1829.
14. "able to act like one." Samuel D. Ingham correspondence, Ms. Coll. 889, box 1, folder 19, Kislak Ctr. U. Penn, Eaton to Ingham, 18 June 1831.
15. "Judas." Hamilton, 227.
16. "integrity unquestionable" Hamilton, *Reminiscences*, 87.
17. "keep these gentlemen about him." Ibid., 104.
18. "assistance of a friend." Ibid., 97.
19. "I want you to be near me" Ibid., 140.
20. "hydra of corruption" Ibid., 167.
21. "scholar and a statesman," Biddle, Nicholas, "Eulogium on Thomas Jefferson, Delivered Before the American Philosophical Society" (Philadelphia: Robert H. Small, 1827), 43.
22. "imbued by learning," Ibid., 6.
23. "still unconquered spirit," Ibid., 16.
24. "beamless descent." Ibid., 38.
25. "burthen of public duties," Ibid., 44.

CHAPTER TWELVE : FOR JACKSON OR THE BANK

1. "I have been afraid of banks." McGrane, memorandum, Nicholas Biddle, regarding his conversation with Jackson, 93.
2. "Parent Board." Ibid., 94.
3. "Continuance of the Bank . . ." McGrane, 99, Nicholas Biddle to William B. Lewis, 8 May 1830.
4. "on the subject . . ." McGrane, 103, William B. Lewis to Nicholas Biddle, Washington, 25 May 1830.
5. "Presidential Election." McGrane, 105, Henry Clay to Nicholas Biddle, 14 June 1830.
6. "That party." Ibid., 111, Clay to Nicholas Biddle, 11 September 1830.
7. "President of the U.S . . ." Ibid., 110.
8. "inexpedient." McGrane, 115, Nicholas Biddle to Clay, 3 November 1830.

9. "love of postponement." Ibid.

10. "an application now." Ibid.

11. "exist in its preset form" was the conclusion. *Niles'*, vol. 39, 11 December 1830, Address to Congress, 7 December 1830.

12. "which is much misunderstood . . ." McGrane, 122, Biddle to Robinson, 20 December 1830.

13. "he is in danger." Ibid., 131, Memorandum, 19 October 1831.

14. "communication with the people." Ibid., 123, Biddle to William Lawrence, 8 February 1831.

15. "appreciate the organization." Ibid., 125–26, Biddle to Joseph Gales, 2 March 1831.

16. "ought to be immediately followed." Ibid., 145, D. Webster to Nicholas Biddle, 18 December 1831.

17. "If pressed into a *Corner*" Ibid., 138, Samuel Smith to Nicholas Biddle, 7 December 1831.

18. "separate himself from Jackson . . ." McGrane, 122, Roswell Colt to Biddle, 29 January 1831.

19. "as safe as Tennessee," Hamilton, *Reminiscences*, 247.

20. "immediately repair to Washington . . ." Ibid., 250.

21. "secure its recharter." Ibid., 244, Jackson to Hamilton, 28 March 1832.

22. "end of June 1831." Gammon, Samuel Rhea, *The Presidential Campaign of 1832* (Baltimore: Johns Hopkins Press, 1922), 120.

23. "your enemies to the South . . ." McGrane, 140, Charles F. Mercer to Biddle, 12 December 1831.

24. "his ox nor any of his asses . . ." Ibid., 179–80, Biddle to Charles Jared Ingersoll, 11 February 1832.

25. three years and a half ago." *Niles'*, 42:337, 7 July 1832.

26. arrived in time to decide all doubts." *Poulson's*, 3 July 1832.

27. "I will kill it!" Remini, Robert, V. *The Life of Andrew Jackson* (New York: Harper & Roe, 1988), 227.

28. "bill would be approved." *Niles'*, 353, 14 July 1832.

29. "people debtors to aliens." Ibid., 365.

30. "potent more powerful." Ibid.

31. "our country in war?" Ibid., 366.

32. "these just principles." Ibid., 368.

33. "despotic power" Remini, 231.

34. "perversion of the veto power." Ibid., 231

35. "these miserable people." McGrane, 196.

36. "How he nicks them." Williams, Michael, 1832, LOC Prints and Photographs Division.

37. "unbounded lust for power." *Poulson's*, July 31.

38. "his overseer." Ibid., August 20.

39. "brutal and ferocious." Ibid., September 20.

40. "good sense of the people" Gammon, 136, Campaign 1832.

41. "driven a friend from us." Gammon, 149, VB to Donelson, 26 August 1832.

42. "destined to be the most popular act of his life." Hamilton, *Reminiscences*, 247.

43. TYRANNY appeared in bold face. *Niles'*, 43:154, 3 November 1832.

44. "any previous one . . ." Ibid., 145, November 3.

45. "both houses of congress." Ibid., 177, November 17.

46. "systematic corruption of the Press." *Newark Sentinel*, 6 November 1832.
47. "money of the people." *Niles*, 43:246, 8 December 1832.
48. "limits of this state." Ibid., 231.
49. "CONSTITUTIONAL LIBERTY" Ibid., 233.
50. "dissolution of the union" Ibid., 234.
51. "such a power." Ibid., 232.
52. "the breath of its life." *Poulson's*, 24 October 1832.
53. "repelling force by force." Ibid., December 6.
54. "slaves of a [Turkish] Divan?" Ibid., December 27.
55. "their arguments lead and steel." *Poulson's*, 3 November 1832.

CHAPTER THIRTEEN : SAVING THE BANK

1. "we will perish amidst the ruins." *Niles*, 43:233–34, 1 December 1832.
2. "destruction of the union." Ibid., 15 December 1832.
3. "will not be preserved." Ibid., 29 December 1832.
4. "the dictator's throne," Ibid.
5. "our rights and liberties." Ibid., 312, 5 January 1833.
6. "against South Carolina." Ibid., 317, 12 January 1833.
7. "maimed for life." *Poulson's*, vol. 42, 3 January 1833.
8. "four pistols and two dirks" *Poulson's*, January 7.
9. "cannot be acknowledged." *Niles*, 342, 19 January 1833.
10. "resistance by violence." *Poulson's*, 25 January 1833.
11. "the architects of ruin." *Poulson's*, March 18.
12. "be safely continued." *Poulson's*, March 6.
13. "behave himself with some decency." McGrane, 200.
14. "wherever they may be deemed useful . . ." *Poulson's*, 22 February 1833.
15. "the Bank business at this place." Andalusia, Autographs Letters L-Z, no. 262, John Mullanphy to Biddle, August 1831.
16. "Autocrat of all Russias." *Poulson's*, "Another Veto," March 12.
17. "President de facto" Ibid., March 16.
18. "his approbation and consent." Ibid.
19. "control elections and subvert states." Ibid., April 6.
20. "Mr. Biddle and the managers of the national bank . . ." Hammond, 416.
21. "does not dare trust his master out of his sight." *Poulson's*, May 8.
22. "you would not try to do any more injury." *Poulson's*, "The President and the Indians," 11 June 1833.
23. "Dulce et decorum est, pro patria mori." *Niles*, 348, 20 July 1833.
24. "winding up its concerns." Ibid., 251, Hamilton to Jackson, 28 February 1833.
25. "The reputation of your Administration may not escape unquestioned." Ibid., 252.
26. "my feelings and temperament." Ibid., 252.
27. "destroy the liberty of our country." Catterall, 287.
28. "little knowledge of the subject." Ibid., 271.
29. "inclination to do mischief." Ibid., 265.
30. "unconstitutional." *Niles*, 45:73, September – December 1833, Jackson "Manifesto," 28 September 1833.
31. "no character and no money." McGrane, 207, Nicholas Biddle to J.S. Barbour, 16 April 1833.

32. "between Chestnut St. and Wall St." Ibid., 209, Nicholas Biddle to Thomas Cooper, 6 May 1833.

33. "THE PUBLIC DISTRESS" *Niles'*, 45:396, 8 February 1833.

34. "given way to despair." Ibid., 425, February 22.

35. "tottering" in March. *Niles'*, 46:18, 8 March 1834.

36. "Biddle as a 'money-king.'" Ibid., 98.

37. "Your humble servant, A DEMOCRAT" *Niles'*, 45:436, 22 February 1834.

38. "sober and industrious." *Niles'*, 46:390–92, 7 February 1835, "Assault on the President".

39. "exciting only an abortive ambition." *Niles'*, 44:349, Nicholas Biddle speech, Girard College, 4 July 1833.

40. "godsend to society if all such were put down." Ibid., 270, Andrew Jackson to Hamilton, 2 February 1834.

41. "destroy the Bank of the United States . . ." Ibid., 280.

42. "considered a failure by his own friends . . ." Ibid., 282, Lewis to Hamilton, March 30.

43. "currency and the recharter of the Bank." Catterall, 330, Nicholas Biddle to William Appleton, 27 January 1834.

44. "of the constitution, and of civil liberty." *Niles'*, 46:126, Clay speech Senate, 14 April 1834.

45. "no right to interfere." *Niles'*, 46:121, 19 April 1834.

46. "sustained and protected me" *Niles'*, 46:144, 26 April 1834.

47. "rights and privileges of the senate." *Niles'*, 46:134, 26 April 1834.

48. "that resistance will be supported by the country." *Niles'*, 46:162, Webster, 21 April 1834.

49. "rights and privileges ought to be met." *Niles'*, 46:215-16, "Debate on the Protest."

50. "recharter of the Bank," McGrane, 231, Nicholas Biddle to John S. Smith, 9 May 1834.

51. "entirely out of our control." Ibid.

52. "sit there as spies?" *Niles'*, 46:203, 24 May 1834.

CHAPTER FOURTEEN : "THE PUBLIC TREASURE – WHERE IS IT?"

1. "engage lodgings in Arabia." McGrane, 221, Nicholas Biddle to Joseph Hopkinson, 21 February 1834.

2. "concentrate its thoughts." Ibid., 226, Nicholas Biddle to Samuel Jaudon, 11 March 1834.

3. "A HORRIBLE PRECIPICE." *Niles'*, 46:20–21, 8 March 1834.

4. "frustrate his designs in relation to it." Ibid., 27, 8 March 1834.

5. "decidedly friendly to the Bank." McGrane, 224, Nicholas Biddle to Samuel Breck, 1 March 1834.

6. "patriotism." Ibid.

7. "of the banking system." Ibid., 226, Nicholas Biddle to Samuel Smith, 2 April 1834.

8. "circulating medium to the confederacy" *Niles'*, 46:221, 31 May 1834, "Reports on the U. States Bank."

9. "supposed violations [were]." Ibid., 221–24.

10. "house of representatives committed." Ibid.

11. "deceit, collusion and corruption." Ibid., 238, June 7.

12. "The Plot Thickens" *Poulson's*, 28 May 1834.

13. "deliberate efforts to destroy the Bank," McGrane, 231, Nicholas Biddle to John Smith, 9 May 1834.

14. "wanton corruption" within the Post Office. *Poulson's*, 20 June 1834.

15. "what little of freedom remains." McGrane, 230, Thomas Cooper to Nicholas Biddle, 1 May 1834.

16. "force only is wanting." *Niles'*, 46:215, 24 May 1834, "Debate on the Protest."

17. "old tactician", as Calhoun called the President, Ibid.

18. "truly alarming." *Niles'*, 46:324, 5 July 1834.

19. "services and sacrifices." Ibid., 326.

20. "Amos Kendall, Cashier." *Poulson's*, 63:19 May 1834.

21. "approved 10th April, 1816." Ibid., 328, "Report on Finance."

22. "the tortures of ten Spanish inquisitions" *Niles'*, 46: 9, 1 March 1834.

23. "swollen almost to bursting" *Poulson's*, 20 June 1834.

24. "the commercial interests of the country." *Niles'*, 46:355, 19 July 1834.

25. "relief to the community," Ibid.

26. "require the most relief." Ibid.

27. "their future business." Ibid.

28. "'greatest and the best'." *Poulson's*, 9 July 1834.

29. "judge of Biddle's sincerity." *Niles'*, 427, 23 August 1834.

30. "pretensions of wealth and aristocracy." Ibid., 428.

31. "Nicholas Biddle's paper" *Poulson's*, 24 July 1834.

32. "Gold instead of Paper" *Niles'*, 330, 12 July 1834.

33. "Rich Will Take Care of the Poor." *Poulson's*, August 12.

34. "to save the country." *Poulson's*, October 28.

35. "lined with gold." *Poulson's*, September 20.

36. "bloodshed and devastation" *Poulson's*, 27 March 1835.

37. "unprovoked aggressions upon our commerce." *Niles'*, 47:225, December 6 [delivered December 2], "Twenty-Third Congress – Second Session."

38. "confiscation or destruction" of American vessels. Ibid., 226.

39. "will be a stain upon our national honor." Ibid., 226.

40. "popular governments." Ibid., 228.

41. "an evil of such magnitude" Ibid., 228.

42. "fight, for fighting's sake", Ibid., 290.

43. "popular effect." *Poulson's*, 1 January 1835.

44. "The war-whoop was sounded from the Kitchen" Ibid., January 19.

45. "French property." Ibid., January 14.

46. "ill humor of the President" Ibid., February 17, *Courier Français*.

47. "mistaken and unskillful (*et une faute et une maladresse*)." Ibid., *Journal du Commerce*.

48. "between France and the United States." Ibid., February 28.

49. "Suppressed letters" Ibid., March 5.

50. "ardent defense of a foreign nation." *Niles'*, 47:271, 20 December 1834.

51. "protested French bill" Ibid., 284.

52. "declare war upon us. Congress", he said, "will not declare [it.]" Ibid., March 11.

53. Van Buren his "legitimate successor." *Poulson's*, 4 April 1835.

54. "uncontrollable acts of the present administration." Ibid.

55. "Slippery Elm" was soon to replace the "Hickory Tree." Ibid., June 6.

56. "will be a paradise compared with this, in a few years." *Poulson's*, 5 September 1835.

57. "the monarch of this country disguised as a republican." *Poulson's*, 14 September 1835, "Opinions Abroad."

58. "a blood relation of President Biddle." *Poulson's*, 31 August 1835.

59. "friend of the Bank." *Poulson's*, November 20.

60. "to the shavers in Wall Street." *Poulson's*, November 30.

61. "or recognized by law." Ibid., December 1.

62. "at the present period." Ibid., December 9.

63. "brought France to terms." Ibid., 28 December 1835.

CHAPTER FIFTEEN : THE DEATH OF ONE BANK, THE BIRTH OF ANOTHER

1. "absolutely and inflexibly silent . . ." McGrane, 255, Biddle to Herman Cope, 11 August 1835.

2. "interests and fame" Govan, 284.

3. "break the president's heart." Ibid.

4. "perfectly reckless of [his] popularity," *Poulson's*, 11 February 1836.

5. "commenced by Andrew Jackson." *Niles'*, 49:361, 30 January 1836.

6. "their 'awful fears'." Ibid.

7. "force the matter tomorrow." McGrane, 264, Charles Baker to Biddle, 5 February 1836.

8. "large sums of money" to vote pro-bank. *Poulson's*, 13 February 1836.

9. "most foul mouthed and violent opposers" of a national bank. Ibid., 15 February 1836.

10. "safe regulator of political power" *Niles'*, 49:253, 12 December 1835.

11. "You will live to see the laws reestablished." Nicholas Biddle Address to the Alumni Association Nassau Hall, Annual Commencement, 30 September 1835, Andalusia: Nicholas Biddle, Jr. Collection, Pamphlets, folder 8.

12. "scene of unparalleled distress is at hand." *Poulson's*, 16 March 1836.

13. "to the unexpected sum of $11,000,000." *Niles'*, 49:252, 12 December 1835.

14. "plant the stars and stripes upon the walls of Paris?" *Poulson's*, 9 January 1836.

15. "offensive language." Ibid., January 21.

16. "buy them on credit." *Niles'*, 48:159–60, 2 May 1835, "Frauds in Land Sales."

17. "secret societies." *Poulson's*, 11 October 1836.

18. "buried six hundred foreigners" *Poulson's*, 11 May 1836.

19. "the restoration of slavery." Andalusia, Autograph Letters, A-K, no. 11, JQ Adams to Biddle, 12 June 1836.

20. "a more sound and healthy state." *Poulson's*, 13 June 1836.

21. "a scarcity of money." Ibid.

22. "integrity and truth . . ." *Niles'*, 50:23–25, 12 March 1836, "Bank of the United States."

23. "crude experiment succeeds another," *Niles'*, 51:14, 3 September 1836.

24. "resident." *Niles'*, 50:436, 27 August 1836.

25. "cupidity of the white man" as a letter to *Poulson's* declared. *Poulson's*, 12 October 1836.

26. "the assaults we made upon each other." *Niles'*, 51:42, 17 September 1836.

27. "an implacable opponent" of the bank. *Poulson's*, 8 September 1836.

28. "abused their charter." Ibid.

29. "insanity" Ibid., September 10.

30. "decayed morality?" Ibid., September 12.

31. "ultra nullifier" Ibid., September 19.

32. "He will not go out of his way for nothing," *Poulson's*, 17 August 1836.

33. "bank aristocracy." Ibid., October 17.

34. "GENERAL HARRISON IS YOUR FRIEND" *Poulson's*, 31 October 1836.

35. "continuation of that institution." *Niles'*, 51:232–36, 10 December 1836, "The Annual Message."

36. "inextricable confusion." *Niles'*, 51:244–45, 17 December 1836, "The State of the Currency – Letter from Mr. Biddle."

37. "the rich richer, and the poor poorer." Ibid.

38. "resort to the states." *Niles'*, 52:22–23, 11 March 1837, "Farewell Address of Andrew Jackson."

CHAPTER SIXTEEN : "A GREAT DISASTER HAS BEFALLEN THE COUNTRY"

1. "disappointed both friends and foes." Ibid., 17.

2. "his well-spent life." Ibid., 18.

3. "ruled by the Bank." *Poulson's*, 16 January 1837.

4. "THEIR PRICES MUST COME DOWN" *Poulson's*, 15 February 1837.

4. "Loco-Foco Revolution." Byrdsall, Fitzwilliam, *Loco-Foco, or Equal Rights Party* (New York: Clement & Packard, 1842), Preface.

6. "remained profoundly silent" throughout the interview, and Biddle left without achieving his goal. *Niles'*, 52:146, 6 May 1837.

7. "I think this is the moment." McGrane, 272, Thomas Cooper to Nicholas Biddle, 29 April 1837.

8. "at your disposal." McGrane, 278, Nicholas Biddle to Patterson, 8 May 1836.

9. "at present, or in prospect . . ." Ibid., 278–80, Cooper to Biddle, 14 May 1837.

10. "agree with me in opinion, decidedly." Ibid., 280, Cooper to Biddle, 24 May 1837.

11. "the success of my proposal." Ibid., 282, Cooper to Biddle, 1 July 1837.

12. "before the destruction of the Bank?" Ibid., 273, Joel Poinsett to Nicholas Biddle, 6 May 1837.

13. "electric and decisive." Ibid., 274, Nicholas Biddle to Poinsett, 8 May 1837.

14. "neither party would desire to have perpetuated." Ibid., 274-6, Nicholas Biddle to Poinsett.

15. "this poor bleeding country of ours." Ibid., 277, Nicholas Biddle to Patterson, 8 May 1837.

16. "the Flying Dutchman" *Poulson's*, 14 February 1837.

17. "under existing circumstances, to interfere." *Poulson's*, 10 May 1837.

18. "disaster has befallen the country." *Niles'*, 52:182, 20 May 1837, "Letter from Mr. Biddle."

19. "policy which originated with President Jackson." *Poulson's*, 22 July 1837.

20. "peace and prosperity of our country." *Niles'*, 52:312–13, 15 July 1837, "Gen. Hamilton's Letter, May 18.

21. "the constitutional currency of gold and silver." *Niles'*, 52:341–43, 29 July 1837, "Anti-Bank Convention."

22. "purely with the view of gratifying Biddle." Hammond, Bray, *Banks and Politics in America* (Princeton: Princeton University Press, Oxford Reissue, 1991), 491.

23. "the best metallic conductors in political storms." *Niles'*, 52:358, 5 August 1837.

24. "her unalloyed prosperity." *Poulson's*, 5 September 1837.

25. "more annoying to the money projects than the banks have been." Ibid., October 11.

26. "separating our State from those desperadoes." McGrane, 299, Nicholas Biddle to Henry Clay.

27. "Burn this – as it is libellous [*sic*] in the extreme." McGrane, 310, attributed by handwriting to Webster, n. d., presumed May 1838.

28. "most of them good, a few otherwise . . ." Andalusia, Autograph Letters, vol. 1, A-K, Clay to Nicholas Biddle, 30 April 1838.

28. "proceed to take measures for resumption." McGrane, 311, Biddle to Samuel Jaudon.

30. "not thro' mere receivers." Ibid., 314, Biddle to Jaudon, 23 June 1838.

31. "notes, bills, and other obligations in gold and silver" Govan, 335.

32. "re-establishment of the currency." Hammond, 489.

33. "caused their defeat." Ibid., 490.

34. "the least shock to the business of the country." Caterall, 473.

35. "the termination of the war" McGrane, 318, Biddle to R.M. Blatchford, 31 July 1838.

36. "proper tone" for all communications. Ibid., 318, Blatchford to Biddle, 1 August 1838.

37. "So is that very able man Webster." Ibid., 333, Cooper to Biddle, 1 October 1838.

38. "you ought to occupy." Ibid.

39. "facetious and in intimate conversation. . . ." Hamilton, *Reminiscences*, 312.

40. "the personal welfare of you all." *Poulson's*, 30 March 1839.

41. "I am in truth profoundly sensible." Andalusia: Nicholas Biddle Jr. Collection, Biddle Diary 1838–39.

42. "May this feeling last during my life." Ibid.

43. "the cost of transmitting that gold and silver." Hammond, 527.

CHAPTER SEVENTEEN : DEFEAT

1. "necessary to kill him off." *Poulson's*, 6 April 1839.

2. "in the "field" again, Ibid., 14 June 1839.

3. "mercy of the legislature." *Niles'*, 57:123, "Suspension of Specie Payments."

4. "shipwreck of our highest interests." *Poulson's*, 22 October 1839, "Prediction and Fulfillment."

5. "private capital is destroyed." Ibid., 2 November 1839.

6. "Grain grows rich when armies bleed and die." Ibid., "The Better Currency."

7. The "monster is dead" had been taken to refer to the former president, rather than Biddle's Bank. Ibid., 7 November 1839.

8. Van Buren pointedly used the word "revolution." Van Buren's annual message to Congress. *Niles'*, 57:279–84, 29 March 1839.

9. "These are the maudlin lamentations of men unfit to lead a great nation." Andalusia, Nicholas Biddle Scrapbook, *American*, 1 June 1840.

10. "servile adulation." Ibid., 78.

11. "able, brilliant, agreeable, plausible, cultivated" Ibid., 93.

12. "Biddle 'got out of the scrape just in time.'" Ibid., 78.

13. "its most influential members." Ibid.

14. "let those laugh who win" Ibid.

15. "has a task extremely repugnant to his pride." McGrane, 337–38, Nicholas Biddle to Webster.

16. "'Tobacco men' had Austria in their pocket." Ibid., 339, Webster to Biddle.

17. "had no greatness about him, either of mind or character." *Pennsylvania Magazine of History and Biography*, vol. 77, no. 1 (January 1953), 78, "The Diaries of Sidney George Fisher, 1839–40."

18. "lending money to the Reading Railroad" *Public Ledger*, 19 April 1841.

19. "miserable intriguers" Ibid.

20. "late proceedings touching the Bank of the United States" Ibid.

21. "insanity as respects the Bank itself." Ibid., 26 April 1841.

22. "conspiracy to defraud the stockholders of the Bank of the United States." *Niles'*, 61:320, 15 January 1842, "U.S. Bank Officers Arrested."

23. "former distinguished 'lions' of the Bank of the United States" *Philadelphia Gazette and Commercial Advertiser*, Philadelphia, 14 January 1842.

24. "tasteful soirées that this capital has seen for many years." Ibid., 31 January 1842.

25. "appeared rather as advocate than Judge," *Philadelphia Gazette*, 24 February 1842.

26. "worthless pile of trash." Ibid., February 16.

27. "released from responsibility under the criminal process" *Niles'*, 62:5, March 1842.

28. "turned all its immense weight and influence on the government." *The Pennsylvanian* (Philadelphia: Mifflin & Parry), 28 March 1842, "The President's Message."

29. "acquitted of all just blame on account of them." Ibid.

30. "President without a party." Ibid., 23 April 1842.

31. "Broken and Defunct Banks." Ibid., 14 February 1842.

32. "prudence and economy in his expenditures." Ibid., 25 April 1842. "Remarks of Mr. Buchanan."

33. "he is more truly happy who never has need of a friend." *Philadelphia Gazette* , March 15, "The United States Bank."

34. "abuses practiced by a vicious banking system" *Pennsylvanian*, 2 May 1842.

35. "defect in the administration of justice." Ibid., May 6.

36. "unjustly held responsible." Ibid., April 2. Response to *Public Ledger*.

37. "sold at auction the 2nd of July." *Niles'*, 62:272, 25 June 1842.

38. "Some transcendentalist – some cobweb spinner?" McGrane, 344, Biddle to Webster.

39. "a riotous sleigh party" HSP, Craig-Biddle Papers (Collection 1451B), box 1, folder 10, Fanny Kemble Butler to Jane, n. d.

40. "I have been very sick – and what is harder – very much doctored." HSP, Roswell L. Colt Papers 1883, box 10, file 16.

41. "Dulcamara, and calomel powder." Ibid.

42. "the Bank Organ in the city." Andalusia, Scrapbook, Nicholas Biddle, Bank and Misc.

43. "in the army and navy of the United States." Ibid.

44. "the noblest object to which knowledge and morals can be devoted." Ibid.

BIBLIOGRAPHY

Ammon, Harry. *James Monroe: The Quest for National Identity*. Charlottesville: University of Virginia Press, 1990.

Biddle, Charles. *Autobiography of Charles Biddle, Vice President of the Supreme Executive Council of Pennsylvania 1745-1821*. Privately Printed. Philadelphia: E. Claxton and Company, 1883.

Biddle, C. Miller, M.D. *William and Sarah Biddle, 1633-1711: Planting a Seed of Democracy in America*. Privately Printed. Saline, MI: McNaughton & Gunn, Inc., 2012.

Biddle, Nicholas. Journals Europe 1804-1807. The Historical Society of Pennsylvania.

Biddle, Nicholas. Personal Letters. The Historical Society of Pennsylvania.

Biddle, Nicholas. *Ode to Bogle*. Philadelphia: Privately Printed for Ferdinand J. Dreer, 1865.

Biddle, Nicholas. *The Correspondence of Nicholas Biddle Dealing with National Affairs, 1807-1844*. Edited by Reginald C. McGrane. Boston: Houghton Mifflin, 1919.

Biddle and Craig Family Papers. The Historical Society of Pennsylvania.

Biddle Papers. Library of Congress.

Biddle Papers. Andalusia. Autograph Letters. Bound Volumes.

Byrdsall, Fitzwilliam. *The History of the Loco-Foco, or Equal Rights Party*. New York: Clement & Packard, 1842.

Catterall, Ralph Charles Henry. *The Second Bank of the United States*. Chicago: University of Chicago Press, 1903.

Clark, William Bell. *Captain Dauntless: The Story of Nicholas Biddle and the Continental Navy*. Louisiana State University Press, 1949.

Cooper, James Fenimore. *The History of the Navy of the United States of America*. In Two Volumes. Philadelphia: Lea and Blanchard, 1840.

Fisher, Sidney, George. *The Laws of Race, as Connected with Slavery*. Philadelphia: Willis P. Hazard, 1860.

Gammon, Samuel Rhea. *The Presidential Campaign of 1832*. Baltimore: Johns Hopkins Press, 1922.

Govan, Thomas Payne. "Nicholas Biddle at Princeton" Princeton University Library Chronicle. Vol. IX, No. 2, Feb. 1948.

Govan, Thomas Payne. *Nicholas Biddle, Nationalist and Public Banker 1786-1844*. Chicago: The University of Chicago Press, 1959.

"An Unfinished Novel by Nicholas Biddle" – with an introduction by Thomas. P. Govan. Princeton University Library Chronicle Vol. X, No. 3, April 1949.

Hamilton, James A. *Reminiscences of James A. Hamilton: Or, Men And Events, At Home And Abroad, During Three Quarters of a Century.* New York: C. Scribner & Co., 1869.

Hammond, Bray. *Banks and Politics in America: From the Revolution to the Civil War.* Princeton: Princeton University Press, 1957.

Eliza Cope Harrison, Editor. *Philadelphia Merchant: The Diary of Thomas P. Cope.* South Bend: Gateway Editions, 1978.

Jones, William, Edward W. DuVal, and Fritz. Redlich. "William Jones' Resignation from the Presidency of the Second Bank of the United States." *The Pennsylvania Magazine of History and Biography* 71, no. 3. 1947.

Kahan, Paul. *The Bank War: Andrew Jackson, Nicholas Biddle, and the Fight for American Finance.* Yardley, PA: Westholme Publishing, 2015.

Kendall, Amos. *Autobiography of Amos Kendall.* New York: Peter Smith, 1949.

Mihm, Stephen. *A Nation of Counterfeiters.* Cambridge: Harvard University Press, 2007.

Nash, Gary B. *The Urban Crucible: Social Change, Political Consciousness, and the Origins of the American Revolution.* Cambridge: Harvard University Press, 1979.

Niles, William Ogden, -1857, and Hezekiah Niles. *Niles' Weekly Register.* Baltimore: H. Niles, 1814-1837.

Oberholtzer, Ellis Paxson. *The Literary History of Philadelphia.* Philadelphia: George W. Jacobs & Co, 1906.

The Port Folio. Oliver Oldschool, Esq. Joseph Dennie nom de plume – later Nicholas Biddle. Philadelphia: Smith & Maxwell, various volumes.

Poulson's American Daily Advertiser. Philadelphia: Printed by Zachariah Poulson.

Philadelphia: A Three-Hundred Year History. Russell F. Weigley, Editor. New York: W. W. Norton, 1982.

Remini, Robert, V. *The Life of Andrew Jackson.* New York: Harper & Row, 1988.

Scharf, J. Thomas, and Thompson Westcott. *History of Philadelphia, 1609-1884.* Philadelphia: L.H. Everts & Co., 1884.

Strangeways, Thomas. *Sketch of the Mosquito Shore, including the Territory of Poyais.* Edinburgh: Sold by William Blackwood, 1822.

Strickland, William. *Reports on Canals, Railways, Roads, etc. Made to "The Pennsylvania Society For The Promotion of Internal Improvement"* Philadelphia: Carey & Lea, 1826.

Thomas, Louisa. *Louisa: The Extraordinary Life of Mrs. Adams.* New York: Penguin Press, 2016.

The United States Gazette. Philadelphia: Hart & Chandler.

The War of 1812. Hickey, Donald R., Editor. New York: Literary Classics of the United States, 2013.

Webster, Daniel. *The Private Correspondence of Daniel Webster.* Edwin D. Sanborn, and Fletcher Webster, Editors. Boston: Little, Brown and Company, 1857.

Webster, Pelatiah. *Political Essay on the Nature and Operation of Money, Public Finances and Other Subjects*. Philadelphia: Joseph Crukshank, 1791.

Wilson, Janet. "The Bank of North America and Pennsylvania Politics: 1781-1787." *The Pennsylvania Magazine of History and Biography* 66.1. 1942.

Wright, Robert E. *The First Wall Street: Chestnut Street, Philadelphia, & the Birth of American Finance*. Chicago: The University of Chicago Press, 2005.

INDEX

ABOUT THE AUTHOR

Cordelia Frances Biddle is an author with a passion for history. Her nonfiction work *Saint Katharine: The Life of Katharine Drexel* explores the transformation of a Philadelphia heiress into a champion for social justice, while her novels (*Sins of Commission, The Actress, Without Fear, Beneath the Wind*, etc.) draw upon history to tell captivating fictional stories. You can learn more about her at:

CordeliaFrancesBiddle.com

www.ingramcontent.com/pod-product-compliance
Lightning Source LLC
Chambersburg PA
CBHW021352090426
42742CB00009B/825